VISUAL QUICKPRO GUIDE

FINAL CUT PRO 2

FOR MACINTOSH

Lisa Brenneis

Peachpit Press

Visual QuickPro Guide
Final Cut Pro 2 for Macintosh
Lisa Brenneis

Peachpit Press
1249 Eighth Street
Berkeley, CA 94710
510/524-2178
800/283-9444
510/524-2221 (fax)
Find us on the World Wide Web at: http://www.peachpit.com
Peachpit Press is a division of Pearson Education

Editor: Jill Marts Lodwig
Production Coordinator: Connie Jeung-Mills
Copyeditor: Judy Ziajka
Compositor: Maureen Forys
Indexer: Emily Glossbrenner
Cover Design: The Visual Group

ISBN 0-201-71979-7

9 8 7 6 5 4 3 2 1

Printed and bound in the United States of America

Dedication

To family and friends.

My land, sea, and sky.

Acknowledgments

Thanks to the Peachpit Press people: editor Jill Marts Lodwig and production coordinator Connie Jeung-Mills, smart, sane women with nerves of steel; Lisa Theobald and Kelly Ryer, the first edition editors who built a fine foundation for this edition; and indelible thanks to Marjorie Baer.

Thanks to the whole Final Cut Pro Team at Apple Computer, particularly Brian Meaney, Erin Skitt, and John Malm—genuinely kind, helpful people who work very hard.

Thanks to Alexis Van Hurkman, (uncredited) author of Apple's Final Cut Pro 2 User's Manual.

Thanks to my collaborator and friend Brett Spivey, who concocted the Compositing and Special Effects chapter with me.

Thanks to Lauren Ward (sharp eyes, sharp mind, sharp pencil) for all the great help.

Thanks to all the men and women of the 2-pop.com Final Cut Pro discussion forums. I started assembling a list by name, and it was too long to print. You lead the FCP community by example, and I am indebted to you. Keep posting.

Finally, thanks to a group of very important people who defy classification: Ralph Fairweather, Michael Wohl, Andrew Baum, Charles McConathy, Cawan Starks, Ross Jones, Philip Hodgetts, Josh Mellicker, Larry Jordan, Elina Shatkin, Tom Wolsky, Bill Davis, Kevin Monahan, Michael Horton, Ken Stone, Ned Soltz, Lowell Kay, Michael Rubin, and Ramy Katrib.

TABLE OF CONTENTS

INTRODUCTION

When the two Steves started Apple back in 1976, they dreamed of making a computer that people could use as a tool to change the world. Final Cut Pro is an Apple program worthy of the founders' vision. A community has formed around this tool, and people are making movies who weren't able to before. FCP is changing the way stories are told, because it changes who's telling them.

Final Cut Pro 2, released in Spring 2001, is the first major upgrade since April 1999, when Apple debuted this remarkable desktop video editing, effects creation, and compositing program.

Wow. A lot has happened in two years.

If you are already using FCP 1, the good news is that FCP 2 is still Final Cut Pro as you know and love it. The Final Cut Pro team has built on its great beginning, adding significant new features that many of us have been requesting, and many, many small thoughtful gifts that editors will love as they live with the program.

Even though the basic operation of Final Cut Pro has not changed, there are changes scattered throughout the program, and major revisions in a couple of areas. This book, *Final Cut Pro 2 for Macintosh: Visual QuickPro Guide*, is a revision of the original *Final Cut Pro for Macintosh: Visual QuickPro Guide*. This edition describes the operation of FCP 2 only. If you are using Final Cut Pro version 1.2.5 or earlier, you'll need a copy of *Final Cut Pro for Macintosh: Visual QuickPro Guide*.

"New in 2" sidebars appear throughout this revision, pointing out significant feature changes in FCP 2.

But the changes won't stop here; the Final Cut Pro team is still relentlessly adding features as I write this introduction (and probably as you're reading it). For example, we should be seeing a Mac OS X version of FCP in the near future.

Who should use this book

Final Cut Pro 2 for Macintosh: Visual QuickPro Guide is designed to be used by intermediate to advanced Mac users with some basic knowledge of video editing terms and procedures; explaining basic video production and editing is beyond the scope of this book. Final Cut Pro is designed to be easy to use, but it's still a professional level video editing and compositing program. If you are not new to the Macintosh, but you're completely new to video editing, consider some basic training in the fundamentals of video editing before you plunge into this program. Try Apple's free iMovie program—it's a great way to get a taste of basic video editing in a stripped-down program that's a little easier for beginners to use.

What's in this book

The first part of the book covers hardware setup, program installation, and specifying program preferences. You'll also find "A Tour of Your Desktop Post-Production Facility," a quick feature overview of the entire program.

The next section introduces the Log and Capture, Browser, and Viewer windows—the Final Cut Pro tools you use for logging, capturing, and organizing media in preparation for an edit.

The third part of the book details the variety of ways you can use Final Cut Pro's editing tools to assemble and refine an edited sequence. This section covers basic editing procedures and the operation of the Timeline, Canvas, and Trim Edit windows; and it includes a chapter on rendering techniques and strategies.

The last section includes chapters on creating final output, on making the best use of Final Cut Pro's media management tools, and on the program's special effects and compositing tools.

How to use this book

This guide is designed to be a Final Cut Pro user's companion, with an emphasis on step-by-step descriptions of specific tasks. You'll encounter some of the following features:

◆ **"Anatomy" sections** introduce the major program windows with large annotated illustrations identifying interface features and operation. If you are not a "step-by-step" kind of person, you can pick up quite bit of information just by browsing these illustrations.

◆ **"FCP Protocol" sidebars** lay out the protocols (the programming "rules") that govern the way Final Cut Pro works. These sections are highly recommended reading for anyone interested in a serious relationship with this program.

◆ **Sidebars** throughout the book highlight production techniques, project management ideas, and tips for streamlining your workflow.

◆ **Tips** are short bits that call your attention to a neat trick or a cool feature, or that warn you of a potential pitfall in the task at hand.

Learning Final Cut Pro

Here are some tips to help you get up and running in Final Cut Pro ASAP.

Basic theory

Two sidebars, one in Chapter 2 and another in Chapter 4, are referred to throughout this book. You don't absolutely have to read these to operate the program, but understanding some of the basic concepts underlying the design of the program is going to make Final Cut Pro much easier to learn.

"What is Nondestructive Editing?" in Chapter 2 explains how nondestructive editing works and how it impacts the operation of Final Cut Pro.

"FCP Protocol: Clips and Sequences" in Chapter 4 explains the protocols governing clip and sequence versions, which is one of the keys to understanding how Final Cut Pro works.

FCP is context-sensitive

The Final Cut Pro interface is context-sensitive, which means that the options available in the program's menus and dialog boxes can vary depending on any of the following factors:

◆ The external video hardware you have attached to the system

◆ The setup configuration you specify when you install the program

◆ What program window is currently active

◆ What program selection you just made

The logic behind the context-sensitive design is sound: to simplify your life by removing irrelevant options from your view. However, because the interface is context-sensitive, the menus and dialog boxes in your installation of Final Cut Pro may occasionally differ from the illustrations shown in this guide.

Test, test, test

Many times, what you are able to produce with Final Cut Pro depends on the capabilities of your external video hardware and the video format you are working in. So before you rush out and submit a budget or sign a contract, take your entire Final Cut Pro system, including your external video gear, for a test drive.

Keyboard commands

Final Cut Pro was designed to support a wide variety of working styles ranging from heavy pointing, clicking, and dragging to entirely keyboard-based editing. More keyboard commands are available than those listed in the individual tasks in this book. You'll find a comprehensive list of keyboard commands in Appendix B.

Shortcut menus

Final Cut Pro makes extensive use of shortcut menus. As you are exploring the program, Control-clicking on items and interface elements is a quick way to see your options in many areas of the FCP interface, and it can speed up the learning process.

Refer to the manual

I'm happy to be able to recommend the official *Final Cut Pro 2 User's Manual* that ships with the program (that's why the box is so heavy). Apple documentors packed this book with basic FCP information, and added explanatory sections for beginning editors, complete lists of FCP filters, shots of every shortcut menu in the program, 126 pages devoted to working with audio, and so on. I'll occasionally refer you to specific sections of the official manual that cover a topic in much more detail that this book can accommodate. (Still, they did miss a few items covered here, and this Visual QuickPro Guide is much easier to carry around.)

Check out the Tech Info Library

Apple posts a steady stream of valuable Final Cut Pro articles and updates in its Technical Information Library (TIL). The company also posts information about FCP "known issues" (that's corp-speak for "bug") as TIL articles. See Appendix A for information on locating the TIL online.

INTRODUCTION

The Web is your friend

Using the World Wide Web is an essential part of using Final Cut Pro. Apple, as well as the manufacturers of the video hardware you'll be using with Final Cut Pro, rely on the Web to inform users of the latest developments and program updates and to provide technical support. You'll find a starter list of online resources in Appendix A and specific Web references sprinkled throughout this book. There are some great sources of information, technical help, and camaraderie out there. If you get stuck or encounter difficulties getting underway, go online and start asking questions. After you've learned the program, go online and answer questions. Helping other people is a great way to learn.

Where to find more information

Check out Appendix A, "Online Resources," for a listing of helpful Web sites.

BEFORE YOU BEGIN

This chapter walks you through the process of assembling the necessary hardware, hooking everything up, and installing Final Cut Pro. Topics include Final Cut Pro system requirements, as well as the hardware components and configurations for both a basic setup and a more full-featured system.

Note that hardware selection, configuration, and installation can involve a wide range of input and output devices and several manufacturers' hardware protocols. This chapter covers Apple's recommended configurations and suggests some sources for getting up-to-the-minute information and advice on hardware.

This chapter also introduces you to Apple's FireWire protocol, the high-speed data transfer protocol underlying the powerful digital video handling in this program.

At the end of this chapter are suggestions for optimizing performance, including recommendations for running Final Cut Pro on a minimal "base-case" system, and tips for troubleshooting Final Cut Pro.

New in 2: More Hardware Options

Final Cut Pro's open program architecture is designed to allow video hardware manufacturers to develop products that integrate smoothly with FCP operation. In the years since FCP's release, the list of compatible hardware has grown to include decks, cameras, and capture systems that range from simple consumer-quality DV camcorders to systems capable of editing uncompressed high-definition (HD) video.

Hardware-assisted real-time video effects are the latest addition to Final Cut Pro's open architecture. Here's what you need to know before diving in:

FCP program design allows video card developers to pick and choose which individual effects their real-time system will support. Effects that aren't programmed into that system's hardware are handled by Final Cut Pro's software, but they don't play back without rendering. Because different real-time systems offer different capabilities, you need to pay close attention to the specifications of any system you are considering.

Some developers are adding real-time effects support to their existing analog video capture systems. Matrox's RTMac and Pinnacle's Targa CinéWave are two examples of combination capture/real-time effects systems.

The bottom line? There's a wide world of hardware available to expand your FCP system, but do your homework (and ask your mom to check it for you) before you buy.

A good place to start your investigation is Apple's Final Cut Pro Web site, which offers a list of compatible products and news of upcoming developments: http://www.apple.com/finalcutpro/specs.html.

What's the Difference Between DV and Digital Video?

When you refer to *digital video*, you could be talking about any video format that stores image and audio information in digital form—it's digital video whether you store it on a D1 tape or on a DVD disc.

DV is a specific digital video format whose identifying characteristic is that conversion from analog to digital information takes place in the DV camera. So *DV* is a camera-based digital video format.

There are a few different flavors of DV; the differences between them come down to tape format and tape speed.

◆ DV usually refers to MiniDV.

◆ DVCAM prints the same DV bitstream to a larger, more robust tape stock.

◆ DVC Pro uses a professional-grade tape as well and also supports a high-quality mode— DVC Pro 50—which supports digitizing at twice the data rate.

System Requirements

Except for maybe long-range weather forecasting, editing digital video on a desktop computer remains one of the most power-hungry tasks you can ask your system to perform. Final Cut Pro 1.0 was conceived as a DV post-production system that would run on a Macintosh G3 computer. Introduced two years after the program's initial release, FCP 2 has slightly stiffer minimum system requirements.

With the support of FireWire technology to move the video data at 400 megabits per second, ATI video support, and multiprocessor CPUs, the G4 has reached a performance level capable of handling uncompressed HD (high-definition) video, as well as DV. Final Cut Pro 2 supports a wider variety of video hardware and heftier video formats.

Apple is continuously testing and qualifying third-party software and third-party external devices for compatibility with Final Cut Pro. To review the latest list of Apple-approved video hardware and software, go to the Final Cut Pro Web site: http://www.apple.com/finalcutpro.

Final Cut Pro 2 minimum system requirements are:

◆ Macintosh computer Power Macintosh with a 300-megahertz (MHz) or faster G3 or G4 processor. Apple specifies Blue and White G3/300s as the low end of their minimum standard. Beige G3 models are not officially supported.

◆ PowerBook G3/300 MHz or faster, with a Final Cut Pro–qualified video capture card.

◆ iMac DV, 350 MHz or faster.

◆ Mac OS9.1 or later. FCP 2 is not certified for Mac OS X or OS X Classic mode.

◆ 192 MB of RAM, or 105 MB of RAM available for FCP 2.

◆ CD-ROM or DVD-ROM drive.

◆ 6 GB A/V (audio/video rated) drive (16 GB recommended).

◆ True-color (24-bit) display.

◆ ATI built-in video support on G3/4 models (required for DV).

If you want to be able to capture and output video from the computer to an external video device (a video deck or camcorder), you'll also need *one of the following:*

◆ A DV source connected to a computer equipped with an Apple FireWire port. Most blue and white G3 and all G4 models come equipped with FireWire ports, but you can add FireWire to an older G3 with an Apple PCI card.

◆ An analog video source and a Final Cut Pro–qualified video capture card or device.

In addition to one of the above video devices, you'll also need the correct FireWire or device control cable and any additional cables you may need for connecting your deck or camcorder to your computer.

Real-Time Effects: About Matrox RTMac

Matrox RTMac is the first (but not the last) real-time hardware available for Final Cut Pro. The RTMac package includes a PCI board, cable, and breakout box and lists for an additional $999 over the price of FCP 2.

Here's what the Matrox RTMac will do for you: The breakout box has analog video and audio inputs and outputs (S-video and composite RCA jacks), so you can connect the output from the breakout box to an analog deck and monitor analog previews of the RTMac's output. You also can capture analog video through the breakout box's analog inputs and transcode it to DV in real time. RTMac's PCI card can also drive a second computer monitor.

What does the RTMac process in real time? RTMac supports up to three layers in real time—two video and one graphics layer, or two graphics layers and one video layer. You can do text superimposition and video-stream scaling and motion, with keyframes, but no filter processing. You can crop, scale, or reposition the video image and adjust opacity, but you can't alter the individual pixels in real time, like you can with color correction, blurring, and stylizing filters.

Details on the Matrox RTMac Board can be found at the Matrox site: http://www.matrox.com.

Real-Time System Requirements

If you want to enhance your Final Cut Pro setup with video hardware (such as the Matrox RTMac) that supports real-time effects, you'll need a beefier system. Current minimum requirements call for a G4 400 MHz system equipped with 256 MB of RAM.

For more information on real-time system capabilities, see Chapter 10, "Rendering."

For details on FCP-compatible real-time systems, visit Apple's Final Cut Pro web site: http://www.apple.com/finalcutpro.

System Configuration

A hardware configuration for Final Cut Pro should handle basic digital video post-production from start to finish.

A basic DV configuration (Figure 1.1) includes a DV camcorder or deck, a computer, and a high-resolution monitor. In a DV configuration, the digitizing of video takes place in the DV deck or camcorder at the time you shoot or record your footage to tape. So when you capture DV into Final Cut Pro, you are not digitizing it; you are transferring already digitized media.

DV camcorder or deck: The DV camera or deck feeds digital video and audio into the computer via FireWire and records DV output from Final Cut Pro.

Computer: Final Cut Pro, installed on the Mac, captures and then stores digital video from the DV camera or deck on an A/V hard drive. Qualified Macs are equipped with FireWire; no additional video digitizing card is needed. You use your computer's speakers to monitor your audio. You edit your DV footage with Final Cut Pro and then send it back out to tape through FireWire to your DV camcorder or deck.

High-resolution computer monitor: You view the results of your work on the computer's monitor.

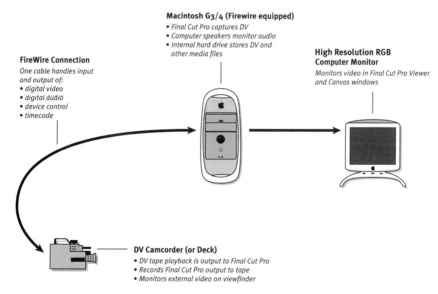

Figure 1.1 A basic DV hardware configuration.

A basic analog video configuration
(**Figure 1.2**) includes an analog video camcorder or deck, a qualified video capture card, a computer, and a high-resolution monitor. In an analog video configuration, the video capture card (installed in your computer) digitizes your video as you capture your video footage in Final Cut Pro, and then converts your digital video back to analog when you output your Final Cut Pro project back to tape.

Analog camcorder or deck: The analog camera or deck feeds analog video and audio into the video capture card installed in your computer and records analog output from the video capture card.

Serial device control: The serial connection from the deck through a serial USB adapter to the computer's USB port (or directly into a computer modified with an added serial port) carries timecode and device-control information in both directions.

Video capture card: The capture card digitizes analog video and audio when you capture into Final Cut Pro. It converts digital video and audio to analog when you output to tape.

Computer: Final Cut Pro, installed on your Mac, captures and then stores digital video from the video capture card on an A/V hard drive.

You edit your digital video footage with Final Cut Pro and then output back to tape through the video capture card to your analog video device.

High-resolution monitor: You view the results of your work on the computer's monitor. You use your computer's speakers to monitor your audio.

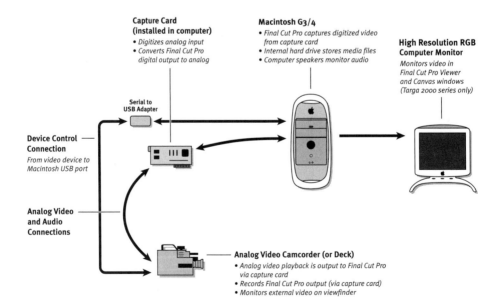

Figure 1.2 A basic analog video hardware configuration.

Frame-Accurate DV Capture Options

If you are designing a Final Cut Pro system based on DV and FireWire, be aware that DV device control is not reliably frame accurate. The discrepancies are minor and do not affect audio/video sync, but the start frame of recaptured clips could be one or two frames offset from your original capture.

If your post–production plan includes recapturing your footage after editing in FCP, you will probably want frame-accurate In and Out points for every clip you log and capture, and you should design your system to include serial device control. That means that you'll need a DV deck or camcorder that has both a FireWire port and a serial port.

Your captured video stream will still come into the Mac via the FireWire connection, but Final Cut will use the serial connection for frame-accurate device control. The new *Final Cut Pro 2 User's Manual* has details on setting up a DV system using serial device control.

For more information on device control and FCP, see "Connecting Video Devices and Monitors" later in this chapter.

FCP Protocol: Disk Names

When you are naming hard drives, partitions, and folders that you intend to use with Final Cut pro, you should observe these special requirements:

◆ Each hard disk must have a name that does not contain the entire name of another disk or partition. For example, disks named "Inferno" and "Inferno 1" could cause FCP to experience media management problems later.

◆ Don't use double-byte characters in the names of disks and folders. If you do, Final Cut Pro may not be able to export or import EDLs (Edit Decision Lists) accurately. (Double-byte character sets are required for writing languages with a large number of characters.)

A recommended setup (Figure 1.3)
enhances your monitoring capabilities with
the addition of an NTSC or PAL video monitor and external speakers to the basic configuration. Additional drives for expanded media
storage capacity are also recommended.

◆ A video monitor is highly recommended
for previewing video output from your
hard disk if you intend to output to videotape or broadcast on television. Final Cut
Pro outputs video to the video monitor
through your camcorder or deck. Many
video camcorders have built-in LCD displays that you can use as an external video
monitor. Connect the NTSC or PAL monitor to your video deck or camcorder using
the component, S-video, or composite
output jacks.

◆ External speakers, monitoring the audio
output from your video camcorder or
deck, will provide you with higher-quality

audio output. Final Cut Pro audio output
is played through the camcorder or deck
when you are printing or editing video
with audio to tape.

✔ Tips

■ If you are going to use an external NTSC
or PAL monitor as you edit, connect your
external speakers to monitor the audio
output of your camcorder or deck, so that
the audio from the external speakers will
be synchronized with the video displayed
on the video monitor. You need to do this
because audio coming from your computer's built-in audio outputs is slightly
out of sync with the NTSC or PAL monitor.

■ FCP's default settings mute the audio feed
to your computer's speakers whenever
you've set it to output to an external video
device. So if you want to monitor audio
and video through the computer, choose
View > External Video and select Off.

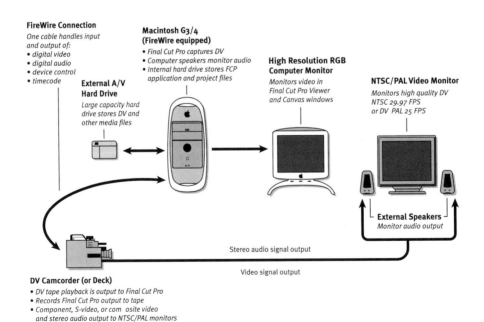

FireWire Connection
*One cable handles input
and output of:*
• *digital video*
• *digital audio*
• *device control*
• *timecode*

**External A/V
Hard Drive**
*Large capacity hard
drive stores DV and
other media files*

**Macintosh G3/4
(FireWire equipped)**
• *Final Cut Pro captures DV*
• *Computer speakers monitor audio*
• *Internal hard drive stores FCP
application and project files*

**High Resolution RGB
Computer Monitor**
*Monitors video in
Final Cut Pro Viewer
and Canvas windows*

NTSC/PAL Video Monitor
*Monitors high quality DV
NTSC 29.97 FPS
or DV PAL 25 FPS*

External Speakers
Monitor audio output

Stereo audio signal output

Video signal output

DV Camcorder (or Deck)
• *DV tape playback is output to Final Cut Pro*
• *Records Final Cut Pro output to tape*
• *Component, S-video, or com osite video
and stereo audio output to NTSC/PAL monitors
and external speakers*

Figure 1.3 A recommended DV hardware configuration.

Storage Strategy for Final Cut Pro

Digital video files are space-hungry critters. If you're going to edit anything substantial at all, you should consider additional hard drive storage for your system.

Some overall considerations when selecting a storage option:

Any storage system you select must be fast enough (a minimum transfer rate of 7 or 8 megabytes per second is recommended by some experts) to keep up with the data transfer rates required. Many storage formats do meet the speed requirement, but as you weigh your speed/capacity/price trade-offs, don't shortchange yourself in the speed department.

RAID (Redundant Array of Independent Disks)—multiple disk arrays that share the work of transferring and storing data—can be configured to improve your system's performance by increasing the speed of data transfer. RAID isn't necessary to editing in Final Cut Pro, but it is in wide use on high-performance systems.

Hard disk storage is available in a variety of formats, and the number of formats is always growing. Rather than discuss a variety of specific hard disk options, here's a set of strategic questions to help you steer to the storage option that's best for you.

How much space do I need?

DV requires 3.6 megabytes of storage per second of program material.

That's 216 megabytes of storage per one minute of DV.

Or one gigabyte of storage per five minutes of DV.

When you are calculating your storage needs, remember that a good rule of thumb is to add the final program lengths of the total number of projects you want to keep online and then multiply by four to accommodate any render files, undo's, scratch copies, or test exports you may generate during your editing process. Be more generous if want to capture much more footage than you ultimately use.

Do I need a dedicated drive just for media storage?

A dedicated drive for storing your media will improve the performance of your system because it contains no operating system software, other applications, or files that can fragment the disk. Fragmentation can interfere with the continuous data flow of video and audio to and from the disk.

Here's another reason to keep your media files and program files on separate drives: Your media drive, because it works harder, is more likely to crash than your program drive. In the event of a media drive crash, you may lose your media files, but you won't lose your edit data, which should make it easier to recover from the crash. A dedicated drive or drives for media storage is almost always a great investment.

Should I go with internal or external storage?

What kind of workflow do you anticipate? Whether to invest in internal drives (which could be less expensive) or external drives (which allow you to switch between projects quickly by swapping out drives on your workstation, or move a project and its media from one workstation to another quickly) depends on your individual needs.

Connecting Video Devices and Monitors

Connect video devices to your computer through a FireWire connection or a dedicated video capture card (such as Pinnacle's Targa CinéWave).

◆ You use a FireWire cable to connect your DV camcorder or deck to your computer. DV devices with FireWire transmit device control data, timecode, video, and audio over a single FireWire cable.

◆ If you are using an analog video capture card, device control and timecode signals are transmitted over one cable, while video and audio data use a separate set of cables. The type of audio and video connection cables depends on the type of analog video device you're connecting. See your video capture card's manual or manufacturer's Web site for details.

To connect a DV device to your computer with FireWire:

1. Start with a 6-pin to 4-pin FireWire cable. Plug the 6-pin connector into the 6-pin Apple FireWire port (**Figure 1.4**) and the 4-pin connector into your video device's DV port. (FireWire ports on external devices are sometimes labeled IEEE 1394, DV IN/OUT, or iLink.) Both connectors snap into place when properly engaged.

2. Turn on the DV camcorder or deck.

3. Switch the DV device to VCR mode (sometimes labeled VTR).

✔ Tip

■ If your DV device is Apple FireWire compatible, connecting it to the computer and turning it on before installing Final Cut Pro will allow the installation program to automatically receive setup information from your DV camcorder or deck.

Figure 1.4 The FireWire logo labels the FireWire ports on the back of your computer.

FireWire Cables: Handle with Care

You should use a 6-pin to 4-pin FireWire cable to connect a DV deck or camcorder to your computer.

Before you start hooking up your FireWire connectors, take a careful look at the connector ends (the 4-pin connector is the smaller end). They are easy to connect, but the 4-pin connectors and ports can be especially fragile. Before connecting a 4-pin connector to its corresponding port, be sure it is aligned properly by matching an indent on the connector to the indent in the port. Do not force the two together.

The 6-pin connector (the larger end) plugs into one of the FireWire ports on the back of your Mac. Don't try to force the 4-pin connector into the computer's 6-pin FireWire port.

CONNECTING VIDEO DEVICES AND MONITORS

Connecting an external NTSC or PAL monitor

Final Cut Pro is designed to make use of the audio and video outputs of your DV deck or camcorder to feed an external NTSC or PAL monitor. Because the monitor receives output from Final Cut Pro through your deck or camcorder's outputs, you must have your deck or camcorder on and the FireWire connection established to your computer, or you won't be able to view FCP's output on your monitor while you are working in Final Cut Pro.

To connect an external NTSC or PAL monitor:

1. Position your video monitor so that it is at a comfortable viewing distance when viewed from your computer monitor and keyboard.

2. *Do one of the following:*

   ▲ Connect the audio and video outputs of your video deck or camcorder to the audio and video inputs of your NTSC or PAL monitor.

   ▲ If you are using additional external speakers, or if your monitor has no speakers, connect only the video output from your video device to the video input of your video monitor. Use your video device's audio outputs to feed your external speakers.

3. After you have installed Final Cut Pro, you will be able to check your viewing settings in the External Video pop-up menu on the Summary tab of the Audio/ Video Settings window (**Figure 1.5**).

✔ Tip

■ If you choose to monitor Final Cut Pro's output though an external NTSC or PAL monitor, you may see a difference in the playback quality in the Canvas window. If you enable FireWire output to your video device, the Canvas will play back at 15 frames per second. Final Cut Pro is designed to give CPU priority to the FireWire output to ensure that there are no dropped frames in that output signal.

CONNECTING VIDEO DEVICES AND MONITORS

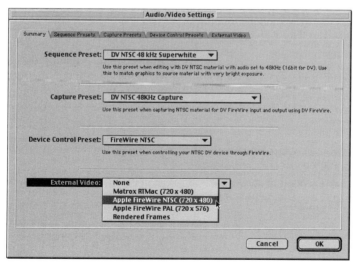

Figure 1.5 Check your viewing preferences in the External Video pop-up menu on the Summary tab of the Audio/Video Settings window.

Controlling video devices with Final Cut Pro

Final Cut Pro can control external video devices through a FireWire cable or a serial cable. If your camcorder or deck supports one of the device control protocols listed in the FCP Protocol sidebar, Final Cut Pro can transmit and receive timecode and transport control data to and from the device and may support remote control of the deck's search mechanisms.

You can also connect DV and non-DV camcorders or decks that do not support device control to capture video clips and export edited sequences.

Whenever you want to use an external video device, connect and turn on the device before opening Final Cut Pro so the application can detect the device.

If you want to use a camcorder as your playback/record deck, you must switch it to VCR mode. In VCR mode, the camcorder uses the video and audio connectors or FireWire for input and output. Because a camcorder in Camera mode has switched its inputs to receive information from the CCD sensor and microphone, Final Cut Pro cannot record to the camcorder while it is in Camera mode.

For more information on controlling your deck or camcorder during video capture, see Chapter 3, "Input: Getting Digital with Your Video."

For more information on controlling your deck or camcorder as you output to tape, see Chapter 11, "At Last: Creating Final Output."

About Apple FireWire

Apple FireWire is a high-speed serial bus that allows simultaneous transfer of digital video, digital audio, timecode information, and device control, all through a single cable. Many Power Macintosh G3/4s come with built-in FireWire ports on the back. FireWire's usefulness is not limited to digital video, however, and the future should bring a wide variety of hard drives, printers, scanners, audio mixers, and other peripheral devices that take advantage of FireWire's high speeds and advanced features.

FireWire (IEEE 1394) serial bus technology is currently supported by many professional and consumer-level camcorders and decks. However, not all manufacturers have implemented the full FireWire specification in their products, so some decks and camcorders won't fully support Final Cut Pro's device control. That is why Final Cut Pro provides two versions of the FireWire protocol in its Device Control presets: Apple FireWire and Apple FireWire Basic.

If your deck or camcorder uses FireWire, try selecting the Apple FireWire protocol first. This is the default protocol if you select DV during the installation setup. With Apple FireWire as your selected device protocol, your FireWire deck or camcorder should support the most basic functions like returning timecode and accepting basic transport commands. If you discover that your deck or camcorder does not accurately go to specified timecodes or fails to execute special commands, switch to the Apple FireWire Basic protocol. To learn how to switch between FireWire protocols in Final Cut Pro, see "Specifying Device Control Settings" in Chapter 2.

✔ Tip

- FireWire Basic is a simplified device control protocol only. Using FireWire Basic as your device control protocol will have no effect on the input or output quality of your digital video and audio.

FCP Protocol: Controlling External Video Output

The External Video display options in Final Cut Pro require a little explanation. There are two control points. The first, the External Video pop-up menu on the Summary tab of the Audio/ Video Settings window, is where you select an output format and/or a destination for your video output. This menu is context sensitive; you will see only the options that your currently connected hardware supports.

Selecting Rendered Frames instead of Targa Video Output, Apple FireWire DV NTSC, or Apple FireWire DV PAL will output rendered frames as well as any video that does not require rendering.

Once you have selected your output format and destination, your second point of control is accessed from the Menu bar. Think of View > External Video as a valve at the end of a pipe, which can be closed (Off), activated on demand (Single Frame), or wide open (All Frames).

If you're building some heavy effects, waiting for all your frames to render before you can watch playback on your external monitor could be too time consuming, and that's where the External Video settings in the View menu come in handy.

With Rendered Frames as your Audio/Video Settings External Video selection:

◆ If you choose View > External Video > All Frames, FCP will play all video that does not require rendering, and it will also render the currently displayed frame automatically whenever you are parked on a frame.

◆ If you choose View > External Video > Single Frames, FCP will play all video that does not require rendering, but will render and display a single frame only when you press F15 or Shift-F12. This setting allows you to preview a single frame of an effected clip on your NTSC or PAL monitor before committing to a full rendering operation.

◆ If you choose View > External Video > Off, you shut off the external video output.

There's a spot of confusion for Targa users here. If you have a Targa card, you would think the best Targa setting would be Targa Video Output, the one analogous to the DV default of Apple FireWire DV NTSC or PAL, right?

But noooo; you want to select Rendered Frames from the pop-up menu. Selecting Targa Video Output will actually play only rendered frames, but it won't display any video that does not require rendering. Don't ask. Just select Rendered Frames.

FCP Protocol: Device Control

Final Cut Pro supports a variety of hardware manufacturer's device control protocols, as well as Apple's own FireWire. Many of these require the use of a serial cable.

If your Macintosh does not have a serial port, you can install a third-party built-in serial port. The Stealth Gport serial adapter kit consists of a serial port and an internal card and replaces the internal modem in your G3/G4. Be sure to order the correct port type for your G3/G4 model. You can also use a third-party adapter, such as the Keyspan USB serial adapter, to attach serial devices to the USB port. Final Cut Pro supports these device control protocols:

◆ Apple FireWire or Apple FireWire Basic

◆ JVC RS-232

◆ Panasonic RS-232 or RS-422

◆ Sony RS-422 or RS-232

◆ Sony VISCA or LANC

(Note that the Panasonic RS-422 and Sony RS-422 protocols require special cables.)

For more information about the various device control protocols and their cables, see Chapter 2 in the *Final Cut Pro User's Manual* or visit the Final Cut Pro Web site: http://www.apple.com/finalcutpro.

CONNECTING VIDEO DEVICES AND MONITORS

Figure 1.6 The application folders on the FCP CD are thoughtfully arranged in the order you need to use them. Work through the folders from top to bottom to complete an installation.

Installing Final Cut Pro

It's a good idea to set up and connect your additional hardware before you install the Final Cut Pro software, because the type of capture hardware you will be using with Final Cut Pro determines how the software is configured during installation. If you have not yet installed and configured the additional hardware you will be using with your computer, read the "System Configuration" and "Connecting Video Devices and Monitors" sections earlier in this chapter. If you already have your system configured with capture hardware and a camcorder or deck, proceed with the installation instructions in this section. If you don't have your hardware yet, it's okay to proceed with the installation of the Final Cut Pro software.

You don't need external hardware to follow the tutorial.

If you can, install the Final Cut Pro application on a separate partition of your drive, with its own System Folder. It's generally fine to keep other graphics programs in the same partition, but programs like Web browsers, e-mail, and even the newest versions of Microsoft Office make use of an Internet or network connection. The extensions those network-dependent programs install in your system's extension folder are the ones most likely to cause conflicts that could interfere with the smooth operation of Final Cut Pro.

It's also important to install your software in the recommended order. Your view of the application folders on the Final Cut Pro CD has been arranged in the order you need to use the folders to complete an installation (**Figure 1.6**). Just work through them from top to bottom.

Upgrading to Final Cut Pro 2

Here's a few tips for users upgrading to Final Cut Pro 2 from an earlier version:

◆ If you're an FCP user who has purchased the upgrade version of FCP 2, you'll need a properly installed version of FCP version 1.2.5 on your computer or the upgrade will not install. If you're running FCP version 1.2.1 or earlier, you'll need to download and install version 1.2.5 before you run the FCP2 upgrade installer. You can find the Final Cut Pro 1.2.5 installer at http://www.apple.com/finalcutpro/download/.

◆ Be sure to allocate enough memory to FCP 2 to handle your current projects.

◆ You can update project files created with FCP 1.x, but the format update requires you to specify how FCP will interpret color space in these files. Older versions of QuickTime used DV codecs that converted YCrCb (the color space used by DV video) to RGB (the color space used by computers) whenever rendering was required. This conversion could generate noticeable color or luminance shifts. If your old project has links to render files created with the old DV codec, you'll probably want to discard those and re-render your project in FCP 2.

  ▲ Before you do anything, though, make a backup copy of your project file. Once you've updated a project file to FCP 2 format, you won't be able to open it in earlier versions of FCP.

  ▲ For details on project upgrade procedures, see Chapter 7 in the *Final Cut Pro 2 User's Manual*.

Figure 1.7 Double-click the QuickTime Installer icon.

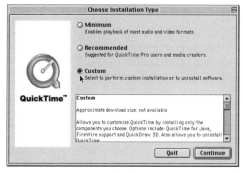

Figure 1.8 Choose the QuickTime Custom installation option.

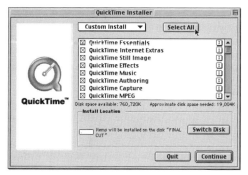

Figure 1.9 Click Select All in the QuickTime Installer window.

Installing QuickTime first

Before you install Final Cut Pro on your system, you'll need to install QuickTime. Much of Final Cut Pro's functionality is based on the QuickTime "engine." To be sure you are installing the correct version of QuickTime, check Apple's Web site for the latest information on QuickTime updates and Final Cut Pro version compatibility.

To install QuickTime components:

1. Insert the Final Cut Pro CD into your CD- or DVD-ROM drive.

2. Double-click the Final Cut Pro CD icon and then double-click the QuickTime folder.

3. Double-click the QuickTime Installer icon (**Figure 1.7**) and follow the onscreen instructions.

4. In the Choose Installation Type window, select Custom (**Figure 1.8**).

5. In the QuickTime Installer window, click Select All and then click Continue (**Figure 1.9**).

   This QuickTime installation will replace any previous versions of QuickTime and will install the complete set of QuickTime components that Final Cut Pro requires.

6. Complete the QuickTime installation process by restarting your computer.

To unlock QuickTime Pro:

1. From the Apple menu in the Finder, choose Control Panels > QuickTime Settings to open the QuickTime control panel.

2. In the QuickTime Settings window, choose Registration from the pop-up menu (**Figure 1.10**) and then click the Edit Registration button.

3. In the Registered To field, type **QuickTime Pro**.

4. In the Registration Number field, enter the QuickTime Pro serial number that came with your Final Cut Pro software and then click OK (**Figure 1.11**).

5. Close the QuickTime Settings window.

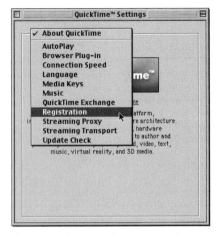

Figure 1.10 Choose Registration from the pop-up menu on the QuickTime Settings control panel.

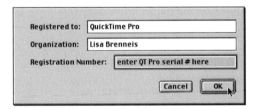

Figure 1.11 Enter your name and the QuickTime Pro registration number that came with your FCP software and then click OK.

Where to Install FCP?

Here's a recommended installation configuration for a Final Cut Pro system with two hard drives available:

You should leave your fastest drive completely free for media files only. Media files include captured audio and video, as well as rendered media files and any computer-generated graphics or motion graphics.

You should partition your other drive into two partitions, installing your office/internet applications and a system folder on one partition, and Final Cut Pro, along with the other video and graphics programs you use, on the other partition. The partition where FCP is installed should have its own system folder, with an extension set optimized for running FCP. That's the best way to avoid possible extension conflicts. Keep your Final Cut Pro project files on the same drive as the Final Cut Pro application.

You should also back up your project files to removable media with such frequency that your behavior seems obsessive to a casual observer. Go ahead, let 'em laugh

Figure 1.12 Double-click the Install Final Cut Pro icon.

Figure 1.13 Review the "Before You Install Final Cut Pro 2" notes and then click Continue.

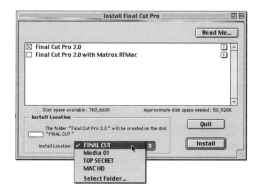

Figure 1.14 Choose a destination disk from the pop-up list and click Continue.

To install Final Cut Pro:

1. Be sure any external video hardware is connected and turned on before you start the installation procedure, so that Final Cut pro can automatically detect your video capture equipment.

2. If it's not already loaded, insert the Final Cut Pro CD into your CD- or DVD-ROM drive; then double-click the Install Final Cut Pro icon (**Figure 1.12**).

3. Read the Software License Agreement and click Continue; then *do one of the following:*

   ▲ Click Disagree to cancel the installation.

   ▲ Click Agree to continue with the installation.

4. If you click Agree, the "Before You Install Final Cut Pro 2" notes appear in the window. Review the material and then click Continue (**Figure 1.13**).

5. In the Install Final Cut Pro window, *select one of the following* installation options:

   ▲ Choose Final Cut Pro 2.0 if you are not using a Matrox real-time card.

   ▲ Choose Final Cut Pro 2.0 with Matrox RTMac if you are using a Matrox real-time video card with Final Cut Pro.

6. Choose a destination disk from the pop-up list (**Figure 1.14**) and click Install.

7. When the installation is complete, click Quit.

Allocating memory to Final Cut Pro

Before you launch Final Cut Pro for the first time, it's a good idea to set the application's RAM allocation. Systems including a real-time system or video capture card could require 256 MB or more allocated for FCP. However, DV/FireWire setups should be fine with the FCP's default memory allocation. You can check the amount of RAM you have available for FCP by quitting all open applications and then choosing About This Computer from the Apple Menu (**Figure 1.15**).

Subtract at least 15 MB from the Largest Unused Block total: that's the maximum memory allocation you could safely assign to Final Cut Pro.

To allocate memory to Final Cut Pro:

1. Click the Final Cut Pro application icon to select it.

2. Choose File > Get Info > Memory.

3. In the Final Cut Pro Info window, enter a value in the Preferred Size field (**Figure 1.16**).

4. Enter a value in the Minimum Size field and then close the window.

✔ Tip

■ Once you have a project underway in FCP, it's a good idea to check FCP's RAM utilization with your projects open. See "Check Your Memory" later in this chapter for details.

■ Real-time system users should allow additional unassigned RAM to accommodate the real-time system's still cache.

Figure 1.15 Check About This Computer to determine how much memory you can safely allocate for Final Cut Pro.

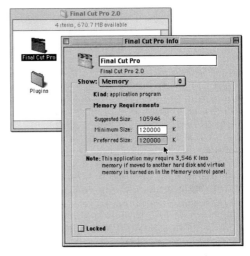

Figure 1.16 Set memory allocation in the Final Cut Pro Info window.

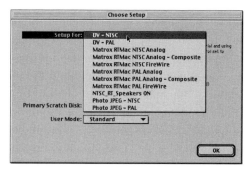

Figure 1.17 In the Choose Setup window, pick the Easy Setup that matches your system's video format and hardware.

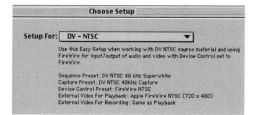

Figure 1.18 When you choose an Easy Setup, a brief description and summary of its settings appears below its name.

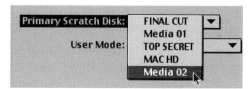

Figure 1.19 Choose the disk you want to use to store your captured media from the Primary Scratch Disk pop-up list.

Registering and choosing an initial setup

If you haven't done so already, be sure any external video hardware is connected and turned on before you launch Final Cut Pro for the first time, so that FCP can detect your video-capture equipment and streamline the Initial Setup process. With standard hardware setups, your Initial Setup selections should correctly configure all your Final Cut Pro Audio/Video settings automatically.

To choose your initial setup:

1. Open the Final Cut Pro 2 application and enter your registration information and serial number.

2. In the Choose Setup window, choose an Easy Setup from the Setup For pop-up menu (**Figure 1.17**).

   A brief description and summary of your selected Easy Setup appears below the pop-up menu (**Figure 1.18**). Choose the setup that matches your system's video format and hardware.

3. From the Primary Scratch Disk pop-up menu, choose the disk you want to use to store your captured video, audio, render, and cache files (**Figure 1.19**). It is recommended that you save captured media files on a different disk than the disk where Final Cut Pro is installed.

   continues on next page

4. From the User Mode pop-up menu, *choose one of the following* (**Figure 1.20**):

▲ Standard: Allows access to Final Cut Pro's full feature set.

▲ Cutting Station: Allows access to basic editing functions only and disables effects and keyframing features.

5. Click OK.

Final Cut Pro is now configured to use a standard set of preferences and preset controls based on information you supplied during initial setup. You may want to review the default preference settings before you dive into a project. For details on modifying preferences and presets, see Chapter 2, "Welcome to Final Cut Pro."

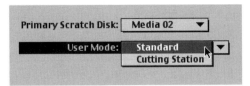

Figure 1.20 Choose Standard or Cutting Station from the User Mode pop-up menu.

INSTALLING FINAL CUT PRO

What's an Easy Setup?

An Easy Setup is one preset configuration of multiple Final Cut Pro settings: Device Control, Capture, Sequence Preset, and External Video. Instead of choosing several presets and external video settings using various tabs, you can now choose them all in a single window—Easy Setup.

Your selected Easy Setup becomes your default setup, so all projects and sequences use these settings until you change them. FCP offers several standard Easy Setup configurations, but you also have the option of customizing an Easy Setup

Any customized setups are stored in the Custom Settings folder in the Final Cut Pro Documents folder, which makes your custom setups portable.

You don't need to change the Easy Setup unless you change your video hardware or source media. Switching to a different Easy Setup affects only the projects that you create after you switch. It doesn't change settings of previously created or currently open projects.

If you are using FCP with a variety of hardware, Easy Setup should make switching system configurations more idiot proof.

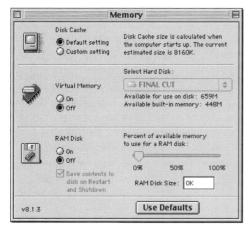

Figure 1.21 On the Memory control panel, use the default disk cache settings and turn off virtual memory.

Figure 1.22 Overlapping the video display areas of the Canvas and the Viewer will interfere with smooth playback.

Optimizing Performance

Here's a rundown of settings and maintenance tips that can help Final Cut Pro
perform more efficiently:

Settings

◆ Turn off virtual memory on the Memory
control panel .

◆ Set your disk cache to the default setting
(**Figure 1.21**).

◆ Turn off AppleTalk in the AppleTalk
Control Panel.

◆ Turn off file sharing on the Control Strip.

◆ Avoid running other applications
and processes, especially networking
software and screensavers that run in
the background.

◆ Do not set Final Cut Pro's memory allocation to an amount higher than the
currently available RAM.

Display

◆ Make sure that windows displaying
video are not obscured or overlapped
(**Figure 1.22**).

◆ Don't place program windows so that
they are split across dual monitors.

Disk maintenance

◆ Store your project files on your startup disk, and store your media and rendered files on a separate hard disk.

◆ Defragment disk drives regularly, especially those used for capturing.

◆ When a project is finished and archived, delete all files from the disk you used to create the project. Defragment the drive with a disk-optimizing utility. This helps prepare the disk for the next project.

◆ Final Cut Pro will perform poorly if you try to work with remote media files over a network connection. Copy files from the network to a local disk before importing them

◆ It's a good idea to run Apple's Disk First Aid utility once or twice a month to check your drive's data directory.

Figure 1.23 This memory utilization bar indicates that about half of the RAM allocated for FCP is in use—that's just about right.

Check Your Memory

Running Final Cut Pro too close to the limits of its memory allocation can seriously impair performance. So after you've started working on projects in Final Cut Pro, you might want to check and see if you have the right amount of RAM allocated to FCP.

Depending on the size of your projects, you should allocate an extra 20 to 60 MB more RAM for FCP than the RAM required to open your average project load.

Here's how to check out your FCP RAM utilization: With your project open and sequences loaded in the Timeline, switch to the Finder and choose About This Computer from the Apple menu. (Save your project first, just to be safe.) If the bar indicates that you're using 50 to 75 percent of your FCP RAM allocation (**Figure 1.23**), that's just about right.

If you see that the Final Cut Pro bar is only 10 percent filled, you can probably reduce your RAM allocation. Some users prefer to allocate the same amount of RAM for both minimum and preferred settings. That way they know that FCP will always be operating with the same memory allocation.

The extra RAM won't hurt anything, but wouldn't you like to be able to run Photoshop and FCP at the same time?

OPTIMIZING PERFORMANCE

The Bottom Line: Running FCP on a G3/300

To get the best performance possible from Final Cut Pro running on a slower G3, you'll have to give up a little flexibility in your display options, but you may find that the improved responsiveness and playback quality is worth it.

1. Eliminate display scaling. Scaling the video to match the size of the playback window in the Viewer or Canvas is handled by the computer's ATI video card, but it takes a lot of processing power to pull it off. To reduce the ATI card's demands on your CPU, set your display option to match DV's native display format: 50 percent, non-square pixels. Go to the Zoom pop-up menu in the Canvas, set the View size to 50 percent, and then uncheck the View as Square Pixels box.

2. On the Monitors control panel, set your monitor resolution to 1024 by 768 or lower and your color depth to Millions.

3. The latest ATI components shipped with FCP require QuickDraw 3D in order to function. Check the Extensions Manager to make sure that you have all your ATI and QuickDraw 3D extensions enabled.

4. On the General tab of the Preferences window, reduce the number of undo's as well as the number of recent items to free up more RAM. If necessary, turn off playback in the Canvas altogether, and monitor only on your external NTSC or PAL monitor, by unchecking Mirror on Desktop during Playback on the External Video tab of the Audio/Video Settings window.

5. Keep your projects lean by deleting old versions of sequences that you no longer need to reference. Smaller projects reduce the amount of RAM necessary to track an open project file.

6. Reinitialize your drives. Quite often, old drive software and/or drivers will impair performance.

OPTIMIZING PERFORMANCE

Troubleshooting

You probably won't encounter any of these problems. But if you should have problems after installing Final Cut Pro and configuring your hardware, the following tips may help.

Many of the tips presented here involve checking and adjusting preferences. But before you start changing individual preference settings, try this: Choose Edit > Easy Setup and make sure you're still using the correct Easy Setup for your video format and hardware.

Chapter 2, "Welcome to Final Cut Pro," contains a guide to setting preferences and presets.

You can't establish a device control connection with your camcorder or deck.

◆ Make sure your device control cable or FireWire cable is properly connected.

◆ Verify that the camcorder is set to VCR mode.

◆ If your device has a Local/Remote switch, be sure it's set to Remote.

◆ Turn on the device and restart Final Cut Pro.

◆ Make sure the appropriate protocol for your device is selected on the Device Control Preset pop-up menu on the Summary tab of the Audio/Video Settings window.

You can't control certain functions of your camcorder or deck.

◆ Make sure your device control cable or FireWire cable is properly connected.

◆ Make sure you've selected the correct protocol for your camcorder or deck on

the Device Control Preset pop-up menu on the Summary tab of the Audio/Video Settings window.

◆ If you are using a device with FireWire, try switching the device control protocol from Apple FireWire to Apple FireWire Basic.

◆ If your deck has a local/remote switch, make sure it's switched to remote.

◆ A few DV camcorders and decks require special scripts for device control to operate properly. The scripts are available on the Final Cut Pro CD and should be installed in the Final Cut Pro Plugins folder. Check Apple's Final Cut Pro Web site to see if your equipment requires a script.

You don't hear audio on your computer's speakers when playing video from your camcorder or deck.

◆ Make sure your audio cables are properly connected.

◆ When you enable your external video output (FireWire or other) to monitor video externally, your audio and video are routed to your external monitor or video device, and your computer's speakers are not receiving any audio. Make sure your external monitor and speakers are on and the volume turned up. To disable external video output, choose View > External Video and select Off.

◆ Check your QuickTime audio settings on the Capture Presets tab of the Audio/Video Settings window. For more information on audio sample and source settings, see the section on setting capture preferences in Chapter 2, "Welcome to Final Cut Pro."

Video is not visible on an external NTSC or PAL monitor.

◆ Make sure your cables are properly connected.

◆ Verify that the camcorder is set to VCR mode.

◆ Make sure the appropriate hardware setting is selected on the View External pop-up menu on the Summary tab of the Audio/Video Settings window.

◆ Choose Rendered Frames from the View During Playback Using pop-up menu on the External Video tab of the Audio/Video Settings window to render frames before they are output to NTSC or PAL video.

◆ Choose All Frames or Single Frames from the External Video submenu of the View menu.

◆ Make sure the Log and Capture window is closed.

You noticed dropped frames on your NTSC or PAL monitor during DV playback from the Timeline.

Like the common cold, dropped frames are frequently a symptom of an over-worked system. Refer to Appendix A of the *Final Cut Pro User's Manual* for a comprehensive list of possible causes for dropped frames. But here are a few easy things to try first:

◆ Make sure you have allocated enough RAM to the Final Cut Pro application memory partition.

◆ Reduce the Canvas or Viewer view size to 50 percent.

◆ Disable View as Square Pixels in the Zoom pop-up menu.

◆ Turn off Mirror on Desktop during Playback on the External Video tab of the Audio/Video Settings window.

◆ Reduce the number of RealTime Audio Mixing tracks specified on the General Preferences tab.

◆ Turn off AppleTalk and file sharing.

◆ Turn off virtual memory on the Memory control panel.

Video playback on the computer screen seems a little blurry.

◆ DV is set to play on older G3s at low quality, because these systems can't process software decompression any faster than that. You'll see the picture snap into focus when you stop DV play-back in the Viewer or Canvas. That's because FCP substitutes a high-quality still frame when you pause playback. So to play back DV at 29.97 fps in full quality, you need to connect an NTSC or PAL monitor to the video output of your external DV device.

You are experiencing poor playback and stuttering video when you try to edit.

◆ Make sure you are not editing with media using keyframe compression such as Sorenson or Cinepak.

◆ Recompress the media without keyframes using Final Cut Pro or Media Cleaner.

TROUBLESHOOTING

WELCOME TO FINAL CUT PRO

2

Welcome to Apple's Final Cut Pro—a combination digital video editing, compositing, and special effects program.

Final Cut Pro is tightly integrated with Apple's G3 and G4 Macintosh processors, FireWire high-speed data transfer technology, and QuickTime multimedia format. It supports DV, the digital-video format, M-JPEG, and all QuickTime formats, as well as QuickTime's built-in effects generators. It also supports Adobe After Effects third-party plug-in filters.

Final Cut Pro provides a professional level of editing functionality: three-point editing, slip editing, rolling and ripple edits, and match frame. It also supports a variety of editing styles, from strictly drag-and-drop edits to entirely keyboard-based editing.

This chapter contains a brief overview of Final Cut Pro features. You'll be introduced to the main interface windows you'll be using for editing and for creating effects, and you'll learn how to customize the arrangement of these windows in a variety of screen layouts.

You'll also learn about Final Cut Pro's media management tools, import and export options, and functions for undoing changes.

Finally, this chapter contains detailed information on how to configure the settings in the Preferences window and how to configure other presets.

Touring Your Desktop Post-Production Facility

Four program windows form the heart of the Final Cut Pro interface: the *Browser*, the *Viewer*, the *Canvas*, and the *Timeline*.

Because the program combines so many editing and effects creation capabilities in a single application, each of these program windows performs multiple functions. Final Cut Pro's elegant use of tabbed windows to stack multiple functions in a single window makes maximum use of your screen real estate.

A small, floating Tool palette contains tools you can use to make selections, navigate, and perform edits in the Timeline and Canvas.

Useful features

Following are a few useful features that apply throughout the program:

Tabbed windows: Every major program window in the Final Cut Pro interface uses tabs. In the Viewer and Preferences windows, tabs give you access to multiple functions within the window (**Figure 2.1**). In the Canvas, Timeline, and Browser, tabs give you access to multiple sequences or projects (**Figure 2.2**). You can drag a tab out of the Browser, Viewer, Canvas, or Timeline window and display the tab as a separate window. You can also return a tab to its original window by dragging the tab back to the tab header of the parent window. Review the sample screen layouts in "Customizing Your Work Environment" later in this chapter.

Figure 2.1 Tabs give you access to multiple functions in the Viewer window.

Figure 2.2 Tabs give you access to multiple sequences in the Timeline.

Roll Edit – R

Figure 2.3 Rest the cursor over a button in the Tool palette, and a ToolTip—a label with the tool's name—will appear. ToolTips also display keyboard shortcuts for tools and buttons.

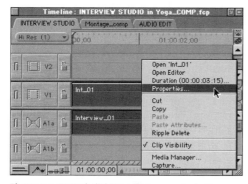

Figure 2.4 Control-clicking a sequence clip in the Timeline calls up a shortcut menu with a list of functions related to that clip.

ToolTips: You can use the ToolTips feature to identify most of the control buttons in the Viewer and Canvas windows and on the Tool palette (**Figure 2.3**). ToolTips also display the keyboard shortcut for a tool or button. Rest the cursor over the button and wait a second, and a label will appear. Switch on ToolTips on the General tab of the Preferences window.

Menus, shortcuts, and controls

Final Cut Pro offers several methods for performing video editing tasks. Experiment to find out which control methods work best for you. Some people work fastest using keyboard shortcuts; others prefer to use the menu bar or shortcut menus as much as possible. Apart from the menu bar and window buttons, you can use several other means to access Final Cut Pro's functions.

Shortcut menus: Shortcut menus can speed your work and help you learn Final Cut Pro. Control-click an item in one of the four main interface windows and select from a list of common functions specific to that item (**Figure 2.4**). Control-click often as you're learning your way around the program just to see your options in a particular area of the FCP interface.

Keyboard shortcuts: You'll find a complete list of keyboard shortcuts in the appendix of this book. You may find that these shortcut keys help you work more efficiently.

Timecode entry shortcuts: Final Cut Pro provides a number of time-saving shortcuts for timecode entry. See "FCP Protocol: Entering Timecode Numbers" in Chapter 5.

Onscreen help

Final Cut Pro has a built-in context-sensitive help feature, Final Cut Pro Help (**Figure 2.5**). The information in the help feature is simple, well written, and hyperlinked. You'll find helpful bits of information in the onscreen help that don't appear in the manual. FCP's onscreen Help also offers a series of tutorials—floating palettes that overlay the Final Cut Pro program interface and step you through basic tasks.

To access onscreen help:

◆ Choose Help > Context Sensitive Help; or press F1.

✔ Tip

■ The files of the onscreen Context Sensitive Help feature are in HTML format, so you can open them from any Web browser if you want to keep a reference copy on a computer that does not have FCP installed. FCP installs its Final Cut Pro Help folder in your system's Help folder. Copy the folder Final Cut Pro Help from your system's Help folder to your other computer; then use the Open File command in your browser to open the Table of Contents file, also called Final Cut Pro Help. The hyperlinks will work, but the search feature won't.

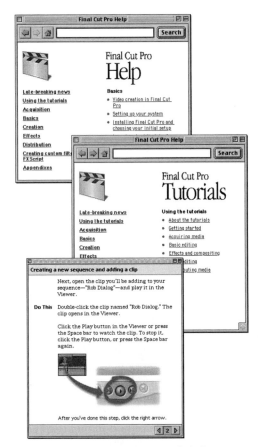

Figure 2.5 The Final Cut Pro onscreen help feature includes tutorials that step you through tasks right in the program interface.

What Is Nondestructive Editing?

Nondestructive editing is a basic concept that distinguishes digital, nonlinear editing systems from analog editing systems.

To find an example of truly destructive editing, you have to go all the way back to film cutting. When a film editor cuts a shot, a piece of film is literally cut from the rest; as editing continues, the editor extends a shot, which means reattaching the bit of footage that was trimmed off and hung up in a trim bin. (A hearty sigh from everybody who has ever had to dive head first to the bottom of the bin in search of a couple of frames.)

In a tape-based editing system, constructing an edit means selecting shots from one tape and then recording them in order on another tape. Once you've recorded the shots, you're limited to the shots as recorded and in the order recorded. If you want to go back and extend the length of a shot, you simply have to re-record that longer version of the shot from your source tape. That's the good news. The bad news? You'll also have to re-record every shot that came after it, because you can't slip the back end of your program down the tape to make room. (A hearty sigh from everybody who has ever had to spend *that* extra hour in the editing suite.)

When you edit on a digital, nonlinear editing system like Final Cut Pro, constructing a digital edit means constructing a *playlist.* A playlist is instructions to the editing program to play a certain bit of Media File A, and then cut to a bit of Media File B, and then play a later bit of Media File A, and so on. The full length of each captured media file is available to the editor from within the edited sequence. That's because in Final Cut Pro, the "clip"—the basic media element you use to construct edited sequences—is nothing more or less than a set of instructions referring to an underlying media file. When you go to play back your edited sequence, it only *looks* like it's been spliced together: Final Cut Pro is actually assembling it on the fly. Since you're viewing a simulation of an edited sequence, and the full length of each captured file is available at the edit point, extending a shot is simply a matter of rewriting the editing program's playlist to play a little more of Media File A before switching to Media File B. In Final Cut Pro, you do this by modifying the clip's length in your edited sequence.

Nondestructive editing is key to editing in a program like Final Cut Pro, which allows you to make use of your media source files multiple times across multiple projects, or to access the same source file but process it in a number of different ways.

Having many instances of a clip (which, in Final Cut Pro, is just a set of instructions) all referring to the same media file saves disk space and offers you flexibility throughout your editing process.

When you reach the limit of Final Cut Pro's ability to assemble your edited sequence on the fly, it's time to render. The rendering process computes all your modifications, superimpositions, and transitions into a single new media file that resides on your hard disk and plays back as part of your edited sequence.

For more information on protocols governing clips, see Chapter 4, "Preparing Your Clips."

For information on rendering, see Chapter 10, "Rendering."

YOUR DESKTOP POST-PRODUCTION FACILITY

Editing and Effects Windows

Four editing and effects program windows form the basis of Final Cut Pro's desktop editing suite. The following brief descriptions of each window's features and functions are simplified summaries of the full list of features. Final Cut Pro's designers went all out to support a wide variety of editing styles, and they have produced a very flexible editing system.

The Browser

The Browser (**Figure 2.6**) is the program window you use to organize and access all the media elements used as source material for your projects. It also contains your projects' sequences: the data files that contain your edited playlists.

The Browser's Effects tab is your source for Final Cut Pro's effects, filters, and generators, including the text generator (**Figure 2.7**).

The Browser is not like a folder on your computer's desktop—it's not a collection of actual files. Instead, a Browser item is a *pointer* to a file on your hard disk. File storage is independent of Browser organization. That means that you can place the same clip in multiple Browser projects, and each instance of the clip will refer to the same media file on your hard drive. For detailed information about the Browser, see Chapter 4, "Preparing Your Clips."

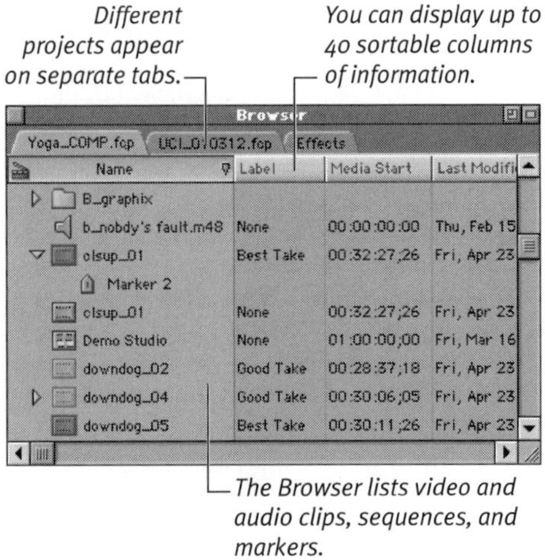

Different projects appear on separate tabs. *You can display up to 40 sortable columns of information.*

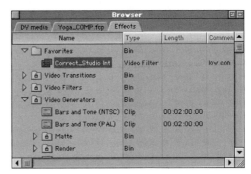

The Browser lists video and audio clips, sequences, and markers.

Figure 2.6 Use the Browser window to organize the media elements in your projects.

Figure 2.7 The Browser's Effects tab displays Final Cut Pro's effects, filters, and generators as well as your own customized effects.

The Viewer

The Viewer window is bursting with functions. When you're editing, the Viewer acts as your source monitor: You can review individual video and audio clips and mark edit points. You can also load clips from the current sequence into the Viewer to refine your edits, apply effects, and create titles—and much, much more.

"How," you ask, "can I do so much in one humble window?"

The FCP interface uses a stack of tabs in the Viewer window to organize and display audio and video plus the controls for any effects you apply to a clip. Here are quick summaries of the functions available on each of the tabs.

The Viewer's Video tab

◆ **Video tab (Figure 2.8):** View video frames and mark and refine edit points. This is the default playback window for a video clip.

Different Viewer window functions appear on separate tabs.

Enter a timecode in the Current Timecode field to navigate to a specific frame.

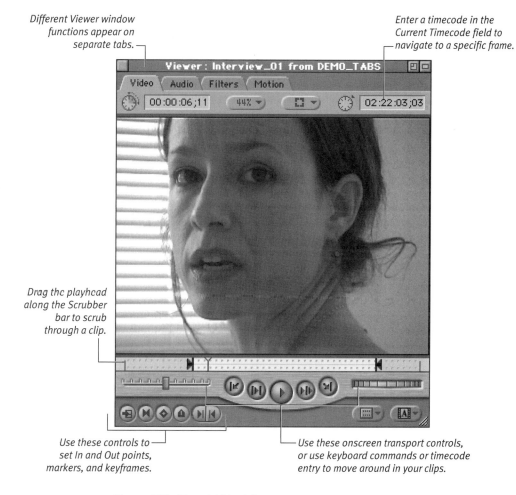

Drag the playhead along the Scrubber bar to scrub through a clip.

Use these controls to set In and Out points, markers, and keyframes.

Use these onscreen transport controls, or use keyboard commands or timecode entry to move around in your clips.

Figure 2.8 The Viewer's Video tab.

The Viewer's Audio tab

◆ **Audio tab (Figure 2.9):** Audition and
mark edit points in audio-only clips. Set
level and pan or spread settings. The
Audio tab displays the audio portion
of an audio+video clip. Clips with two
channels display two audio tabs.

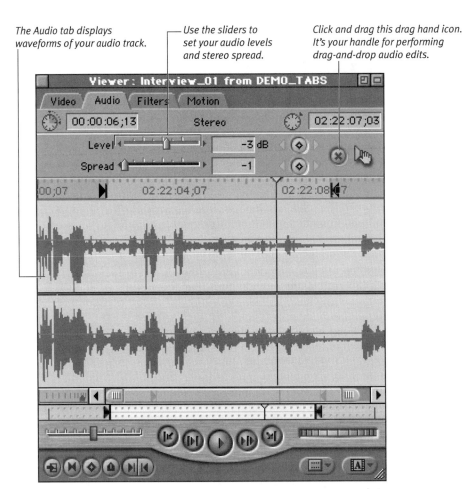

Figure 2.9 The Viewer's Audio tab contains a few controls that don't appear on the
Video tab.

The Viewer's Effects tabs

◆ **Controls tab (Figure 2.10):** Adjust the settings for a generator effect, such as the text generator.

◆ **Filters tab:** Adjust the settings and set keyframes for any filter effects you have applied to a clip.

◆ **Motion tab:** Apply and modify motion effects.

For more information on the Viewer, see Chapter 5, "Introducing the Viewer."

To learn about creating effects, see Chapter 13, "Compositing and Special Effects."

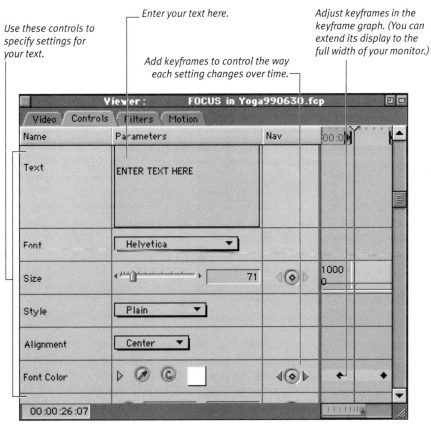

Use these controls to specify settings for your text.

Enter your text here.

Add keyframes to control the way each setting changes over time.

Adjust keyframes in the keyframe graph. (You can extend its display to the full width of your monitor.)

Figure 2.10 A text generator, on the Viewer's Controls tab. The Controls tab contains the tools you need to adjust the settings for a generator effect. Filters and Motion tabs perform the same function, but for different classes of effects.

EDITING AND EFFECTS WINDOWS

The Canvas

Analogous to a record monitor, the Canvas plays back your edited sequence as you are creating it. The Canvas window (**Figure 2.11**) looks similar to the Viewer and has many of the same controls. You can use the controls in the Canvas window to play sequences, mark sequence In and Out points, add sequence markers, and set keyframes. In addition to using the Viewer-like marking controls, you can perform various types of drag-and-drop edits in the Canvas edit overlay (**Figure 2.12**), which appears automatically when you drag a clip into the Canvas. You can also use the Canvas window to plot out effects.

For more information on the Canvas, see Chapter 7, "Using the Timeline and the Canvas."

Learn about applying filters and effects in Chapter 13, "Compositing and Special Effects."

Multiple open sequences appear on separate tabs in the Canvas window.

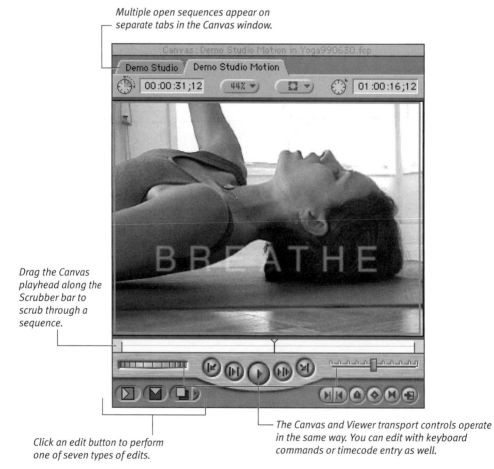

Drag the Canvas playhead along the Scrubber bar to scrub through a sequence.

Click an edit button to perform one of seven types of edits.

The Canvas and Viewer transport controls operate in the same way. You can edit with keyboard commands or timecode entry as well.

Figure 2.11 The Canvas window.

Figure 2.12 The Canvas window, with the Canvas Edit overlay displayed. Drag a clip from the Viewer or Browser and drop it on the type of edit you want to perform.

The Timeline

The Timeline displays your edited sequence as clips arrayed on multiple video and audio tracks along a time axis (**Figure 2.13**). As you drag the playhead along the Timeline ruler, the current frame of the sequence is updated in the Canvas window, and if you update the value in the Canvas window, it's reflected in the playhead. If you have multiple sequences open, the Timeline and Canvas will display a tab for each sequence. You can edit by dragging clips directly from the Browser or Viewer and dropping them in the Timeline.

Multiple open sequences appear on separate tabs in the Timeline window.

Drag the playhead along the ruler to scrub through a sequence.

Adjust keyframes and access effects controls from the Filter and Motion bars.

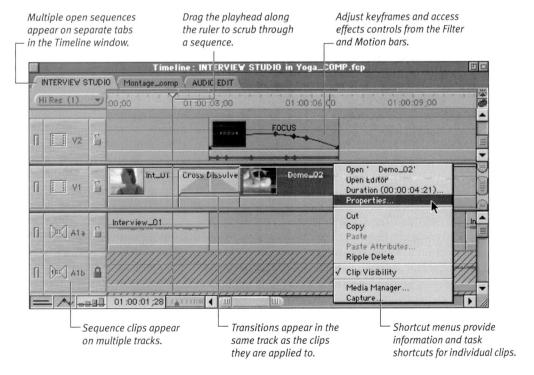

Sequence clips appear on multiple tracks.

Transitions appear in the same track as the clips they are applied to.

Shortcut menus provide information and task shortcuts for individual clips.

Figure 2.13 The Timeline displays a chronological view of your edited sequence.

The Tool palette

The Tool palette (**Figure 2.14**) contains tools for selecting and manipulating items in the Timeline, Canvas, and Viewer. For a listing of each tool, see Chapter 7, "Using the Timeline and the Canvas."

Input and Output Windows

Although most of your editing tasks are performed in Final Cut Pro's main editing and effects windows, you'll need to use a couple of other windows to shape your program's input and output.

Log and Capture

Use the Log and Capture window (**Figure 2.15**) to capture video and audio media in Final Cut Pro. Log and Capture supports a range of capturing options, from capturing live video on the fly to automated batch capture with full device control. Log and Capture functions are explained in detail in Chapter 3, "Input: Getting Digital with Your Video."

Edit to Tape

The Edit to Tape window (**Figure 2.16**) replaces and works like the Canvas. In the Edit to Tape window, you can edit directly from Final Cut Pro onto your video deck or camcorder. You must have a controllable video device to use Edit to Tape. (If your deck or camera doesn't support device control, you can still use Print to Video.) For more information on the Edit to Tape window, see Chapter 11, "At Last: Creating Final Output."

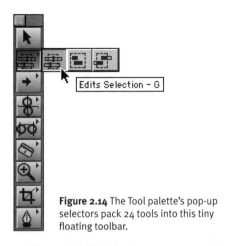

Figure 2.14 The Tool palette's pop-up selectors pack 24 tools into this tiny floating toolbar.

Figure 2.15 The Log and Capture window supports a range of capturing and logging techniques, including automated batch capture after you've logged all your reels.

Figure 2.16 Use the Edit to Tape window to assemble material output from Final Cut Pro onto videotape.

Figure 2.17 Use the Media Manager to trim unused portions of your source media files from a project.

Figure 2.18 The Make Offline ommand offers three ways to remove a clip from your project.

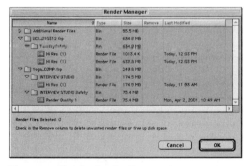

Figure 2.19 Use the Render Manager to manage your render files.

Media Management Tools

The following tools can help you manage your wonderland of media files.

Media Manager

The new Media Manager replaces FCP 1's Sequence Trimmer and Media Mover. You can still trim sequences for batch recapture and copy or move sequences and clips, along with their source media files, to another drive location. New in FCP 2 is the power to delete all or part of a media file from inside the program. That means that you can trim off the unused portions of the clips you're using in your sequence and actually delete them from your drive (**Figure 2.17**).

FCP 2 offers more control over the links between Final Cut Pro projects and their associated media and render files. Use the Reconnect Media command to restore links between projects and their media or render files. Control-click a clip (or multiple clips) and choose the Make Offline command, which offers three options: break the clip's link to its source media file but leave the source file on the disk, move the source file to the Trash, or delete the source file from the disk (**Figure 2.18**).

Render Manager

Use the Render Manager (**Figure 2.19**) to delete render files for deleted or obsolete projects or for removing obsolete render files from your current projects. The Render Manager finds and lists render files from unopened projects as well as open projects and displays their modification dates to help you decide which files to remove. For information on the Render Manager, see Chapter 10, "Rendering."

Import and export options

Final Cut Pro's media handling is based on Apple QuickTime, and that means you have a lot of import and export format options. If QuickTime can handle it, so can Final Cut Pro. You can also import and export Edit Decision Lists (EDLs), FXBuilder scripts, and logging information.

◆ You can import QuickTime-compatible media files into a Final Cut Pro project.

◆ You can import audio directly from a CD.

◆ You can import still images in a full range of formats.

◆ You can import a layered Adobe Photoshop file (**Figure 2.20**). Final Cut Pro preserves the layers, importing the file as a sequence. Each layer in Photoshop corresponds to a video track in the sequence.

◆ You can import an EDL created on a linear editing system or another nonlinear editing system and use it to create sequences.

◆ You can export clips, sequences, or portions of either as QuickTime movies or in a variety of image and sound formats.

◆ You can export a sequence as an EDL and use this to create sequences on another linear or nonlinear editing system.

Customize Your Environment

The power of the Final Cut Pro interface lies in its flexibility. You perform a wide range of tasks in FCP: database management, editing, effects design, titling, and many others. Here are a few sample screen layouts that can help you make the most of your screen real estate. Final Cut Pro saves every detail of your workspace status each time you quit the program, so the next time you relaunch Final Cut Pro, each program window will contain the same project, sequence, clip, and frame—just as you left it.

Figure 2.20 When you import a layered Photoshop file into Final Cut Pro, you can maintain control over the individual layers.

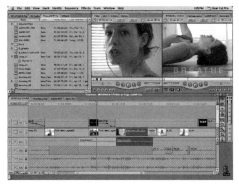

Figure 2.21 Use a screen layout with a wide Timeline when you need to get the big picture of your sequence layout.

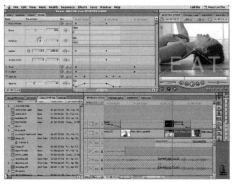

Figure 2.22 Use a screen layout with an expanded Effects tab to improve your access to effects controls and keyframe graphs.

Figure 2.23 This screen layout features large monitor views for video editing.

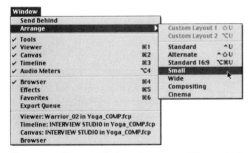

Figure 2.24 Choose Window > Arrange and then select from four preset and two custom screen layouts.

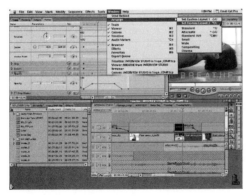

Figure 2.25 Holding down the Option key while selecting Custom Layout from the Arrange submenu of the Window menu saves the current screen layout as a custom preset.

Figure 2.21 is an example of a screen layout with a wide view of the Timeline.

Figure 2.22 is an example of an effects creation layout, with the Effects tab expanded for a better view of the keyframe graphs.

Figure 2.23 is an example of a video editing layout, with large picture-viewing monitors.

✔ Tip

- Final Cut Pro program windows are programmed to "windowshade"—to collapse when you double-click the program window's title bar. To activate windowshading, choose Apple Menu > Control Panels > Appearance and then select the Options tab. Check Double-Click Title Bar to Collapse Windows.

To select a preset screen layout:

- Choose Window > Arrange (**Figure 2.24**) and then select a screen layout from the four presets and two custom layouts available.

To customize a screen layout:

1. Arrange the four main windows in the layout and sizes you want.

2. Hold down the Option key and choose one of the two custom layouts from the Arrange submenu of the Window menu (**Figure 2.25**).

    The next time you open Final Cut Pro, you can choose the layout you created from the Arrange submenu of the Window menu.

CUSTOMIZE YOUR ENVIRONMENT

Undoing Changes

You can undo every action you perform in your projects, sequences, and clips. You can also redo actions that you have undone. You can configure FCP to store up to 99 actions across multiple projects. You set the number in the Levels of Undo preference.

To undo the last action:

◆ Choose Edit > Undo (**Figure 2.26**).

To redo the last undone action:

◆ Choose Edit > Redo.

To specify the number of actions that can be undone:

1. Choose Edit > Preferences.

2. On the General tab of the Preferences window, set the levels of undo operations to a number between 1 and 99 (**Figure 2.27**).

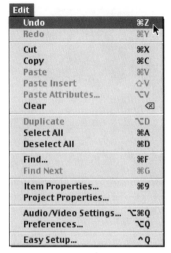

Figure 2.26 Choose Edit > Undo to undo your last action.

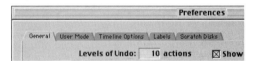

Figure 2.27 You can set the levels of undo to any number between 1 and 99 on the General tab of the Preferences window.

FCP Protocol: Undoing Changes in Multiple Projects

FCP's Undo feature can track up to 99 changes across multiple projects, but it makes no distinction between projects. If you are working with more than one sequence or project, check to be sure that you are in the correct sequence or project when you choose Undo. Even so, the change you undo may not occur in the current project, so take care when undoing multiple changes.

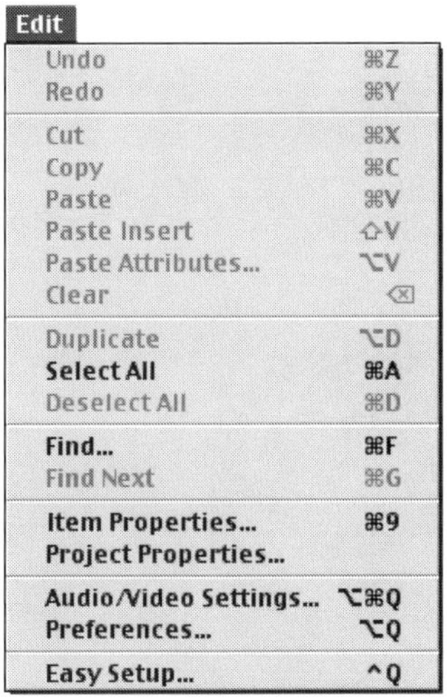

Edit	
Undo	⌘Z
Redo	⌘Y
Cut	⌘X
Copy	⌘C
Paste	⌘V
Paste Insert	⇧V
Paste Attributes...	⌥V
Clear	⌫
Duplicate	⌥D
Select All	⌘A
Deselect All	⌘D
Find...	⌘F
Find Next	⌘G
Item Properties...	⌘9
Project Properties...	
Audio/Video Settings...	⌥⌘Q
Preferences...	⌥Q
Easy Setup...	^Q

Figure 2.28 Preference settings are accessed from three Edit menu choices: Easy Setup, Audio/Video Settings, and Preferences

How to "Trash Your Prefs"

FCP 2 has made setting up preferences simpler, but you still may find that you need to delete your FCP preferences file (or "trash your prefs") to force FCP to restore all your program settings to default values.

In the Finder, go to System/Preferences/ Final Cut Pro Data and remove your current preferences file, called Final Cut Pro 2.0 Preferences, from the folder. Then relaunch Final Cut Pro with all of your external hardware on and connected. You'll see the Choose Setup window. Here's your chance to reset your preferences from scratch.

Using Presets and Preferences

Final Cut Pro's designers have carefully organized the tools you use to configure settings and preferences. The goal of this organization is to make it much easier for editors using the most common hardware and video formats to configure FCP, and much more difficult for users to unintentionally modify individual settings within a preset configuration.

Capture, device control, and sequence settings are all organized into preset configurations, and these Audio/Video presets are grouped into master presets called *Easy Setups.*

Any of these preset configurations are completely customizable, but the vast majority of FCP users should be able to choose an Easy Setup based on their hardware and video format, specify a scratch disk for media capture on the Scratch tab of the Preferences window, and forget about settings until they change their external hardware.

FCP 2 preference settings are accessed from three menu choices: Easy Setup, Audio/Video Settings, and Preferences (**Figure 2.28**).

Easy Setup

An Easy Setup is one master preset configuration of multiple Final Cut Pro settings: a Device Control preset, a Capture preset, a Sequence preset, and an External Video setting. Instead of choosing several presets and external video settings using various tabs, you can now make one selection in a single window: Easy Setup. FCP offers several standard Easy Setups, but you also have the option of customizing an Easy Setup.

If you are using FCP with a variety of hardware, Easy Setup should make switching system configurations more idiot proof. Any customized setups you create are stored in the Custom Settings folder in the Final Cut Pro Documents folder, which makes your custom setups portable.

Audio/Video Settings

FCP's Audio/Video settings have their own preference window, called Audio/Video Settings. That's where you can make detailed adjustments to your Sequence presets, Capture presets, Device Control presets, and External Video settings, should the need arise. Your Audio/Video settings are summarized on the front tab in the Summary window. If, for some reason, you want to modify your underlying basic QuickTime settings, you access them through the tabs in the Audio/Video Settings window.

Preferences

Unlike the Audio/Video settings, which are largely dictated by your hardware and video format, a preference is a setting that specifies how *you* want to work with your media in Final Cut Pro. The settings in the Preferences window affect all your Final Cut Pro projects. The Preferences window contains five tabs: General (which contains general program preferences), User Modes, Clip Labels, Timeline Options, and Scratch Disks.

Modifying the Settings of an Existing Item

If you change the settings on the Easy Setup, Audio/Video, or Timeline Options tab of the Preferences window, your change will be reflected in new projects, sequences, or items created after you changed the settings. How and where do you change the settings of a project, sequence, or clip you have already created?

- **Item Properties:** Control click the item's icon in the Browser or Timeline and then select Item Properties from the shortcut menu.

- **Sequence Settings:** Control click the sequence's icon in the Browser and then select Sequence Settings from the shortcut menu.

- **Project Properties:** Open the project and then choose Edit > Project Properties.

- **Details on your settings** options appear at the end of this chapter.

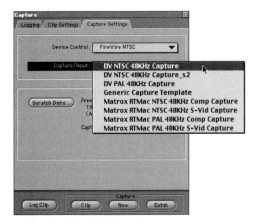

Figure 2.29 Selecting a Capture preset from the Input pop-up list located on the Capture Settings tab of the Log and Capture window.

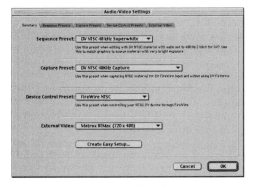

Figure 2.30 Your change is reflected on the Summary tab of the Audio/Video settings window. Both windows reference the same set of Capture preferences.

Accessing Preference Settings

Frequently, Final Cut Pro provides more than one route to access your preset and preference settings. For example, you can access the capture preferences from the Capture Presets tab in the Audio/Video Settings window, and also directly in the Log and Capture window by selecting a preset from the Capture/Input pop-up list located on the Capture Settings tab (**Figure 2.29**). The list of capture presets you access directly from the Log and Capture window is labeled Capture/Input, but the list of capture presets is the same, and any changes you make on the Log and Capture window's Capture Settings tab will be reflected on the Audio/Video Settings' Summary tab (**Figure 2.30**) and in the Easy Setups window.

One of the reasons FCP's designers based their configuration scheme on presets is because they wanted to make it easy to completely configure the program settings without having to alter individual settings. And it is easy to get confused. Some settings windows look the same but actually modify different program settings. For example, sequence presets and capture presets have separate QuickTime settings options. Mismatch between capture settings and sequence settings makes clips play back poorly when you start to edit them in the Timeline, and settings mismatch has been one of the primary causes of user difficulties with FCP.

So how can you avoid problems and confusion? When you launch Final Cut Pro for the first time after installing it, your answers to the Initial Setup questions determine the settings you see in the Easy Setup, Audio/Video Settings, and Preferences windows. It's best to start with the default settings, use the recommended Easy Setup, and make changes only if you have a specific problem. If you do make changes, your troubleshooting will be most effective if you make one change at a time.

Using Easy Setups

An Easy Setup is a single preset configuration of multiple Final Cut Pro settings: a Device Control preset, a Capture preset, a Sequence preset, and an External Video setting. FCP offers several standard Easy Setups, but you also have the option of customizing an Easy Setup.

You selected an Easy Setup as part of the initial setup process. Once you have an Easy Setup that works for your Final Cut Pro system, you shouldn't need to change it unless you change your video hardware or video format. If your FCP system includes a variety of external hardware, Easy Setups make it simple to switch FCP's configuration quickly and accurately.

Easy Setups are portable; you can create a custom Easy Setup and install it on another FCP system or e-mail it to a colleague. In this section, you'll learn how to switch to a different Easy Setup, how to find the folder where Easy Setups are stored so you can add and remove Easy Setups, and how to customize an Easy Setup.

Easy Setups to Go

One of the great things about Easy Setups is that they're portable. You can copy your customized Easy Setups from the folder where Final Cut Pro stores them and take them with you if you move to a different FCP system. You can e-mail them to a client or colleague (or to your dad when he's having trouble configuring his FCP system).

Here's the protocol for FCP's custom settings folders:

Customized Easy Setups—the ones you make yourself (or receive from your dad)—are stored in the Custom Settings folder. Here's the directory path: **System Folder: Preferences: Final Cut Pro Data: Custom Settings**.

Add or remove Easy Setups by copying them or deleting them in the Custom Settings folder. Easy Setups in this folder are unlocked.

FCP's stock Easy Setups files are stored in the Hardware Settings folder. Here's the directory path: **Final Cut Pro: Plugins: Final Cut Pro Settings: Hardware Settings.** Easy Setups in the Hardware Settings folder are locked and cannot be modified, so if you have a custom Easy Setup you want to protect, drag it into the Hardware Settings folder.

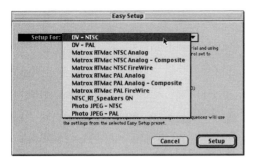

Figure 2.31 From the Setup For pop-up menu, select an Easy Setup.

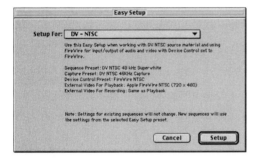

Figure 2.32 A summary of your selected Easy Setup appears below the pop-up menu.

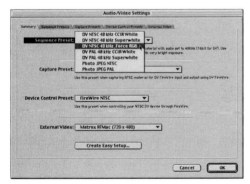

Figure 2.33 Select from the preset pop-up menus on the Summary tab of the Audio/Video Settings window to compose your custom Easy Setup.

To switch to a different Easy Setup:

1. Choose Edit > Easy Setup.

2. From the Setup For pop-up menu, select an Easy Setup (**Figure 2.31**).

   A summary of your selected Easy Setup appears below the pop-up menu (**Figure 2.32**).

3. Click Setup.

   The new Easy Setup affects only new projects and sequences and doesn't change settings for existing projects and sequences.

To create a custom Easy Setup:

1. Choose Edit > Audio/Video Settings.

2. On the Summary tab, select from the preset pop-up menus to compose your custom Easy Setup (**Figure 2.33**), or make more specific preset modifications on the settings tabs. Information on specifying presets appears earlier in this chapter.

3. Specify an external video setting.

4. Click Create Easy Setup.

continues on next page

USING EASY SETUPS

5. In the Easy Setup dialog box, enter a name and description. Check Enable Verification of Device Control in First Start Dialog if you want FCP to check the device control status each time you launch the program; then click Create (**Figure 2.34**).

6. The file dialog box appears, with the Custom Settings folder (the default storage location for Easy Setups) selected (**Figure 2.35**). Enter a file name and navigate to your desired folder location if you don't want to use the defaults.

7. Click Save.

Your new Easy Setup becomes the selected Easy Setup and appears in the Setup For pop-up menu of the Easy Setups window (**Figure 2.36**).

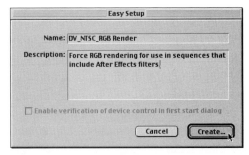

Figure 2.34 In the Easy Setup dialog box, enter a name and description. Specify whether you want FCP to check the device control status each time you launch the program; then click Create.

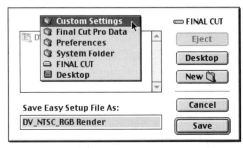

Figure 2.35 The Custom Settings folder is the default storage location for custom Easy Setups.

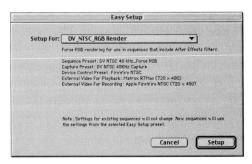

Figure 2.36 Your new Easy Setup appears as the selected Easy Setup in the Easy Setups window.

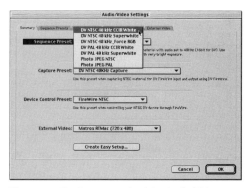

Figure 2.37 The Summary tab of the Audio/Video Settings window.

Using Audio/Video Presets

A preset is a group of saved settings that are automatically applied any time you create a new project or sequence. The beauty of a preset is that you can configure all your settings correctly with a single selection, because these settings have already been tested with your video hardware and format.

In the Audio/Video Settings window, the Summary tab (**Figure 2.37**) displays the currently selected preset for each setting—Sequence, Capture, and Device Control, plus your External Video setting—that make up your current Easy Setup. If you need to modify your current Audio/Video preset settings, you can select a different preset from the pop-up menus on the Summary tab, or you can open the tab for the setting you need to modify and specify custom settings. Try to use the stock presets before you start tinkering with your settings. This section will explain how to choose, edit, and delete an existing preset and how to create a new preset. For detailed information on your settings options for the different types of Audio/Video presets, see "Specifying Sequence Settings," "Specifying Capture Settings," "Specifying Device Control Settings," and "Using External Video Settings" later in this chapter.

Finding Additional and Third-Party Presets

Final Cut Pro loaded its default preset files when you installed the program, but you can find additional presets on the Final Cut Pro CD in the Extras folder. Check with the manufacturers of any third-party hardware or software you are using with FCP; they may have created a custom FCP preset. Having the correct custom preset for your external hardware can make configuration of Final Cut Pro a whole lot easier.

To install additional and third-party presets, just copy them into the correct folder. Here is the directory path to that folder: **Final Cut Pro: Plugins: Final Cut Pro Settings: Hardware Settings**.

The next time you open Final Cut Pro, the presets will be available in the Audio/Video Settings window.

To switch to a different preset in your current Easy Setup:

1. Choose Edit > Audio/Video Settings.

2. On the Summary tab, choose a different preset from one of the pop-up menus (**Figure 2.38**); then click OK.

   If your newly selected preset configuration doesn't match an existing Easy Setup, Final Cut Pro switches your Easy Setup designation to Custom Setup and summarizes your new settings in the Easy Setup window (**Figure 2.39**). If your new settings match an existing Easy Setup, FCP switches to that Easy Setup.

To view settings for a preset:

1. Choose Edit > Audio/Video Settings.

2. In the Audio/Video Settings window, click the tab for the preset settings you want to view.

3. On the preset tab, click the preset's name (**Figure 2.40**).

   The Summary box lists the properties of the selected preset. The default preset is indicated by a check mark in the left column.

4. When you're done, click OK to close the Audio/Video Settings window.

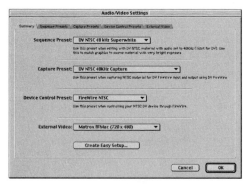

Figure 2.38 You can modify your Easy Setup by switching to a different preset on the Summary tab of the Audio/Video Settings window.

Figure 2.39 Your Easy Setup designation switches to Custom, and your new settings are summarized in the Easy Setup window.

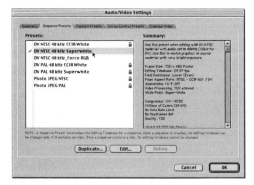

Figure 2.40 Click the preset's name to view its settings in the Summary box on the right side of the preset tab. Careful; if you click in the left column, you'll switch the default preset.

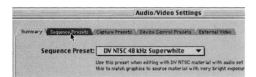

Figure 2.41 In the Audio/Video Settings window, click the tab for the type of preset you want to edit.

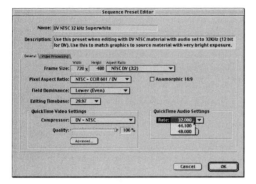

Figure 2.42 Enter a new name and description for your preset; then modify its settings in the Preset Editor window.

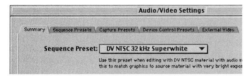

Figure 2.43 The modified preset becomes the currently selected preset and appears on the appropriate Summary tab pop-up menu.

To edit an existing preset:

1. Choose Edit > Audio/Video Settings.

2. In the Audio/Video Settings window, click the tab for preset type you want to edit (**Figure 2.41**).

3. On the preset tab, click the preset you want to edit; then *do one of the following*:
   ▲ Click Duplicate to open an editable copy of this preset in the Preset Editor. This is the only way to edit Final Cut Pro's presets, which are locked by default.
   ▲ Click Edit to modify an existing unlocked preset.
   The Preset Editor window appears.

4. In the Preset Editor window, enter a new name and description for your preset, modify its settings (**Figure 2.42**), and then click OK.

   The modified preset becomes the currently selected preset, appearing in the appropriate Summary tab pop-up menu (**Figure 2.43**).

5. When you've finished editing the preset, click OK to save your changes.

To create a new preset:

◆ There is no way to create a new preset entirely from scratch. Duplicate and then edit the preset whose settings are closest to the custom preset you require.

To delete a preset:

1. In the Audio/Video Settings window, click the tab for the preset you want to delete.

2. On the preset tab, click the preset you want to delete; then click Delete (**Figure 2.44**).

✔ Tips

- You won't be able to delete the currently selected preset (that's the one with the check mark next to it) or any locked preset (presets with a lock icon displayed in the right column).

- Think before you delete a preset, because you can't undo this action. Once you delete a preset, it's gone. You can restore FCP's stock presets though, by reinstalling the program.

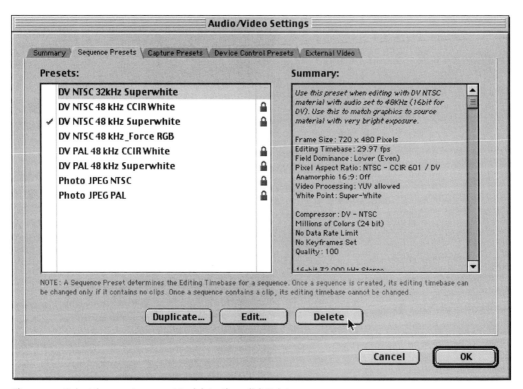

Figure 2.44 Select the preset you want to delete; then click Delete.

Specifying Sequence Settings

Final Cut Pro provides sequence presets you use to quickly create new sequences with the same settings every time. You can also choose to be prompted to specify the preset for each new sequence you create. The Preset Editor window allows you to create and edit sequence presets. The preset you choose will be applied to all new sequences until you change it. Sequence settings for existing sequences are not affected.

You can open and review or modify any individual existing sequence's settings in the Sequence Settings window. For more information, see "Changing the Settings of an Existing Sequence" later in this chapter.

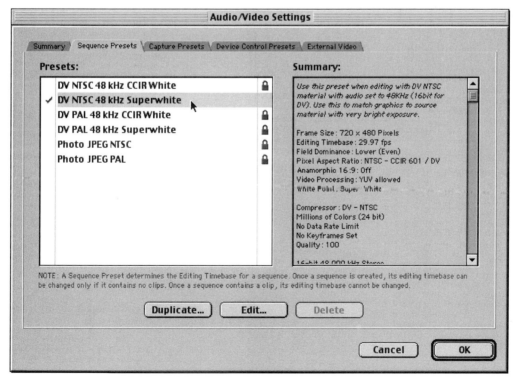

Figure 2.45 Select the preset you want to edit on the Sequence Presets tab of the Audio/Video Settings window; then click the Edit button.

To edit general sequence settings for the current preset:

1. On the Sequence Presets tab of the Audio/Video Settings window, select a preset (**Figure 2.45**); then click the Edit button.

   If the preset is locked, a dialog box appears indicating that a copy will be made for editing; then the Sequence Preset Editor window appears. Sequence settings are available on the Sequence Preset Editor's General tab and Video Processing tab.

2. On the General tab, you can modify the default settings for any of the following (**Figure 2.46**):

   ▲ **Name:** Enter a name for the preset.

   ▲ **Description:** Enter a description of the preset. If it's based on an existing preset with one or two changes, you might note the base preset plus the changes.

   ▲ **Frame Size:** Specify the frame size for the output of the sequence. Enter a custom frame size in the Width and Height fields or choose a predefined frame size in the Aspect Ratio pop-up menu.

▲ **Pixel Aspect Ratio:** Specify a pixel aspect ratio in this pop-up menu that is compatible with your source video.

▲ **Anamorphic 16:9:** If your source video is 16:9, checking this box ensures that FCP will interpret and display your source media's pixel aspect ratio properly.

▲ **Field Dominance:** Specify the field to be displayed first on an NTSC monitor. DV and Targa both default to the Lower (Even) setting. If field dominance is set incorrectly, moving areas of the image will have jagged edges.

▲ **Editing Timebase:** This field displays the currently selected editing timebase. Ideally, the editing timebase should be identical to the frame rate of the source clips in the sequence. All source clips with a frame rate that does not match the editing timebase are converted to the sequence's editing timebase and will require rendering. You can modify an existing sequence's timebase only if there are no clips in it.

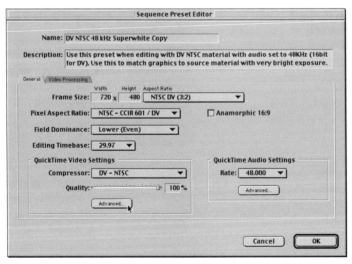

Figure 2.46 The General tab of the Sequence Presets tab of the Audio/Video Settings window.

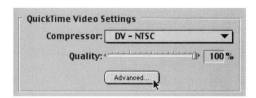

Figure 2.47 Click the Advanced button In the QuickTime Video Settings section to access QuickTime video compression settings.

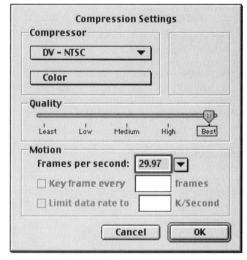

Figure 2.48 These QuickTime compression settings determine the compression format of any material you render in your sequence.

Specifying QuickTime settings for sequence presets

The current video compression codec settings for the selected sequence preset are displayed under QuickTime Video Settings. The current audio sample rate setting for this preset is displayed under QuickTime Audio Settings. Unless you have a specific reason to make a change, stick with the default settings. Selecting the appropriate sequence preset in the main Audio/Video Settings window should load the correct values for all other settings. Refer to the *Final Cut Pro User's Manual* for details on your QuickTime settings options.

To access the QuickTime video compression settings for the current preset:

1. In the QuickTime Video Settings section of the Sequence Preset Editor window, click the Advanced button (**Figure 2.47**).

   The Compression Settings window appears (**Figure 2.48**). The compression settings determine the compression format of any material you render in your sequence.

2. Select the codec that matches your clip's capture settings. You can modify the default settings for any of the following:

   ▲ **Compressor:** Choose a compression method (codec) to be applied to your sequence from the first Compressor pop-up menu. The second Compressor pop-up menu may have additional color depth resolutions available depending on the type of codec chosen. Certain codecs display an Option button next to the Cancel button. This button provides access to additional options specific to that codec.

continues on next page

▲ **Quality:** Use this slider to adjust the video image quality. Least quality yields a high data compression. Best quality yields the lowest data compression.

▲ **Frames per Second:** Enter a value or choose a preset value from the pop-up menu to specify the number of frames sampled per second. Your frame rate should match the editing timebase of your sequence preset.

▲ **Key Frame Every _n_ Frames:** Check this box to manually assign keyframe intervals. Type a numeric value in the field to define the number of frames between keyframes.

▲ **Limit Data Rate to _n_ K/Second:** Check this box to manually limit the data rate while capturing video. Type a numeric value in the field to define the data throughput in Kps.

To access the QuickTime audio compression settings for the current preset:

1. On the General tab of the Sequence Preset Editor window, click Advanced.

The Sound Settings window appears (**Figure 2.49**). The compression settings determine the compression format of any audio you render in your sequence.

2. You can modify the default settings for any of the following:

▲ **Compressor:** Choose None.

▲ **Rate:** Enter a value in this field to specify the output rate for the audio, or choose a predefined value from the pop-up menu to select from a list of standard sample rates.

▲ **Size:** Choose a bit resolution for the audio.

▲ **Use:** Choose Mono or Stereo output for the audio in your sequence.

✔ Tips

■ Editing with compressed audio will cause Final Cut Pro to lose sync, and it could cause a crash. Don't do it.

■ Compressing audio should be the very last step in your post-production process. Trying to mix or filter compressed audio can produce distorted tracks. Don't compress your final audio unless you absolutely have to.

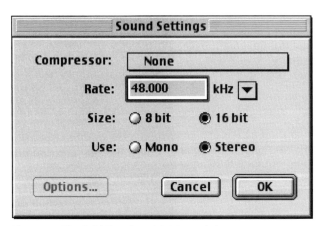

Figure 2.49 The QuickTime Sound Settings window.

Specifying Video Processing Settings

The settings on the Video Processing tab allow you to specify how FCP will interpret color space when rendering clips used in sequences created with this sequence preset.

Older versions of QuickTime used DV codecs that converted YUV (the color space used by DV video) to RGB (the color space used by computers) whenever rendering was required. This conversion could generate noticeable color or luminance shifts. Now, because QuickTime has added support for rendering in YUV (also known as YCrCb) color space, you have a choice. If you selected a QuickTime codec that supports YUV color space, you'll be able to set additional options on the Video Processing tab.

To edit Video Processing settings for the current preset:

On the Video Processing tab of the Sequence Preset Editor window (**Figure 2.50**), you can modify the following default settings:

◆ **Always Render in RGB:** Check this box to force codecs that normally process color using the YUV (or YCrCb) color space to render in RGB color space. This may cause slight color shifts in rendered material.

◆ **Process Maximum White As** (note that this pop-up menu only appears if Always Render in RGB is not selected):

▲ **Super-White:** Choose this to match the maximum brightness of imported clips from RGB color space to the super-white levels of clips from DV camcorders.

▲ **White:** Choose this to limit the maximum brightness of imported clips created in RGB color space to 100 IRE.

continues on next page

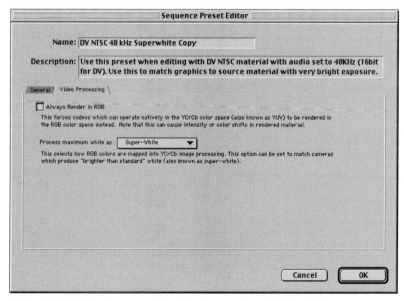

Figure 2.50 The Video Processing tab of the Sequence Preset Editor window.

This setting allows you to match the brightness levels of DV video source clips to integrate better with RGB elements. Many DV camcorders record video with white values (known as super-white) that are brighter than 100 IRE. Brightness levels in these DV clips with super-white white values may not match other elements in your sequence—for example, imported graphics files or Adobe After Effects clips created in RGB color space.

✔ Tip

■ You might choose Always Render in RGB if you want to use After Effects filters and Final Cut Pro filters in the same project. After Effects filters can render in RGB space only, so you'd choose this option to force the Final Cut Pro filters—which render in YUV by default—to render in RGB as well, thus ensuring a consistent result.

Specifying Capture Settings

Capture settings determine the quality at which Final Cut Pro captures video, and you must set your capture preferences before you can capture any media. Your capture settings will determine your clip's native format. Capture preferences specify the capture board you are using, compression method, frame rate, frame size, and audio sampling rate. Final Cut Pro sets capture preferences for you automatically when you install the program, so unless you change your hardware or know the change you want to make, don't feel you need to alter the default settings. One exception to this guideline: You'll want to check the audio settings before you capture to specify which audio channels you want captured, adjust your audio input levels, and specify a sample rate. For more information, see Chapter 3.

✔ Tip

■ If you are using a third-party video capture card with your Final Cut Pro system, check the manufacturer's documentation or Web site for the latest information on configuring the product to work smoothly with Final Cut Pro. A custom preset may be available for you to download and install, or you may find details on configuring the capture preset correctly.

To edit settings for the current capture preset:

1. On the Capture Presets tab of the Audio/Video Settings window, select a preset; then click the Edit button.

   If the preset is locked, a dialog appears indicating that a copy will be made for editing; then the Capture Preset Editor window appears (**Figure 2.51**).

2. You can modify default settings for the following:

   ▲ **Name:** Enter a name for the preset.

   ▲ **Description:** Enter a description of the preset. If it's based on an existing preset with one or two changes, you might note the base preset plus the changes.

   ▲ **Frame Size:** Choose a preset frame size from the Aspect Ratio pop-up menu, or choose Custom and then enter a custom value in the Width and Height fields.

   ▲ **Anamorphic:** Check this box if you are capturing 16:9 media.

   ▲ **Capture Card Supports Simultaneous Play Through and Capture:** Check this box if your video capture card is equipped to display video on an external video monitor while the Log and Capture window is open and you're capturing video. Check your capture card documentation.

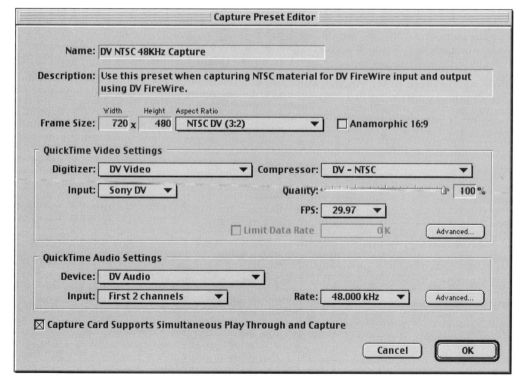

Figure 2.51 The Capture Preset Editor window.

Specifying QuickTime settings for video and audio

The current video settings for this Capture preset are displayed under QuickTime Video Settings. The current audio settings for this preset are displayed under QuickTime Audio Settings. The video and audio options that appear in the pop-up menus depend on the video hardware you have connected to your FCP system. It's critical that your capture settings match the hardware you're using. Unless you have a specific reason to make a change, stick with the default settings that match your capture hardware. Selecting the appropriate capture preset in the main Capture Preferences window should load the correct values for all other settings.

✔ Tip

■ Final Cut Pro 2 has incorporated the QuickTime settings you use the most into pop-up menus in the Capture Preset Editor. Now you can modify most Quick-Time settings for your Capture preset right in the Preset Editor window (without having to surf through all those default QuickTime settings windows).

To modify QuickTime video settings for the current capture preset:

In the QuickTime Video Settings section of the Capture Preset Editor window (**Figure 2.52**), you can modify default values for any of the following:

◆ **Digitizer:** Choose a capture interface from this pop-up menu to specify the digitizer hardware to be used.

◆ **Input:** Choose an input device from this pop-up menu to specify which video input you want to capture from. Some capture cards have multiple inputs to choose from.

◆ **Compressor:** Choose a codec from this pop-up menu to select a compression method for captured video. DV/FireWire systems should choose DV-NTSC or DV-PAL. Capture card users should select the codec recommended for their hardware.

◆ **Quality:** Adjust this slider to determine the image quality for your video. DV/FireWire systems should choose medium. Capture card users should consult hardware documentation for a recommendation.

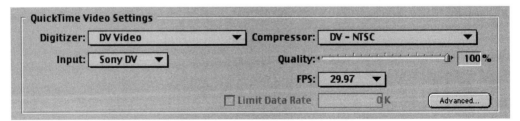

Figure 2.52 The QuickTime Video Settings section has pop-up menus for the QuickTime settings you use the most. You can modify most QuickTime settings for your Capture preset right in the Preset Editor window.

◆ **FPS:** Select a frames-per-second rate for capture from this pop-up menu. Select 29.97 for NTSC standard; select 25 for PAL standard.

◆ **Limit Data Rate to n K/Second:** Check this box to manually limit the data rate while capturing video. Type a numerical value in the field to define the data throughput in kilobytes per second. This applies only to certain codecs.

◆ **Advanced:** Click this button to access additional QuickTime video settings. Your advanced options are described in the next section.

To specify video source settings:

1. In the QuickTime Video Settings section of the Capture Preset Editor window, click the Advanced button.

   The Video window appears.

2. Choose Source from the pop-up menu in the upper-left corner of the Video window.

   If Final Cut Pro is receiving the video signal from your video input device, the preview window on the right side of the Video window should display video when your video input device is playing (**Figure 2.53**).

3. You can modify the default settings for any of the following:

   ▲ **Digitizer:** Choose a digitizer method from this pop-up menu to specify the digitizer hardware to be used.

   ▲ **Input:** Choose an input device from this pop-up menu to specify the playback hardware to be used.

   ▲ **Format:** Choose a format standard from this pop-up menu to specify the broadcast format to be used.

   ▲ **Filter:** Select the type of filter to be used when processing the source video.

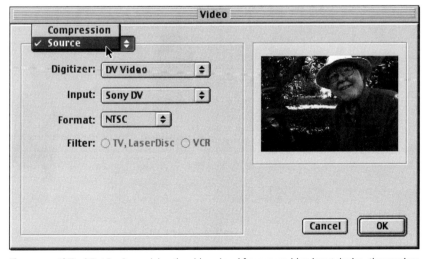

Figure 2.53 If Final Cut Pro is receiving the video signal from your video input device, the preview window on the right should display video when your video input device is playing.

To specify video compression settings:

1. Choose Compression from the pop-up menu in the upper-left corner of the Video window (**Figure 2.54**).

2. You can modify the default settings for any of the following:

   ▲ **Compressor:** Choose a codec from this pop-up menu to select a compression method for captured video.

   ▲ **Depth:** Choose a color depth from this pop-up menu to specify a bit-depth resolution for captured video.

   ▲ **Quality:** Adjust this slider to determine the image quality for your video. Least image quality yields a high data compression. Best image quality yields the lowest data compression.

   ▲ **Frames per Second:** Enter a value in this field or choose a preset value from the pop-up menu to specify the number of frames sampled per second.

   ▲ **Key Frame Every *n* Frames:** Check this box to manually assign keyframe intervals. Type a numerical value in the field to define the number of frames between keyframes. This applies only to certain codecs.

   ▲ **Limit Data Rate to *n* Kbytes/ Second:** Check this box to manually limit the data rate while capturing video. Type a numerical value in the field to define the data throughput in kilobytes per second. This applies only to certain codecs.

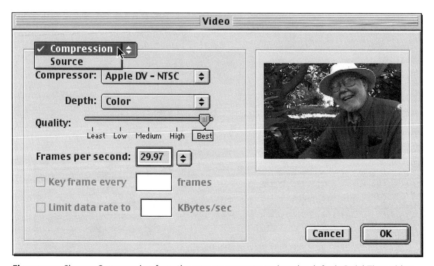

Figure 2.54 Choose Compression from the pop-up menu to review the default QuickTime video compression settings.

To modify QuickTime audio settings for the current capture preset:

In the QuickTime Audio Settings section of the Capture Preset Editor window (**Figure 2.55**), you can modify default values for any of the following:

◆ **Device:** Choose a capture interface from this pop-up menu to specify which of the Mac audio inputs you want to capture from. Choices include DV Audio, Internal CD, Built-in (the Mac's built-in mini audio input), and None. If you choose None, the other Audio Settings options disappear.

◆ **Input:** Select the audio channels you want to capture from this pop-up menu. If you have source material with four audio channels, this is the place to specify capture from the second pair of channels.

◆ **Rate:** Choose an audio sample rate from this pop-up menu. Be sure the sample rate matches the sample rate of your source material.

◆ **Advanced:** Click this button to access additional QuickTime audio settings. Your advanced options are described in the next two sections.

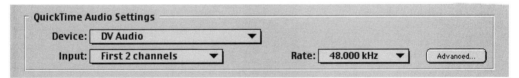

Figure 2.55 The QuickTime Audio Settings section has pop-up menus for the device, input source, and sample rate settings.

SPECIFYING CAPTURE SETTINGS

To specify source settings:

1. In the QuickTime Audio Settings section of the Capture Preset Editor window, click the Advanced button.

2. Choose Source from the pop-up menu in the upper-left corner of the Sound window.

3. You can modify the default settings for any of the following:

   ▲ **Device:** Choose a device type from this pop-up menu to specify the type of audio input device you are using.

   ▲ **Input:** Select the audio channels you want to capture from this pop-up menu (**Figure 2.56**).

   ▲ **Speaker:** Choose Off, On, or Off While Recording from this pop-up menu to specify the state of the speaker.

   ▲ **Volume:** Adjust this slider to set the speaker's volume.

   ▲ **Gain:** Adjust this slider to set the audio levels to be used when recording. If this slider is disabled, use the Gain slider on the Clip Settings tab of the Log and Capture window to set your audio input levels.

To specify sample settings:

1. In the QuickTime Audio Settings section of the Capture Preset Editor window, click the Advanced button.

2. Choose Sample from the pop-up menu in the upper-left corner of the Sound window (**Figure 2.57**).

3. You can modify the default settings for any of the following:

   ▲ **Rate:** Choose a predefined rate from this pop-up menu to specify an audio sample rate.

   ▲ **Size:** Choose a bit size or resolution for the audio sample.

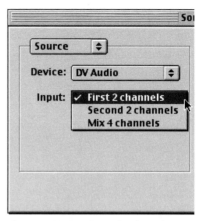

Figure 2.56 Select the audio channels you want to capture.

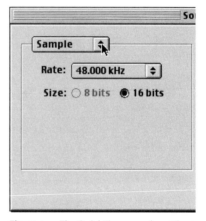

Figure 2.57 The QuickTime sample settings in the Sound window.

Specifying Device Control Settings

Before you can begin logging and digitizing source footage, you need to specify device control settings. Even if your external video deck or camcorder doesn't support device control, you'll still have limited capture and output capabilities, but to get the benefits of Final Cut Pro's batch capture and recapturing functions, device control is a must. Try the recommended device control preset for your external deck or camcorder first, before you modify the default settings. The Device Control Preset Editor window allows you to create and edit device control presets.

To edit settings for the current device control preset:

1. On the Device Control Presets tab of the Audio/Video Settings window, select a preset; then click the Edit button.

   If the preset is locked, a dialog box appears indicating that a copy will be made for editing; then the Device Control Preset Editor window appears.

2. You can modify the default settings for any of the following (**Figure 2.58**):

   Name: Enter a name for the preset.

   Description: Enter a description of the preset. If it's based on an existing preset with one or two changes, note the base preset plus the changes.

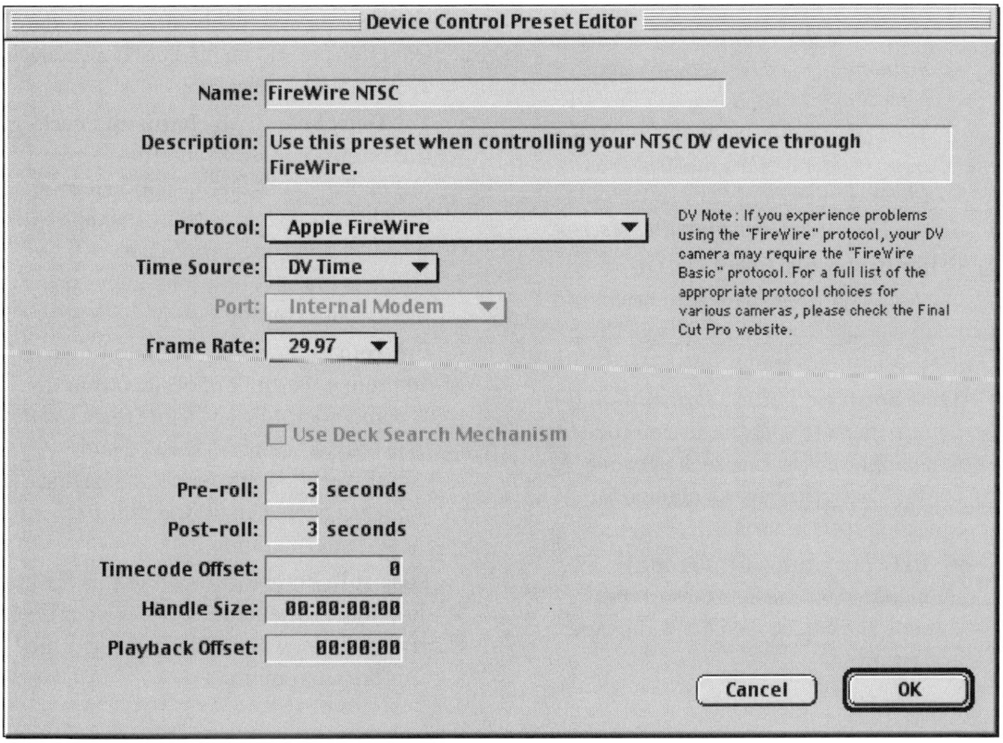

Figure 2.58 The Device Control Preset Editor.

Protocol: From this pop-up menu, choose the device control protocol your camcorder or deck uses:

▲ **FireWire (IEEE 1394):** If your deck or camcorder uses FireWire, try selecting the Apple FireWire protocol first. This is the default protocol if you select DV during the installation setup. With Apple FireWire as your selected device protocol, your FireWire deck or camcorder should support the most basic functions, such as returning timecode and accepting basic transport commands. If you discover that your deck or camcorder can't move to specified timecodes or fails to execute special commands, switch to the Apple FireWire Basic protocol. For more information, see "About Apple FireWire" in Chapter 1.

Note: Some DV cameras require the installation of a DV Tuner script to work properly with Final Cut Pro. DV Tuner scripts are available from the Extras folder on the Final Cut Pro CD. Check Apple's Final Cut Pro Web site to see if your equipment requires a script.

Other protocols: Check your deck or camcorder manual for the correct protocol type and then select it from the Protocol pop-up menu.

Time Source: Choose a format from this pop-up menu to specify the timecode format supported by your deck or camcorder. Check the device's manual for timecode specifications.

▲ **LTC:** Longitudinal timecode is recorded on a linear track of the tape and can be read while the tape is moving.

▲ **VITC:** Vertical interval timecode is contained in the vertical blanking of a signal and can be read when the tape is paused on a frame.

▲ **LTC+VITC:** A combination of longitudinal timecode and vertical interval timecode ensures that timecode can be read while the tape is in motion or paused.

▲ **Timer:** This format specifies a clock-based value as the timecode.

▲ **DV Time:** Digital video timecode is available for FireWire, Sony VISCA, and LANC protocols and should be selected when using DV formats.

Port: Choose a port from this pop-up menu to specify the computer port to which your device control cable is connected.

Frame Rate: Select the correct frame rate for your system's broadcast standard from this pop-up menu. For NTSC, select 29.97. For PAL, select 25.

Use Deck Search Mechanism: Check this box to use a deck's internal search mechanism. Turn off this option if your deck has problems shuttling the tape to a specified timecode during capture. This option is available only for systems using serial device control.

Pre-roll: Enter a duration in this field to determine the amount of video your deck or camcorder will play before the Capture In point you specify in the Log and Capture window. If your deck is having problems cueing up during capture, increase this duration.

Post-roll: Enter a duration in this field to determine the amount of video your deck or camcorder will play after the specified Capture Out point.

Timecode Offset: Enter a value in this field to calibrate your system to your tape deck when using Log and Capture. You may not need to offset your timecode, but if the timecode you capture doesn't match the timecode on your video deck, you may need to change the timecode offset or playback offset. See Chapter 3, "Input: Getting Digital with Your Video."

Handle Size: Enter a duration (in seconds) in this field to determine handle sizes for batch-captured clips. Handles provide extra frames on either end of the captured clip for editing flexibility.

Playback Offset: Enter a duration (in seconds) in this field to compensate for delays between the start of playback and the start of recording on the deck when editing to tape. Playback offset normally is set to zero. Enter a positive number to start playback before your deck starts to record. Enter a negative number to start playback after recording begins. If you discover that the first few frames laid to tape during Edit to Tape operation are duplicates, enter a positive value in this field equal to the number of frames being repeated. After you've specified device control preferences, you should capture some footage from a tape with burned-in timecode to determine whether you need to calibrate your system. You may not need to offset your timecode, but if the timecode you capture doesn't match the timecode on your video deck, you may need to change the timecode offset or playback offset. See Chapter 3 for more information on calibrating timecode offsets.

Using External Video Settings

External Video settings specify how Final Cut Pro feeds video and audio to your external video camcorder or deck, which in turn feeds your external video monitors and audio speakers. You control Final Cut Pro's External Video settings in three locations:

◆ The External Video pop-up menu on the Summary tab of the Audio/Video settings window displays the external video setting for your current Easy Setup. You can use the pop-up menu on the Summary tab to select a different setting. FCP will use this setting to route video output for both playing and recording. This menu is context sensitive; you will see only the options that your currently connected hardware will support.

◆ The External Video tab of the Audio/Video Settings window offers the complete array of external video settings. You can select one output destination for playing your video output, and a different output routing for recording video output.

◆ The View > External Video menu selection is the third control point for external video output. You can use this control to turn off FCP's external video output or to control display of rendered frames on external video monitors. To learn more about choreographing FCP's external video settings, see "FCP Protocol: Controlling External Video Output" in Chapter 1.

To select an external video setting from the Audio/Video Settings Summary:

1. Choose Edit > Audio/Video Settings.

2. From the External Video pop-up menu on the Summary tab, *choose one of the following* settings options (**Figure 2.59**); then click OK:

   ▲ **None:** Choose this option to turn off external video output.

   ▲ **Apple FireWire NTSC:** Choose this option to send the contents of the Canvas or Viewer to the connected NTSC FireWire device.

   ▲ **Apple FireWire PAL:** Choose this option to send the contents of the Canvas or Viewer to the connected PAL FireWire device.

▲ **Rendered Frames:** Choose this option to show frames rendered if All Frames or Single Frames is selected in the External Video submenu of the View menu.

▲ **Other video capture interface:** If you are using FCP with a third-party capture system, it will appear as an option in this list. Choose this option to send FCP's video output to your capture system.

Specifying External Video Settings

The External Video tab of the Audio/Video Settings window contains two pop-up menus: View During Playback, and View During Recording. Both pop-up menus contain identical options—the same external

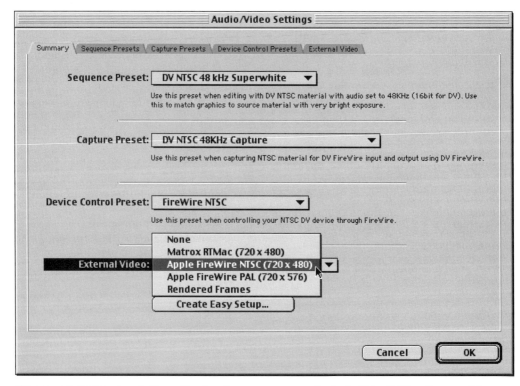

Figure 2.59 Select an external video setting from the pop-up menu on the Audio/Video Settings Summary tab.

video setting choices that appear on the Summary tab—but the two independent routing controls allow you the option of selecting one output destination for external monitoring of video playback, and a different routing for video output you're recording to tape. You can also enable or disable "mirroring" (video playback in the Canvas or Viewer) while playing back external video.

To configure additional external video settings:

1. Choose Edit > Audio/Video Settings.

2. On the External Video tab (**Figure 2.60**), modify any of the following default settings; then click OK:

   ▲ **View During Playback Using:** Choose an external video output routing to use when playing sequences and clips from the Viewer or Canvas. See Step 2 of the previous section, "To select an external video setting from the Audio/Video Settings Summary tab" for a list of your settings options.

▲ **Options:** If your video card requires it, click Options to access decompression options. Check your hardware documentation for more information.

▲ **Mirror on Desktop During Playback:** Check this box to display video in the Viewer or Canvas window on your computer monitor when playing back external video.

Disable this option if you notice dropped frames in your external output during video playback.

▲ **View During Recording Using:** Choose a video output routing to use when you're using Print to Video or Edit to Tape. FCP users with real-time systems that preview real-time effects in analog might select their real-time system to receive video output during playback, but choose a DV/FireWire option for their final output to tape. See Step 2 of the previous section, "To select an external video setting from the Audio/Video Settings Summary tab" for a list of your settings options.

▲ **Options:** If your video card requires it, click Options to access decompression options. Check your hardware documentation for more information.

▲ **Mirror on Desktop During Recording:** Check this box to display video in the Viewer or Canvas window on your computer monitor when using the Print to Video function. Disable this option if you notice dropped frames in your external output while you're using the Print to Video or Edit to Tape function.

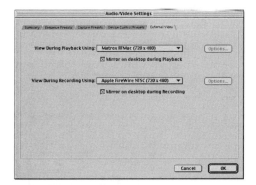

Figure 2.60 Specify how and where you monitor your video on the External Video tab of the Audio/Video Settings window.

Specifying Preference Window Settings

The settings in the Preferences window affect all of your Final Cut Pro projects. The Preferences window contains five tabs: General (which contains general program preferences), User Mode, Timeline Options, Labels, and Scratch Disks.

To set general preferences:

◆ Choose Edit > Preferences.

The General tab will appear as the front tab in the Preferences window (**Figure 2.61**).

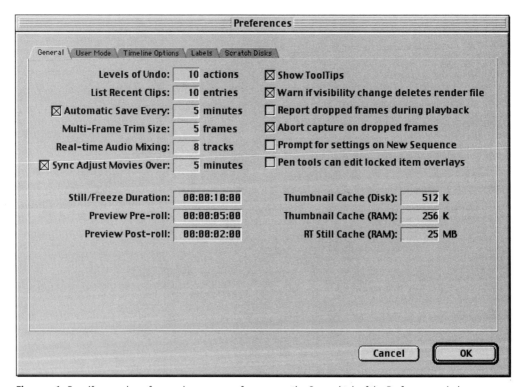

Figure 2.61 Specify a number of general program preferences on the General tab of the Preferences window.

General preferences settings

You can specify settings for the following:

◆ **Levels of Undo:** Specify the number of actions that can be undone. Specifying a large number of undo's can make significant demands on your available RAM.

◆ **List Recent Clips:** Set the number of recently accessed clips available on the Viewer's Recent Clips pop-up menu.

◆ **Automatic Save Every:** Check the box to save projects automatically at regular intervals. Enter a number to specify a time interval in minutes.

◆ **Multi-Frame Trim Size:** Set the multi-frame trim size by specifying the number of frames (up to nine) in this field. The specified number appears in the multi-frame trim buttons in the Trim Edit window.

◆ **Real-Time Audio Mixing:** Specify the number of audio tracks that Final Cut Pro mixes in real time. The default setting is eight tracks. The maximum number of tracks you will be able to mix depends on multiple factors. Reduce the number of tracks if you experience audio playback problems, such as video stuttering or audio pops or dropouts.

◆ **Sync Adjust Movies Over:** Sync Adjust's only function is to compensate for audio sync problems in long, continuous clip captures from video shot on certain cameras, notably certain models of Canon cameras. *Unless you are experiencing sync problems in long captures, turn the Sync Adjust function off by unchecking its box.* If you are capturing long clips from source tapes shot by cameras whose audio sampling rates are not exactly 48.000 KHz, enter a number of minutes in this field to

specify a minimum capture length. Final Cut Pro will sample rate convert the clip's audio on the fly to compensate for the sync problem. For details, see Chapter 3, "Input: Getting Digital with Your Video."

◆ **Still/Freeze Duration:** Enter a duration (in seconds) in this field to specify a default duration between In and Out points for imported still images, generators, and Adobe Photoshop files. Feel free to change this setting at will to increase your efficiency, for example when you're producing a series of freeze frames of a uniform length.

◆ **Preview Pre-roll:** Enter a number of seconds in this field to specify how much media to play before the edit point when you click the Play Around Current button or the Play Around Edit-Loop button.

◆ **Preview Post-roll:** Enter a number of seconds in this field to specify how much media to play after the edit point when you click the Play Around Current button or the Play Around Edit-Loop button.

◆ **Show ToolTips:** Check this box to toggle the display of ToolTips labels on buttons and tools.

◆ **Visibility Warning:** Check this box if you want Final Cut Pro to display a warning dialog box whenever making tracks invisible would cause render files to be deleted.

◆ **Report Drops:** Check this box if you want Final Cut Pro to display a warning dialog box whenever frames are dropped during playback.

◆ **Abort Capture on Dropped Frames:** Check this box to automatically stop the capture process if dropped frames are detected during the capture process.

continues on next page

◆ **Prompt for settings on New Sequence:**
Check this box if you want to see a list of
sequence presets each time you create a
new sequence.

◆ **Pen Tools Can Edit Locked Item
Overlays:** Check this box to enable the
Pen tools to edit keyframe overlays on
items on locked tracks in the Timeline.

◆ **Thumbnail Cache (Disk):** Specify the
amount of disk space to allocate for storing thumbnails.

◆ **Thumbnail Cache (RAM):** Specify the
amount of memory to allocate for storing
thumbnails. Increase this value to
improve the program's performance.

◆ **RT Still Cache (RAM):** This preference
appears only on RTMac-equipped systems. Specify the amount of memory to
allocate for storing graphics. The recommended minimum is 25 MB, but you
should increase this value if your projects
include large numbers of graphics.

✔ **Tip**

■ Displaying video on the computer monitor while printing to video or editing to
tape taxes the computer's processing
power and can cause performance problems. If you notice dropped frames in
your output when performing these operations, check out the tips for optimizing
performance in Chapter 1, "Before You
Begin," before giving up and disabling
your desktop video playback. You may
want to increase the size of your thumbnail caches if you are working with a
large number of clips and want to display thumbnails, or if you are using the
Browser's Icon view. If you often scrub
through thumbnails in the Browser's Icon
view, you can optimize the performance
of this feature by increasing the size of
the thumbnail RAM cache. Set a location
for the thumbnail cache on the Scratch
Disk tab of the Preferences window.

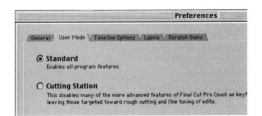

Figure 2.62 Specify Standard or Cutting Station user mode by clicking the appropriate radio button.

Setting User Mode Preferences

Final Cut Pro offers a choice of user modes. Standard, which includes Final Cut Pro's full feature set, is the default mode. Cutting Station mode offers a more limited feature set. You could benefit from choosing Cutting Station if:

◆ You are new to Final Cut Pro, and you want to simplify your work environment by removing a group of features.

◆ You are preparing a project that will be exported as an EDL. Cutting Station mode removes many features that do not export successfully in EDL. Hiding incompatible features could simplify the editing process.

◆ You selected a user mode as part of the initial setup process when you installed Final Cut Pro, but you can switch modes on the User Mode tab of the Preferences window.

To switch user mode preferences:

1. Choose Edit > Preferences; then select the User Mode tab.

2. On the User Mode tab (**Figure 2.62**), click the appropriate radio button to *select one of the following*:

   ▲ Standard: Allows access to Final Cut Pro's full feature set.

   ▲ Cutting Station: Allows access to basic editing functions only and disables effects and keyframing features.

3. Click OK.

4. Quit and then relaunch Final Cut Pro to switch to the new user mode.

FCP Protocol: Cutting Station Feature List

Here's a rundown of Cutting Station user mode features:

◆ Limited to two video and four audio tracks per sequence.

◆ Limit of seven audio and video filters per sequence.

◆ Transition effects are limited to Oval Iris, Edge Wipe, Page Peel, and Rectangle Iris.

◆ No keyframing of motion effects, but you can make a global adjustment to an entire clip.

◆ No speed changes

Now if Microsoft would only invent Cutting Station mode for Word....

Customizing the Timeline Display

The Timeline display options you specify on the Timeline Options tab in the Preferences window will become the default display settings for subsequent new projects and sequences. If you want to modify the Timeline display options for an existing sequence, you will need to make the change in the Sequence Settings window for that sequence. See "Changing the Settings of an Existing Sequence" later in this chapter.

To customize your default Timeline display settings:

1. Choose Edit > Preferences.

   Click the Timeline Options tab. On the Timeline Options tab (**Figure 2.63**), you can modify the default settings for any of the following:

   Starting Timecode: Enter a value in this field to set the starting timecode for your sequence. The hour value can be used to help you identify sequences. The default starting timecode is 01:00:00;00.

   Drop Frame: Check this box if you want drop-frame timecode displayed in the sequence Timeline.

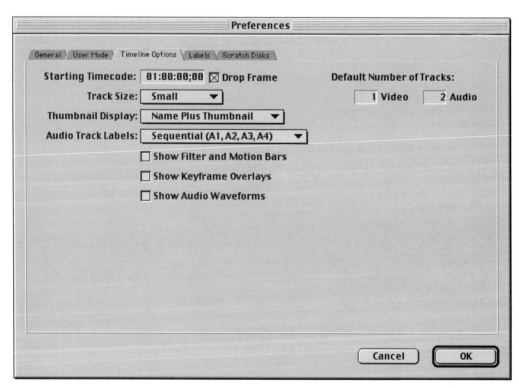

Figure 2.63 Customize your default Timeline display options on the Preference window's Timeline Options tab

CUSTOMIZING THE TIMELINE DISPLAY

Track Size: Choose a setting from this pop-up menu to specify a default track size.

Thumbnail Display: Select one of three thumbnail display options from this pop-up menu:

▲ Name displays the name of the clip and no thumbnail images.

▲ Name Plus Thumbnail displays the first frame of every clip as a thumbnail image and then the name of the clip.

▲ Filmstrip displays as many thumbnail images as possible for the current zoom level of the Timeline.

Audio Track Labels: Select one of two track labeling options from this pop-up menu:

▲ **Paired (A1a, A1b, A2a, A2b):** This is a good labeling scheme if you are working with stereo tracks.

▲ **Sequential (A1, A2, A3, A4,):** This is a good labeling scheme if you are working with a collection of single tracks, such as dialog tracks.

Show Filter and Motion Bars: Check this box to display filter and motion bars below the clip in the Timeline.

Show Keyframe Overlays: Check this box to display opacity keyframe overlays on video clips and level keyframe graphs on audio clips in the Timeline.

Show Audio Waveforms: Check this box to display the audio waveform along the audio clip in the Timeline.

Default Number of Tracks: Specify the number of video and audio tracks to be included in a new sequence, and then click OK.

Your custom Timeline display settings will become the defaults for subsequent new sequences.

Setting Label Preferences

Final Cut Pro offers color-coded icons with customizable names. You can apply these labels to Browser and Timeline clips and use the Label and Label 2 columns in the Browser to sort by label type. Label colors are not customizable.

To customize label names:

1. Choose Edit > Preferences.

2. Click the Labels tab.

3. Click the text field to make it active; then enter your custom label name (**Figure 2.64**).

4. Click OK.

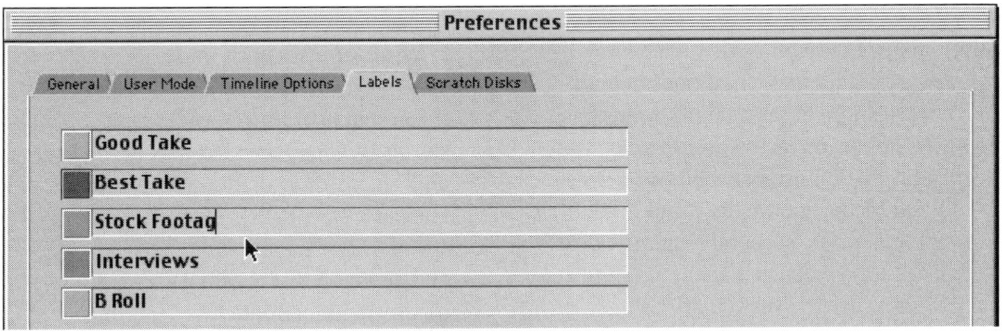

Figure 2.64 Enter a custom label name in the text field.

Setting Scratch Disk Preferences

A *scratch disk* is a folder on a hard disk where Final Cut Pro stores your captured media source files and render files. The default scratch disk location is the same hard disk where your Final Cut Pro application is installed. You can specify multiple scratch disk locations, either to improve performance by capturing audio and video on separate drives (not recommended for DV) or to provide the necessary storage capacity for your project media.

You should use your fastest disk drives as your scratch disks. For best performance, avoid setting the system hard disk as the scratch disk.

When a disk or folder is added to the scratch disk list, Final Cut Pro automatically creates a folder on that disk called Final Cut Pro Documents. That folder contains subfolders (one for each type of media file your project will generate) named Capture Scratch, Audio Capture Scratch, and Render Files, Audio Render Files, Thumbnail Cache Files, and Waveform Cache Files (**Figure 2.65**). If you are capturing DV, your captured media files will be stored in a folder, bearing your project's name, inside the Capture Scratch folder.

✔ Tip

- Final Cut Pro requires that each hard disk have a distinct name that does not contain the entire name of another media drive. For example, the program will not reliably distinguish between two drives named Media and Media 1, but Media 1 and Media 2 are acceptable names. Bear this in mind when you are assigning names to hard drives you are using with Final Cut Pro.

Figure 2.65 The Final Cut Pro Documents folder contains a subfolder for each type of media file that your project will generate.

FCP Protocol: Scratch Disks

Unless you specify otherwise, Final Cut Pro uses the disk with the most available space as its storage area for rendered files. If you specify multiple scratch disks, Final Cut Pro will use the next disk in the list with the most available space when the current disk runs out of space. You can specify separate disks for captured video and audio files to obtain better capture quality at higher data rates and improved playback performance.

To specify scratch disk preferences:

1. Choose Edit > Preferences.

2. Click the Scratch Disks tab.

3. You can specify settings for the following (**Figure 2.66**):

   ▲ **Video Capture, Audio Capture, Video Render, and Audio Render:** Check these boxes to specify the types of files to be stored on each disk. Specify more than one disk for increased storage space. When the current disk runs out of space, Final Cut Pro automatically switches to the next specified disk for storing capture files or to the disk with the most space available for storing render files.

▲ **Clear:** Click the Clear button to remove a disk from the list of available disks.

▲ **Set:** Click the Set button to choose a disk or a folder on a hard disk. You can specify up to five disks.

▲ **Capture Audio and Video to Separate Files (not recommended for DV):** Check this box if you want to optimize playback for QuickTime files with higher data rates. This feature allows you to write the video and audio tracks in a QuickTime movie to separate files on separate disks during the capture process. Video and audio files have the same name with _v appended to video and _a appended

continues on next page

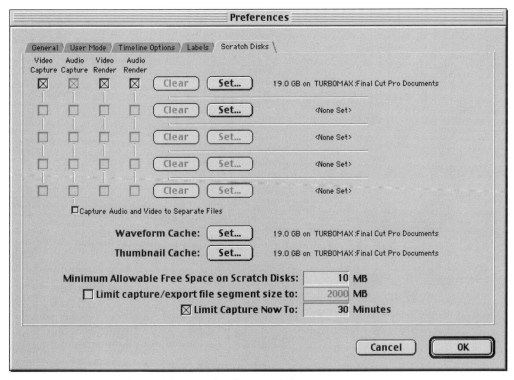

Figure 2.66 The Scratch Disks tab of the General Preferences window.

to audio files. Note that separate files must be captured to different disks; the two files cannot be captured to different directories on the same disk.

▲ **Waveform Cache:** Click the Set button to specify a folder or disk to store waveform cache files (graphical representations of audio signals). The default location is the Final Cut Pro Documents folder on your scratch disk.

▲ **Thumbnail Cache:** Click the Set button to specify a folder or disk to store thumbnail cache files. The default location is the Final Cut Pro Documents folder on your scratch disk.

▲ **Minimum Allowable Free Space on Scratch Disks:** Enter a limit value in this field. When disk space falls below this minimum, a disk will no longer be used as a scratch disk, and files will be stored on the next disk in the list.

▲ **Limit Capture/Export File Segment Size To:** Enter a limit value in this field. The default value is 2 gigabytes. Final Cut Pro 2 allows capture and export of single files larger than 2 gigabytes, but if you're planning on moving your files to another system that has a file size limitation, or you are sharing media files over a network, you should enable this option. Files that are larger than your specified limit will be spanned (written as separate, but linked, files).

◆ **Limit Capture Now To:** Enter a limit value in this field. The default limit is 30 minutes.

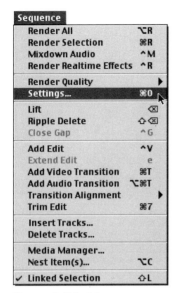

Figure 2.67 Select the sequence; then choose Sequence > Settings.

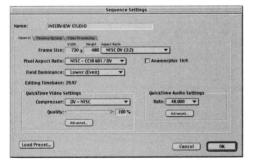

Figure 2.68 The Sequence Settings window contains the same options as the Sequence Preset Editor, plus a Timeline Options tab where you can customize display options for the selected sequence. Modifying settings for an individual sequence changes the settings for that sequence only.

Changing the Settings of an Existing Sequence

You can open and review or modify any individual sequence's settings in the Sequence Settings window. The Sequence Settings window contains the same options as the Sequence Preset Editor, plus a Timeline Options tab where you can customize a sequence's display options. When you modify settings for an individual sequence, you are changing the settings for that sequence only.

To change the settings for an individual sequence:

1. Make the sequence active by selecting it in the Browser or Timeline.

2. Choose Sequence > Settings (**Figure 2.67**).

   The Sequence Settings window appears (**Figure 2.68**).

   Review or modify your sequence settings; then click OK.

   For a list of your options on the General and Video Processing tabs, see "Specifying Sequence Settings" earlier in this chapter. For a list of your options on the Timeline Options tab, see "Customizing the Timeline Display," also earlier in this chapter.

To switch a sequence's settings to a different sequence preset:

1. Make the sequence active by selecting it in the Browser or Timeline.

2. Choose Sequence > Settings.

   The Sequence Settings window appears.

3. Click the Load Preset button (**Figure 2.69**).

4. Choose a different preset from the Select pop-up menu in the Select Preset dialog box (**Figure 2.70**); then click OK.

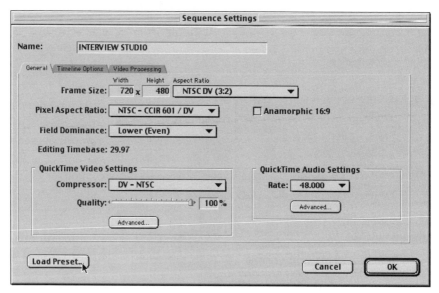

Figure 2.69 Click Load Preset to select replacement sequence settings from a list of sequence presets.

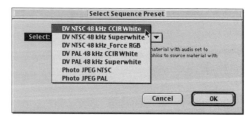

Figure 2.70 Choose a different sequence preset to replace the settings of your selected sequence.

Viewing and Setting Item Properties

The Item Properties window is the central location for information about an individual clip. Three tabs in the Item Properties window allow you to view or change the properties of a clip.

✔ Tip

■ What if you have changed the name of a clip and removed all traces of the original source media file it references? You can consult the Item Properties window for the renamed clip to trace the underlying source media file name and location.

To open a clip's Item Properties window:

1. Select the clip in the Browser or Timeline or open it in the Viewer.

2. *Do one of the following:*
   ▲ Choose Edit > Item Properties.
   ▲ Control-click the item; then choose Properties from the shortcut menu.
   ▲ Press Command-9.

To get information about the format of a clip:

1. In the clip's Item Properties window, click the Format tab (**Figure 2.71**) to open it. This tab displays data on the location of the clip's source media file, file size, and format characteristics.

2. The following Format properties can be modified:
   ▲ **Field Dominance:** Specify the dominant field by making a selection from the pop-up menu.
   ▲ **Alpha Type:** Select an alpha channel type for the video clip.
   ▲ **Reverse Alpha:** Reverse the alpha channel of the video clip.
   ▲ **Composite Mode:** Select the mode to be used when compositing the video clip.
   ▲ **Pixel Aspect Ratio:** Select a pixel aspect ratio for this clip.
   ▲ **Anamorphic 16:9:** If your clip's source media is 16:9, checking this box ensures that FCP will interpret and display the clip's pixel aspect ratio properly.

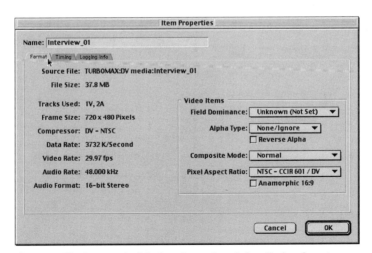

Figure 2.71 The Format tab of the Item Properties window displays format information on an individual clip or sequence.

VIEWING AND SETTING ITEM PROPERTIES

To get information about the timing of a clip:

1. In the clip's Item Properties window, click the Timing tab to open it (**Figure 2.72**).

2. In the Clip section, you can modify the following Timing properties (on Browser clips only):

   ▲ **In:** Enter or modify the In point of a clip.

   ▲ **Out:** Enter or modify the Out point of a clip.

   ▲ **Duration:** Enter or modify the duration of a clip.

3. The Media section of the Timing tab displays the total media length and the start and end timecode values of the clip's source media file.

   The Speed section of the Timing tab displays the clip's current speed and frame blending status.

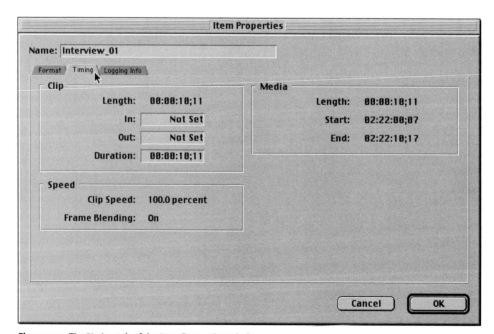

Figure 2.72 The Timing tab of the Item Properties window.

VIEWING AND SETTING ITEM PROPERTIES

To get logging information for a clip:

1. In the clip's Item Properties window, click the Logging Info tab (**Figure 2.73**).

   This tab provides logging information for a clip.

2. You can review or modify the following:

   ▲ **Reel:** Enter or modify the name of the clip's source tape.

   ▲ **Description:** Enter or modify descriptive details for a clip.

   ▲ **Scene:** Enter or modify tracking information for a clip.

   ▲ **Shot/Take:** Enter or modify tracking information.

▲ **Log Note:** Enter or modify a log note.

▲ **Capture:** Specify the status of a clip as Not Yet, Captured, or Queued.

▲ **Label and Label 2:** Enter or modify any labels you have assigned to this clip.

▲ **Mark Good:** Click the Mark Good check box to mark the clip as good.

▲ **Comments 1–4:** Enter or modify additional comments for the clip in these fields. Note: If you customized Comment column names in the Browser, they won't appear here.

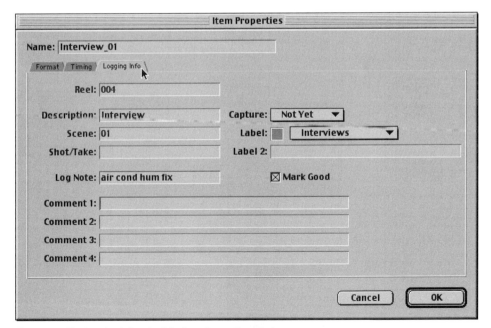

Figure 2.73 The Logging Info tab of the Item Properties window.

Viewing and Setting Project Properties

Each project has a set of properties that are saved with it. The project's properties apply to all sequences in a project and are independent of the project's sequence presets.

To view or change the properties of a project:

1. In the Browser window, click the Project tab.

2. Choose Edit > Project Properties (**Figure 2.74**).

3. In the Project Properties window (**Figure 2.75**), do any of the following:

   ▲ Display timecode or frames in the browser's Duration column. Choosing Frames displays the total number of frames for clips and sequences in the Duration column.

   ▲ Edit render qualities for the project. (For more information on editing render qualities, see Chapter 10, "Rendering.")

   ▲ Edit the heading labels for the Comment columns that appear in the Browser window.

✔ Tip

■ Any comments you enter in the Comment 4 column can be included in an exported EDL if you should export an EDL of your FCP project.

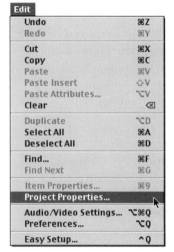

Figure 2.74 Choose Edit > Project Properties.

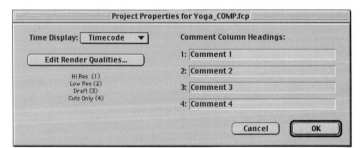

Figure 2.75 The Project Properties window.

INPUT: GETTING DIGITAL WITH YOUR VIDEO

This chapter explains how to use Final Cut Pro's input features. The logging and capture functions have been designed to facilitate some common post-production strategies.

Logging and capturing are independent operations in Final Cut Pro. You can use the logging process to assess all your material for the entire project when you are getting underway. Your logged, offline clips are ready to be captured when you're ready for them, and they won't be taking up space on your hard drives.

You can use the Log and Capture window to review and log the media on an entire source tape and then capture all the clips that you want from that tape in one operation, called a *batch capture*.

Recapturing media is another vital process in most desktop video editing post-production plans. For more information, see the sidebar "The Wonders of Batch Recapture" later in this chapter.

This chapter also includes details on importing audio, still images, and other media files.

It's important to note that you will not be able to use the most powerful automated capture and output features unless your external video hardware supports device control. You still can capture clips that are logged and manually captured while the tape is playing, but you won't be able to perform automated batch capture and recapture or assemble segments of your project using the Edit to Tape feature when you're ready to output your final product to tape.

Before you plunge into your project, take a moment to plan your route. There's a lot to think about when you start to assemble your project, and your media input strategy has a big impact on whether you get the most out of FCP.

Anatomy of the Log and Capture Window

Use the Log and Capture window to capture video and audio media in Final Cut Pro. Log and Capture supports a range of capturing options, from capturing live video on the fly to automated batch capture with full device control.

Final Cut Pro logs shots by creating offline clips that it stores in a Browser bin of your choice.

Logging and capturing are independent operations in Final Cut Pro, so you can log all the footage for your entire program before you capture a single clip. When your disk storage space is tight (and disk storage space is *always* tight), having a detailed inventory of your material online means you can make use of the Browser's powerful database features to sort out your source material and develop a game plan before you start capturing media. For more information on the Browser's capabilities, see "How the Browser Can Save Your Sanity" in Chapter 4.

✔ Tip

■ The size of your Log and Capture window is determined by the size of the Canvas and Viewer windows in your workspace arrangement. If you're using the large size for the Canvas and Viewer, your Log and Capture window will be large as well. Small Canvas and Viewer windows will result in a small Log and Capture window.

Preview window

Many of the controls in the Preview section of the Log and Capture window also appear in the Viewer window. For more information, review "Onscreen Controls and Displays" in Chapter 5.

Figure 3.1 shows an overview of the Log and Capture window.

◆ **Current Timecode field:** This field displays the current timecode location of your source tape. Enter a timecode number in this field to shuttle the source tape to that timecode location.

◆ **Timecode Duration field:** This field displays the duration of the currently marked clip.

◆ **Free Space status display:** This display shows the amount of available hard disk space remaining.

◆ **Transport controls:** Use these buttons to control your deck or camcorder transport controls if you have device control enabled. Transport control operation is described in Chapter 5, "Introducing the Viewer."

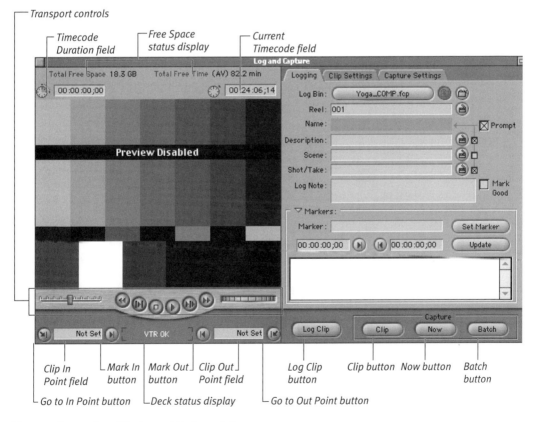

Figure 3.1 An overview of the Log and Capture window.

◆ **Deck status display:** This display shows the status of communication between your deck or camcorder and Final Cut Pro.

◆ **Go to In Point button:** Click to shuttle tape to the currently marked clip's In point.

◆ **Clip In Point field:** This field displays the timecode location of the currently marked clip's In point.

◆ **Mark In button:** Click to mark an In point for your capture.

◆ **Mark Out button:** Click to mark an Out point for your capture.

◆ **Clip Out Point field:** This field displays the timecode location of the currently marked clip's Out point.

◆ **Go to Out Point button:** Click to shuttle tape to the currently marked clip's Out point.

✔ Tip

■ Not only can you copy and paste time-codes from one field to another; you can Option-click and then drag and drop a timecode to copy it into another time-code field—a useful procedure while you're logging.

Log and capture controls

The Log and Capture control buttons appear below the tabbed portion of the window. The Log Clip button is used to log a clip without capturing it, and the other three buttons perform different kinds of capture operations.

◆ **Log Clip button:** Click this button to log the current clip in the log bin.

◆ **Clip button:** Click this button to capture a single clip immediately. This kind of captured clip can be saved directly to your Capture Scratch folder and need not be associated with a specific project. However, any log information you enter won't be automatically added to the Browser; you must save the clip manually. For more information, see "Capturing Video with Device Control" later in this chapter.

◆ **Now button:** Click this button to capture without setting In or Out points. This procedure is useful if your deck or camcorder doesn't have device control, or if you want to capture long clips without setting the Out point in advance. For more information, see "Capturing Video without Device Control" later in this chapter.

◆ **Batch button:** Click this button to batch capture a group of previously logged clips. For more information on batch capturing, see "Batch Capturing Clips" later in this chapter.

Logging tab

The Logging tab (**Figure 3.2**) contains fields and shortcut tools you use to enter the information you need to log a clip.

◆ **Log Bin button:** Click to open the current log bin (the Browser bin where offline clips are stored during logging).

◆ **Up button:** Click to move the log bin selection up a level from the currently selected log bin.

◆ **New Bin button:** Click to create a new log bin inside the currently selected log bin.

◆ **Reel field:** Enter the name of your current source tape in this field. Control-click the text field to select from a list of recent reel names.

◆ **Reel Slate button:** Click to add a number at the end of the name for incremental labeling. Click again to increment the number by 1. Option-click to clear the contents of the field. All the Slate buttons on the Logging tab perform the same functions for their respective fields.

◆ **Name display:** The name in this field is compiled from information entered in the Description, Scene, and Shot/Take fields. This is the name that will appear in the Browser's Name column.

◆ **Prompt check box:** Check this box for a prompt to name a clip when you click the Log Clip button at the bottom of this tabbed window.

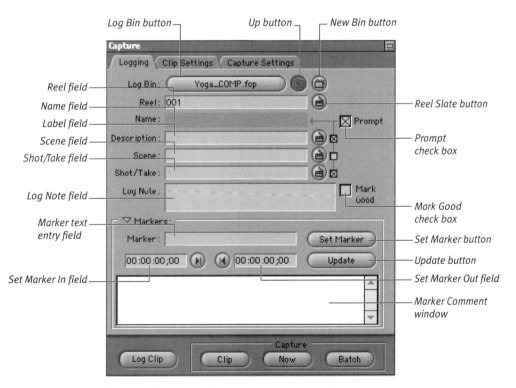

Figure 3.2 The Log and Capture window's Logging tab.

◆ **Description field:** Enter descriptive text in this field. Check the box at the right to include this description in the Name field.

◆ **Scene field:** Enter descriptive text in this field. Check the box at the right to include this description in the Name field.

◆ **Shot/Take field:** Enter descriptive text in this field. Check the box at the right to include this description in the Name field.

◆ **Log Note field:** Enter descriptive text in this field. Control-click the text field to select from a list of recent log notes.

◆ **Mark Good check box:** Check this box to place a marker in the Browser's Good column. When you're done logging, you can use the Browser's sort function to group all the clips you've marked "Good."

◆ **Marker text entry field:** Enter a marker name or remarks in this field. For more information, see "Using Markers" in Chapter 5, "Introducing the Viewer."

◆ **Set Marker In field:** Click to set a Marker In point, or enter a timecode in the field.

◆ **Set Marker Out field:** Click to set a Marker Out point, or enter a timecode in the field.

◆ **Set Marker button:** Click to log the marker.

◆ **Update button:** Click to modify a previously entered marker.

◆ **Marker Comment window:** This window displays marker information for the current clip.

Capture Settings tab

The Capture Settings tab (**Figure 3.3**) provides shortcut access to the Device Control, Capture/Input, and Scratch Disks settings. The Free Space status display shows the amount of space currently available on designated scratch disks. The Capture Now limit indicates the time limit currently specified in the Scratch Disks preference window.

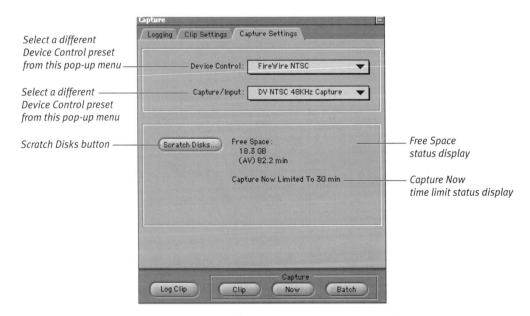

Select a different Device Control preset from this pop-up menu

Select a different Device Control preset from this pop-up menu

Scratch Disks button

Free Space status display

Capture Now time limit status display

Figure 3.3 The Log and Capture window's Capture Settings tab.

Clip Settings tab

The Clip Settings tab (**Figure 3.4**) contains controls for calibrating and formatting your input. Once you've configured clip settings, the same settings will apply to subsequent captured clips until you change the settings again.

◆ **Image quality controls for video:** Use the sliders to adjust the image quality settings for video you are digitizing (not applicable for DV capture).

◆ **Use Digitizer's Default Settings button:** Click to restore the manufacturer's default audio/video settings for your capture card.

◆ **Gain slider:** Adjust the slider to set incoming audio levels. (The Gain slider has no effect on audio levels for DV capture.)

◆ **Capture Format selector:** Select video, audio, or video and audio.

◆ **Audio Input Format selector:** Select an audio channel configuration for capture from the pop-up menu.

◆ **Waveform Monitor and Vectorscope button:** Click to access the waveform monitor and vectorscope. Use the waveform monitor and vectorscope to calibrate input settings for video you are digitizing. See "Calibrating capture settings with color bars and audio tone" later in this chapter.

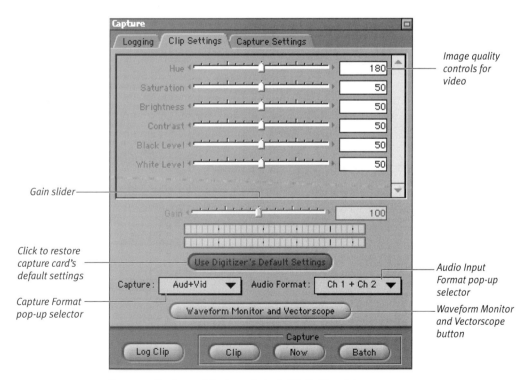

Figure 3.4 The Log and Capture window's Clip Settings tab.

To open the Log and Capture window:

◆ Choose File > Log and Capture (**Figure 3.5**).

✔ Tips

■ When you open the Log and Capture window for the first time after launching FCP, the screen will say "Preview Disabled." Don't freak out. That's standard operating procedure—the warning disappears when you click Play. If it doesn't—then you can start worrying.

■ For best performance, the Log and Capture window should be completely visible on your computer monitor, with nothing overlapping the window—not even the cursor.

■ If you have been capturing clips, FCP will not play back clips in your external monitor until you close the Log and Capture window.

Figure 3.5 To open the Log and Capture window, choose File > Log and Capture.

Setting Up for Capture

If you are new to Final Cut Pro, take a moment to read Chapters 4 and 5, which contain details on Browser and Viewer operation, before you start a capture process. You'll need to use both of these windows in the capture operation. Capturing video is probably the first thing you're going to want to do, but a little general knowledge of the FCP interface will make your first captures go more smoothly.

You may also need to review Chapter 2, "Welcome to Final Cut Pro," for details on preference and preset settings.

Capturing is important, and you should set up for it correctly. Here's an overview of the setup procedure and your objectives in each step:

◆ *Check device control settings.* You want to ensure that your video, audio, timecode, and device control connections between your deck or camcorder and Final Cut Pro are operational.

◆ *Check scratch disk preferences.* You want to ensure that any media you capture will be written to the correct hard disk or folder, that your designated scratch disk is fast enough to handle the data transfer, and that you have enough space to accommodate the media files you want to capture.

◆ *Checking capture settings.* You want to be sure that you've selected the proper capture preset. Your capture settings should match the video hardware and tape format you're using. Select the correct audio channels and sample rate to match the media you want to capture.

◆ *Calibrate the timecode signal input.* You want to compensate for any offset between the timecode of your source video and your captured video.

◆ *Calibrate input signals (for non-DV systems only).* You want to adjust the incoming video signal to ensure the best image quality or to match the quality of media you've already captured.

◆ *Check clip settings.* Clip settings are just customized capture settings that you can adjust for an individual clip only. In a DV system, even though you can't make adjustments to a clip's video or audio (DV capturing is a straight transfer of digital information), you can adjust the audio channel or sample rate clip settings for an individual clip. In a non-DV system, you can adjust the clip's hue, saturation, brightness, contrast, sharpness, black level, white level, and gain settings.

✔ Tips

■ If your DV clips need image-quality adjustments, you can fix them post-capture by applying the appropriate image control filters. To learn how to use FCP's filters, see Chapter 13, "Compositing and Special Effects."

■ Before you start logging and capturing your footage, you should use color bars to check the image quality on your external video monitor as well. Your monitor is a critical tool for evaluating your footage, so set it up right, and once you've calibrated it, leave the monitor's image settings alone. See Appendix F in Apple's *Final Cut Pro User's Manual* for instructions.

Is Your System Capture-Ready?

Capturing video puts your entire FCP system—including your external hardware—to the test. Any conditions that impair its performance can show up as dropped frames, audio sync drift, or error messages—not a good start for your project.

Apple's Technical Information Library (also known as TIL) has a good article on the subject: "Final Cut Pro: Dropped Frames and Loss of Audio Sync" (article ID 58640).

Here's a checklist (summarized from the TIL article) you can use to avoid the most common causes of capture troubles:

◆ Allocate sufficient memory to FCP. A realistic minimum is 106 MB.

◆ AppleTalk should be off. Use the AppleTalk Control Panel to turn it off.

◆ Virtual memory should be off. Use the Memory control panel to turn it off.

◆ The Canvas size should be set to Fit to Window or smaller. If you can see scroll bars in the Canvas, you have a problem. Analog capture cards may have other limitations on video scaling in the Canvas.

◆ Your computer monitor's refresh rate should be set to 75 Hz or higher in the Monitor's control panel.

◆ On PowerBook FCP systems, turn off processor cycling on the Advanced Settings panel of the Energy Saver control panel.

◆ You should be using FCP-qualified drives. If your drives are overly full, or if the data is too fragmented, drive performance can be impaired.

See "Optimizing Performance" in Chapter 1 and "Troubleshooting Capture Problems" later in this chapter for more tips on improving Final Cut Pro's performance.

Figure 3.6 Click the Capture Settings tab in the Log and Capture window.

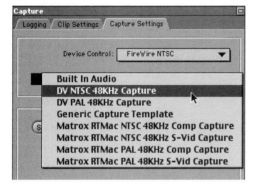

Figure 3.7 Use the Capture/Input pop-up menu if you need to switch to a different capture preset.

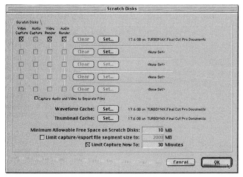

Figure 3.8 Click OK to save your scratch disk preference settings.

Checking preferences

You can review your device control, scratch disk, and capture settings on the Capture Settings tab in the Log and Capture window. If you need to, you can switch to a different preset without leaving the Capture Settings tab, by making a selection from the pop-up menus. For an itemized list of the preference options and specification procedure, see Chapter 2, "Welcome to Final Cut Pro."

To access preference settings:

1. In the Log and Capture window, click the Capture Settings tab (**Figure 3.6**).

2. On the Capture Settings tab, *do one of the following:*

   ▲ Review your device control preset setting in the Device Control pop-up menu.

   ▲ Review your current capture preset in the Capture/Input pop-up menu (**Figure 3.7**).

   ▲ Click the Scratch Disks button to access preference settings.

   Follow Chapter 2 procedures for reviewing or modifying your scratch disk settings; then click OK (**Figure 3.8**).

✔ Tip

■ If you make a mistake or two while you're adjusting your preference settings, you can restore default settings by quitting FCP and deleting your Final Cut Pro Preferences file. See "How to "Trash Your Prefs" in Chapter 2 for details.

SETTING UP FOR CAPTURE

97

Capture Settings: Try These First

Final Cut Pro provides a variety of ways to adjust your capture settings and clip settings. But do you really need to make adjustments to the default settings? Which settings apply to your capture system?

For FCP users with DV/FireWire systems that use common external video devices, perfecting your preference settings should be as easy as selecting DV NTSC or DV PAL from the Easy Setups window's pop-up menu.

For users running more complex systems including third-party capture cards, getting the perfect configuration could take more effort. Check to see if your card's manufacturer offers a custom FCP Easy Setup, or configure your own using the documentation that comes with the hardware. Don't forget to check the manufacturer's Web site for the latest instructions or driver updates.

Once you have perfected your settings, you should save your settings configuration as a custom Easy Setup to protect your work. To learn how to save a custom Easy Setup, see "Using Easy Setups" in Chapter 2.

Here's a suggested configuration for DV/FireWire systems:

◆ Capture preset: DV NTSC or DV PAL.

◆ Clip settings: The only clip settings controls that have any effect on DV capture are Capture Format and Audio Input Format. You can monitor, but not adjust, your audio input levels. You can adjust your DV audio levels in Final Cut Pro after you have captured the files. (If your DV audio levels are too high, you won't be able to fix clipping and distortion after capture.)

◆ Audio sample rate: The sample rate should match the sample rate of your deck or camcorder.

◆ Sequence preset: DV-NTSC or DV PAL.

◆ If you specified a DV Easy Setup when you installed the Final Cut Pro software, the correct capture settings (except the audio sample rate) were configured automatically.

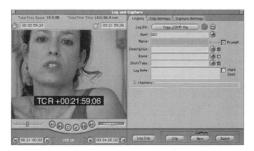

Figure 3.9 Capture a test clip.

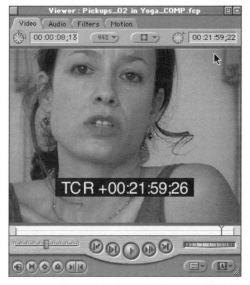

Figure 3.10 Compare the burned-in timecode visible in the video frame with the timecode value that appears in the Viewer's Current Timecode field.

TCR +00:21:59;26

minus ⊘ 00:21:59;22

= +4 frames

Figure 3.11 Burned-in timecode minus Current Timecode value equals duration of the offset.

Calibrating the timecode signal input

Computer hardware can introduce an offset between the timecode signal and the video signal, which causes the timecode and video to be offset when they are captured.

If the timecode you capture doesn't match the timecode on your video deck, you'll need to set a timecode offset. To do this, you'll need a test tape with timecode visible in the frame (a window dub), or you'll need a deck or camcorder with a timecode display option.

To calibrate timecode:

1. Capture video from the window dub test tape or from another tape with the time-code display option for your deck turned on (**Figure 3.9**).

2. In the first frame of your test capture clip, compare the burned-in timecode visible in the video frame with the timecode value that appears in the Viewer's Current Timecode field (**Figure 3.10**). (If you use the display option, the number will appear in your camera's viewfinder or on your external monitor.)

3. Calculate the duration of the offset by subtracting the Current Timecode field's timecode value from the burned-in time-code value (**Figure 3.11**).

   If the timecode value in the Current Timecode field is less than the burned-in timecode value, you should get a positive number for the offset duration. If the burned-in timecode value is greater than the Current Timecode field's value, you should get a negative number.

   continues on next page

SETTING UP FOR CAPTURE

4. You'll need to edit your device control preset in order to enter the timecode offset Choose Edit > Audio/Video Settings, and then click the Device Control Presets tab.

5. On the Device Control Preset tab, select your current capture preset (it should be checked), and then click Edit.

6. In the Device Control Preset editor window, enter the calculated duration of the offset in the Timecode Offset field; then click OK (**Figure 3.12**).

7. Repeat the test to double-check your work.

✔ Tip

■ You should recheck your timecode calibration every time you switch video decks or cables! If you regularly switch between a couple of decks, you can incorporate each deck's timecode offset into a customized Easy Setup. Simply switch Easy Setups when you switch decks. It's that simple.

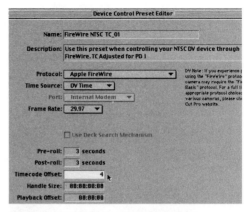

Figure 3.12 On the Device Control tab of the Preferences window, enter the calculated duration of the offset in the Timecode Offset field.

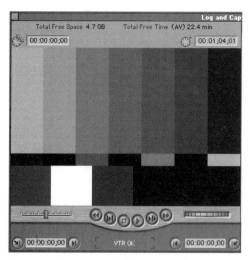

Figure 3.13 Use the Log and Capture window's transport controls to play the color bar portion of your tape.

Figure 3.14 Click the Waveform Monitor and Vectorscope button.

Calibrating capture settings with color bars and audio tone

If you are using Final Cut Pro with a capture card, your setup procedure should include calibration of your capture settings using color bars and an audio tone from your source video tape.

Calibrating a tape to color bars and an audio tone matches the color and audio level settings for a whole tape to the settings present when that tape was recorded. The settings you make are saved with each logged clip and applied when you capture the clip.

A single calibration operation per tape may be enough, but if you need to, you can also use the Clip Settings tab in the Log and Capture window to customize settings for individual clips. Customized clip settings will be saved with that clip.

Final Cut Pro includes a waveform monitor and vectorscope that let you see adjustments and examine the quality of the incoming signal. You make these adjustments on the Clip Settings tab. This procedure will be easier if you record at least 30 seconds of standard color bars on each tape to use when making baseline adjustments.

To adjust clip settings with bars and tone (non-DV only):

1. Choose File > Log and Capture.

2. In the Log and Capture window, use the transport controls to play the color bar portion of your tape (**Figure 3.13**).
   The tape must be playing for the measurements in the waveform and vectorscope to be accurate.

3. Click the Clip Settings tab to open it.

4. On the Clip Settings tab, click the Waveform Monitor and Vectorscope button (**Figure 3.14**).

continues on next page

The waveform monitor will be updated only while the Log and Capture window is active.

5. Use the Waveform Monitor and Vectorscope window (**Figure 3.15**) to review and calibrate the following:

▲ Adjust the black level so that the black reference bar in the waveform monitor is at the desired level (7.5 IRE for NTSC). The waveform monitor displays the luminance and chrominance values of the incoming signal. The vertical axis displays the dynamic range of the signal from black at the bottom (7.5 IRE) to white at the top (100 IRE).

▲ If black level and white level controls are not available, use the brightness and contrast controls.

▲ Adjust the white level so that the white reference bar in the waveform monitor is at the desired level (100 IRE for a 100 percent white reference bar).

▲ Adjust the hue so that the ends of the lines in the vectorscope are as near the color target boxes as possible. The diagonal line marker FT is the flesh tone target. All flesh tones should center around this line. The vectorscope displays the hue and saturation values of the incoming signal. The hue is represented by the angle of a line within the circle (its 12 o'clock position). The saturation is represented by the length of the line from the circle's center point. The vectorscope displays targets for the optimum values for the six primary colors (red, green, blue, yellow, magenta, and cyan) in a standard color bar pattern.

▲ Adjust the saturation so that the ends of the lines in the vectorscope are as close as possible to the center of the target boxes.

▲ Use the transport controls to shuttle the tape to a portion with a 1-KHz audio reference tone; then use the Gain slider to adjust the audio signal to 0 dB or so that it does not peak into the red areas of the audio meters.

6. After you've adjusted your settings, close the Waveform Monitor and Vectorscope window before capturing.

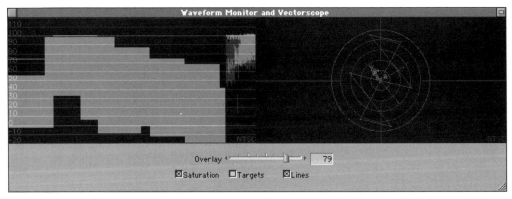

Figure 3.15 Use the Waveform Monitor and Vectorscope window to review and calibrate image quality parameters. This procedure is for analog-to-digital captures only.

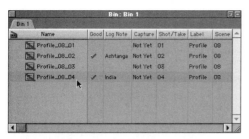

Figure 3.16 Offline clips in a Browser bin. Note the Capture status column, which shows that these clips haven't been captured yet.

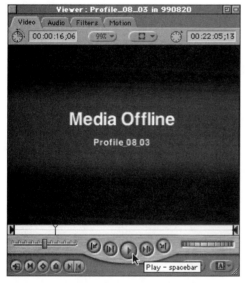

Figure 3.17 An offline clip displayed in the Viewer. Note that the timecode and duration can be displayed for the offline clip.

About Logging

Logging is the process of reviewing your source video tapes, labeling and marking the In and Out points of usable clips. As you do this, you're compiling a log: a list of timecode locations, shot and take numbers, and production notes. You can also mark clips as "good," so that you can easily select just the clips you think you'll use. When you log a shot, Final Cut Pro creates an offline clip, which is stored in a logging bin you select (**Figure 3.16**).

Final Cut Pro treats offline clips just like online clips. The only difference is that online clips are linked to captured media files on disk. The offline clips appear in the Browser; you can even edit them, but you won't see or hear anything on the screen while you're editing.

An offline clip (**Figure 3.17**) is just a reference to a media file you haven't captured to disk yet. Remember: When you specify a logging bin for your logged clips, you're making an entry in a database; you are not specifying a hard disk location for the actual media file. You specify disk location for captured media files in the scratch disks preferences.

To use all of the logging options in Final Cut Pro, you need device control over your video deck or camcorder. If you don't have a controllable video deck, you can log only the duration and In and Out points for individual clips. Final Cut Pro logs content by storing offline clips in the Browser bin of your choice. Offline clips specify capture preferences for video or audio you capture later. Clips logged from different tapes cannot be captured unattended. When you complete logging, you can select the offline clips you want to capture and digitize them in a batch.

The Art of File Naming

When you capture or import media into Final Cut Pro, you name each file as a part of the process. You'll be living with these file names for a long time. Since it's not a trivial matter to change file names once you've assigned them, you should develop a file naming system before you start your project. Write it down, distribute it to your production team, and stick to it.

Much of the logic behind file naming schemes involves constructing file names in a way that allows you to make use of the computer's Sort and Find functions and to identify the file's content, file type, and version number. In Final Cut Pro, an added level of flexibility is available to you because clips and their underlying media files do not need to have the same name.

A directory structure is the planned organization of folders you use to store your project's media elements. A complete file naming system should also be extended to the naming and organization of your files into folders. If you can, create your folder structure before you start acquiring your media elements. This will make it easier to file your elements correctly after the pace of production heats up.

Final Cut Pro imposes an automated directory structure for captured media files, automatically generating folders named after your current project inside the Capture Scratch folder. This complicates the process of filing media elements according to your own system, but if you're organized, you can work around it. After you capture, you can move your captured clips into your own folder system and then import them into a project before you start assembling sequences.

Here are a few guidelines to help you develop file names that will remain useful throughout the life of your project:

◆ Incorporate file names into your shooting scripts, voice-over scripts, and storyboards early in production. Some projects actually enter the entire script into a database and use that script/database to track media elements.

◆ File names should contain the shot's scene and take numbers, if appropriate.

◆ Avoid duplicate file names.

◆ File suffixes are traditionally used as file type indicators. There are some standard file suffixes in use, but don't be shy about making up your own system of file type abbreviations. Be sure to document them.

◆ Audio file names should incorporate a code that indicates sample rate, file format, and whether the files are stereo or mono files.

◆ Your file naming system should include a code for version control. Don't rely on a file's creation or modification date as your only means of identifying the latest version of a file.

◆ If you're planning on exporting an EDL of your Final Cut Pro project, make sure the file names for your reels are consistent with the EDL format you're using. EDL naming restrictions differ, so check out the naming requirements before you start, or use a conservative naming scheme if you don't know your destination format.

Figure 3.18 Click the New Bin button on the Logging tab to create a new bin inside the current logging bin and select it as the current logging bin.

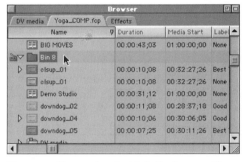

Figure 3.19 The new logging bin in the Browser. The clapstick icon indicates the current logging bin.

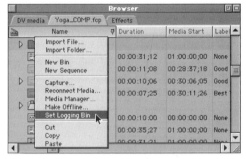

Figure 3.20 Control-click the bin; then select Set Logging Bin from the bin's shortcut menu.

Selecting a logging bin

A logging bin (or log bin) is the Browser bin where your offline clips are stored during logging. The default location for a new logging bin is the top level of a project tab in the Browser window. You can set a logging bin in the Log and Capture window or in the Browser window.

To set a logging bin in the Log and Capture window:

On the Logging tab of the Log and Capture window, *do one of the following*:

◆ Click the New Bin button (**Figure 3.18**) to create a new bin inside the current logging bin and select it as the current logging bin (**Figure 3.19**).

◆ Click the Log Bin button to open the new logging bin you created.

◆ Click the Up button to set the bin hierarchically above the current logging bin as the new logging bin.

A little clapstick icon appears next to the current logging bin.

To set a logging bin in the Browser window:

1. In the Browser, select the bin that you want to set as the logging bin.

2. *Do one of the following:*

   ▲ Control-click the bin; then select Set Logging Bin from the bin's shortcut menu (**Figure 3.20**).

   ▲ Choose File > Set Logging Bin.

A little clapstick icon appears next to the current logging bin.

ABOUT LOGGING

105

Speed Logging Tips

Each time you log a clip, Final Cut Pro resets several fields on the Logging tab to prepare for your next logging operation:

◆ The Out point from your last logged clip is assigned as the new In point.

◆ The Reel, Description, and Shot/Take fields that make up the clip's name will automatically be updated. Only the last field with the Use This Field check box checked will be incremented.

◆ When you log a clip by pressing F2, Final Cut Pro will automatically reset the Out point to the current tape position.

With automatic updating of the name fields and In and Out points, you can log your tape simply by pressing F2 whenever you want to log a new clip. With your source tape rolling, press F2 whenever you want to end a shot and begin a new one.

If you want to trim your logged shots a little more tightly, you can adapt this technique: Press I (the letter "i") to mark the clip's In point; then press F2 to mark the Out point and capture the clip in one keystroke.

Other logging tips

◆ Click the Logging Bin button to display the selected logging bin on the front tab of the Browser.

◆ Control-click the Reel field to access a pop-up menu displaying all the reel names you've used in the current project. Selecting your reel name from the pop-up list helps you be sure you're entering exactly the same name each time. That's critical to successful batch capture.

◆ Option-click a field to clear it.

◆ Use the Good check box to mark your best stuff. You can use the Find feature to search the Browser's Good column and select only the clips you've marked "Good" for batch capture.

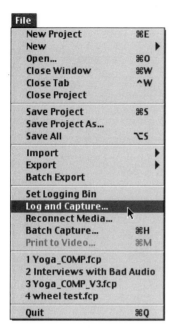

File

New Project	⌘E
New	▶
Open...	⌘O
Close Window	⌘W
Close Tab	^W
Close Project	
Save Project	⌘S
Save Project As...	
Save All	⌥S
Import	▶
Export	▶
Batch Export	
Set Logging Bin	
Log and Capture...	
Reconnect Media...	
Batch Capture...	⌘H
Print to Video...	⌘M
1 Yoga_COMP.fcp	
2 Interviews with Bad Audio	
3 Yoga_COMP_V3.fcp	
4 wheel test.fcp	
Quit	⌘Q

Figure 3.21 Choose File > Log and Capture.

Logging

Before you begin logging, make sure your video deck is properly connected and device control is operational. If you're capturing with an analog capture card, calibrate your image and audio quality before you start capturing. Your clip settings will be saved with the logged takes. And don't forget: the best time to check the timecode calibration for your deck or camcorder is before you start logging.

To log footage:

1. Load the source tape you want to log into your deck.

2. Choose File > Log and Capture (**Figure 3.21**).

3. In the Log and Capture window, specify a logging bin by one of the methods described in the previous task.

continues on next page

FCP Protocol: Auto-Incrementing on the Logging Tab

The rules governing the behavior of the Description, Scene, and Shot/Take fields on the Logging tab are too many to list in this sidebar. Here, however, are a few handy rules that should help you get more efficiency out of the auto-entry features built into the Logging tab:

◆ The check box to the right of a field's name controls whether the field will be included in the clip's name.

◆ The last checked field is the one that will increment automatically. Here are some examples:

▲ If you check only the Description field, just the Description field will increment.

▲ If Scene is the last checked field, the scene number automatically increments, even if you entered a number in the Shot/Take field but left it unchecked.

▲ If Shot/Take is the last checked field, the Shot/Take field increments, and the scene number remains unchanged until you click its Slate button to increment it. Clicking the Scene field's Slate button resets the Shot/Take field to 01 (FCP assumes that your new scenes start with Take 01).

You can include a Shot/Take number only if you include a scene number.

4. In the Reel field, *do one of the following:*

▲ Enter a name for the reel (the tape or other video source you are currently logging).

▲ Click the Reel Slate button to have the program add a numeric reel name.

▲ Control-click the field; then choose from a pop-up list of recent reel names (**Figure 3.22**).

5. In the Description field, *do one of the following:*

▲ Enter a name for the clip.

▲ Select Prompt if you want to name each clip as you log it (**Figure 3.23**).

6. In the Description, Scene, and Shot/Take fields, *do any of the following:*

▲ Click the check boxes next to the fields you want to incorporate into the clip's name.

▲ Enter any identifying text you want to use in the text field.

▲ Click the Slate button to have the program add an automatically incremented numeral to the corresponding text field (**Figure 3.24**).

Final Cut Pro's automatic naming function creates clip names by combining the fields you selected, such as Description_Scene01_Take01, into the Name field. This is the name that will appear in the Browser's Name column, and it is the name of your source media file on disk.

7. Use the transport controls in the Log and Capture window to control your source deck and locate the footage that you want to log. If you have full device control enabled, you can also navigate to a specific timecode location on your source tape by entering a timecode value in the Current Timecode field.

Figure 3.22 Control-click the Reel field; then select from a list of recent reel names.

Figure 3.23 Check Prompt if you want to name each clip as you log it.

Figure 3.24 Click the Slate buttons to add an incremented numeral to any of the text fields.

ABOUT LOGGING

Figure 3.25 Click the Mark Out button to set an Out point for the capture.

Figure 3.26 Click Log Clip to create an offline clip.

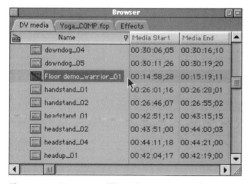

Figure 3.27 Your new offline clip appears in the selected logging bin.

8. To mark media In and Out points for a clip, *do one of the following:*

▲ Click the Mark In and Mark Out buttons (**Figure 3.25**); or press I (the letter "i") to set the In point and press O (the letter "o") to set the Out point.

▲ Enter specific timecodes in the timecode fields at the bottom of the Log and Capture window. Enter the In point in the left timecode field and the Out point in the right timecode field.

9. To log a clip, *do one of the following:*

▲ If the Prompt option is on, click Log Clip and then enter your clip's name.

▲ If the Prompt option is off, click the Slate button next to the fields you want to increment and then click Log Clip (**Figure 3.26**) or press F2.

An offline clip appears in your selected logging bin (**Figure 3.27**). After you log your first clip, the Name fields will be incremented automatically.

✔ Tip

■ When you mark In and Out points for a clip during logging, the points you specify will appear in the captured clip as the Media Start and Media End frames. However, if you add handles to your logged clip before capture, the Media Start and End frames will reflect the addition of the handles. When you open the captured clip, the Viewer's playhead will be located at the media In point you logged before you added the handles, but you won't see any In and Out point icons in the scrubber bar.

ABOUT LOGGING

To add a marker to a clip while logging:

1. To access the marking controls, click the triangle indicator next to Markers at the bottom of the Logging tab.

2. Enter a marker name or comment in the Marker field.

3. To set the In and Out points of the marker, *do one of the following:*

   ▲ Enter timecode values in the In and Out timecode fields. You can Option-drag values from any timecode fields in the Log and Capture window to copy them into these fields.

   ▲ Click the Mark In and Mark Out buttons.

4. Click Set Marker (**Figure 3.28**).

   The marker In and Out points and any information entered in the Marker field appear in the Marker Comment window (**Figure 3.29**).

   These markers appear as subclips in the Browser once a clip is captured.

✔ Tip

■ If you need to modify your marker data after you've set the marker, you can enter the revisions in the Marker fields and then click the Update button to save your changes.

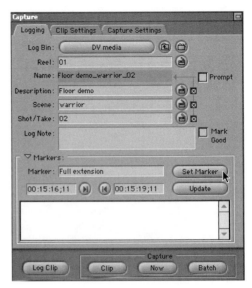

Figure 3.28 Click Set Marker to enter the marker In and Out points as well as any information entered in the Marker field in the Marker Comment window.

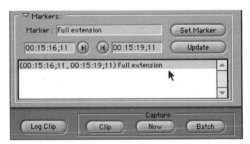

Figure 3.29 The logged information appears in the Marker Comment window. When the clip is captured, this information will be used to create subclips within the master clip.

Figure 3.30 Drag the clip from the Browser and drop it on the preview area of the Log and Capture window.

Figure 3.31 The clip's current data settings load into the Log and Capture window.

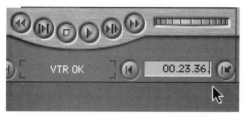

Figure 3.32 Modify the logged clip data on the Logging tab or by setting new media start and end points.

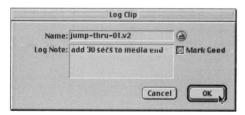

Figure 3.33 Give the clip a new name and description if desired; then click OK.

Modifying logged clip data

Even if you've organized your logging operation to a fare-thee-well, you'll probably need to go back and modify clip data on your logged clips before your project is complete. One common relogging operation is changing the tracks that are specified for capture. You may have a number of clips you're using as video-only inserts, or you might want to go back and capture just the audio from an interview because you find you're going to use it as voice-over. Final Cut Pro offers a couple of different ways to make it easy to change your mind.

To modify logged clip data:

1. Drag the clip you want to relog from the Browser and drop it on the Preview area of the Log and Capture window (**Figure 3.30**).

   The clip's current data loads into the Log and Capture window (**Figure 3.31**).

2. Modify the logged clip data as outlined in the "To log footage" task earlier in this chapter (**Figure 3.32**) and then press F2 to relog the clip.

3. In the Log Clip dialog box, give the clip a new name and description if desired and then click OK (**Figure 3.33**).

   The relogged clip appears as a new offline clip in the Browser (**Figure 3.34**).

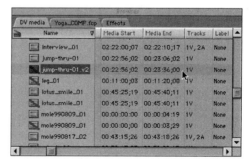

Figure 3.34 The relogged clip appears as a new offline clip in the Browser.

To modify logged clip data in the Browser:

1. In the Browser, select the offline clips whose data you want to modify. Command-click to select multiple clips (**Figure 3.35**).

2. Control-click in the data column for the setting you want to change and select a new setting (**Figure 3.36**). (Note that not all Browser columns offer this shortcut.)

   All of the offline clips you selected will be switched to the new setting (**Figure 3.37**).

Capturing Video with Device Control

Capturing a clip with device control combines logging tasks (marking In and Out points, naming the clip, entering comments) and specification of the clip's settings for this capture on the Clip Settings tab.

When you capture a single clip by clicking the Clip button at the bottom of the Log and Capture window, Final Cut Pro runs a batch capture procedure with a single clip as the batch list, and the captured clip is saved in your Capture Scratch folder but outside the current project.

Unless you're picking up very few shots scattered about on different reels, it will be quicker to log your shots and capture them as a batch. Batch capture is easier on your video deck, camcorder, and source tapes as well.

For more information on logging clips for batch capture, see "About Logging" earlier in this chapter.

For more information on batch capture, see "Batch Capturing Clips" later in this chapter.

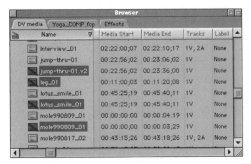

Figure 3.35 Command-click to select multiple offline clips.

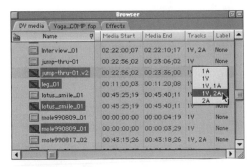

Figure 3.36 Control clicking in the Tracks column and selecting a new track format from the shortcut menu.

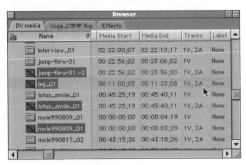

Figure 3.37 All the selected offline clips are switched to the new setting.

Figure 3.38 Choose File > Log and Capture.

Figure 3.39 Use the transport controls in the Log and Capture window to control your video deck and locate the footage that you want to capture.

Figure 3.40 Click the Mark Out button to set an Out point for the capture. You could also enter a timecode value in the Out point timecode field.

To capture a clip with device control:

1. Make sure your video deck is properly connected and device control is operational. If the deck has a Local/Remote switch, make sure the switch is set to Remote.

2. Choose File > Log and Capture (**Figure 3.38**).

3. Use the transport controls in the Log and Capture window to control your source deck and locate the footage that you want to capture (**Figure 3.39**). If you have full device control enabled, you can also navigate to a specific timecode location on your source tape by entering a timecode value in the Current Timecode field.

4. In the Log and Capture window, click the Logging tab.

5. To enter logging information for your clip, follow steps 4 through 6 in "To log footage" earlier in this chapter.

6. Click the Clip Settings tab; then follow steps 2 through 7 (detailing clip setting procedures) in the task in the next section, "To capture a clip without device control."

7. To mark a clip, *do one of the following:*
   ▲ Click the Mark In and Mark Out buttons (**Figure 3.40**); or press I to set the In point and press O to set the Out point.
   ▲ Enter specific timecodes in the timecode fields at the bottom of the Log and Capture window. Enter the In point in the left timecode field and the Out point in the right timecode field.

continues on next page

8. Click the Clip button located at the bottom of the window (**Figure 3.41**).

Final Cut Pro captures the clip, and the captured clip appears in a Viewer window. Your captured clip has been saved in the current project, in your designated logging bin.

Capturing Video without Device Control

If you don't have a video device that your computer can control, you can still capture video in Final Cut Pro by using the controls on your video deck or camcorder to search and play your source tape.

To log clips without the benefits of device control, you'll need to manually enter the clip's starting and ending timecodes and other information in the appropriate fields in the Log and Capture window. The clip information you enter in the Log and Capture window will be used to identify the clip when you save it.

The captured clip opens in the Viewer as an untitled, unsaved clip that is not associated with any project.

You can't capture previously logged clips unless you have a deck with device control.

✔ Tip

■ Before you start capturing, check your Capture Now time-limit setting on the Capture Settings tab of the Log and Capture window. The default limit is 30 minutes. Very long Capture Now time limits can increase the lag between the time you click the Capture Now button and the time capture begins, so specify a time limit not much longer than the longest clip you're planning to capture.

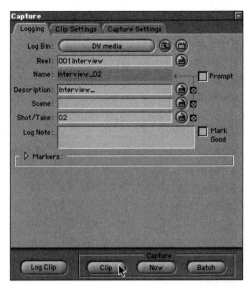

Figure 3.41 Click the Clip button located at the bottom of the Logging tab.

Figure 3.42 Click the Clip settings tab in the Log and Capture window.

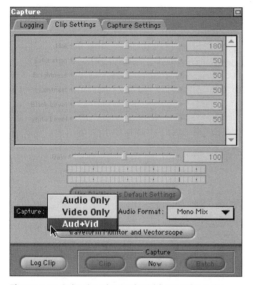

Figure 3.43 Selecting the Aud+Vid format from the Capture pop-up menu.

Figure 3.44 Selecting Stereo from the Audio Format pop-up menu.

To capture a clip without device control:

1. Make sure your video deck is properly connected.

2. Choose File > Log and Capture.

3. In the Log and Capture window, click the Clip settings tab (**Figure 3.42**).

4. On the Clip Settings tab, select a capture format from the Capture pop-up menu (**Figure 3.43**). You have three options:
   ▲ Audio Only
   ▲ Video Only
   ▲ Aud(io)+Vid(eo)

5. Select an audio capture format from the Audio Format pop-up menu (**Figure 3.44**). The available audio formats are as follows:
   ▲ **Ch 1 + Ch 2:** Capture both tracks, but configure them as separate channels that can be adjusted independently of one another.
   ▲ **Ch 1 (L):** Capture only the left audio channel from the tape (Ch 1), with pan centered. (See Chapter 5 for information on pan settings.)
   ▲ **Ch 2 (R):** Capture only the right audio channel from the tape (Ch 2), with pan centered.
   ▲ **Stereo:** Capture both channels as a stereo pair. Stereo pairs are always linked, and anything that is applied to one track is applied to both.
   ▲ **Mono Mix:** Capture both channels from the tape, mixed into a single track.

6. If you are digitizing an analog video source, you can use the image quality slider controls to calibrate the incoming signal.

7. If you are digitizing an analog video source, you can use the Gain slider control to adjust your audio input levels (**Figure 3.45**).

Figure 3.45 If you are digitizing an analog video (or audio) source, you can use the Gain slider control to adjust your audio input levels.

8. Use your deck's controls to locate the footage you want to capture, rewind 7 to 10 seconds, and then press the deck's Play button.

9. Click the Now button at the bottom of the Log and Capture window 1 to 5 seconds before the deck reaches the first frame in your clip (**Figure 3.46**).

Figure 3.46 Click the Now button (at the bottom of the Log and Capture window) 1 to 5 seconds before the first frame in your clip appears.

There's a slight delay after you click the button before capture begins—how long a delay depends on your Capture Now time limit and the number of scratch disks you have assigned to FCP.

10. To stop recording, press the Escape key; then stop playback on your deck.

The captured clip appears in a Viewer window (**Figure 3.47**).

11. Play the clip to make sure it contains the video you want. You may need to close the Log and Capture window, as some video capture hardware won't play the captured clip while this window is open.

Figure 3.47 The captured clip appears in a Viewer window. You'll still need to save it.

Figure 3.48 Click in the image area of the unsaved clip in the Viewer; then drag the clip to the Browser and drop it in your selected bin.

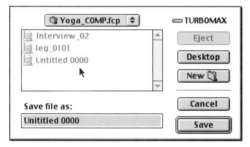

Figure 3.49 The unsaved clip, labeled Untitled 0000, has already been written to your Capture Scratch folder.

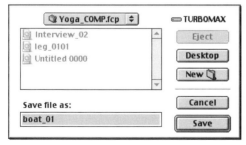

Figure 3.50 Entering a name for your captured clip in the Save File As field.

12. To save your captured clip, *do one of the following:*

▲ Click in the image area of the unsaved clip in the Viewer; then drag the clip to the Browser and drop it in your selected bin (**Figure 3.48**).

▲ Click in the image area of the unsaved clip in the Viewer; then drag the clip into the Timeline and drop it in an open sequence.

▲ To save the captured clip outside the current project, choose File > Save Clip As.

▲ The Save dialog box appears, already open to the Capture Scratch Folder where your captured clip is stored (**Figure 3.49**).

13. Enter a name for your captured clip in the Save File As field (**Figure 3.50**); then click Save.

✔ Tip

■ If you're using a camcorder, you can use Capture Now to capture live footage. Your live footage won't have a timecode track unless your camcorder is recording to tape as you capture the live footage in Final Cut Pro.

Capturing analog audio

You can use the Macintosh's built-in sound input capabilities (if your Mac model has an audio input) to digitize analog audio from a cassette player, TV, or other source and capture it in Final Cut Pro. This can be a great convenience if you want to capture temporary rough voice-over or music.

To capture analog audio:

1. Connect the output of your analog audio device to the Mic In port on the back of the Macintosh.

2. On the Capture Presets tab of the Audio/Video Settings window, duplicate a preset from the Presets list so you can create an analog-audio–only capture preset (**Figure 3.51**).

3. In the QuickTime Video Settings section of the Capture Preset Editor window, choose None from the Digitize pop-up menu.

4. In the QuickTime Audio Settings section of the Capture Preset Editor window, adjust the settings as follows:

   ▲ **Device:** Select Built-in.

   ▲ **Input:** Select External Mic.

   The sample rate will automatically switch to 44.1 KHz, the Mac's built-in audio sample rate (**Figure 3.52**).

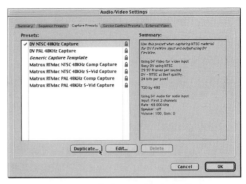

Figure 3.51 In the Audio/Video Settings window, duplicate a preset from the Capture Presets list so you can create an analog-audio–only capture preset.

Figure 3.52 When you select Built-in from the Device pop-up menu, the sample rate will automatically switch to 44.1 KHz, the Mac's in-in audio sample rate.

5. Name your new audio preset (**Figure 3.53**); then click OK.

6. Open the Log and Capture window; then click the Clip Settings tab.

7. On the Clip Settings tab, choose Audio Only from the Capture pop-up menu (**Figure 3.54**) and double-check your audio input levels.

8. To capture your analog audio, follow steps 8 though 13 (detailing capture and file saving procedures) in "To capture a clip without device control" earlier in this chapter.

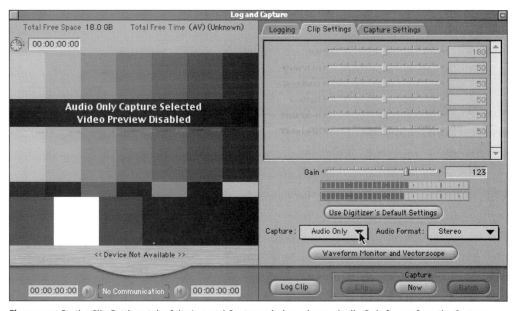

Figure 3.53 Name your new audio preset on the Capture Preset Editor tab; then click OK.

Figure 3.54 On the Clip Settings tab of the Log and Capture window, choose Audio Only format from the Capture pop-up menu.

Batch Capturing Clips

You can use the Log and Capture window to review and log the media on an entire source tape and then capture all the clips that you want from that tape in one operation, in a batch capture. Final Cut Pro uses the clip log you've created and automatically captures only the clips you select. You don't need to capture every clip you have logged.

Most digital video tape formats are delicate, so you want to minimize the amount of wear and tear you put on your video source tapes, particularly if you won't be capturing the final versions of your media files until late in the editing process. Logging and batch capture are important tools for minimizing the amount of time your precious original tapes spend shuttling back and forth in your tape deck.

You can batch capture clips from these sources:

◆ Clips you've logged with Final Cut Pro.

◆ Clips in a text log you've imported from another program or another Final Cut Pro project. See "Importing a Batch List" later in this chapter.

◆ Clips from an imported Edit Decision List (EDL) file. See "Importing an Edit Decision List (EDL)" later in this chapter.

If you need to interrupt a batch capture, you can use the Batch Capture command to automatically redigitize all clips not captured previously, by choosing the Aborted Clips option from the Capture pop-up menu.

Automated, unattended batch capture is limited to clips from one tape. You can set up an automated batch capture that involves clips from several reels, but you'll need to hang around and feed new tapes to your video deck during the process.

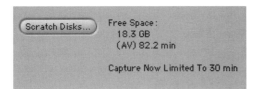

Figure 3.55 Available storage space estimate as it appears on the Log and Capture window's Capture Settings tab.

Total Media Time: 00:01:22:04

Total Disk Space: 297.1 MB needed / 17.6 GB available

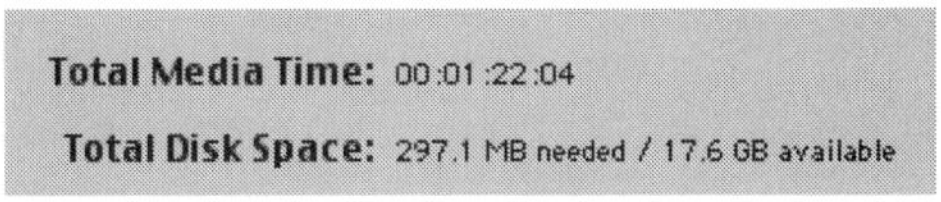

Figure 3.56 An estimate of the space needed for this batch capture appears in the Batch Capture dialog box.

Preparing for a batch capture

Batch capture is an automated process. It's worthwhile to prepare carefully before you kick off an automated capture because, well, things can happen while your back is turned. Here are some suggestions:

◆ Check your currently selected capture preset and scratch disk preferences. Make any changes you want applied to this batch capture; you won't be able to change these settings after you open the Batch Capture dialog box.

◆ Answer these questions: Are your capture settings correct for this batch capture? Is the estimated space available on your designated scratch disk sufficient to contain your incoming media files?

◆ On the Log and Capture window's Capture Settings tab, make a note of the available space estimate (**Figure 3.55**); you'll want to compare this value to the estimate of space needed in the Batch Capture dialog box (**Figure 3.56**). This comparison can yield clues that can help you debug your batch capture list. For example, a 10-second subclip from a 20-minute master clip can throw your whole capture scheme out of whack; Final Cut Pro would capture the entire 20-minute master clip.

◆ Before batch capturing clips, be sure your tape does not contain timecode breaks. If it does, Final Cut Pro won't be able to accurately locate your offline clips, and that can cause your batch capture to go seriously haywire. (Timecode breaks can be caused by shutting down the camera or ejecting your tape in mid reel and not re-cueing on the last bit of previously recorded timecode.)

To batch capture clips:

1. To select which clips to capture; *do one of the following:*

   ▲ To capture clips you've just logged, click Batch Capture in the Log and Capture window (**Figure 3.57**). This captures clips in the selected logging bin.

   ▲ To capture all offline clips in a project, set the project tab as the logging bin, make sure nothing is selected in the Browser, and then choose File > Batch Capture.

   ▲ To capture selected offline clips in your project, see the next section, "To batch capture a selection of clips."

2. In the Batch Capture window, check the Coalesce Clips box if you want Final Cut Pro to save disk space by combining overlapping clips plus clips within 2 seconds of each other on the source reel in a single media file.

3. *Do one of the following:*

   ▲ Check the Use Logged Clip Settings check box if you want Final Cut Pro to capture all clips using the customized clip settings you have saved with individual clips.

   ▲ Uncheck the Use Logged Clip Settings check box if you want Final Cut Pro to bypass your individual clip settings (**Figure 3.58**). Disk space calculations are based on the data rate settings specified in the current capture preset.

4. Enter a duration to set the handle size of offline clips (this is optional) (**Figure 3.59**). Handles add extra frames beyond the In and Out points of a captured clip.

5. Select a capture preset option from the Capture pop-up menu.

Figure 3.57 Click the Batch Capture button in the Log and Capture window to capture clips in the currently selected logging bin.

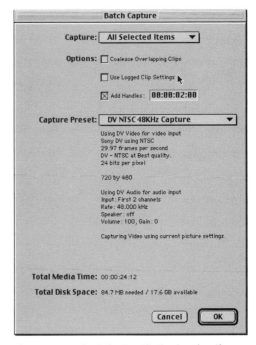

Figure 3.58 Uncheck the Use Clip Settings box if you want Final Cut Pro to bypass your individual clip settings.

Figure 3.59 Setting the handle size for offline clips.

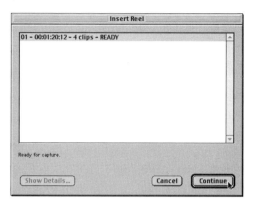

Figure 3.60 Load the reel you want to capture into your deck, select it from the list, and click Continue. When it's finished capturing all the clips from that reel, FCP will prompt you to select the next reel.

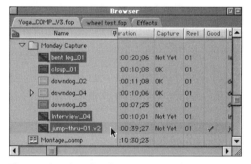

Figure 3.61 Select the clips you want to batch capture. You can select a combination of offline and online clips.

Figure 3.62 Choose a capture selection option from the Capture pop-up menu.

6. Click OK.

The Insert Reel Dialog box appears, displaying a list of all the reels required for this batch capture operation.

7. Load the first reel you want to capture into your deck, select it from the list, and click Continue (**Figure 3.60**).

8. To interrupt batch capture, press Escape or click the mouse button.

If you interrupt batch capture, Final Cut Pro labels all clips that were not captured as "aborted." This indicator appears in the Browser's Digitize column.

To batch capture a selection of clips:

1. In the Browser window, select the clips you want to batch capture (**Figure 3.61**); then choose File > Batch Capture.

Your selection can include both offline clips and online clips, but all clips must be within a single project.

2. In the Batch Capture window, choose a capture selection option from the Capture pop-up menu. The available capture selection options vary depending on the items you've selected in your batch (**Figure 3.62**).

Follow steps 2 through 8 in "To batch capture clips" in the previous section.

✔ Tip

■ If you recapture online clips into the same scratch disk folder where the original clip's media files are stored, the original media files will be overwritten. If you recapture into a different folder, the original media files will be preserved.

BATCH CAPTURING CLIPS

To restart and complete an interrupted batch capture:

1. Choose File > Batch Capture.

2. In the Batch Capture window, select Aborted Items Only from the Capture pop-up menu (**Figure 3.63**).

3. Follow steps 2 through 7 in "To batch capture clips" earlier in this chapter.

   You can use the Batch Capture command to automatically redigitize all clips not captured previously, by choosing the Aborted Clips in Login Bin option from the Capture pop-up menu.

Figure 3.63 In the Batch Capture window, select Aborted Clips in Logging Bin from the Capture pop-up menu. Note how the pop-up menu's selections have changed to reflect current circumstances.

The Wonders of Batch Recapture

Final Cut Pro's basic design assumes that you will at some point want to use the Media Manager to analyze your edited project and batch recapture your source clips. The Media Manager offers several options for trimming your project files (you can read about them in detail in Chapter 12, "Big Picture: Managing Complex Projects"), but batch recapture is one of the most commonly used. The Media Manager constructs a trimmed, offline sequence that includes just the media you are actually using in your final product. Your next step would be to select the trimmed offline sequence and batch recapture just that footage from your original source tapes and then reconnect the recaptured media files to your existing project.

Batch recapturing can increase your post-production efficiency in a number of other ways:

◆ You can capture your footage and then convert it to a low-resolution codec like Photo-JPEG. Photo-JPEG not only saves disk space, but your clips will render faster while you're editing. When you've settled on a final version of your edited sequence, you can batch recapture at high resolution only the clips you're using in the final version.

◆ Some editors capture entire tapes and then select and log their shots by marking subclips within the long master. Then they export their logged subclips as a batch list and use it to recapture their selected material as individual online clips. This process allows random access to locations throughout the long master—you'll log faster because you won't be waiting for your video deck's transport mechanism to move the tape around. Your capture process is streamlined, too, saving wear and tear on your gear and your tapes.

◆ You use batch recapture when you are moving a production from another editing system to Final Cut Pro. You import your production's EDL (or any tab-delimited file with the right data) as a batch list and then use it to recapture your footage. See "Importing a Batch List" and "Importing an Edit Decision List (EDL)" later in this chapter.

◆ If you lose your media files, batch recapture can speed reconstruction of your project—a good reason to back up your files and store them outside your computer.

BATCH CAPTURING CLIPS

Importing a Batch List

A *batch list* is a log containing the information that Final Cut Pro uses to pull clips from your source tapes in a batch capture. You can export a batch list from Final Cut Pro and then reimport it, or you can import a log that you've created with another application to use for batch capture. For example, you can log clips with a field log during production and then import the log to Final Cut Pro.

The batch list function was specifically designed to work with standard text files from popular database and spreadsheet programs like Excel and FileMaker Pro. Use your logging application to save the log as a tab-delimited text file.

When you import the file into Final Cut Pro, the logged clips appear as offline clips that you can then capture.

The minimum requirement for an imported batch list is that the first record must have field headers that match at least the Name, Duration, In, and Out column headers in the Browser.

Other import protocols include the following:

◆ Final Cut Pro will accept any additional data fields that correspond to a Browser column type.

◆ Column names must match the names in the Browser exactly.

◆ Capitalization is ignored.

◆ Subsequent records are the tab-delimited data.

For information on exporting a batch list, see Chapter 11, "At Last: Creating Final Output."

To import a batch list:

1. In the Browser window, open a Browser bin to receive the batch list (**Figure 3.64**).

2. Choose File > Import > Batch List (**Figure 3.65**).

3. In the dialog box, select the file that you want to import as a batch list (**Figure 3.66**); then click Open.

   The imported batch list appears in the Browser bin (**Figure 3.67**).

✔ Tip

■ To get a surefire template for a properly formatted batch list, start by exporting a batch list with the data columns you want from FCP and then opening the list in the text editor or spreadsheet program you plan to use for logging.

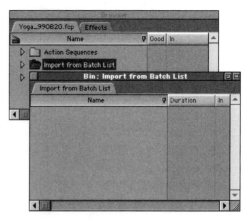

Figure 3.64 Select a Browser bin to receive your imported batch list.

Figure 3.65 Choose File > Import > Batch List.

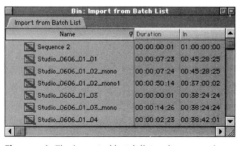

Figure 3.67 The imported batch list as it appears in the Browser bin.

Figure 3.66 Select the file that you want to import as a batch list.

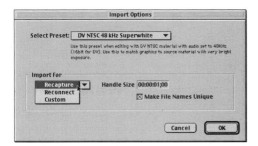

Figure 3.68 Select the Recapture import configuration if you are planning on using the imported EDL data to recapture your media.

Importing an Edit Decision List (EDL)

You can import an EDL created on a linear editing system and use it to re-create your edited sequences in Final Cut Pro.

After you import an EDL, a sequence appears in the Browser that re-creates the edit sequence of your EDL. If the EDL was exported from a nonlinear system, there's a chance the original clip names will be successfully imported. In all other cases, Final Cut Pro uses the reel number and starting timecode number as the clip name: for example, 0001 01:07:24:10.

✔ Tip

- Apple's Final Cut Pro 2 User's Manual has extensive information on the ins and outs of EDLs and FCP2—recommended reading for FCP users who are working with EDLs.

To import an EDL:

1. Choose File > Import > EDL.

2. In the Import Options dialog box, you can specify the following EDL import options:

   Select Preset: Select a sequence preset for your imported EDL from this pop-up menu.

   Import For: Selecting an import configuration from this pop-up menu will automatically configure the Import settings:

   ▲ **Recapture:** Select this configuration if you are planning on using the imported EDL data to recapture your media. This setting makes clip names for recaptured media files unique and adds handles to the front and back of clips. The default handle size is 1 second (**Figure 3.68**).

continues on next page

▲ **Reconnect:** Select this configuration if you are reconnecting existing media files to a sequence generated from imported EDL data. This setting leaves clip names untouched (for easier relinking) and does not add handles to the front and back of clips (**Figure 3.69**).

▲ **Handle Size:** Specify the handle duration. The number of frames you specify will be added to front and back of clips. This setting is not available in Reconnect mode, because your files are already on disk.

▲ **Make File Names Unique:** Check the box to ensure unique clip names for recaptured media files. Leave this option unchecked if you are reconnecting media files.

3. Locate and select the EDL's file name and then click Open (**Figure 3.70**).

Your EDL appears as a new sequence in the Browser window (**Figure 3.71**).

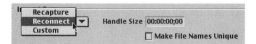

Figure 3.69 The Reconnect configuration, designed for reconnecting EDL data with media files already on disk, leaves clip names untouched and does not add handles.

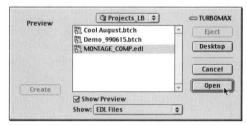

Figure 3.70 Select the EDL file that you want to import.

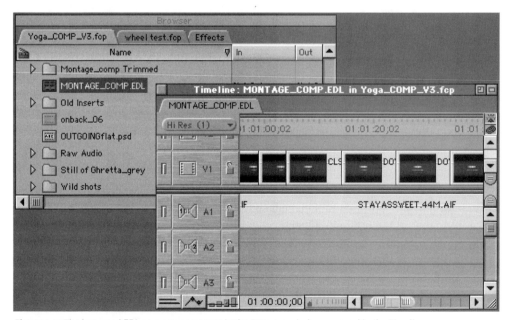

Figure 3.71 The imported EDL as a new sequence In the Browser window, opened in the Timeline.

IMPORTING AN EDIT DECISION LIST (EDL)

Figure 3.72 Control-click the Viewer's Current Timecode field and select from a list of timecode viewing options. You can view a clip using the source, Aux1, or Aux2 timecode.

Changing Your Source Timecode

You can modify the source timecode of any clip in Final Cut Pro. When you use the Modify Timecode feature to modify a clip's source timecode, the change is written as a permanent change in the clip's source media file on disk. The source timecode modification will be reflected in every use of that clip in all projects.

Auxiliary timecodes allow you to assign an additional timecode reference to a clip without modifying its source timecode. Final Cut Pro clips have two auxiliary timecode fields. You can view a clip using the source, Aux1, or Aux2 timecode (**Figure 3.72**).

There are no hard and fast rules about when to modify timecodes and when to reference auxiliary timecode fields. Generally speaking, Modify is an appropriate choice if your Final Cut Pro source timecodes need to be adjusted to conform to the timecode of your master tapes—the ones you're going to be using to cut the finished version of the program. For example, you would modify the source timecode of your Final Cut Pro files to conform to master tapes if you needed to create an EDL whose timecode values would reference your master tapes, rather then the Final Cut Pro files.

Auxiliary timecodes are useful for synchronizing material from a variety of sources to a master timecode without modifying any clip's source timecode (synchronizing multiple shots to a music track in a music video, for example).

To change a clip's timecode:

1. Double-click a clip in the Browser (**Figure 3.73**) or Timeline to open it in the Viewer.

2. Move the playhead to the frame where you want to establish the new timecode.

3. Choose Modify > Timecode.

4. In the Set pop-up menu at the top of the Timecode dialog box, *do one of the following:*

   ▲ Choose Current Frame to set the currently displayed frame to the timecode value you enter in the Source field.

   ▲ Choose Starting Frame to set the first frame of the clip's underlying media file to the timecode value you enter in the Source field (**Figure 3.74**).

5. Enter a new timecode value in the Source field and click OK.

   The timecode value of the media file on disk is modified to reflect the change.

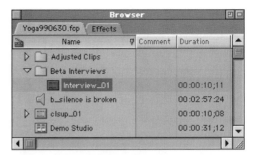

Figure 3.73 Double-click the clip in the Browser to open it in the Viewer window.

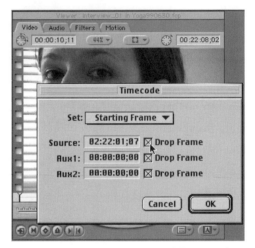

Figure 3.74 Select Starting Frame, and the timecode value you enter in the Source field will be applied to the first frame of the clip's underlying media file.

Figure 3.75 Position the playhead on the frame where you want to establish the new timecode.

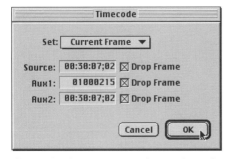

Figure 3.76 After you've entered a new timecode value in the Aux1 field, click OK.

Figure 3.77 Control-click the Current Timecode field and then select View Using Aux1 from the shortcut menu.

To change a clip's auxiliary timecode:

1. Double-click a clip in the Browser or Timeline to open it in the Viewer.

2. Move the playhead to the frame where you want to establish the new timecode (**Figure 3.75**).

3. Choose Modify > Timecode.

4. In the pop-up menu at the top of the Timecode dialog box, *do one of the following:*

   ▲ Choose Current Frame to set the timecode value at the currently displayed frame.

   ▲ Choose Starting Frame to set the timecode value at the first frame of the clip.

5. Enter a new timecode value in the Aux1 or Aux2 field and click OK (**Figure 3.76**). Auxiliary timecodes can be changed only one clip at a time.

To view a clip's auxiliary timecode:

◆ In the Viewer or Canvas, Control-click the Current Timecode field and then select View Using Aux1 (or Aux2) from the shortcut menu (**Figure 3.77**).

✔ Tip

■ Drop Frame or Non-Drop Frame? That is the question. If you are unsure about whether your clips were originally recorded or shot using drop or nondrop frame timecode, you can identify your clip's original timecode format. Control-click any timecode field in the Viewer, Canvas, Timeline, or Log and Capture window. The shortcut menu lists View as Non-Drop Frame, View as Drop Frame, and View as Frames. The clip's original timecode format is shown in bold.

CHANGING YOUR SOURCE TIMECODE

131

Troubleshooting Capture Problems

If you experience problems during video capture, you may see an error warning. Final Cut Pro monitors the state of controlled devices and reports an error if the problem is due to a camcorder or deck malfunction. Cancel the operation before proceeding and consult your camcorder or deck manual for troubleshooting information.Here are some basic troubleshooting tips that may help you get back on the road.

If the message "No Communication" appears in the Deck Status area of the Log and Capture window (**Figure 3.78**):

◆ Check to make sure that your deck is plugged in, switched on, and properly connected to your computer.

◆ A quick check of the Audio/Video Settings window's Summary tab can tell you if an external device is considered "missing" (**Figure 3.79**).

◆ Turn on the deck and restart the computer. If your deck's power was not switched on when you started your computer, the device may not be recognized.

◆ Connect the serial cable and restart the computer. If your deck's serial cable (FireWire serial cable as well) was not connected properly when you started your computer, the device may not be recognized.

Figure 3.78 The "No Communication" message appears in the Deck Status area of the Log and Capture window if device control is disabled.

Figure 3.79 The Summary tab of the Audio/Video Settings window indicates that the selected external video device is considered "missing."

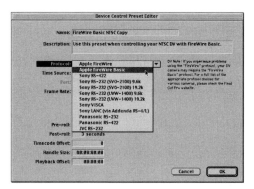

Figure 3.80 If Apple FireWire doesn't provide reliable device control, switch to the Apple FireWire Basic protocol by modifying your device control preset.

If you experience problems controlling your deck or camcorder:

◆ If your deck has a Local/Remote switch, be sure it's set to Remote.

◆ If you're using the Apple FireWire protocol, try Apple FireWire Basic instead. Edit the FireWire (NTSC or PAL) device control preset. In the Device Control Preset Editor window, choose the Apple FireWire Basic protocol from the Protocol pop-up menu (**Figure 3.80**).

◆ Check that you're using the device control protocol specified for your deck or camcorder. Device control protocols are listed in the Device Control Preset Editor window.

◆ Not all decks and camcorders support all functions, such as hard recording, high-speed searching, insert editing, assemble editing, preview editing, or accurate movement to timecodes entered. You may need to use a different protocol.

◆ Check Apple's Final Cut Pro Web site to see if your deck or camcorder requires a special DV Tuner script to work properly with FCP. Some tuner scripts are available on the Final Cut Pro application CD.

Here's the URL for the FCP 2 Device Qualification page (**Figure 3.81**):

`http://www.apple.com/finalcutpro/`
`qualification.html`.

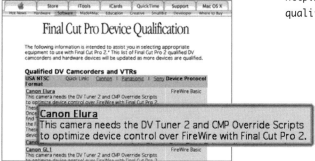

Figure 3.81 Check Apple's Final Cut Pro Web site to see if your video gear requires a DV Tuner script.

If you encounter a "Bus error" error message when you try to capture:

♦ Something went wrong when your captured data crossed the bus, the data delivery interface between your computer and the outside world. Bus errors can be caused by a number of things, but you can try making sure that your cables are hooked up completely, that any hardware cards you are using are seated properly, and that you don't have an extensions conflict.

If you encounter a "Batch Capture: Unable to lock deck servo" error message when you try to capture:

♦ Your camcorder or deck needs more pre-roll time before capture starts. Increase the Pre-roll capture setting in the Device Control Preset Editor window (**Figure 3.82**).

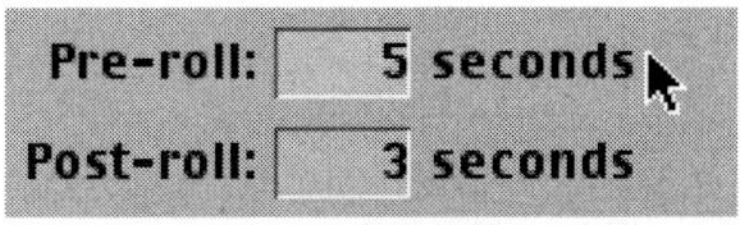

If your captured audio and video play back out of sync:

♦ The video displayed in the Viewer and Canvas will not appear to play back in sync if you are monitoring your audio through external speakers connected to your deck or camcorder. The audio from the external speakers will be synchronized with video displayed on the video monitor.

♦ The audio sample rate of your original source tape must match the audio sample rate of your capture settings. Check the source tape's audio sample rate against your capture settings.

♦ Your FCP system may be dropping frames during capture or playback. See "Is Your System Capture-Ready?" earlier in this chapter for a list of possible causes for dropped frames.

Figure 3.82 Increase the Pre-roll capture setting in your device control preset.

FCP Protocol: Sync Adjust Movies feature

The Sync Adjust Movies feature (formerly known as the AutoSyncCompensator) is designed to compensate for audio sample rate discrepancies in video tape that has been shot on certain cameras, notably certain models of Canon cameras.

When you enable the Sync Adjust Movies (SAM) feature in General Preferences, Final Cut Pro checks the actual audio sample rate of any captured or imported media file whose duration is longer than the duration you specified in the preferences, and then it marks those files to be played back at a sample rate that will compensate for the sync problem.

Enabling the Sync Adjust Movies feature does not affect the sample rate during capture.

SAM restores synchronization by converting the audio sample rate of your captured clips on the fly and then playing back the result.

Converting the sample rate of audio files in real time has a slight impact on performance and quality. If you're not using long sync takes and you don't perceive any sync problems, you might want to disable the Sync Adjust Movies feature.

However, if you are noticing audio/video sync drift in long takes, you might want to enable the SAM feature and see if that corrects your sync problem. The only serious downside to leaving SAM enabled is that you risk serious sync loss if you attempt to capture a tape with timecode breaks in it.

Because SAM doesn't flag files until after capture, you won't need to recapture clips to disable SAM.

However, because files are flagged at the time they are relinked or imported, even if you disable the Sync Adjust Movies feature in Preferences after a clip has been imported or relinked, a SAM-flagged file will remain affected until you reimport or relink it.

TROUBLESHOOTING CAPTURE PROBLEMS

Importing Media

You can import most types of QuickTime-compatible files into a Final Cut Pro project. This includes video clips, still images, and sound files. Final Cut Pro recognizes all QuickTime-compatible file formats.

The Read Me file for QuickTime Pro (installed with Final Cut Pro) contains a complete list of supported file formats; here's a list of common FCP-supported QuickTime formats:

◆ **Graphics:** BMP, FlashPix, GIF, JPEG/ JFIF, MacPaint (PNTG), Photoshop (PSD), PICS, PICT, PNG, QuickTime Image File (QTIF), SGI, TARGA (TGA), and TIFF

◆ **Video:** AVI, QuickTime Movie

◆ **Audio:** AIFF, Audio CD Data (Macintosh), Sound, and Wave

◆ **Other:** Macromedia Flash (video only)

You can import an entire folder or organization of multiple folders in a single operation. When you import a folder, Final Cut Pro imports all files it recognizes in the folder, as well as all recognized files in any subfolders. Folders are imported with their internal hierarchies intact.

FCP Protocol: File Location Is Critical

When you import a file into a Final Cut Pro project, that file is not copied into the FCP project file. Importing a file places a clip in your Browser, but that clip is a reference to the current hard disk location of your imported media file at the time you import it.

In Final Cut Pro, any clip's link to its underlying media file is entirely location based. If you move media files to another disk location after you've used them in a project, you break their link to the clip references in your FCP projects. You can use the Reconnect Media command to restore those clip-to-media file links, but a little forethought before you import files can save you a lot of hassle later. The Reconnect Media function is discussed in Chapter 12, "Big Picture: Managing Complex Projects."

Before you import a file into FCP, be sure to copy it to its permanent folder location in your project's media assets directory structure. Importing files directly from a removable media storage device (such as a Zip disk) is going to cause your file to be marked "offline" in your project once you remove that disk from your system. The same principle applies to audio imported from a CD.

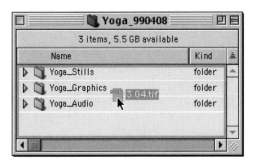

Figure 3.83 Before you import a file, copy or move the file into the correct asset folder in your project.

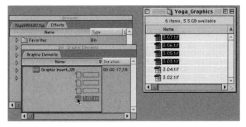

Figure 3.84 Drag the desired files or folders directly from your desktop into Final Cut Pro.

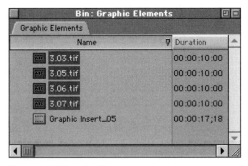

Figure 3.85 Drop the files on a project tab or in a bin within the Browser.

To import a file or folder:

1. Copy or move the file that you want to import into the correct asset folder in your project (**Figure 3.83**).

2. In the Browser, to select a destination for your incoming file, *do one of the following*:
   ▲ To import files or folders into the top level of a project, click the project's Browser tab.
   ▲ To import files into a bin within a project, double-click the bin to open it.

3. *Do one of the following:*
   ▲ Choose File > Import; then choose File or Folder from the submenu, select the item, and click Open.
   ▲ In the Browser or any Browser bin window, Control-click and then choose Import File (or Import Folder) from the shortcut menu.
   ▲ Drag the desired files or folders directly from your desktop (**Figure 3.84**) to a project tab or to a bin within the Browser (**Figure 3.85**).
   ▲ Drag the desired files or folders from your Finder desktop to an open sequence in the Timeline. This places a clip reference to the media in the Timeline, but does not place a reference in the Browser.

IMPORTING MEDIA

Importing still images

Final Cut Pro's default format for imported still images is a clip containing 2 minutes of identical video frames, with a default duration of 10 seconds between In and Out points. You can change the default duration by specifying new values for the Still/Freeze Image Duration option on the General tab in the Preferences window.

If you edit still images into a sequence, they won't be visible on your NTSC external monitor until they are rendered.

Final Cut Pro supports all QuickTime-compatible graphics file formats. Check the QuickTime Read Me file or Apple's QuickTime Web site for a complete list of compatible file formats.

✔ Tip

■ Final Cut Pro does not import EPS files.

Importing layered Photoshop files

Final Cut Pro preserves the layers in a layered Photoshop file, importing the file as a sequence. Each Photoshop layer is represented by a clip on a track in that sequence.

Because imported layered Photoshop files appear in FCP as sequences, your Still/Freeze Image Duration preference will set the total length of the imported file, with no allowance for handles. If you want to increase its length after you import, you'll have to open the Photoshop file sequence and extend the length of the individual layers inside.

When you place a layered Photoshop file into your FCP sequence, you're actually *nesting* it; placing a sequence within another sequence. Nesting sequences is a powerful tool, and knowing the rules governing the behavior of nested sequences will help you plan your work better. See "Working with Multiple Sequences" in Chapter 12.

For more information on working twith Photoshop files in Final Cut Pro, see Chapter 13, "Compositing and Special Effects."

FCP Protocol: Layered Photoshop Files

◆ A layered Adobe Photoshop file imported into a Final Cut Pro project retains its transparency information, visibility, and composite mode.

◆ Layer opacity settings and layer modes are preserved, but layer masks and layer effects are not.

◆ If a Photoshop layer mode has no corresponding compositing mode in Final Cut Pro, the layer mode is ignored.

◆ Any changes you make to a layered Photoshop file (once you've imported it into FCP) will not be reflected in your FCP sequence. To update your sequence, delete the original imported file from your FCP project and then import the updated file.

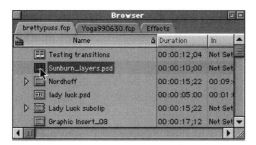

Figure 3.86 A layered Photoshop file appears as a sequence when it's imported into Final Cut Pro. Double-click the Photoshop file to open it.

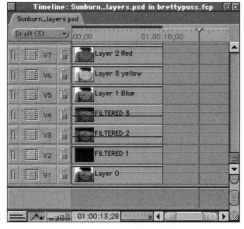

Figure 3.87 The Photoshop file opens as a sequence in the Timeline. Individual layers appear as clips.

To view individual layers in imported Photoshop files:

◆ In the Browser, double-click the Photoshop file, which appears as a sequence (**Figure 3.86**).

The Photoshop file opens as a sequence in the Timeline. Individual layers appear as clips aligned on separate video tracks (**Figure 3.87**).

✔ Tips

■ Once you've opened your multilayer Photoshop file as an FCP sequence, you can drag individual layer "clips" out of the sequence and drop them in the Browser. You can then use the individual layers as independent clips.

■ To import a layered Photoshop file as a clip instead of a sequence, flatten the image in Photoshop before importing it.

Importing audio files

You import digital audio files into Final Cut Pro just as you do any other digital media. You can import files in any QuickTime-supported audio format.

You can capture audio at its originally recorded sample rate and use it in the same sequence with audio recorded at other sample rates. When you play back the sequence, Final Cut Pro will convert the sample rate in real time for any audio clips with sample rates that do not match the sequence settings.

Letting Final Cut Pro convert the sample rates in real time is not always the best solution, as real-time sample rate conversion is optimized for speed, not audio quality. You can convert the sample rate of your non-conforming audio by using Final Cut Pro's Export feature to make a copy of your audio file at the correct sample rate. See Chapter 11, "At Last: Creating Final Output."

Importing audio files from audio CDs

You can import audio tracks from an audio CD into a Final Cut Pro project. When you import a CD track, QuickTime converts the audio tracks to digital audio files that can be edited within Final Cut Pro.

You can import an entire audio track or select a portion of a track. It is not recommended that you import audio tracks by dragging directly from an audio CD to Final Cut Pro's Browser window, because once you remove the CD from your computer, your project will no longer have access to the audio file.

Once you've imported the CD track, you should convert the sample rate of the CD audio from 44.1 KHz to the sample rate you are using in your sequence settings. You can convert the sample rate by exporting the audio at the sample rate that matches your sequence audio rate and then importing the exported copy back into your project. See Chapter 11, "At Last: Creating Final Output."

Figure 3.88 Control-click the Browser's Name column, then choose Import file from the shortcut menu.

Figure 3.89 Navigate to the CD, locate the audio track that you want to import, and click Convert.

Figure 3.90 After you've set an audio sampling rate, bit rate, and audio format (Stereo or Mono) that matches your sequence settings, click OK.

Figure 3.91 After you name the audio track and specify a location to save it, click Save.

To import audio tracks from a CD:

1. *Do one of the following*:
   ▲ Choose File > Import > File.
   ▲ In the Browser window, Control-click in the Name column; then choose Import File from the shortcut menu (**Figure 3.88**).

2. In the Import dialog box, locate the audio track that you want to import and click Convert (**Figure 3.89**).

3. In the file dialog box, click Options.

4. In the Audio CD Import Options window, *do any of the following*:
   ▲ To audition the track, click Play.
   ▲ Drag the timecode marker in the slider bar to jump to a different location in the CD track.
   ▲ To convert only a portion of the track, mark In and Out points by entering starting and ending times in the Start and End text boxes or drag the ends of the sliders to set the starting and ending times.

5. Select a bit rate and audio format (Stereo or Mono) that matches your sequence settings; then click OK (**Figure 3.90**). Note that the 48 KHz sample rate is not available; leave the sample rate at 44.1 KHz.

6. Name the audio track and specify a location to save it; then click Save (**Figure 3.91**).

✔ Tip

■ Be sure to navigate to a location on your hard disk before you try to save, or you won't be allowed to save your CD track.

FCP Helper: iTunes Converts to 48 KHz on Import

If you are using a lot of material from audio CDs in your FCP projects, consider downloading iTunes, an audio jukebox application, from Apple's Web site. (It's free.) You can set up iTunes' preferences to convert 44.1 KHz audio to 48 KHz as it imports the CD audio track (**Figure 3.94**). Check the tracks you want to import, click the Import button (**Figure 3.93**), and you'll get 48 KHz AIFF files, all ready to import into your FCP project.

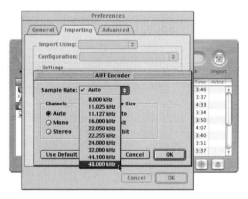

Figure 3.92 Set iTunes' preferences to sample rate convert to 48 KHz on import.

Figure 3.93 Just check the tracks you want, and click the Import button.

PREPARING YOUR CLIPS

Modern media is a postmodern thing. Seems like every time you switch on the TV, there's Elvis singing to some cartoon character, or Fred Astaire and Elton John dancing with a vacuum cleaner. Even if the project you're cutting was all shot at the same time, you've still got to track title art, transitions, and credits, as well as successive versions of your edits.

Enter the modern science of asset management. Media professionals have spent countless hours and many thousands of dollars on the best schemes to track the flood of media snippets that come together to form a film, video, or multimedia project. This expenditure of time and effort usually comes just after they have spent hours and dollars searching for (and then reshooting) a bit of lost footage. The introduction of computers into the film/video production process has brought the whole media world around to a computer-centric asset management system.

This chapter introduces Final Cut Pro's system of organizing your wonderland of little bits of media, so when the time comes to get it all together, it's already together. You'll get an overview of Final Cut Pro's organizing frameworks—projects and sequences—and a listing of Final Cut Pro's media types. We'll introduce the Browser and the Viewer, the two program windows you'll use to review your source material in preparation for editing:

- The Browser is equipped to offer you powerful tools to track and organize your stuff.

- The Viewer is your monitor to view, audition, mark, and apply effects to a clip.

This chapter deals with the Browser in detail; the next chapter covers the Viewer. You'll need a working knowledge of both of these windows to prepare your material for editing, so you might want to take a look at Chapter 5, "Introducing the Viewer," before you jump in and try to drive this thing.

Anatomy of the Browser

The Browser is the program window you use to organize and access your clips, audio files, graphics, and offline clips—all the media elements you use in your project. It also includes the project's *sequences*—the files that contain your edits.

The Browser is not like a folder on your computer's desktop; moving a batch of program resources from one bin to another in the Browser does not change the location of the resources' corresponding files on your hard drive. File storage is independent of Browser organization, so you can place the same clip in several Browser projects, and each instance of the clip will include a reference to the same file on your hard drive.

Figure 4.1 shows the Browser window interface.

New in 2: Browser Features

You can sort by almost any column in the Browser.

New Browser columns include:

◆ The Media Start and Media End columns, which display the starting and ending timecode number of a clip's source media.

◆ The Last Modified column, which shows a time/date stamp for clips and sequences, putting an end to guessing which version of a sequence you worked on last.

You can use the Set Poster Frame feature to select which frame will be displayed in a clip's Thumbnail and Large Icon view.

You can use a new Find feature to display unused clips in the Browser. This feature is useful for streamlining your project or for hunting down an unused cutaway.

Finder-style Labels add color-coded icons and customizable categories to the arsenal of organizing tools.

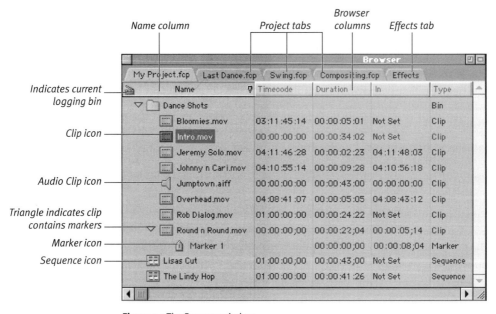

Figure 4.1 The Browser window.

Browser columns

The Browser window can display up to 40 columns of data, but you can customize the Browser to display only the columns you are using and hide the rest. You can add remarks and other types of information in the columns to help you keep track and sort information about your clips. **Table 4.1** contains a complete list of the columns available for use in the Browser.

Browser window icons

Along the left side of the window, you'll notice icons that accompany each item listed in the Browser. These icons represent file types in Final Cut Pro. Following are the icons and descriptions of each.

Sequence: A structured arrangement of media clips, edit information, render properties, and output information

Clip: A media file; can contain audio, video, graphics, or other media imported into Final Cut Pro

Subclip: A portion of a clip defined by In and Out points; any number of subclips may be referenced to one master clip

Offline Clip: Placeholder clip referencing media not currently on the local hard drive

Marker: Reference point in a clip

Audio Clip: Media clip composed of audio samples

Video Transition: Transition effect; can be applied to a video track

Audio Transition: Transition effect; can be applied to an audio track

Video Filter: Effects filter, can be applied to a video clip

Audio Filter: Effects filter; can be applied to an audio clip

Generator: Effects utility; generates screens, tones, and text for program transitions

Graphic: Clip is in a single layer graphic file format (Multilayer Photoshop files appear with a sequence icon)

ANATOMY OF THE BROWSER

Table 4.1

Browser Columns and Functions	
COLUMN	FUNCTION
Name	Name of the media element; rename clips and sequences here
Alpha	Alpha channel present
Anamorphic	Indicates if clip is flagged to be displayed in anamorphic (16:9) aspect ratio
Aud Format	File format of audio clip
Aud Rate	Frequency and bit rate of audio clip
Aux TC 1-2	Reference timecode numbers for use in synchronizing clips
Capture	Capture state of a clip in the Batch Capture list
Comment 1-4	Used for logging information
Composite	Composite mode used by this clip
Compressor	Indicates compression codec
Data Rate	Rate of data flow per second
Description	Displays information entered in Logging window's Description field
Duration	Duration between a clip's In and Out points
Frame Size	Video frame size, in pixels
Good	Indicates a clip marked "Good" in Log and Capture window
In	In point specified on a clip
Label	Displays Finder-style colored label info
Label 2	Displays descriptive text entered in the Log and Capture window
Last Modified	Displays the time and date of an item's last modification
Length	Length of the source media file on disk
Media Start	Starting timecode number of clip's source media
Media End	Ending TC number of clip's source media
Log Note	Used for logging information
Out	Out point specified on a clip
Pixel Aspect	Pixel aspect ratio
Reel	Lists reel number entered at time of capture
Reverse Alpha	Reverse Alpha Channel present
Scene	Displays information entered in Logging window's Scene field
Shot/ Take	Displays information entered in Logging window's Shot/Take field
Size	File size, in megabytes
Source	Pathname of the media file on disk
TC	Timecode currently displayed in the Viewer; can be the source timecode or an auxiliary timecode
Thumbnail	Displays poster (or first) frame of the clip; click and drag a thumbnail to scrub through the clip
Tracks	Number of video and audio tracks in the item
Type	The type of each item; possible types: sequence, clip, subclip, sequence, bin, effect
Vid Rate	Video frame rate

FCP Protocol: Clips and Sequences

A *clip* is the basic unit of media in Final Cut Pro.

A clip can be a movie, still image, nested sequence, generator, or audio file.

A clip is a reference to the actual media file stored on your hard disk. But a clip can also reference material that is not currently online. If you delete the original media file, the clip will still appear in the Browser and Timeline, but you won't see the frames and you won't be able to play it.

When you apply special effects and perform edits on clips, you are *not* affecting the media file on disk.

Using Clips in Sequences

When you insert a clip from a project into a *sequence*, the clip is *copied* into the sequence. The copy of the clip you placed in the sequence refers directly back to the actual media file on the disk and is not a reference to the clip in the project file.

This protocol is important to understand because it affects how and where you should make changes to your clips. So let's lay out the rules:

◆ You can open a clip from the Browser (outside a sequence) or from the Timeline (within a sequence).

◆ If you make changes to a clip in the Browser and then insert the clip into a sequence, the clip that is placed in the sequence *includes* the changes that have been made in the Browser.

◆ Any changes you make to a clip from within a sequence are *not* made to the clip in the Browser.

◆ After you've inserted a clip into a sequence, any further changes you make to that clip from the Browser will not be reflected in any sequence where the clip is used.

◆ Clips that appear in multiple sequences are independent of one another. Changes to one will not affect the others.

◆ If you want to make further revisions to a clip that's already in a sequence, open the clip from the Timeline and then make the changes.

◆ If you want to make changes to a clip and have the changes show up in all the sequences in which that clip is used, open the clip from the Browser and make the changes. Then reinsert the revised clip into each sequence in which you want the updated clip to appear.

◆ Final Cut Pro identifies clips that have been opened from the Timeline by displaying two lines of dots in the Scrubber bar. No dots appear in the Scrubber bar of clips that have been opened from the Browser.

ANATOMY OF THE BROWSER

About Projects

A *project* is the top level of the organizing framework. It's a Final Cut Pro file that stores references (file location information) to all the media files you have used to complete a particular program, along with the sequencing information (your "cut") and all settings for special effects you have applied to any clip in the project. This information is used to re-create the timing, sequencing, and transitions and effects you have specified for a particular cut, *without altering or changing the storage location of your original source files*. (Note: If you haven't read the section "What Is Non-Destructive Editing?" in Chapter 1, please do so now. It's key to understanding how Final Cut Pro works.)

To start a new project in Final Cut Pro, you create a new project in the Browser window and then start adding clips and sequences as you shape your project. Sequences can be exported independently as movies or clips, but they can't be saved separately from a project.

To create a new project:

◆ Start in the Browser window. Choose File > New Project (**Figure 4.2**); or press Command-E.

Your new project will appear in the Browser window (**Figure 4.3**).

To open a project:

1. Start in the Browser window; choose File > Open or press Command-O.

2. Locate and select the project file that you want to open (**Figure 4.4**).

3. Click Open.

To save a project:

◆ Start in the Browser window. Choose File > Save Project; or press Command-S.

Figure 4.2 Choose New Project from the File menu.

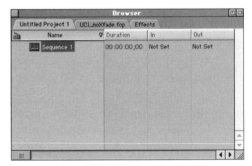

Figure 4.3 The Browser window with a new, untitled project. Sequence 1 appears automatically when you create a new project.

Figure 4.4 Locate the project file you want to open.

Figure 4.5 Choose Save Project As from the File menu.

Figure 4.6 After you've typed the new name for your project, click Save.

Figure 4.7 Choose Save All from the File menu.

Figure 4.8 For each project, type the new name and then click Save.

To save a project with a different name:

1. Start in the Browser window. Choose File > Save Project As (**Figure 4.5**).

2. In the dialog box, type a name for the project in the Save Project As field.

3. Choose a destination folder from the pull-down menu at the top of the dialog box.

4. Click Save (**Figure 4.6**).

To save all open projects:

1. Choose File > Save All (**Figure 4.7**).

2. In the dialog box, type a name for your first new project.

3. Choose a destination folder from the pull-down menu at the top of the dialog box.

4. Click Save (**Figure 4.8**).

   Repeat steps 2 through 4 for each new project that you want to save. Previously saved open projects will save automatically.

Using Save As to Protect Your Work

Opening, modifying, and then saving the same project file day after day increases the chance that your precious project file will become corrupt and unusable.

Use the Save As command to back up your project file every day or so. Save As makes a copy of the project file.

Give the duplicate copy a version number, and then continue working in the new duplicate version.

If your project file were to fail one day, you could always go back to the previous day's version and not lose more than a day's work.

ABOUT PROJECTS

149

To close a project:

1. Control-click in the project's tab (**Figure 4.9**).

2. From the shortcut menu, choose Close Tab (**Figure 4.10**).

Or do one of the following:

◆ In the Browser window, click the project's tab to bring it to the front (**Figure 4.11**). Then choose File > Close Project (**Figure 4.12**).

◆ In the Browser window, press Command-W. For all projects you've modified, Final Cut Pro will ask which projects you want to close.

✔ Tips

■ To close all open projects, close the Browser window.

■ Be consistent about where you store your project files. Make sure that all files relating to a project are stored in the same place.

■ Back up your project files frequently on a removable disk or in another safe location to avoid losing files in case of a power outage or another technical problem. Project files contain all your time and hard work. Without the editing information in the project files, your media files have no sequencing information.

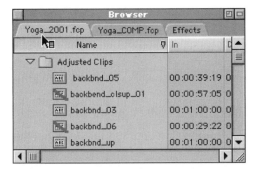

Figure 4.9 Control-click in a Project's tab to bring up the Shortcut menu; note the special cursor.

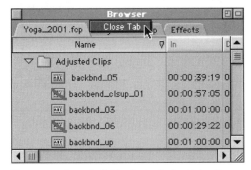

Figure 4.10 Control-clicking in the Project tab will result in only one choice; choose Close Tab to close the project.

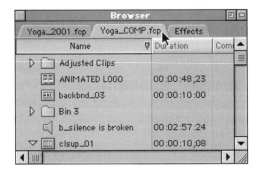

Figure 4.11 Click in a project's tab to bring it to the front of the Browser.

Figure 4.12 Choose Close Project from the File menu.

Figure 4.13 Choose Project Properties from the Edit menu.

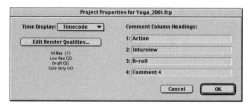

Figure 4.14 You can edit render-quality settings, rename Comment-column headings, and choose timecode or frames-display format from the Project Properties window.

To view or change the Properties of a project:

1. Start in the Browser window.

2. Click the Project tab.

3. Choose Edit > Project Properties (**Figure 4.13**).

4. In the Project Properties window (**Figure 4.14**), *do one of the following:*

   ▲ Display timecode or frames in the Duration column (see Chapter 2).

   ▲ Edit render qualities for the project (see Chapter 10).

   ▲ Edit the heading labels for Comment columns.

5. After you make your changes, click OK.

The Autosave Option

Final Cut Pro lets you autosave all open projects as you work, at a time interval that you select. The autosaved version is a backup copy that includes all changes you've made (up to the last autosave time) in the project file that you're currently working on (The project file is modified only when you invoke the Save or Save All command.) If your computer powers off or crashes while you're working in Final Cut Pro, when you restart you'll have a choice of opening the autosaved version of the project or the original and then returning to the program. The autosaved version of your project file will always be saved in the same folder as the project file it's backing up.

◆ If you open the original version, the autosaved backup will not be deleted until you invoke the Save or Save All command and save over the original.

◆ If you open the autosaved version, Final Cut Pro will treat it as a separate project file and leave the original untouched. If you save the autosaved version, it will be saved as a separate file from the original version.

You can set autosave preferences in the General tab of the Preferences window.

ABOUT PROJECTS

How the Browser Can Save Your Sanity

The Browser is a powerful tool for organizing all your program elements in a way that makes sense to you. You could construct a multilevel folders-within-folders structure by organizing your material in multiple bins, or you could use one long list containing every element in the same display. You might want to keep separate bins for your stock and production footage; or in a classroom situation, you might want to use a separate bin for each student's editing assignment.

You can search for your clips based on any clip property and sort from most Browser columns. Any markers you've placed in a clip will be noted in the Browser. You can use the Browser shortcut menu to modify some clip and sequence properties, or you can add or modify most clip information directly by double-clicking a Browser column entry.

To select an item in the Browser:

Do one of the following:

◆ Click the item you want to select.

◆ Use the arrow keys to step through the item list until you arrive at the item you want.

◆ Use the Tab key to move between items alphabetically from A to Z. Use Shift-Tab to move alphabetically from Z to A.

◆ Type the first few letters of an item's name and the corresponding item will be highlighted.

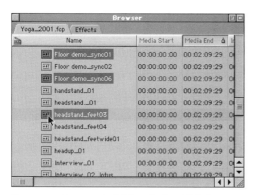

Figure 4.15 Command-click to select multiple Browser items individually.

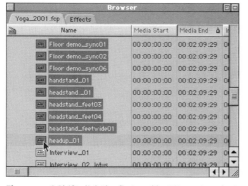

Figure 4.16 Shift-click the first and last items to select a contiguous range of Browser items.

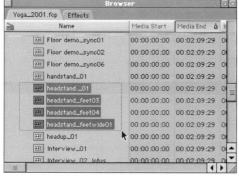

Figure 4.17 You can select a group of items by dragging a bounding box around them.

Selecting multiple Browser items

Item selection in FCP's Browser works differently than it does in the Macintosh finder. Shift-clicking a selection in a Finder window on the desktop will select multiple individual items. But in FCP's Browser, Command-clicking selects multiple items individually. Shift-clicking in the Browser will select a range of items.

To select multiple items in the Browser:

Do one of the following:

- ◆ Command-click the individual items you want to select (**Figure 4.15**).

- ◆ Shift-click the first and last items in the list to select a range of items (**Figure 4.16**).

- ◆ Drag a bounding box around a group of list items or icons (**Figure 4.17**).

- ◆ To add or subtract single items from a multiple selection, Command-click the item.

Sorting items

Final Cut Pro allows you to sort by almost every column you see in the Browser. You can use a series of secondary sorts (up to eight) to further refine your list order.

To sort items in the Browser:

1. Click the column header to select the primary sort column (**Figure 4.18**).

   The primary sort column is indicated by a green arrow in the column header.

2. Click again to reverse the sort order (**Figure 4.19**).

3. Shift-click the additional column headers to select secondary sort columns (**Figure 4.20**).

4. Shift-click again to reverse the sort order.

   Secondary sort columns are indicated by a light blue arrow in the column headers.

Customizing the Browser display

Different Browser display modes offer different functionality. List view, for example, offers a multitude of data, arranged in sortable columns, and those sexy scrubbable Thumbnail clips. Large Icon view allows you to drag your clips into any order you choose. Final Cut Pro will save your custom Browser arrangement between sessions, but your custom arrangement does not propagate to new bins created within the project.

✔ Tip

■ Make an empty template bin with your customized column selection, arrangement, and comment column names when you start a project. Copy the template bin to create new bins, and your custom arrangement will be intact in the new bins.

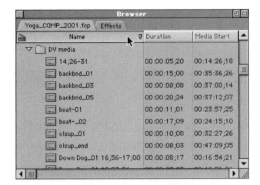

Figure 4.18 Click in the column header to sort by name; the direction of the tiny arrow on the right of the header indicates ascending order.

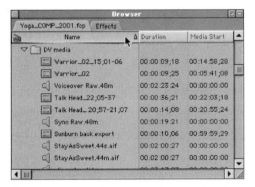

Figure 4.19 Click again to reverse the sort order; the direction of the tiny arrow now indicates a descending order.

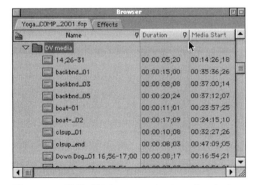

Figure 4.20 Shift-click in a second column header to select a secondary sort column; a green arrow indicates the primary sort column, and light blue shows a secondary sort.

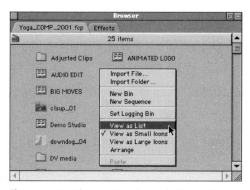

Figure 4.21 Another way to select a display option: control-click in the Name column, and then select from the shortcut menu.

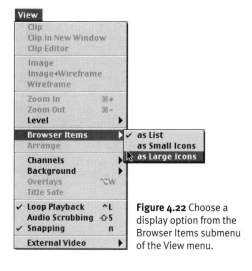

Figure 4.22 Choose a display option from the Browser Items submenu of the View menu.

You can customize the Browser in the following ways:

- Make items appear as icons or as a text list.

- In List view, rearrange, resize, hide, or show as many columns as you like. (Note: You can't hide the Name column.)

- Sort by most columns.

- Set a standard arrangement of columns, and switch between that preset and another preset column arrangement for logging clips. Both presets are selectable from the column header's shortcut menu.

- Change the Comment column headers.

To display items as a list or as icons:

1. In the Browser window, Control-click the Name column.

2. Select a display option from the shortcut menu (**Figure 4.21**).

Or do this:

- Choose View > Browser Items, and then select a display option from the submenu: as List, as Small Icons, or as Large Icons (**Figure 4.22**).

To display thumbnails in List view:

1. In the Browser window, Control-click any Browser column except Name.

2. From the shortcut menu, choose Show Thumbnail (**Figure 4.23**).

✔ Tip

■ You can scrub a clip's thumbnail in the Browser by clicking the thumbnail and then dragging in the direction you want to scrub (**Figure 4.24**). Initially, your thumbnail will display the clip's first frame, but you can select another poster frame by scrubbing through the clip until you locate the frame you want and then pressing the Control key before you release the mouse button. Very slick.

To hide a column:

1. In the Browser window, Control-click the column header.

2. From the shortcut menu, choose Hide Column (**Figure 4.25**).

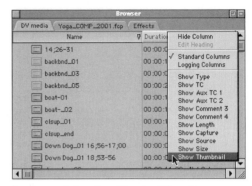

Figure 4.23 Select Show Thumbnail from the shortcut menu.

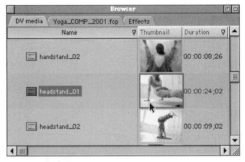

Figure 4.24 Click and drag your cursor across a thumbnail in the Browser; the thumbnail will scrub through the action in that clip.

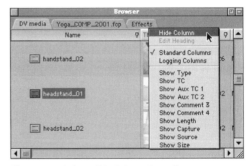

Figure 4.25 Select Hide Column from the shortcut menu.

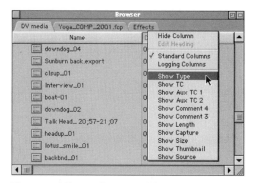

Figure 4.26 Choose the name of the column from the shortcut menu.

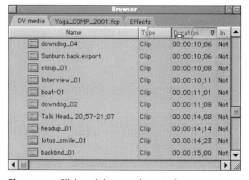

Figure 4.27 Click and drag a column to its new location.

To display a hidden column:

1. In the Browser window, Control-click in the column header to the right of the place you want the hidden column to be displayed.

2. From the shortcut menu, choose the name of the column you want to display (**Figure 4.26**).

✔ Tip

■ Final Cut Pro initially hides some Browser columns by default. Check the shortcut menu in the Browser's column header for a complete list of available columns.

To rearrange columns:

◆ Drag the column header to the new location (**Figure 4.27**).

To resize columns:

◆ Drag the edge of the column header to the new width.

To edit the Comment column name:

1. In the Browser window, Control-click the Comment column header.

2. From the shortcut menu, choose Edit Heading (**Figure 4.28**).

3. Type in the new column name (**Figure 4.29**).

4. Press Enter.

Or do this:

1. Choose Edit > Project Properties.

2. Type the new column name in the Comment text box and then click OK.

✔ Tip

■ Try double-clicking or Control-clicking clip information right in its Browser column. You will find that you can modify lots of clip settings without bothering to open the clip's Item Properties window. You can also modify clip settings for multiple clips in a single operation by selecting the clips and then adjusting the setting of just one of the selected clips.

To apply a label to a clip:

1. In the Browser window, Control-click the clip's icon.

2. From the shortcut menu, choose Label; and then select a label from the submenu. (**Figure 4.30**).

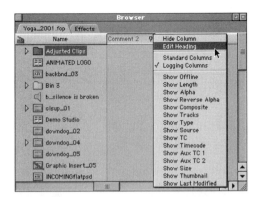

Figure 4.28 Control-click in the Comment column heading, and then choose Edit Heading from the shortcut menu.

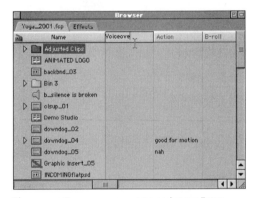

Figure 4.29 Type your new name and press Enter.

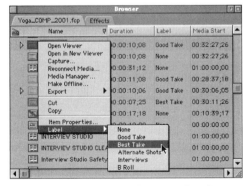

Figure 4.30 Control-click the clip's icon; then choose a label from the shortcut menu. Note the Label column; you can sort your clips by label.

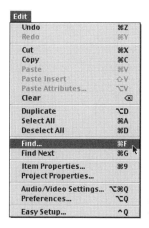

Figure 4.31
Choose Find from
the Edit menu.

Figure 4.32 You can search for a clip by timecode
number.

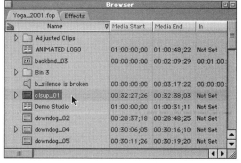

Figure 4.33 The clip with matching timecode is
highlighted in the Browser.

Searching for items in
the Browser

Final Cut Pro has a powerful search engine in
its Find function. You can perform a simple
name search, but you can also search for single or multiple items by timecode, by file
type, by log comment, or you can search your
project for unused clips — clips you have not
yet used in any sequence. Take a moment to
explore the search options available in the
Browser, and imagine how you might plan
your project to make use of them.

To search for a single item:

1. Start in the Browser window. Choose
   Edit > Find (**Figure 4.31**); or press
   Command-F.

2. In the Find window, type in your search
   criteria or select from the search criteria
   options available from the pull-down
   menus along the bottom of the window
   (**Figure 4.32**).

3. Click Find Next.

   Final Cut Pro highlights the found item in
   the Browser (**Figure 4.33**).

To search for multiple items:

1. Start in the Browser window. Choose Edit > Find (**Figure 4.34**); or press Command-F.

2. In the Find window, type in your search criteria, or select from the search criteria options available from the pull-down menus near the bottom of the window (**Figure 4.35**).

3. Select an option from the Results pull-down menu. You can choose to replace the results of your previous Find or add the new results to your previous list of found items (**Figure 4.36**).

4. Click Find All.

   The list of found items that match your search criteria appears in the Find Results window (**Figure 4.37**).

✔ Tip

■ Searching by the Name column in the Browser will return clips whose current name matches the search. But if you renamed your clips after capture, searching by both the Source and Name column will track down all the clips—including those pesky renamed clips—associated with a source media file.

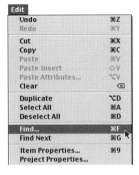

Figure 4.34 Choose Find from the Edit menu.

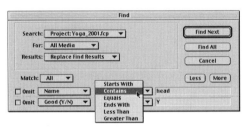

Figure 4.35 This example searches for all clips whose names contain "head," and that have a check in the Good column.

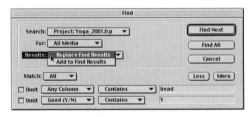

Figure 4.36 Set the Results option to "Replace Find Results."

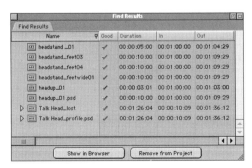

Figure 4.37 The Find Results window with the list of clips that match your search criteria; note the two shortcut buttons at the bottom of the window.

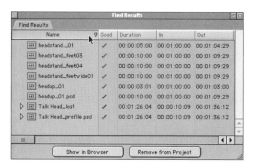

Figure 4.38 The Find Results window with a list of found clips; columns sort just as they do in the Browser window.

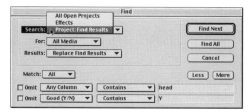

Figure 4.39 Performing a search of the Find Results window.

Using the Find Results window

The Find Results window displays a list of found items that match your search criteria (**Figure 4.38**). This window displays the same clip information as the Browser, and it offers the same flexible sorting and display options. You can perform multiple searches in the Find window and assemble a collection of items in the Find Results window to *do any of the following*:

◆ Copy or move found items to a single bin for assembly into an edited sequence.

◆ Delete found items from a project.

✔ Tip

■ You can search within the Find window. If you have assembled a large group of items in the Find Results window and you want to refine your list or perform an additional search, you can select Project: Find Results from the Search option pull-down menu (**Figure 4.39**).

Search the Project or Search the Sequence?

You can perform two types of searches in Final Cut Pro:

Choose Edit > Find with the Browser window selected, and Final Cut Pro will search all open projects for clips, sequences, graphics, and effects but will not search for items located inside sequences.

Choose Edit > Find with the Timeline selected, and your search will be limited to the currently open sequence. You'll want to search in the sequence if you are looking for the sequence version of a particular clip—a clip you applied effects to after you inserted it into a sequence, for example.

Searching for items in the Timeline is discussed in Chapter 7, "Using the Timeline and the Canvas."

Working with Bins

Final Cut Pro's Browser bins are similar to the folders you use to organize your Mac desktop—with one crucial difference. When you make changes to the contents of a bin, such as moving, renaming, or deleting clips, the changes will not affect the disk files or the folders in which your source material is stored. If you delete a clip from the bin, it is not deleted from the disk. Creating a new bin does not create a corresponding folder on your hard drive. The bin exists only within your project file. (See "What is Non-Destructive Editing?" in Chapter 2 for more information.)

To add a new bin to a project:

1. In the Browser window, Control-click an empty portion of the Name column (**Figure 4.40**).

2. *Do one of the following:*
   ▲ From the shortcut menu, choose New Bin (**Figure 4.41**).
   ▲ Choose File > New > Bin.

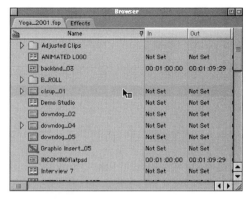

Figure 4.40 Control-click to bring up the shortcut menu.

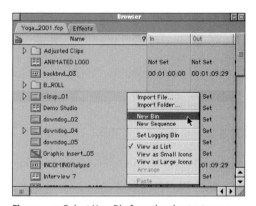

Figure 4.41 Select New Bin from the shortcut menu.

Figure 4.42 The current Log-bin indicator is located on the left edge of the bin's Name column.

What's That Little Doodad?

The tiny clapboard icon (**Figure 4.42**) indicates that the current bin is set as the *Log bin*, the Browser bin where your offline clips will be stored when you are logging footage in the Log and Capture window. For details, see "Selecting a logging bin" in Chapter 3.

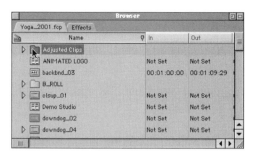

Figure 4.43 Double-click a bin name.

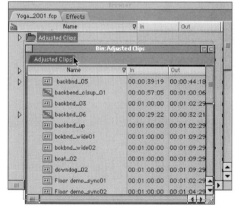

Figure 4.44 The bin opens as a new window; click and drag the tab to the Browser window.

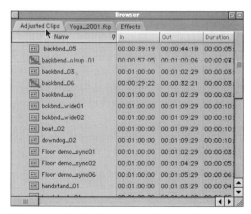

Figure 4.45 The bin is now accessible from its own tab in the Browser window.

To open a bin and create a Browser tab for it:

1. In the Browser window, double-click a bin name (**Figure 4.43**).

2. In the newly opened Bin window, click and drag the tab from the bin header into the area above the Name column in the Browser window (**Figure 4.44**).

   The bin will appear as a tab in the Browser window (**Figure 4.45**).

To move items between bins in List view:

1. Drag the items you want to move onto your selected bin (**Figure 4.46**).

2. Release the mouse button, and drop the items into the bin (**Figure 4.47**).

✔ Tip

■ To move any item to the top level of a project, drag the item to the Name column header in the Browser window.

To make a copy of a Browser item:

1. Hold down the Option key as you drag the item you want to copy (**Figure 4.48**).

2. In the new location, release the mouse button.

   The item is copied and appears in both locations (**Figure 4.49**).

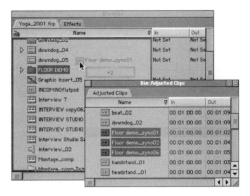

Figure 4.46 Drag selected items to a different bin.

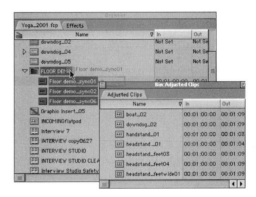

Figure 4.47 Release the mouse over the folder icon of the destination bin.

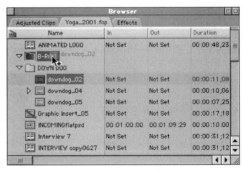

Figure 4.48 Hold down the Option key as you drag an item to copy it to its new location.

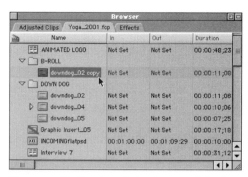

Figure 4.49 The item is copied and appears in both locations.

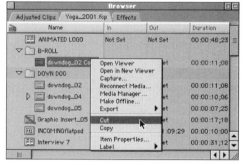

Figure 4.50 Control-click the item you want to delete, and then choose Cut from the shortcut menu.

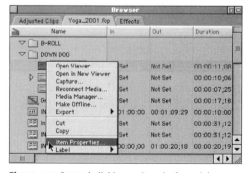

Figure 4.51 Control-clicking an item is the quickest way to access the Item Properties window.

To remove a Browser item from a project:

1. Select the item.

2. Press Delete.

Or do this:

1. Control-click the item you want to delete.

2. From the shortcut menu, choose Cut (**Figure 4.50**).

To modify clip properties in the Browser:

1. Control-click the clip you want to modify.

2. From the shortcut menu, choose Item Properties (**Figure 4.51**).

To make changes to multiple Browser items or entries:

1. Command-click to select the items or entries you want to modify (**Figure 4.52**).

2. Control-click one of the selected items.

3. From the shortcut menu, specify the change you want to make (**Figure 4.53**).

To rename clips, sequences, and bins:

1. Click the icon of the item you want to rename (**Figure 4.54**).

2. Click again on the item's name.

3. Type a new name (**Figure 4.55**).

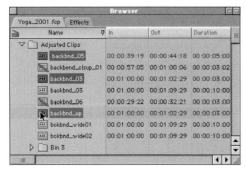

Figure 4.52 Command-click to select multiple items to modify.

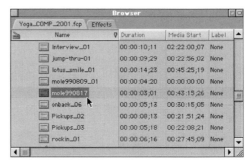

Figure 4.54 Click to select the item you want to rename.

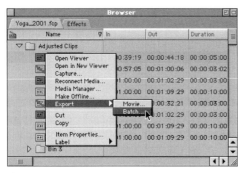

Figure 4.53 Specify the change you want to make in the shortcut.

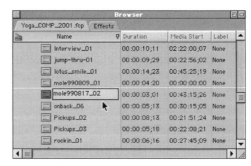

Figure 4.55 Click again on the item's name to open the field, then type a new name.

Introducing
the Viewer

You'll be spending a lot of time in the Viewer window. Not only do you use the Viewer to play clips and mark edit points and keyframes, you'll also work in the Viewer to sculpt your audio and video with effects and filters.

The Final Cut Pro interface uses tabs in the Viewer window to organize and display the clip controls. Following are summaries of the functions available on each tab:

◆ **Video tab:** View video frames and set In and Out points and keyframes. This is the default playback window for a video clip.

◆ **Audio tab:** Audition and mark edit points in audio-only clips. This is where you can set level and pan or spread settings. The Audio tab will display the audio portion of an audio+video clip. Clips with two channels of audio will display the two Audio tabs.

◆ **Filters tab:** Adjust the settings for any filter effects you have applied to a clip.

To learn about applying filters and effects, see Chapter 13, "Compositing and Special Effects."

To learn about applying audio filters, see Chapter 7, "Using the Timeline and the Canvas."

◆ **Motion tab:** Apply and modify motion effects to a clip. You can create animated effects by using a combination of keyframes and changes to motion settings. To learn about creating motion effects, see Chapter 13, "Compositing and Special Effects."

◆ **Controls tab:** Adjust the settings for a generator you have opened. A text entry field for a text generator appears on this tab.

Onscreen Controls and Displays

The Final Cut Pro Viewer has a wide variety of tools for navigating and marking your clips: transport controls, clip-marking controls, pop-up selectors, view selectors, and timecode navigation displays (**Figure 5.1**).

All the Viewer controls listed here, except the pop-up selectors, appear in the Canvas window as well. The controls operate in the same way in the Canvas window as they do in the Viewer.

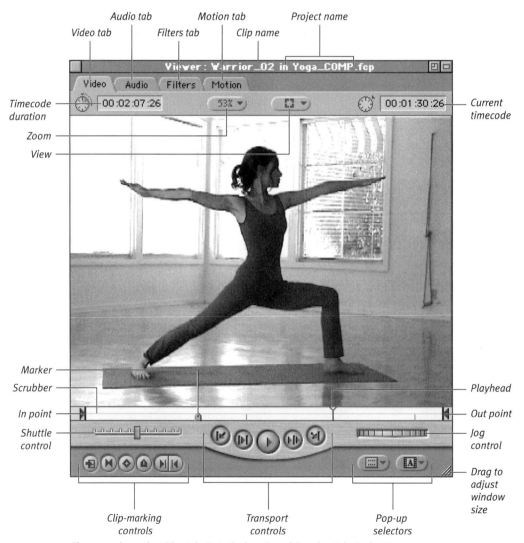

Figure 5.1 shows the Video tab. Note the location of the other tabs in the Viewer.

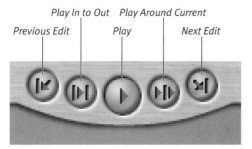

Play In to Out *Play Around Current*

Previous Edit *Play* *Next Edit*

Figure 5.2 The Viewer's transport control buttons.

Figure 5.3 The Shuttle control.

Figure 5.4 The Jog control.

Figure 5.5 The Scrubber and playhead.

Figure 5.2 shows the transport controls that lie horizontally across the bottom of the Viewer window. The next few sections discuss the onscreen controls you'll encounter in the Viewer.

Transport controls

The transport controls are located in the middle of the bottom section of the Viewer:

◆ **Previous Edit button:** Click to jump the playhead back to the previous edit (In or Out point).

◆ **Play In to Out button:** Click to play the clip from the In point to the Out point.

◆ **Play button:** Click to play the clip from the current position of the playhead. Click again to stop.

◆ **Play Around Current button:** Click to play the part of the clip immediately before and after the current position of the playhead. The pre-roll and post-roll settings (in the Preferences window) determine the duration of the playback.

◆ **Next Edit button:** Click to move the playhead to the next edit.

◆ **Shuttle control:** Drag the control tab (**Figure 5.3**) away from the center to fast forward or rewind. Speeds vary depending on the control tab's distance from the center. A green control tab indicates normal playback speed.

◆ **Jog control:** Click and drag your mouse to the left or right (**Figure 5.4**) to step through your clip one frame at a time.

◆ **Scrubber and playhead:** The Scrubber is the strip that stretches horizontally below the image window. Move through a clip by dragging the playhead, or click on the Scrubber to jump the playhead to a new location (**Figure 5.5**).

Clip-marking controls

All the onscreen controls you use to mark clips are grouped in the lower-left corner of the Viewer (**Figure 5.6**):

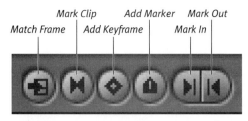

Figure 5.6 The Viewer's clip-marking controls.

- **Match Frame:** Click to display the frame currently showing in the Viewer in the Canvas window. This control is useful for synchronizing action.

- **Mark Clip:** Click to set In and Out points in the sequence. Edit points will be set at the outer boundaries of the clip at the position of the playhead in the target track.

- **Add Keyframe:** Click to add a keyframe to the clip at the current playhead position.

- **Add Marker:** Click to add a marker to the clip at the current playhead position.

- **Mark In (left) and Mark Out (right):** Click to set the In point or the Out point for the clip at the current playhead position.

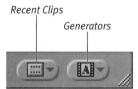

Figure 5.7 Pop-up selectors.

Pop-up selectors

Two buttons at the lower right of the Viewer window provide convenient access to source materials (**Figure 5.7**):

- **Recent Clips:** Select recently used clips directly from this pop-up menu.

- **Generators:** Select a generator effect from this pop-up menu. (To read about generators, see Chapter 13, "Compositing and Special Effects.")

The next few sections discuss the onscreen controls you'll encounter across the top of the Viewer.

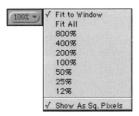

Figure 5.8 The Zoom selector.

Figure 5.9 The View selector.

Figure 5.10 The Timecode Duration display.

Figure 5.11 The Current Timecode display.

View selectors

The view selectors directly above the Viewer window allow you to adjust the window's view.

- ◆ **Zoom:** Adjust the Viewer's image display size (**Figure 5.8**). (This pop-up selector does not affect the actual frame size of the image.)

- ◆ **View:** Select a viewing format (**Figure 5.9**). Title Safe and Wireframe modes are accessible from this pop-up menu.

Timecode navigation and display

Two timecode displays appear in the upper corners of the Viewer window. They are useful for precision navigating to specific timecode locations.

- ◆ **Timecode Duration:** This displays the elapsed time between the In and Out points of a clip. If no edit points are set, the beginning and end of the clip serve as the In and Out points (**Figure 5.10**).

- ◆ **Current Timecode:** This displays the timecode at the current position of the playhead. You can enter a time in the display to jump the playhead to that point in the clip (**Figure 5.11**). Control-click the display to toggle the time view between Drop, Non-drop, and Frames view.

ONSCREEN CONTROLS AND DISPLAYS

Working with Clips in the Viewer

You can open clips from the project's tab in the Browser or from the Timeline. You can open single and multiple clips or open clips you have viewed recently. You can also open clips from outside an open project.

When you open an Audio+Video clip, it appears in a Viewer window with the Video tab selected.

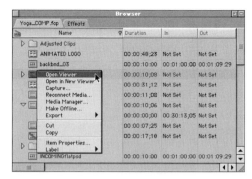

Figure 5.12 Control-click the clip's icon and choose Open Viewer from the shortcut menu.

To open a clip in the Viewer:

Do one of the following:

◆ Double-click the clip's icon in the Browser or Timeline.

◆ Control-click the clip's icon and choose Open Viewer from the shortcut menu (**Figure 5.12**).

◆ Select the clip's icon and press Enter.

◆ Drag a clip's icon from the Browser and drop it in the image area of the Viewer.

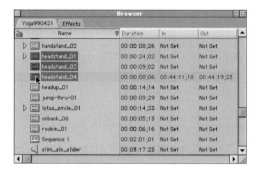

Figure 5.13 Command-click to select multiple clips.

To open a clip in a new window:

1. Select the clip in the Browser or Timeline.

2. Choose View > Clip in New Window.

✔ Tips

■ It's common practice in Final Cut Pro to load an entire sequence into the Viewer and edit it into another sequence, just as if it were a clip. To load a sequence into the Viewer, select the sequence in the Browser, then choose View > Sequence, or drag the sequence's icon from the Browser and drop it in the image area of the Viewer.

■ You can learn more about constructing a project with multiple sequences in Chapter 12, "Big Picture: Managing Complex Projects."

Figure 5.14 Drag the clips to the Viewer and then drop them on the image area.

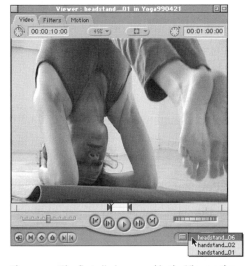

Figure 5.15 The first clip is opened in the Viewer; the rest are listed in the Recent Clips pop-up selector.

Figure 5.16
Select a clip from the Recent Clips control's pop-up list.

To open multiple clips:

1. Command-click to select multiple clips in the Browser (**Figure 5.13**).

2. Drag the clips to the Viewer (**Figure 5.14**). The first clip opens in the Viewer, and the other selected clips are listed in the Recent Clips control (**Figure 5.15**).

To open a recently viewed clip:

◆ Select the clip name from the Recent Clips control's pop-up list in the Viewer (**Figure 5.16**).

✔ Tip

■ You can load an entire folder of clips into the Viewer in one move by dragging the folder from the Browser and dropping it in the image area of the Viewer. The clips in the folder will show up in the Recent Clips control (as long as you have set your List Recent Clips preference high enough to cover the folder's item count).

To open a clip from the Timeline or Canvas:

1. Select the clip in the Timeline.

2. *Do one of the following:*

   ▲ Choose View > Clip to replace the current contents of the Viewer with the selected clip (**Figure 5.17**).

   ▲ Choose View > Clip in New Window to open a new Viewer containing the selected clip (**Figure 5.18**).

   ▲ Control click on the clip in the Timeline, then select Open (clip name) from the shortcut menu.

3. The clip opens in the Viewer. If you positioned the Timeline's playhead over a frame in the clip, the clip opens with the Viewer's playhead located at the same frame.

To open imported clips in the original application:

1. Open the clip in the Viewer or Canvas window.

2. Choose View > Clip Editor (**Figure 5.19**).

3. Clips created in an application other than Final Cut Pro will open in that application (**Figure 5.20**). If the application used to create the clip is not installed on your computer, a dialog box opens that allows you to choose an application in which to edit the clip.

✔ Tip

■ You will need enough RAM on your computer to run both applications simultaneously—and that's a lot of RAM.

Figure 5.17 Choose View > Clip to open a clip selected in the Timeline or Canvas window in the Viewer.

Figure 5.18 Choose View > Clip in New Window to open a clip selected in the Timeline or Canvas window in a new Viewer window.

Figure 5.19 Choose View > Clip Editor to open a clip in the application you used to create it.

Figure 5.20 This clip, captured in Final Cut Pro, has opened in QuickTime Player, because Final Cut Pro clips are QuickTime format files.

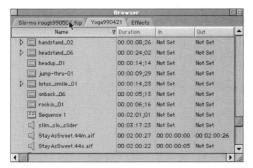

Figure 5.21 Click a project's tab to bring that project to the front of the Browser window.

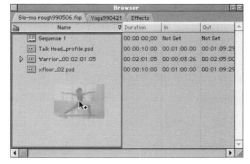

Figure 5.22 Drag a clip into a project in the Browser window. Clip changes will be saved with the project.

To open a clip outside the current project:

1. Choose File > Open.

2. Locate the clip.

3. Select the clip and click Open.

To save changes in a clip outside the current project:

1. In the Browser window, select a project in which to save your modified clip by clicking the tab of that project.

This brings your selected project to the front of the Browser window (**Figure 5.21**).

2. Click and drag from the video frame in the Viewer to the project's tab in the Browser.

Your clip is now inserted in that project, and your changes will be saved with that project (**Figure 5.22**).

WORKING WITH CLIPS IN THE VIEWER

FCP Protocol: Saving Clip Changes

Say you have marked edit points and placed some other markers in a clip you opened outside of your project. To save the changes you made to that clip, you'll need to do the following:

◆ Insert the modified clip into a project that's currently open.

or

◆ Export the clip.

Remember that FCP will save the changes you make only if the clip has been placed in a project or exported as a new file. If you mark changes and close the Viewer window without taking the steps listed here... bye-bye changes. There's no warning dialog box, so take care. One exception to this rule: Any modification of a clip's timecode will be written to the clip's media file immediately.

To open a generator effect in the Viewer:

1. Start in the Browser window with the Effects tab selected.

2. *Do one of the following:*
   - ▲ Double-click the generator icon in the Browser or Timeline (**Figure 5.23**).
   - ▲ Select a generator icon and press Enter.

✔ Tip

- ■ You can select generator effects directly from the Generator pop-up menu in the Viewer window (**Figure 5.24**).

To play a clip in the Viewer:

1. Start with an open clip and the Viewer window selected.

2. Click the Play button (**Figure 5.25**), press the Spacebar, or press L.

3. To stop playback, press the Spacebar or click the Play button.

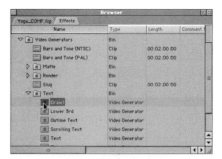

Figure 5.23 Double-click a generator icon to open the generator effect in the Viewer.

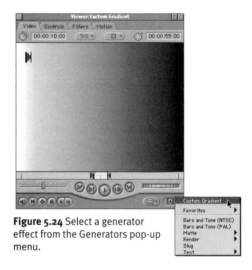

Figure 5.24 Select a generator effect from the Generators pop-up menu.

Figure 5.25 Click the Play button to start clip play. Click Play again to stop play.

Figure 5.26 Click the Play In to Out button to play the section of the clip between the In and Out points.

Figure 5.27 Click the Play Around Current button to play a section of the clip before and after the current playhead position.

To play a clip in reverse:

1. Start with an open clip and the Viewer window selected.

2. Shift-click the Play button, press Shift-Spacebar, or press J.

3. To stop playback, press the Spacebar, click the Play button, or press K.

To play a clip between In and Out points:

1. Start with an open clip and the Viewer window selected.

2. Click the Play In to Out button (**Figure 5.26**); or press Shift-\ (backslash).

3. To stop playback, press the Spacebar or click the Play button.

To play a clip from the current playhead position to the Out point:

◆ Command-click the Play button.

To play a clip before and after the current playhead position:

◆ Click the Play Around Current button (**Figure 5.27**); or press backslash (\).

The clip plays back the specified pre-roll duration before the playhead location, and it plays back the post-roll duration after the playhead location. The duration of video playback is determined by the pre-roll and post-roll preferences.

WORKING WITH CLIPS IN THE VIEWER

To play every frame:

◆ Choose Mark > Play > Every Frame
(**Figure 5.28**).

To loop playback in all playback modes:

1. Choose View > Loop Playback
(**Figure 5.29**).

2. Choose View > Loop Playback again to
turn off looping.

✔ Tip

■ You can toggle looped playback on and
off from your keyboard by pressing
Control-L.

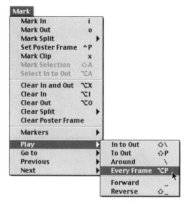

Figure 5.28 Choose Mark > Play > Every
Frame to play every frame of a clip.

JKL Keys: The Way to Move

Early users of FCP 1.0 (especially Avid users) raised their voices and overwhelmingly requested
a remapping of the FCP keyboard commands to support "JKL Keys," the Avid system of controlling variable speed playback. The Final Cut Pro team, in its wisdom, made the switch.

Here's how it works.

The J, K and L keys are located on your keyboard in a row, and you use them to control your
playback speed and direction. The I and O keys, which you use for setting In and Out points, are
located just above the JKL. The comma (,) and period (.) keys, which you can use to trim edits,
are located below the JKL. The Semi-colon (;) and Apostrophe (') keys control Previous and
Next Edit. This arrangement makes it easy to edit with the most commonly used keyboard
shortcuts under one hand. It's easy to see how editors would get attached to this system.

Here's the rundown on J, K and L keyboard command functions:

Press J to play in reverse. Tap J twice to double reverse shuttle speed. Tap J three times for
X4 reverse shuttling speed. Tap J four times for X8 reverse shuttling speed.

Press K to Stop or Pause.

Press L to Play forward. Tap L twice to double forward shuttle speed. Tap L three times for
X4 forward shuttling speed. Tap L four times for X8 forward shuttling speed.

Hold down K and tap J or L to get slow motion shuttling in either direction. A single
"J" or "L" tap, with the K key held down, will step forward or back one frame at a time.

Figure 5.29 Choose View > Loop Playback to loop clip playback. Choose View > Loop Playback again to toggle looping off.

Figure 5.30 Click and drag the playhead across the Scrubber to scrub through a clip.

Figure 5.31 Click and drag the Jog control to step through a clip one frame at a time.

Figure 5.32 Click and drag the Shuttle control to scan through a clip at a range of speeds from slow to fast.

Other ways to move: Jogging, scrubbing, and shuttling

While editing, you can find yourself spending more time playing your material at fast and slow speeds than at normal speed. Use the following tools for high- and low-speed navigation:

◆ To scrub through a clip, drag the playhead along the Scrubber bar above the transport controls (**Figure 5.30**).

◆ To jump the playhead to a location within the clip, click in the Scrubber bar.

◆ To move the playhead frame by frame, use the arrow keys.

◆ To jump the playhead in one-second increments, press Shift as you use the arrow keys.

◆ To jog one frame at a time, drag the Jog control (**Figure 5.31**). You can drag off the control area if you continue to hold down the mouse button.

◆ To play a clip at various speeds, drag the Shuttle control (**Figure 5.32**). Drag further from the center to increase the playback speed. Drag right to play forward; drag left to play in reverse.

WORKING WITH CLIPS IN THE VIEWER

FCP Protocol: Entering Timecode Numbers

Final Cut Pro uses a number of convenient shortcuts for timecode navigation. Final Cut Pro uses standard timecode, which follows the format Hours:Minutes:Seconds:Frames.

For example, typing 01241315 sets the timecode to 01:24:13:15. You don't need to include the colons when you type.

You need to type only the numbers that change. Numbers that don't change, such as the hour or minute, don't need to be entered. Let's look at some examples.

Example 1

1. Start at timecode location 01:24:13:15.

2. To jump to timecode 01:24:18:25, type 1825 (for 18 seconds, 25 frames) and press Enter.

The playhead jumps to timecode location 01:24:18:25. The hour and minute don't change for the new timecode location, so you don't need to reenter the hour or minute.

Example 2

The same idea applies to a new timecode minutes away from your current location.

1. Again start at timecode location 01:24:13:15.

2. To jump to timecode 01:27:18:25, type 271825 (for 27 minutes, 18 seconds, 25 frames) and press Enter.

The playhead jumps to timecode location 01:27:18:25.

Entering durations

Say you just want to move 12 seconds, 27 frames back in your clip. You don't need to calculate the new timecode number yourself.

Type –1227, and your clip jumps back 12 seconds and 27 frames. You can enter the timecode value preceded by a + (plus) or – (minus) sign, and FCP will change the current time by that amount.

You can jump to a new location using the + (plus) and – (minus) keys in two ways: using time (Hours:Minutes:Seconds:Frames) or using the total number of frames, which can be converted to Time plus Frames. Here are some examples using time:

♦ Typing –3723 jumps back 37 seconds and 23 frames.

♦ Typing +161408 moves the time ahead 16 minutes, 14 seconds, and 8 frames.

In the Frames position in the timecode, any two-digit value between 30 and 99 is converted to the correct number of seconds (30 frames = 1 second). Here are some examples using the frame count:

♦ Entering –69 frames jumps back 69 frames, which is 2 seconds and 9 frames.

♦ Entering +36 frames jumps ahead 1 second, 6 frames, which is 36 frames.

One more shortcut

There's one other keyboard shortcut: You can substitute a period (.) for zeros in a timecode value. Each period replaces a set of two zeros in a timecode number. Here's an example:

♦ To jump to timecode location 00:07:00:00, type 7.. (7 and two periods). The periods insert 00 in the Frames and Seconds fields.

♦ Type 11... to move to 11:00:00:00.

Sure beats typing all those colons, huh?

Figure 5.33 Current Timecode display in the Viewer window.

Figure 5.34 Adding 1 second, 15 frames (45 frames), to the current timecode position using a timecode entry shortcut.

Figure 5.35 The playhead is repositioned 1 second, 15 frames later, and the Current Timecode display is updated.

Figure 5.36 Timecode Duration display in the Viewer window. The current clip duration is 10 seconds.

Figure 5.37 Adding 1 second (30 frames) to the current clip duration using a timecode entry shortcut.

Figure 5.38 The Out point is extended by 1 second, and the Timecode Duration display is updated.

Navigating with Timecode

Moving around using timecode values can be the most efficient way to work, especially if your sense of timing is tuned to "frames per second." Final Cut Pro's timecode input functionality is quite flexible. If you know exactly where you want to go, this is the way to get there. Timecode navigation works the same way in both the Viewer and Canvas.

To navigate using timecode values:

1. Start with your clip open and the Viewer window selected. **Figure 5.33** shows the timecode location before repositioning.

2. Enter a new timecode number (or use the shorthand methods detailed in the nearby Tips and sidebar). You don't need to click in the field to begin entering a new timecode—just type the numbers (**Figure 5.34**), and then press Enter.

   The playhead repositions to the location that matches the new timecode value, and the new timecode position is displayed in the Current Timecode field in the upper-right corner of the Viewer (**Figure 5.35**).

To change the Out point using timecode:

◆ To change the Out point for a clip or sequence, enter a new timecode in the Duration field, in the upper-left corner of the Viewer, then press Enter. (See **Figures 5.36–5.38**.)

✔ Tips

- In the Viewer or Canvas, press Tab once to select the Duration field, or twice to select the Current Timecode field.

- You can copy the timecode from one field and paste it into another if the timecode is valid in the location where it is being pasted. You can also drag a timecode from one field to another by pressing Option while dragging.

Working with In and Out Points

The In and Out points determine the start and end frames of the portion of a clip that is used when the clip is placed into a sequence. Determining the usable part of a clip and setting In and Out points is the first step in assembling your edit. Many editing functions are performed by adjusting these points, either within the clip itself or from within a sequence.

To set In and Out points for a clip in the Viewer:

1. In the Browser, double-click the clip to open it in the Viewer.

2. Press the Home key to position the play-head at the beginning of the clip.

3. Use the Play button or the Spacebar to start playing the clip from the beginning.

4. Click the Mark In button (**Figure 5.39**), or press I, when you see (or hear) the beginning of the part you want to use.

5. Click the Mark Out button (**Figure 5.40**), or press O, when you see (or hear) the end of the part you want to use.

6. Click the Play In to Out button to check your In and Out points (**Figure 5.41**).

✔ Tip

■ You don't need to have the clip playing to set its In and Out points. You can drag the playhead to locate a particular frame and then set the edit point.

Figure 5.39 Set an In point by clicking the Mark In button.

Figure 5.40 Set an Out point by clicking the Mark Out button.

Figure 5.41 Click the Play In to Out button to review the edit points you have marked.

Figure 5.42 Use the Scrubber bar's shortcut menu for setting and clearing edit points.

Figure 5.43 Pressing Shift while dragging an edit point slides both the In and Out points.

To change In and Out points in the Viewer:

Do one of the following:

◆ Play the clip again and click Mark In or Mark Out at the new spot.

◆ Drag the In or Out point icon along the Scrubber bar to change its location.

◆ Drag the In or Out point icon off the Scrubber to remove it.

✔ Tip

■ You can use the shortcut menu to set and clear edit points. Control-click in the Scrubber and select an option from the shortcut menu (**Figure 5.42**).

To move the In and Out points simultaneously:

1. Start in the Viewer.

2. Click on either edit point indicator in the Scrubber.

3. Press and hold Shift while dragging the edit point indicator (**Figure 5.43**).

   The marked duration of the clip is not changed, but the frames that are included in the marked clip shift forward or backward. Modifying an edit in this way is called slipping.

WORKING WITH IN AND OUT POINTS

183

About Subclips

Subclips are shorter clips you create from a longer master clip. You can create multiple clips from a single master clip. For example, you can open a 15-minute clip in the Viewer and subdivide it into as many subclips as you need.

As you create subclips, the master clip remains open in the Viewer. Once you've created a subclip, you can open it in the Viewer and work with it in the same way as any other clip. Changes you make to a subclip won't affect the master clip.

Final Cut Pro places new subclips in the same project bin as the master clip, automatically naming each clip as you create it. For example, if the master clip is named "Whole Thing," the first subclip is named "Whole Thing Subclip," the second is "Whole Thing Subclip 2," and so on.

Once you create a subclip, you can rename it and trim the edit points, but you cannot extend the subclip's In and Out points beyond the In and Out points of its master clip.

If you need to extend a subclips' edit points beyond its current duration, you'll need to remove the subclip's limits, restoring your subclip to the full length of the master clip, and then set new In and Out points.

✔ Tips

- You can use subclips to mark selected portions of a long clip (you can even rename them), and then export all those subclips as a batch list. Use that batch list to recapture just the bits of the longer clip you really want to keep. They'll be captured as full-fledged, individual master clips.

New in 2: Media Manager and Subclips

- If you use subclipping to mark your selected footage from a master clip, FCP's retooled Media Manager will now allow you to retain only the marked portions of the master and delete the unused footage without re-capturing. Oh happy day. For details see Chapter 12, "Big Picture: Managing Complex Projects."

- DV Start Stop Detection is akin to the popular "scene detection" feature in iMovie. FCP 2.0 will automatically set markers in your captured clip each time it detects a Start/Stop (Record/Pause) in a long captured clip. Because FCP can use markers to break a clip into individual subclips, you can use the technique outlined below to capture long sections of DV tape and break it up into usable subclip chunks. You can even use the Media Manager to delete your unused footage. For details on Media Manager features, see Chapter 12, "Big Picture: Managing Complex Projects."

- A word of caution: If you select a subclip for recapturing, Final Cut Pro will recapture the entire master clip containing the subclip. Exporting subclips as a batch list breaks the connection to the master clip.

- One more cautionary word: Test ahead of time if you are exporting an EDL of a sequence that includes subclips.

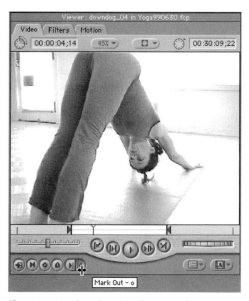

Figure 5.44 Mark an Out point for your subclip.

Figure 5.45 Choose Modify > Make Subclip.

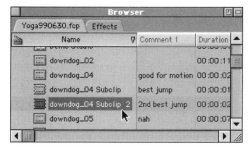

Figure 5.46 A new subclip appears in the Browser, below the master clip.

To create a subclip:

1. Double-click a clip in the Browser or Timeline to open it in the Viewer window.

2. Mark In and Out points (**Figure 5.44**).

3. Choose Modify > Make Subclip (**Figure 5.45**); or press Command-U.

4. A new, automatically named subclip appears in the Browser, below the master clip (**Figure 5.46**).

To adjust a subclip's length:

1. Select the subclip in the Browser, or a sequence subclip from the Timeline.

2. Choose Modify >Remove Subclip limits.

3. Open the subclip in the Viewer

   The full length of the master clip appears. If you have selected a Timeline subclip, the current In and Out points will still be displayed.

4. Set new In and Out points for the subclip.

To find a subclip's master clip:

1. Double-click a subclip in the Browser or Timeline to open it in the Viewer window.

2. Choose Mark > Go To > Master Clip, or press Shift-F.

Using Markers

Markers are reference pointers in a clip or sequence that have a variety of uses. You can

◆ Quickly jump the playhead to markers in clips or sequences.

◆ Align the clip marker to a marker in the sequence.

◆ Align a filter or motion keyframe to the marker.

◆ Mark a range of the clip to use as you might a subclip.

◆ Align other clip markers, clip boundaries, or transition boundaries to a marker in the Timeline.

◆ To learn more about using markers in sequences see Chapter 7, "Using the Timeline and the Canvas."

To add markers to a clip or sequence in the Viewer:

1. Open the clip in the Viewer.

2. Play the clip or sequence.

3. When playback reaches the place where you want to set your marker, click the Add Marker button (**Figure 5.47**); or press M.

4. To add a custom label or comments to the marker, click Add Marker or press M a second time to display the Edit Marker dialog box (**Figure 5.48**).

✔ Tip

■ Save keystrokes! Shift-click the Add Marker button to set a marker and open the Edit Marker dialog box in one move.

Figure 5.47 Click the Add Marker button to set a marker in your clip.

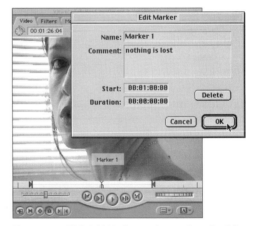

Figure 5.48 Click Add Marker again to call up the Edit Marker dialog box.

USING MARKERS

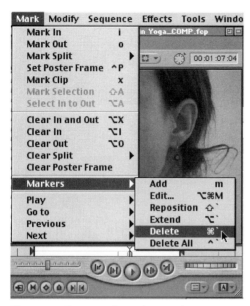

Figure 5.49 Choose Mark > Markers > Delete to remove a marker from your clip.

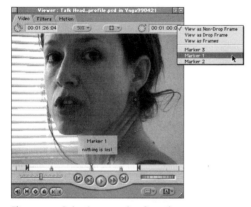

Figure 5.50 Selecting a marker from the shortcut menu. Control-click the Current Timecode display to see the shortcut menu listing of all markers in a clip.

To delete a marker:

1. Move the playhead to the marker.

2. *Do one of the following:*
   - ▲ Choose Mark > Markers > Delete (**Figure 5.49**).
   - ▲ Press Command-` (accent grave, which shares a key with the tilde [~]).
   - ▲ Option-click the Marker button.

To move the playhead to a marker:

Do one of the following:

- ◆ Drag the playhead in the Scrubber bar to the marker location.

- ◆ Control-click the Current Timecode field in the Viewer and choose a marker from the shortcut menu (**Figure 5.50**).

- ◆ Choose Mark > Previous > Marker (or Next > Marker).

To rename a marker:

1. Move the playhead to the marker.

2. Press M to open the Edit Marker dialog box.

3. Type a new name or comment in the corresponding text boxes (**Figure 5.51**).

4. Click OK.

To extend the duration of a marker:

1. Move the playhead to the marker.

2. Press M to open the Edit Marker dialog box.

3. To extend the duration of a marker, enter a duration value (**Figure 5.52**).

   An extended duration marker appears as a marker icon with a bar extending along the Scrubber bar (**Figure 5.53**).

   You can place extended duration markers on audio tracks to visually mark the location and duration of key dialogue or a specific passage in a music track.

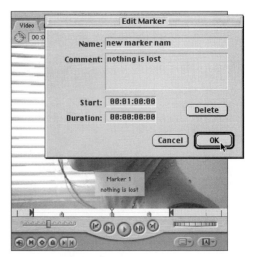

Figure 5.51 Rename a marker or add comments in the Edit Marker dialog box; then click OK.

Figure 5.52 Extend a marker's duration by entering a value in the Duration field of the Edit Marker dialog box.

Figure 5.53 The marker icon displays its duration on the Scrubber bar.

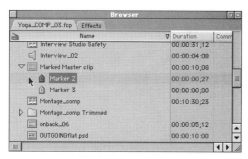

Figure 5.54 Click the clip's twirldown triangle, then select the desired marker from the list.

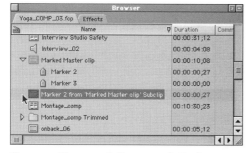

Figure 5.55 The new subclip appears in the Browser. Note the subclip's duration is equal to the extended marker's duration.

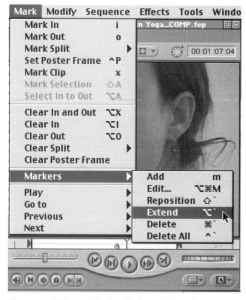

Figure 5.56 Choose Mark > Markers > Extend.

To make a subclip from a marker:

1. In the Browser, click the marked clip's twirldown triangle to reveal a list of its markers, then select the desired marker (**Figure 5.54**).

2. Choose Modify > Make Subclip; or press Command-U.

   The new subclip appears in the Browser. The subclip will have a duration equal to the extended marker's duration (**Figure 5.55**). If the marker has no extended duration, the subclip will extend to the next marker in the clip.

To extend the marker duration to the playhead location:

1. Position the playhead at the location where you want the endpoint of your extended marker.

2. Choose Mark > Markers > Extend (**Figure 5.56**); or press Option-` (the accent that shares a key with the tilde [~]).

   The marker's duration will extend from the original location of the marker to the location of the playhead (**Figure 5.57**).

Figure 5.57
The marker's duration now extends to the playhead position.

To move a marker forward in time:

1. Move the playhead to the location where you want the marker to be repositioned (**Figure 5.58**).

   You can move a marker only forward.

2. Choose Mark > Markers > Reposition (**Figure 5.59**); or press Shift-` (accent).

✔ Tip

- To extend or reposition a marker on the fly during playback, use the keyboard shortcuts listed above. Hit the keys when you see the frame you want to make your new marker location.

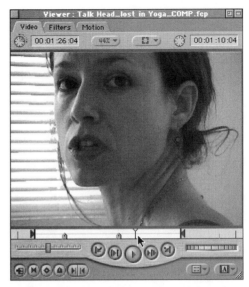

Figure 5.58 Move the playhead to the new desired location for your marker.

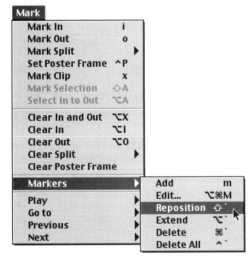

Figure 5.59 Choose Mark > Markers > Reposition.

Marking Shortcuts

FCP offers lots of ways to mark In and Out points. This is something editors do all day long, so it may be worthwhile to try these shortcuts and see which work best for you.

To mark In:

Do one of the following:

- Press I on the keyboard.
- Click the Mark In button in the Viewer.
- Press / (slash) on the keypad.
- From the Mark menu, choose Mark In.

To mark Out:

Do one of the following:

- Press O on the keyboard.
- Click the Mark Out button in the Viewer.
- Press * (asterisk) on the keypad.
- From the Mark menu, choose Mark Out.

To delete edit points:

Do one of the following:

- Press Option-X to clear both In and Out points; or Option-click the Mark Clip button.
- Press Option-I to clear In points; or Option-click the Mark In button.
- Press Option-O to clear Out points ; or Option-click the Mark Out button.

To locate to edit points:

Do one of the following:

- Press Shift-I to go to the In point; or Shift-click the Mark In button.
- Press Shift-O to go to the Out point; or Shift-click the Mark Out button.

USING MARKERS

Adjusting the Viewer Display

You can set up the Viewer to show your clips in a variety of display formats and magnifications. Final Cut Pro is also designed to overlay an array of useful information on your clip image, or it can let you turn everything off. View settings are clip-specific, and are stored with the clip.

Changing magnification and window size in the Viewer or Canvas

Final Cut Pro's interface is very ambitious. Unless you are working with a dual monitor setup, you'll probably be juggling window sizes from time to time to get a really good look at a detail.

To zoom in:

Do one of the following:

◆ Choose a higher magnification level from the Zoom pop-up menu at the top of the Viewer or Canvas (**Figure 5.60**).

◆ Select the Zoom In tool from the Tool palette, and click inside the Viewer or Canvas.

◆ From the View menu, select the amount you want to zoom in from the Level submenu.

◆ Select the Zoom In tool from the Tool palette (**Figure 5.61**). Click the video image, and drag a marquee to zoom in on the desired area of the image (**Figure 5.62**).

Note that clips will not play smoothly when you have zoomed in on a clip in the Viewer.

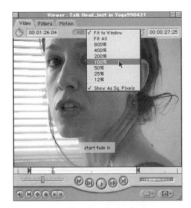

Figure 5.60 Choose a magnification level from the Zoom pop-up menu.

Figure 5.61 Select the Zoom In tool from the Tool palette.

Figure 5.62 Drag a marquee around the area you want to zoom in on.

Figure 5.63 Drag the Hand tool over a magnified image to move it in the Viewer window.

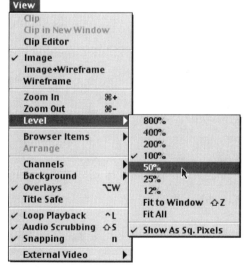

Figure 5.64 Choose View > Level, and select a zoom-out level.

To view different parts of a magnified image:

Do one of the following:

◆ Select the Hand tool from the Tool palette and drag it over the image to move the view (**Figure 5.63**).

◆ Use the scroll bars to move around the image.

To zoom out:

Do one of the following:

◆ Choose a lower magnification level from the Zoom pop-up menu at the top of the Viewer.

◆ Select the Zoom Out tool from the Tools palette, and click inside the Viewer or Canvas.

◆ From the View menu, select the amount you want to zoom out from the Level submenu (**Figure 5.64**).

To fit a clip into the window size:

◆ From the Zoom pop-up menu at the top of the Viewer, choose Fit to Window.

To fit all items into the view plus a 10% margin:

Do one of the following:

◆ From the Zoom pop-up menu at the top of the Viewer, choose Fit All (**Figure 5.65**).

◆ Choose View > Level > Fit All.

✔ Tip

■ Selecting "Fit All" will zoom out to show all of the objects in a multi-layered composited sequence, including those outside the screen area (**Figure 5.66**).

To view at actual size:

◆ From the Zoom pop-up menu at the top of the Viewer, choose 100%.

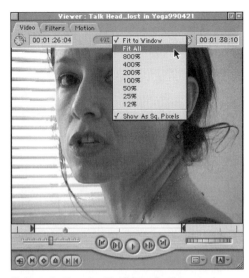

Figure 5.65 Choosing Fit All from the Zoom pop-up menu.

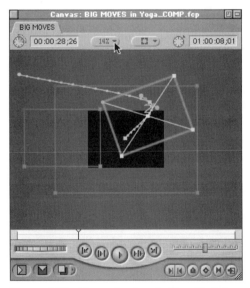

Figure 5.66 The Viewer showing all of the objects in a multi-layered composited sequence. Selecting "Fit All" is the only way to get Viewer zoom level to go below 12.5%.

Figure 5.67 Click the Viewer to make it active.

Figure 5.68 Double-click the Zoom tool in the Tool palette.

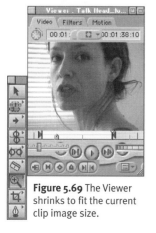

Figure 5.69 The Viewer shrinks to fit the current clip image size.

To shrink the window to the current clip size:

1. Make the Viewer active (**Figure 5.67**).

2. Double-click the Zoom In tool in the Tool palette (**Figure 5.68**).

   The viewer window will shrink to fit the current clip size (**Figure 5.69**).

Viewing Title Safe and Action Safe boundaries

Most NTSC (National Television Standards Committee) television sets don't display the full video image on their screens. Use the Title Safe and Action Safe overlays to be sure that crucial parts of your composition or titles are not cut off at the edges when displayed on a television screen.

✔ Tip

■ Consumer TV sets may trim off the edges of your video, but Web video displays the whole frame, so if you are aiming your show at both Web and TV, you'll need to watch the edges of your frame as well.

To view or hide Title Safe and Action Safe boundaries:

Do one of the following:

◆ Choose View > Title Safe.

◆ From the View pop-up menu at the top of the Viewer, choose Title Safe (**Figure 5.70**).

◆ Choose Title Safe again to switch off the overlay (**Figure 5.71**).

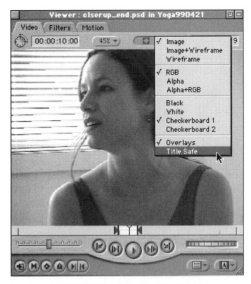

Figure 5.70 Choose Title Safe from the View pop-up menu to display the Title Safe overlay.

Wireframes in the Viewer

Wireframe and Image+Wireframe modes let you view schematic diagrams of the motion effects you apply to a clip or sequence. Wireframe modes are available in both the Canvas and Viewer. You can use the Viewer's View pop-up menu to switch on wireframe mode, but you're more likely to be using wireframe mode in the Canvas. For details on wireframe operation, see Chapter 13, "Compositing and Special Effects."

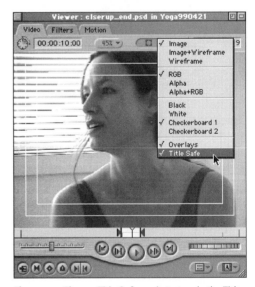

Figure 5.71 Choose Title Safe again to toggle the Title Safe overlay off.

Viewing overlays

Overlays are icons or text displayed on top of the video when the playhead is parked on a significant frame. Overlays indicate significant points, such as In and Out points, in a clip or sequence. Overlays appear only when the Viewer and Canvas are in Pause mode and are not rendered to output. They are displayed by default. Final Cut Pro displays the following overlays **(Figure 5.72)**:

◆ **In and Out points:** These icons appear when the playhead is positioned on the In or Out point frame.

◆ **Start and End of media:** The filmstrip symbol along the left or right side of the video frame indicates the start or end of the video media.

◆ **Start and End of Edits (not shown):** An L shape at the lower left indicates the start of an edit, and a backward L shape at the lower right indicates the end of an edit. These icons appear only in the Canvas.

◆ **Marker:** Marker overlays appear as translucent boxes displaying the marker's name and comment text.

◆ **Title Safe and Action Safe:** Title Safe and Action Safe boundaries are rectangular boxes around the edges of the video.

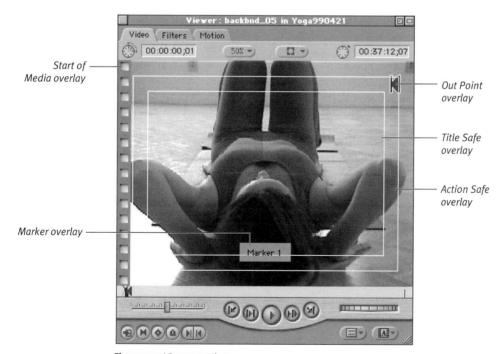

Figure 5.72 Viewer overlays.

To view or hide overlays:

◆ Choose Overlays from the View pop-up menu at the top of the Viewer or Canvas (**Figure 5.73**).

Viewing with different backgrounds

If you are working with a clip that has an alpha channel—say some black generated text that you want to superimpose over video—you can change the default black background of your black text to white, to make the text more visible while you are working with it. Translucent clips will be more visible if you choose a background that emphasizes them. When a clip is rendered, the background is always set to black.

To choose a background for viewing a clip:

Do one of the following:

◆ Choose the desired background from the View Control pop-up menu at the top of the Viewer or Canvas.

◆ From the View menu, select the desired background from the Background sub-menu (**Figure 5.74**).

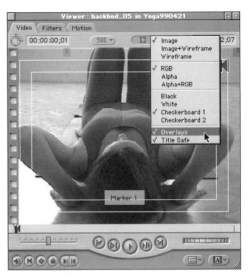

Figure 5.73 Turn off all overlay displays in the Viewer by unchecking Overlays in the View pop-up menu.

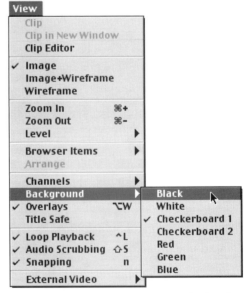

Figure 5.74 Selecting a black background by choosing View > Background > Black.

Anatomy of the Audio Tab

The Audio tab is the Viewer window where you perform review, marking, and editing tasks on single audio clips opened from the Browser or the Timeline. You can see the audio waveforms of your tracks, and in addition to the editing functions, you can also use onscreen controls to adjust the level and stereo pan settings (**Figure 5.75**).

Before you start marking up your audio clips, make sure you understand how and where FCP will save changes you make to your clips. See the sidebar "FCP Protocol: Clips and Sequences" at the beginning of Chapter 4.

✔ Tip

■ Don't use compressed audio as source media when you are editing in FCP. Compressed audio will be distorted during playback and in your final output. It's all right to compress your final output audio when exporting; you have a choice of compression formats.

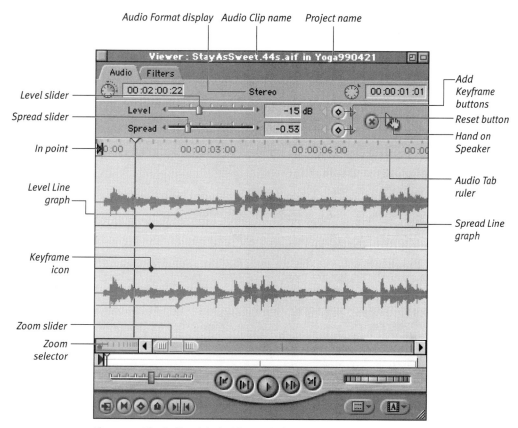

Figure 5.75 The Audio tab in the Viewer window.

Audio tab onscreen controls and displays

Editing digital audio requires different interface tools than editing digital video. When you open an audio clip in the Viewer, a graph of the audio waveform appears on the Audio tab, and the playhead travels across a stationary waveform image.

The Audio tab retains the transport controls from the Video tab interface in the lower part of the window, but it has its own set of onscreen controls in the upper part.

Here's a brief rundown on the onscreen controls unique to the Audio tab (**Figures 5.76 and 5.77**):

◆ **Level slider:** Use to adjust the amplitude or volume of the audio clip.

◆ **Add Keyframe button (top):** Use to place keyframe markers at the current playhead location on the Level line graph in the clip timeline. These keyframe markers can be used for editing audio levels between two points.

◆ **Spread slider:** Use to adjust stereo panning or swapping of left and right channels. Single channel (mono) clips will display a Pan slider here, for left/right positioning of audio.

◆ **Add Keyframe button (bottom):** Use to place keyframe markers at the current playhead location on the Spread line graph in the clip timeline. These keyframe markers can be used for panning audio output between two points.

◆ **Reset (X) button:** Use to delete all marked points in the audio timeline and reset the level and spread values to their original settings.

◆ **Drag Hand:** This is your handle for drag-and-drop editing. Click and drag to move the audio clip with edits to another window, such as the Browser or Timeline.

◆ **Audio tab ruler:** This displays the timecode for the audio displayed. Edit point overlays are displayed along the ruler. You can adjust the time scale with the Zoom slider or the Magnifier.

◆ **Level line graph:** Both a tool and an indicator, it graphs the level changes by indicating the amplitude of the audio. You can also click and drag the Level line graph to adjust the overall level of your audio clip, or you can click and drag keyframes to create dynamic volume effects.

◆ **Spread (or Pan) line graph:** This has the same basic operation as the Level line graph. Click and drag to adjust the spread (for stereo clips) or pan (for mono clips).

◆ **In and Out points:** These appear in both the Scrubber bar and the ruler.

◆ **Zoom selector:** Click to jump between different time scale views.

◆ **Zoom slider:** Use to scroll through your audio file and to adjust the time scale of your view.

✔ Tip

■ You can link two single audio tracks to form a stereo pair. This is a quick way to apply identical level changes to a couple of tracks. You can always unlink them after you have made your level adjustments.

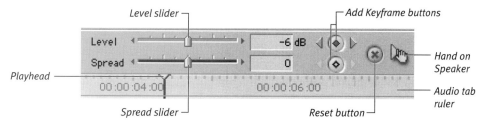

Figure 5.76 Audio tab onscreen controls displayed in the upper half of the window.

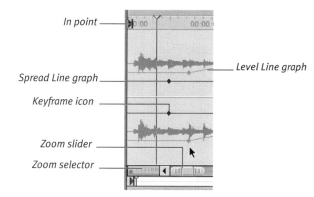

Figure 5.77 Audio tab onscreen controls displayed in the lower half of the window.

ANATOMY OF THE AUDIO TAB

FCP's Audio Formats

When you captured your video clips, you made an audio format selection. The audio format functionality described here applies to the audio captured with video as well as to imported or captured audio-only clips. You can modify the audio format of captured audio using the Modify > Stereo Pair and Modify > Link commands. For example, toggling Stereo Pair off will convert a pair of tracks captured as a stereo pair to Ch 1 + Ch 2 format.

- **Mono Mix:** The audio consists of both channels from the tape mixed into a single track. A single Audio tab appears in the Viewer.

- **Stereo:** Both channels have been captured as a stereo pair. Stereo pairs are always linked, and anything that is applied to one track is applied to both. Waveforms for the two channels that make up the stereo pair appear in a single Audio tab window.

- **Ch 1:** The audio consists of only the left channel from the tape (Ch 1), with pan centered. A single Audio tab appears in the Viewer.

- **Ch 2:** The audio consists of only the right channel from the tape (Ch 2), with pan centered. A single Audio tab appears in the Viewer.

- **Ch 1 + Ch 2:** Both tracks have been captured but are distinct and can be adjusted independently of one another. Two Audio tabs appear in the Viewer.

Using the Viewer's Audio Tab

The capture settings for a clip determine how its audio appears in the Viewer. Stereo clips are panned full left and full right by default, and clips with one or two channels of discrete audio are panned center.

To open an audio clip:

Do one of the following:

◆ Double-click the clip icon in the Browser or Timeline.

◆ Select a clip icon and press Enter.

◆ Select the clip in the Browser or Timeline and choose View > Clip in New Window.

✔ Tip

■ Don't forget: You can stretch the Viewer window across your monitor to make a wide view—great when you're working with audio. You can see more of the clip, which makes marking and level adjustments easier.

To open the audio track for an audio+video clip:

◆ Open the clip in the Viewer and click the Audio tab (**Figure 5.78**).

Figure 5.78 Click the Audio tab to access the audio portion of an audio+video clip.

Figure 5.79 Drag the Zoom slider across the scroll bar to navigate through an audio file. This control doesn't move the playhead, just the view.

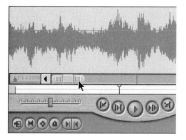

Figure 5.80 Drag the thumb control to vary time scaling. A smaller Zoom slider indicates an expanded time scale.

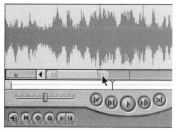

Figure 5.81 Drag the thumb control. A longer Zoom slider indicates a more compressed time scale.

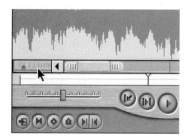

Figure 5.82 Jump to a different time scale with one click using the Zoom selector.

Scaling and scrolling an audio file

The Zoom slider is located along the bottom of the Audio tab. You use it to scroll through your audio file and to adjust the time scale of your view. You can view several minutes of audio in the window or focus on a fraction of a frame. The Zoom slider also appears on the Filters tab, Motion tab, and Timeline.

To scroll through your file:

◆ Drag the Zoom slider across the scroll bar (**Figure 5.79**).

To adjust the time scale:

Do one of the following:

◆ Press CMD-+ (plus) to Zoom in, expanding the time scale, and CMD – (minus) to Zoom out, shrinking the time scale. These Zoom keyboard shortcuts are useful in the Audio tab, because your view stays centered on the current playhead position.

◆ The thumb controls are the ribbed-looking ends of the Zoom slider (**Figure 5.80**). Click on a thumb control and drag it to shrink the time scale and expose more of your audio file (**Figure 5.81**).

◆ Click the Zoom selector to the left of the Zoom slider to jump to a different time scale (**Figure 5.82**).

Setting edit points in the Audio tab

You set In and Out points and markers on the Audio tab in the same way as on the Viewer's Video tab. The overlays for these markers are displayed on the Audio tab ruler at the top of the waveform display.

Because video is captured and stored as frames, the smallest adjustment you can make to a video edit point is a single frame. Digital audio, however, is captured in sub-frames as samples forming a continuous waveform. In FCP, audio edit points can be set to an accuracy of 1/100 frame. The Audio tab is the only place you can make sub-frame adjustments to an audio clip's In and Out points. You are most likely to need this kind of fine-tuning when you are finessing a music edit.

You can also place keyframes with the same precision—a lifesaver when you are working your way through a really good dialogue take with a couple of bad clicks or pops. The sub-frame precision allows you to use audio level keyframes to silence that track just for the few milliseconds it takes to mute the click.

Lost in the Waveforms? Audio Tab Editing Tips

◆ When you're trying to fine tune an audio edit point in the Audio tab, it's easy to lose track of your location as you zoom and scroll through your audio track's waveforms. Here's a navigation method to try while you're editing in the audio tab.:

◆ Start by playing back the clip.

◆ When you hear the spot where you think your edit point should be, tap the space bar to pause the playhead at that spot.

◆ Then use the marquee selection feature of the Zoom tool to draw a narrow selection box around the playhead. You won't lose track of the playhead this way.

◆ When you've zoomed in you can take advantage of the detailed waveform display to get a precision edit. Press I or O to mark your edit point at the current playhead position.

◆ When you're done tweaking, press Option = to Zoom out and fit the clip to the window with a single keystroke.

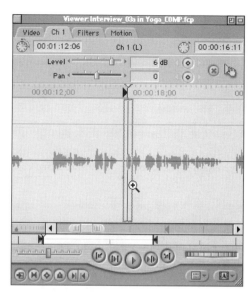

Figure 5.83 Use the Zoom Tool to drag a marquee right around the playhead. When the view zooms in the playhead will still be in view.

To make sub-frame adjustments to an audio clip's edit points:

1. Open the audio clip in the Audio Tab, then jump the playhead to the edit point you want to adjust.

2. Use the marquee selection feature of the Zoom Tool to zoom in until the playhead looks like a bar (**Figure 5.83**).

3. Hold down the Shift key, then click on the Audio tab playhead and drag it to the (sub-frame) location of the new In or Out point (**Figure 5.84**).

4. Press I (or O) to stamp a new In (or Out) point (**Figure 5.85**).

✔ Tip

■ To add an audio keyframe in a location that's not on a frame line, you don't need to adjust the playhead, just zoom way in and use the Pen tool to add the keyframe.

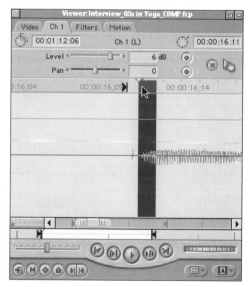

Figure 5.84 Hold down the Shift key, then drag the Audio tab playhead to the exact location of the new In or Out point.

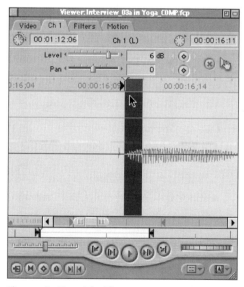

Figure 5.85 Press I (or O) to set a new In point. This In point has been adjusted to trim out the little pop at the beginning of a word.

To drag an audio clip into the Timeline or Canvas window:

1. Start with an open clip and the Viewer window selected.

2. Position the cursor over the Drag Hand icon.

   When the cursor changes to a hand shape, you're in the right spot (**Figure 5.86**).

3. Click and drag from that spot to the Canvas or Timeline.

   This will insert your audio clip into the open sequence (**Figure 5.87**).

Figure 5.86 Click and hold to grab the Drag Hand icon.

Setting audio levels

You can set the volume (level) for individual audio clips in the Viewer's Audio tab by visually editing the line graph that appears as an overlay on your audio waveform.

In the Timeline, you can use the Modify > Levels command to set levels for multiple audio clips in a single operation. See Chapter 7, "Using the Timeline and the Canvas."

Figure 5.87 Drag and drop to insert a clip into a sequence in the Canvas window.

To set audio clip levels:

1. Start with an open clip and the Viewer window selected.

2. *Do one of the following:*

   ▲ Click and drag the Level slider to the right to increase clip volume or to the left to lower clip volume (**Figure 5.88**).

   ▲ Click and drag the pink Level line graph displayed over the audio waveform. Drag higher to increase volume or lower to decrease volume (**Figure 5.89**).

   ▲ Press Control-+ or – to adjust audio levels by single dB increments.

   ▲ Choose Modify > Audio, and make a Gain selection from the submenu (**Figure 5.90**).

Figure 5.88 Dragging the Level slider to the right increases the clip volume.

Figure 5.89 Dragging the Level line graph higher increases the volume.

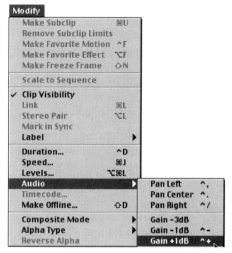

Figure 5.90 Choose Modify > Audio, and make a Gain selection from the submenu. Note the keyboard shortcuts listed to the right of the submenu choices.

Monitor Levels and Mixing

It's important to keep your speaker levels constant when you are adjusting audio levels for a sequence. There's more than one place to adjust your monitoring level. Take a moment before you start working to set up everything, and note your settings so that you can recalibrate if necessary.

If you'll be recording out to an external video deck or camera, check your audio output levels on the recording device's meters. Play the loudest section of your program. If your recording device has no meters, record a test of the loudest section and review the audio quality.

Check the Sound control panel to make sure your computer's sound output level is not set too low. Next, set a comfortable listening level on the amplifier that drives your external speakers. Now you are in a position to make consistent volume adjustments to your clip audio.

To set computer audio levels:

There's no way to adjust computer audio levels within Final Cut Pro. You'll need to adjust your levels from the Sound control panel of your Macintosh (**Figure 5.91**).

Adjusting the pan position

The pan position is the left/right placement of sound for single audio channels. Clips with one or two channels of discrete audio will initially open with pan set to the center.

To set a pan position:

1. Start with an open clip and the Viewer window selected.

2. *Do one of the following:*

    ▲ Click and drag the Pan slider to the right to pan toward the right; drag the slider to the left to pan toward the left (**Figure 5.92**).

    ▲ Click and drag the purple Pan line graph displayed over the audio waveform. Drag higher to pan right; drag lower to pan left (**Figure 5.93**).

    ▲ Choose Modify > Audio, and make a Pan selection from the submenu.

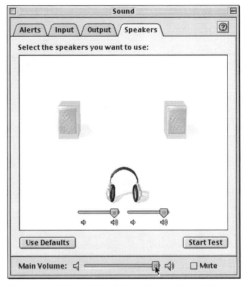

Figure 5.91 The Macintosh Sound control panel.

Figure 5.92 Dragging the Pan slider to the left pans your track toward the left channel.

Figure 5.93 Dragging the Pan line graph lower pans your track toward the left channel.

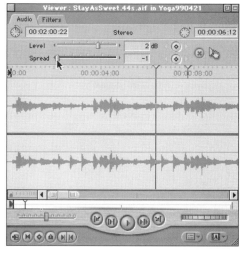

Figure 5.94 Spread slider settings.

Adjusting the spread

The Spread control adjusts the degree of stereo separation, and it adjusts left and right channels simultaneously and equally.

◆ You can use the Spread slider or the Level line graph to adjust the spread. The setting options on the Spread slider are as follows (**Figure 5.94**):

◆ The base setting of –1 outputs the left audio channel to the left and the right audio channel to the right. This setting will accurately reproduce the stereo mix of a track from a music CD.

◆ A setting of 0 outputs the left and right audio channels equally to both sides.

◆ A setting of +1 swaps the channels and outputs the left audio channel to the right and the right audio channel to the left.

To adjust the spread on a stereo track:

1. Start with an open clip and the Viewer window selected.

2. *Do one of the following:*

   ▲ Click and drag the Spread slider to adjust the stereo tracks (see **Figure 5.95**).

   ▲ Click and drag the purple Level line graph displayed over the audio waveform at the center line between the two stereo tracks. Drag away from the center line for a +1 setting; drag toward the center for a –1 setting (**Figure 5.96**).

To turn audio scrubbing off or on:

◆ To turn off audio scrubbing, choose View > Audio Scrubbing (**Figure 5.97**).

◆ To turn audio scrubbing back on, choose View > Audio Scrubbing again.

✔ Tip

■ Turn off audio scrubbing in the Viewer to mute your clip's audio when you scrub the playhead or use the jog wheel.

Figure 5.95 The Spread slider at its base setting of –1. This setting replicates the original mix of a stereo source track.

Figure 5.96 Drag the Spread line toward the center for a –1 setting.

Figure 5.97 Choose View > Audio Scrubbing to enable audible scrubbing in the Viewer.

Figure 5.98 Move the playhead to the location where you want the level change to start.

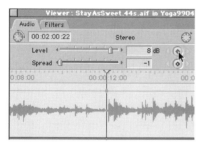

Figure 5.99 Adjust the level with the Level slider and click the Set Keyframe button to set a keyframe.

Figure 5.100 Move the playhead to the next location where you want a level change. Another keyframe will be set automatically.

To create dynamic level changes within a clip:

1. Start with an open clip and the Viewer window selected.

2. Park the playhead where you want to start the level change (**Figure 5.98**).

3. Adjust the level using the Level slider.

4. Set a keyframe by clicking the Set Keyframe button to the right of the Level slider (**Figure 5.99**).

5. Move the playhead to the next location where you want a change in the level.

6. Adjust the level with the Level slider (**Figure 5.100**).

   Another keyframe will be set automatically when you adjust the Level slider.

✔ Tips

- Using the Set Keyframe button in the lower part of the screen will set a keyframe on both the Level and Spread line graphs at the current playhead position.

- There's a lot more you can do with keyframes. Keyframes are discussed in more detail in Chapter 13, "Compositing and Special Effects."

EDITING IN
FINAL CUT PRO

In this chapter, you'll get an overview of the underlying concepts and protocols that govern editing in Final Cut Pro: sequences, three-point editing, multiple media tracks, and various edit types.

You'll learn about the basic procedures for performing edits in Final Cut Pro and how to use the seven edit types available in FCP.

A more detailed discussion of Timeline and Canvas window operations appears in Chapter 7, "Using the Timeline and the Canvas."

The Timeline displays a chronological view of a sequence. All of the media elements you have assembled to create a sequence appear in the Timeline as elements that diagram the sequencing and layering of audio and video tracks. As you drag the playhead along the Timeline ruler, the current frame of the sequence is updated in the Canvas window.

The Canvas looks like the Viewer and has many of the same controls. If you're assembling your edit by dragging clips into the Timeline, the Canvas shows what the sequence will actually look like when it is played (if you have added effects, FCP will need to render the sequence before you can play back the results of your work). You can also edit in Final Cut Pro using only the Viewer (your source monitor) and the Canvas (your record monitor).

The Timeline and Canvas windows work together. Any changes you make to the sequence in the Canvas will be reflected in the Timeline; you'll see results of any Timeline changes when you play your sequence back in the Canvas window.

If you have multiple sequences open, the Timeline and Canvas will display a tab for each sequence.

What's a Sequence?

A sequence is an edited assembly of audio and video clips. Sequences are the middle level of the FCP organizing framework (**Figure 6.1**). A sequence is always part of a project, and you can have multiple sequences in a project.

Once you've assembled a sequence, that sequence can be manipulated as if it were a single clip. You can open a sequence and play it in the Viewer, mark In and Out points, and insert all or parts of that sequence into another sequence, just as if it were a clip. Inserting a sequence into another sequence creates what's known as a nested sequence. (See Chapter 12, "Big Picture: Managing Complex Projects.")

Creating a new sequence

A new project in FCP will automatically gen-erate a new untitled sequence in your default sequence format.

Note that you probably won't need to change sequence presets unless you change your audio or video input device. Final Cut Pro selects your default preset based on setup information you supplied when you installed the program. To learn how to set sequence preset preferences, see "Specifying Sequence Settings" in Chapter 2.

To add a new sequence to the current project:

1. Choose File > New > Sequence; or press Command-N.

    A new sequence with a default, high-lighted name appears at the top level of the current bin (**Figure 6.2**).

2. Type a new name for the sequence to rename it (**Figure 6.3**).

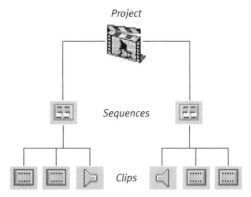

Figure 6.1 Sequences are the middle level of the FCP organizing framework.

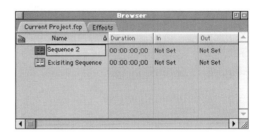

Figure 6.2 New sequence with a default, highlighted name.

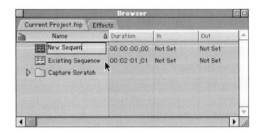

Figure 6.3 Type a new name for the sequence.

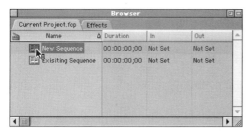

Figure 6.4 Control-click the sequence's icon.

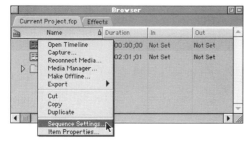

Figure 6.5 Choose Sequence Settings.

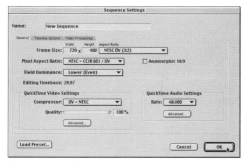

Figure 6.6 Modify the sequence settings and click OK.

✔ Tip

■ You can still select a different sequence preset for a new sequence by pressing the Option key when choosing the New Sequence command.

To modify sequence settings:

1. Control-click the sequence's icon in the Browser (**Figure 6.4**).

2. Choose Sequence Settings from the shortcut menu (**Figure 6.5**).

3. Modify your sequence settings (**Figure 6.6**). Then click OK. See Chapter 2, "Welcome to Final Cut Pro," for information on the options in the Sequence Settings dialog box.

To open a sequence for editing:

Do one of the following:

◆ Double-click the sequence in the Browser (**Figure 6.7**).

◆ Control-click the sequence's icon; then choose Open Timeline from the shortcut menu.

◆ Select the sequence; then choose View > Sequence Editor.

The sequence opens in both the Canvas and the Timeline (**Figure 6.8**).

✔ Tip

■ You can import an Edit Decision List created in another application and use it to create an FCP sequence. For details, see the EDL discussion in Chapter 11, "At Last: Creating Final Output."

To open a sequence in the Viewer:

1. Start in the Browser with the sequence selected.

2. *Do one of the following:*

   ▲ Choose View > Sequence to see the sequence in the Viewer window (**Figure 6.9**).

   ▲ Choose View > Sequence in New Window to see the sequence in a new Viewer window.

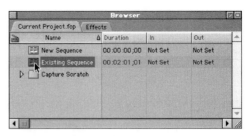

Figure 6.7 Double-click the sequence's icon in the Browser to open it for editing.

Figure 6.8 The sequence opens in the Canvas and the Timeline.

Figure 6.9 Choose View › Sequence to see the sequence in the Viewer.

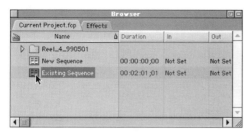

Figure 6.10 Select the sequence in the Browser.

Figure 6.11 Choose Edit › Duplicate.

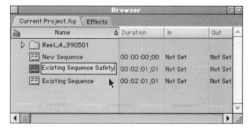

Figure 6.12 Rename the sequence copy.

To duplicate a sequence:

1. Select the sequence in the Browser (**Figure 6.10**).

2. Choose Edit > Duplicate (**Figure 6.11**); or press Option-D.

3. In the Browser, rename the sequence copy with a unique name (**Figure 6.12**).

✔ Tip

■ The copy procedure described here is a convenient way to "safety copy" a version of a sequence and associated media files after a long rendering process. Any changes you make to the duplicate sequence will not affect the original sequence or its render files.

To copy a sequence from one project to another:

1. Select the sequence in the Browser.

2. Choose File > Copy; or press Command-C.

3. Open the second project and select its tab in the Browser.

4. Choose File > Paste; or press Command-V.

   The sequence now appears in both projects. The two copies of the sequence will reference the same source media files on disk, but you'll need to re-render any previously rendered sequence material in the new project location.

✔ Tip

■ You can also create a copy of a sequence by dragging it from one project window and dropping it on the destination project's Browser tab.

New in 2: Time Stamp for Sequences

A small but thoughtful improvement in FCP 2.0: the new Last Modified column in the Browser makes it easy to find the most recently revised version of your sequence—a real life saver when you need to revisit a project after a long absence (or a long night).

WHAT'S A SEQUENCE?

Specifying target tracks

Each time you add clips to a sequence, you can specify which tracks the media will occupy. You specify target tracks using the Timeline's target track controls (**Figure 6.13**): the speaker and film icons located on the left of the Timeline. You can specify a maximum of three target tracks at a time: two for audio and one for video.

To select target tracks in the Timeline:

◆ In the Timeline, click the target track control at the left side of the track you want to use.

The control is highlighted in yellow when targeting is on (**Figure 6.14**).

To use audio only from an audio+video clip:

◆ Click to turn off the video target track before you perform your edit (**Figure 6.15**).

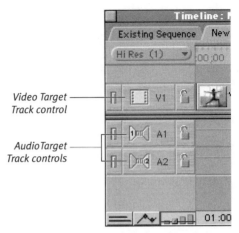

Video Target Track control

Audio Target Track controls

Figure 6.13 The target track controls in the Timeline.

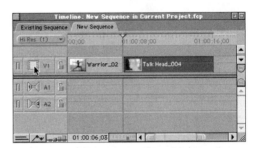

Figure 6.14 Setting a target track by clicking the Video target track control. The control is highlighted in yellow when targeting is on.

Figure 6.15 Click to turn off the Video target track control. Audio tracks remain targeted.

FCP Protocol: Target Tracks

◆ Once you have specified target tracks, your edits will use the same target tracks until you change your target selection.

◆ When you insert a clip into a sequence by dragging it to a specific track in the Timeline, the clip will be placed on that track even if you did not target it previously.

◆ If the target track is locked, it will not accept any additional audio or video.

Figure 6.16 Double-click the new sequence's icon in the Browser to open it for editing.

Figure 6.17 Double-click the clip to open it in the Viewer.

Basic Editing Step by Step

Here's a step-by-step breakdown of a simple rough-assembly-style edit in Final Cut Pro. After you've reviewed this basic editing procedure, find out how to perform more specific types of edits in the sections that follow.

To add the first clip to your sequence:

1. In the Browser, press Command-N to create a new sequence.

2. Double-click the new sequence to open it in the Canvas and Timeline (**Figure 6.16**).

3. In the Browser, double-click the first clip you want to insert in your new sequence to open that clip in the Viewer (**Figure 6.17**).

   Before you insert a clip in a sequence, you need to specify the target tracks (the destination tracks for your clip in the sequence).

4. Set the target tracks for your first clip by clicking the target track controls in the Timeline (**Figure 6.18**).

continues on next page

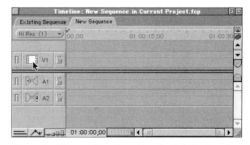

Figure 6.18 To specify a target track, click the target track icon in the Timeline.

BASIC EDITING STEP BY STEP

219

5. Select the portion of the clip you want to use in the sequence by setting In and Out points on your source clip (**Figure 6.19**). (See Chapter 5, "Introducing the Viewer.")

6. Click and drag the clip from the image area of the Viewer to the Canvas window.

The Canvas edit overlay menu will appear.

7. Drop the clip on the Overwrite edit area (**Figure 6.20**). (Overwrite is the default edit type in FCP unless you specify another type.)

The clip will be inserted at the beginning of your new sequence.

Many Ways to Make an Edit

Dragging your source clip to the Canvas edit overlay is just one way to execute an edit in Final Cut Pro. Once you have defined your edit points, you can also do the following:

◆ Drag the clip directly to the Timeline (**Figure 6.21**).

◆ Use the edit buttons on the Canvas (**Figure 6.22**)

◆ Use a keyboard shortcut to perform the edit.

Figure 6.19 Marking an Out point in the source clip.

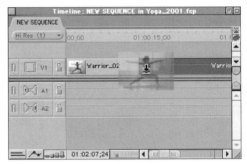

Figure 6.21 You can edit by dragging a clip directly from the Browser or Viewer and dropping it into a sequence in the Timeline.

Figure 6.20 Drag the source clip from the Viewer to the Canvas edit overlay; then drop the clip on the Overwrite edit area.

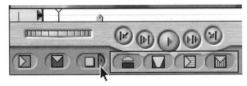

Figure 6.22 You can perform an edit by clicking an edit button in the Canvas. Edit button ToolTips display the keyboard shortcut for that type of edit.

FCP Protocol: Three-Point Editing

To perform most edits, an editing system needs four points specified: In and Out points for your source clip (defining the part of the clip to use) and In and Out points in the sequence you are assembling (defining the clip's new location in the sequence).

In a three-point edit, you can define any three points of an edit, and Final Cut Pro will calculate the fourth point for you.

Here's an example of three-point editing:

1. Specify In and Out points for your source clip.

2. Park the playhead in the Canvas at the sequence In point (the point where you want your new clip to start).

When you insert the new clip into your sequence, Final Cut Pro uses the duration of the new clip insert to calculate the sequence Out point.

At least three edit points must be set in the Viewer and Canvas to perform an edit. But if you specify fewer than three points and perform an edit, FCP will calculate your edit based on the following protocols:

◆ If no In or Out point is set in the Canvas, the Canvas playhead location is used as the sequence In point.

◆ If no In or Out point is set in the source, FCP assumes that you want to use the entire source clip. The playhead's location in the sequence (Timeline and Canvas) is used as the sequence In point. FCP calculates the Out point for the sequence.

◆ If one edit point (In or Out) is set in a source clip, the second point is the beginning or end of media (depending on whether the user-defined point is an In or an Out point). The Canvas playhead is used as the sequence In point, and FCP calculates the Out point.

There are two exceptions to the FCP's three-point editing rules:

◆ Fit to Fill editing requires four user-specified points, because FCP will adjust the speed of the specified source clip to fill a specified sequence duration.

◆ Replace Editing ignores the In and Out points set in the source clip and uses the boundaries of the clip under the Canvas playhead as sequence In and Out points. Replace edits affect the target-track media. To replace an audio track, turn off targeting for all video tracks.

◆ If In and Out points are set for both the source clip and the sequence, FCP ignores the source clip's Out point and uses the clip's In point and the sequence's In and Out points.

To insert additional clips:

1. In the Canvas, park the playhead on the frame where you want your new clip to start (**Figure 6.23**). You can press I to set a sequence In point on that frame, but it's not required.

2. In the Viewer, set In and Out points on your second clip (**Figure 6.24**).

3. Click and drag the clip from the image area of the Viewer to the Canvas window. The Canvas edit overlay menu will appear.

4. Drop the clip on the Overwrite edit area (**Figure 6.25**).

   The second clip will be inserted starting at the sequence In point (**Figure 6.26**).

Figure 6.23 Position the Canvas playhead to set a sequence In point.

Figure 6.25 Drag the second source clip to the Canvas edit overlay; then drop the clip on the Overwrite edit area.

Figure 6.24 The second source clip, displayed in the Viewer with In and Out points set.

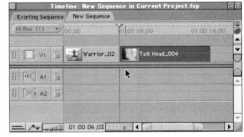

Figure 6.26 The sequence displayed in the Timeline, with the second clip inserted at the sequence In point.

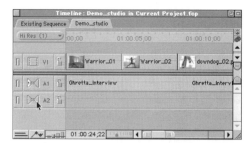

Figure 6.27 With A2 targeting turned off, channel 2 audio is excluded from the sequence.

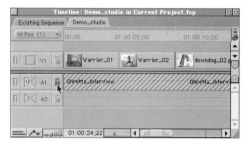

Figure 6.28 Clicking the track lock control prevents further changes in this audio track.

To use one channel of two-channel audio from the source clip:

◆ Click to turn off the target indicator of the track you want to exclude (**Figure 6.27**).

To lock a track:

◆ Click the track lock control on the left of the Timeline (**Figure 6.28**).

Moving the playhead

You can jump the playhead to the edit point of your choice with a single keystroke or mouse click. Most of these shortcuts work in the Viewer as well.

To move the playhead to the In point:

◆ Press Shift-I; or Shift-click the In point icon in the Canvas Scrubber bar.

To move the playhead to the Out point:

◆ Press Shift-O; or Shift-click the Out point icon in the Canvas Scrubber bar.

To jump the playhead to an adjacent edit point:

Do one of the following:

◆ Click the Previous Edit or Next Edit button in the transport controls.

◆ Press the Up or Down Arrow key.

◆ Open the Mark menu and choose from the Next or Previous submenu.

◆ Press Option-E (to go to the previous edit point) or Shift-E (to go to the next edit point).

✔ Tip

■ If you need to define the edit points for a clip, you'll find information on marking In and Out points on a source clip in Chapter 5, "Introducing the Viewer."

BASIC EDITING STEP BY STEP

FCP Protocol: Editing Multiple Tracks in Final Cut Pro

Final Cut Pro sequences can have multiple video and audio tracks. The first video clip you add to a sequence will be the base layer (V1). Any video frames you place on track 2 are superimposed over any video frames at the same point in time on track 1. In a sequence with multiple layers, the base track becomes the background, and media on each higher-numbered track obscures the media on tracks below it. The result appears in the Canvas (after a little rendering).

Audio tracks A1 and A2 are the designated base tracks for stereo audio. Final Cut Pro can mix and play back several audio tracks in a sequence in real time.

How many audio tracks?

The number of audio tracks you use depends on your Macintosh's configuration (available RAM, processor speed, data transfer rate of your hard drive, and so on) and the number of audio transitions you have specified in your sequence. You can specify the number of tracks you want FCP to attempt to handle in real time by setting the Real-Time Audio Mixing preference (see "Using Preferences and Presets" in Chapter 2). However, increasing your real-time audio track budget is no guarantee that you'll be able to play back the number of tracks you specify in Preferences, and if you set this preference too high, you could trigger dropped frames during playback or dropouts in audio.

Eight tracks of real-time audio is the FCP default setup, but you can have up to 99 tracks in a sequence.

In calculating the number of audio tracks you need for a sequence, note that each simultaneous audio crossfade or transition increases the track count by one. So if your sequence requires seven audio tracks, adding a pair of crossfades increases the count to nine tracks and requires rendering to preview.

You can reduce your audio track overhead by choosing Mixdown Audio from the Sequence menu. Mixdown Audio renders all of the audio tracks in a sequence along with their transitions, and it filters and consolidates your tracks into one render file. For more information on nesting items, see "Working with Multiple Sequences" in Chapter 12.

BASIC EDITING STEP BY STEP

Performing Edits in the Canvas

When you perform an edit in Final Cut Pro by dragging a clip directly into the Canvas video frame, the Canvas edit overlay appears with fields for each type of edit (**Figure 6.29**). You can select the type of edit you want to perform by dropping your clip on the appropriate

overlay area. The default edit type is an Overwrite edit.

You can also perform edits in the Canvas by dragging your source clip to one of the edit buttons at the bottom of the Canvas window.

Following is a rundown of the various types of edits you can perform in FCP, along with any variations they impose on the basic editing procedure.

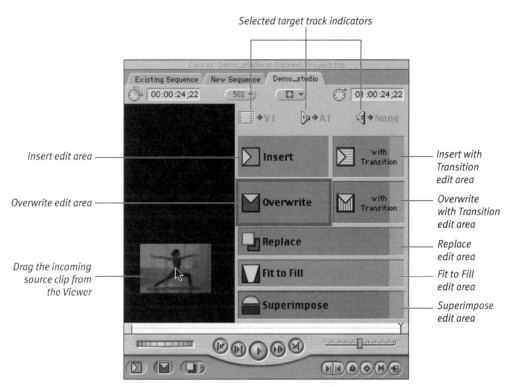

Figure 6.29 The Canvas edit overlay allows drag-and-drop editing for seven types of edits.

Insert edit

An Insert edit puts a source clip into a sequence by pushing back the part of the sequence that's past the sequence In point. This makes room for the new source clip.

To perform an Insert edit:

1. Set the sequence In point by positioning the Canvas playhead where you want the edit to occur (**Figure 6.30**).

2. Drag the clip from the Viewer to the Insert edit overlay or button in the Canvas (**Figure 6.31**); or press F9.

✔ Tip

■ You can set up a back time edit by marking your source and sequence Out points, along with one of your In points. FCP will calculate the other In point and back your clip in.

Figure 6.30 Position the Canvas playhead to set your sequence In point.

Figure 6.31 Drag the source clip from the Viewer to the Canvas edit overlay; then drop the clip on the Insert edit area.

Figure 6.32 Position the Canvas playhead to set your sequence In point.

Figure 6.33 Drag the source clip from the Viewer to the Canvas edit overlay; then drop the clip on the Overwrite edit area.

Overwrite edit

In an Overwrite edit, the source clip overwrites sequence clips past the sequence In point. Overwrite edits use the source In and Out points to calculate the edit duration. The sequence material is replaced by the incoming source clip, with no time shift in the existing sequence.

To perform an Overwrite edit:

1. Set the sequence In point by positioning the Canvas playhead where you want the edit to occur (**Figure 6.32**).

2. Drag the clip from the Viewer to the Overwrite overlay or button in the Canvas (**Figure 6.33**); or press F10.

Replace edit

A Replace edit replaces the contents of a sequence clip with source clip material. You can use a Replace edit to simply replace a shot in a sequence with footage from another shot with the same duration. Replace editing can also be a powerful tool for matching action in a sequence. You can park the Canvas playhead on a particular frame you want to match with a frame from your source clip and then mark In and Out points in the Canvas to select the section of the sequence you want to replace with the new material. The material between the sequence In and Out points is replaced by corresponding material from the source clip on either side of the frame that was matched. The Replace edit uses the Viewer's actual playhead position, not the In and Out points, to calculate the Replace edit; your source In and Out points will be ignored. If you don't set sequence In and Out points, FCP uses the boundaries of the clip under the Canvas playhead.

To perform a Replace edit:

1. Position the Viewer playhead on the frame you want to match with a frame in the Canvas (**Figure 6.34**).

2. Position the Canvas playhead on the frame you want to match with the one selected in the Viewer (**Figure 6.35**).

3. Drag the clip from the Viewer to the Replace overlay or button in the Canvas; or press F11.

   Figure 6.36 shows the Timeline before the Replace edit; **Figure 6.37** shows the Timeline after the Replace edit.

✔ Tip

■ Use the Replace edit technique to replace a clip with an offset copy of itself. This is a shortcut to adjust the timing of action in a clip or to sync action to music.

Figure 6.34 Position the Viewer playhead on the frame you want to match with a frame in the Canvas.

Figure 6.35 Position the Canvas playhead on the frame you want to match with a frame in the Viewer.

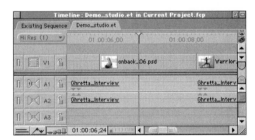

Figure 6.36 In the Timeline, the sequence before the Replace edit.

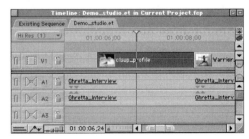

Figure 6.37 The same sequence after performing the Replace edit. The new clip replaces the old, using the match frame you selected as the sync point.

Figure 6.38 Marking a sequence Out point in the Canvas. Setting the sequence In and Out points defines the section you want to fill.

Figure 6.39 Marking a source Out point in the Viewer. Setting source In and Out points defines the section you want to fit into the sequence.

Fit to Fill edit

In a Fit to Fill edit, the speed of the source clip is modified to fill the duration specified by the sequence In and Out points; the clip must be rendered before the edit can be played back.

To perform a Fit to Fill edit:

1. In the Canvas, set the speed of the sequence In and Out points to define the part of the sequence you want to fill (**Figure 6.38**).

2. In the Viewer, set source In and Out points to define the part of the source clip you want to add to the sequence (**Figure 6.39**).

3. Drag the clip in the Viewer to the Fit to Fill overlay or button in the Canvas (**Figure 6.40**); or press Shift-F11.

Figure 6.40 Drag the source clip from the Viewer to the Canvas edit overlay; then drop the clip on the Fit to Fill edit area. The source clip changes speed to fit the sequence In and Out duration.

PERFORMING EDITS IN THE CANVAS

229

Superimpose edit

In a Superimpose edit, the source clip is placed on a new track above the target track, starting at the sequence In point (**Figure 6.41**). The target track is not changed. If the clip has audio, the source audio is added to new tracks below the target audio track.

To perform a Superimpose edit:

1. Position the Canvas playhead or set sequence In and Out points where you want the source clip to start (**Figure 6.42**).

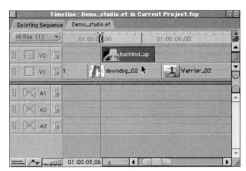

Figure 6.41 The source clip is placed on a new track above the target track, starting at the sequence In point.

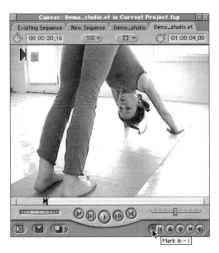

Figure 6.42 Setting a sequence In point where you want your superimposition to begin.

2. In the Viewer, set source In and Out points to define the part of the source clip you want to add to the sequence (**Figure 6.43**).

3. Drag the clip from the Viewer to the Superimpose overlay or button in the Canvas (**Figure 6.44**); or press F12.

Figure 6.43 In the Viewer, set source In and Out points to specify the part of the source clip that you want to superimpose on the sequence.

Figure 6.44 Drag the source clip from the Viewer to the Canvas edit overlay; then drop the clip on the Superimpose edit area.

Figure 6.45 Positioning the Canvas playhead to set a sequence In point.

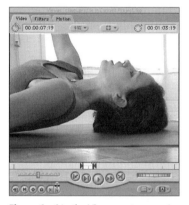

Figure 6.46 In the Viewer, set source In and Out points to specify the part of the source clip that you want to use.

Figure 6.47 Drag the source clip from the Viewer to the Canvas edit overlay; drop it on the Transition edit area.

Transition edits

There are two types of transition edits: Insert with Transition and Overwrite with Transition. A transition edit automatically places your default transition at the head of the edit. You'll have to render transition edits before you can play them back. When using either of the transition edit types, you'll need enough footage in your source clip to create the transition. Each source clip will need additional frames equal to half of the transition's duration.

To perform a Transition edit:

1. Set the sequence In point by positioning the Canvas playhead where you want the edit to occur (**Figure 6.45**).

2. In the Viewer, set source In and Out points to define the part of the source clip you want to add to the sequence (**Figure 6.46**).

3. Drag the clip from the Viewer to either the Insert with Transition or the Overwrite with Transition edit overlay in the Canvas (**Figure 6.47**); or press Shift-0 (zero).

   The source clip is inserted in the sequence with the default transition (**Figure 6.48**).

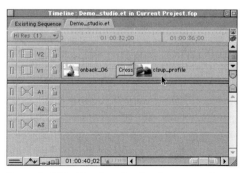

Figure 6.48 The Timeline, showing the source clip inserted into the sequence with the default transition at the head.

To set your default transition:

1. In the Browser, Control-click the effect you want to designate as your default transition (**Figure 6.49**).

2. From the shortcut menu, choose Set Default Transition (**Figure 6.50**)

   The default transition appears underlined in the Browser (**Figure 6.51**).

✔ Tip

■ Once you've customized a transition in your sequence, you can select it in the Timeline, drag it to your Favorites folder in the Browser, and then set it as the default transition. It's so easy to set up a customized default transition that it's worth doing so even if you're building a fairly short sequence.

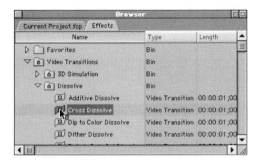

Figure 6.49 Control-click the transition icon to access the shortcut menu.

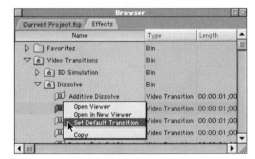

Figure 6.50 From the shortcut menu, choose Set Default Transition.

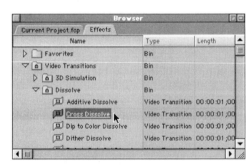

Figure 6.51 The name of the default transition appears underlined in the Browser.

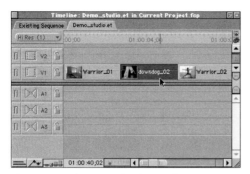

Figure 6.52 A clip selected in the Timeline. Press Delete to perform a Lift edit by deleting the clip from the sequence, or press Command-X to cut the clip for pasting elsewhere.

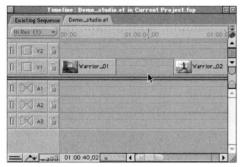

Figure 6.53 The sequence after a Lift edit. The rest of the sequence clips hold their positions.

Deleting clips from a sequence

Two types of edits can be used to remove material from a sequence:

◆ **Lift** removes the selected material, leaving a gap.

◆ **Ripple Delete** removes the selected material and closes the gap.

To perform a Lift edit:

Do one of the following:

◆ Select the clip in the Timeline and press Delete.

◆ Select the clip in the Timeline and then choose Sequence > Lift.

◆ Select the clip in the Timeline and press Command-X (Cut).

◆ Control-click the selected clip in the Timeline; then choose Cut from the shortcut menu. (Use Cut if you want to paste the deleted clip in another location in the sequence.)

Figure 6.52 shows a sequence in the Timeline before a Lift edit; **Figure 6.53** shows the same sequence after a Lift edit.

To perform a Ripple Delete edit:

Do one of the following:

◆ Select the clip in the Timeline and press Shift-Delete.

◆ Select the clip in the Timeline; then choose Sequence > Ripple Delete.

◆ Control-click the selected clip in the Timeline (**Figure 6.54**); then choose Ripple Delete from the shortcut menu (**Figure 6.55**).

The clip is deleted from the sequence, and the material on all unlocked tracks to the right of the sequence is pulled up to close the gap (**Figure 6.56**).

✔ Tip

■ You can delete a precisely defined section of a sequence by setting sequence In and Out points to mark the section you want to remove and then pressing Delete to lift the section or pressing Shift-Delete to ripple delete.

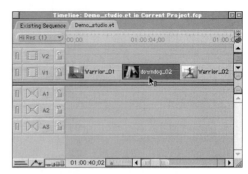

Figure 6.54 Control-click the selected sequence clip to access the shortcut menu.

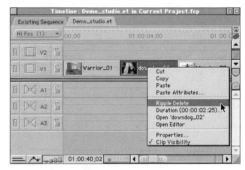

Figure 6.55 From the shortcut menu, choose Ripple Delete.

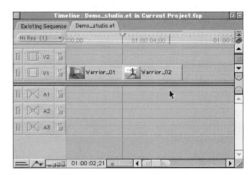

Figure 6.56 The sequence after a Ripple Delete edit. Material to the right of the deleted clip has been pulled up to close the gap.

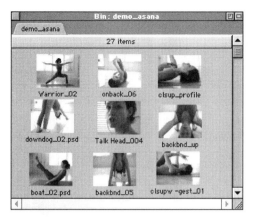

Figure 6.57 Using the Large Icon view of the Browser, arrange clip icons in storyboard order.

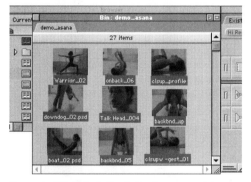

Figure 6.58 Select all clips in the Browser and drag them to the Timeline.

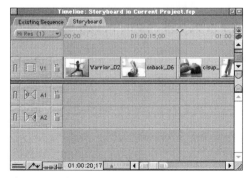

Figure 6.59 The sequence assembles clips in storyboard order.

Performing Edits in the Timeline

Editing in the Timeline can be a faster way to go, particularly when you're in the early stages of assembly.

You have a number of ways to control the size and time scale of the Timeline window. You need the Timeline's "big picture" view of your edited sequence when you're deploying multiple tracks of visual or sound effects, but you can also zoom way in when you need to perform very precise work. See Chapter 7, "Using the Timeline and the Canvas," for details.

◆ You can assemble a sequence by dragging clips directly to the Timeline from the Browser or Viewer.

◆ You can use the Browser Sort function to sort your takes by timecode or by shot number and then drag a whole group of clips from the Browser directly to the Timeline. FCP will place the clips in the Timeline based on your Browser sort order.

◆ You can construct a storyboard in the Browser (use the Large Icon view; **Figure 6.57**) and then drag all of the clips into the Timeline (**Figure 6.58**). If the Browser tab from which you drag the clips is in Icon mode, the clips are placed in left-to-right order, from top to bottom (**Figure 6.59**).

◆ You can designate target tracks in an edit just by dragging a source clip directly to the destination track.

◆ Drag a source clip to the space above your existing tracks, and FCP will automatically create a new track for you.

To perform an Insert edit:

◆ Drag the source clip from the Viewer or Browser to the upper third of the Timeline track (**Figure 6.60**).

The pointer changes to indicate the type of edit.

To perform an Overwrite edit:

◆ Drag the source clip from the Viewer or Browser to the lower two-thirds of the Timeline track (**Figure 6.61**).

✔ Tips

■ If you drag a clip in to the Timeline when it is set to the smallest timeline track size. you'll perform an Overwrite edit. Hold down the Option key to perform an Insert edit.

■ When you drag a clip from the Browser onto a clip or transition in the Timeline, a two-up display appears in the Canvas. This two-up display shows the frame just before your insert on the left, and it shows the frame just after your insert on the right. The names of the sequence clips adjacent to your edit point appear at the top of each display, and the timecode of the displayed frames appears at the bottom of the display (**Figure 6.62**).

Figure 6.60 Dragging a clip to the upper third of the Timeline track performs an Insert edit.

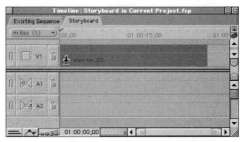

Figure 6.61 Dragging a clip to the lower two-thirds of the Timeline track performs an Overwrite edit.

Figure 6.62 When you drop a clip directly into the Timeline, the Canvas displays details about the two clips adjacent to your edit point.

Figure 6.63 Position the Viewer playhead at the Video In point.

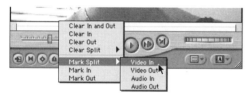

Figure 6.64 Control-click anywhere on the Scrubber bar to call up the shortcut menu; then choose Mark Split > Video In.

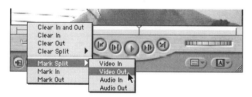

Figure 6.65 Reposition the playhead; then use the Scrubber shortcut menu again to mark the Video Out point.

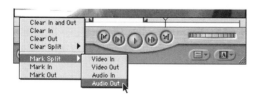

Figure 6.66 Using the Scrubber shortcut menu to mark the Audio Out point. (You can also switch to the clip's Audio tab to do this.)

Performing Split Edits

A split edit sets different In and Out points for video and audio in a single clip. Split edits are commonly used in cutting synchronized dialogue scenes. You can mark a split edit before you insert a clip into a sequence for the first time (as shown here), but a common split edit approach to a dialogue sequence might start by making straight cuts of both video and audio tracks based on the rhythm of the dialogue and then going back and using the Roll tool to adjust the edit points on the video track only.

Another approach is to include only video or only audio in your edit by targeting only the video or audio track in the Timeline.

To mark a split edit:

1. With the clip open in the Viewer, position the playhead where you want the video to begin (**Figure 6.63**).

2. Control-click the Scrubber bar; then choose Mark Split > Video In from the shortcut menu (**Figure 6.64**).

3. Reposition the playhead at your desired Out point and choose Mark Split > Video Out from the shortcut menu (**Figure 6.65**).

4. Repeat the process to set your Audio In and Out points (**Figure 6.66**). You could also choose to switch to your clip's Audio tab and mark the audio there.

✔ Tip

- Check out the appendix for the keyboard shortcuts to mark split edits on the fly.

To move split edit points:

◆ Open the clip in the Viewer. In the Scrubber bar, click and drag either the In points or the Out points to a new position.

The video and audio edit points move in tandem in a split edit (**Figure 6.67**).

To slip all split edit points at once:

◆ In the Scrubber bar, press Shift while dragging any of the edit points.

All of the edit points move in unison (**Figure 6.68**).

The respective video and audio durations specified in the split edit don't change, but the frames that are included in the marked clip shift.

✔ Tip

■ As you slip a split edit, the updated In point frame with the timecode for the edit point you selected is displayed on the Viewer image, and the edit's Out point frame with timecode is displayed on the Canvas. Awesome.

To move only one edit point in a split edit:

◆ In the Scrubber bar, press Option as you drag the edit point you want to modify (**Figure 6.69**).

A display pops up as you drag to indicate the duration of the offset between Video In and Audio In, or Video Out and Audio Out. The Scrubber bar in the Viewer updates to reflect the new edit points.

To remove a split edit point:

◆ In the Scrubber bar, control-click; then choose Clear Split and, from the shortcut submenu, select the point to want to clear (**Figure 6.70**).

Figure 6.67 Moving split In points by dragging them in the Scrubber. The Audio and Video In points will shift in tandem. Video edit points appear in the top half of the Scrubber; audio points appear in the bottom half.

Figure 6.68 Shift-dragging moves all four points at once. The timecode readout in the Viewer displays the current In point location of the point that you drag.

Figure 6.69 Option-click and drag to shift only one edit point in a split edit. The pop-up display shows the offset duration between Video and Audio Out points.

Figure 6.70 Clearing a Video In point using the Scrubber shortcut menu. Control-click the Scrubber to access this menu.

Figure 6.71 In the Timeline, place the playhead over the clip that you want to use to mark the sequence.

Figure 6.72 Check that the selected clip is on the target track. The target track icon is highlighted in yellow.

Figure 6.73 Choose Mark > Mark Clip.

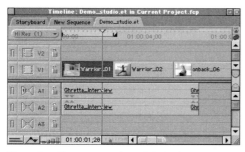

Figure 6.74 The sequence In and Out points are set to match the boundaries of the clip.

Setting Sequence In and Out Points

Use the same commands and keyboard shortcuts that you use to mark In and Out points in the Viewer to mark your sequence In and Out points in the Timeline and Canvas.

FCP also offers a couple of handy commands specifically for marking edit points in a sequence:

◆ Use the Mark Clip command to set the sequence In and Out points to match the edit points of a particular clip in the sequence.

◆ Use Mark Selection to set the sequence In and Out points to match a multiple-clip selection or a selection that includes only part of a clip.

To use the Mark Clip command:

1. Place the playhead over a clip in the Timeline (**Figure 6.71**).

2. Check that your selected clip's track is the target track (**Figure 6.72**).

3. Choose Mark > Mark Clip (**Figure 6.73**). The sequence In and Out points are set to match the boundaries of the clip (**Figure 6.74**).

✔ Tip

■ Mark Clip is a quick way to mark sequence In and Out points if you want to superimpose something over a particular clip.

To use the Mark Selection command:

1. Make a selection in the Timeline. The selection can range from a part of a single clip to an entire sequence (**Figure 6.75**).

2. Check that your selected clips' track is the target track (**Figure 6.76**).

3. Choose Mark > Mark Selection (**Figure 6.77**).

   The sequence In and Out points are set to the boundaries of the selection (**Figure 6.78**).

Figure 6.75 Selecting a region of the sequence. Use Range Select from the toolbar if you want to include just part of a clip.

Figure 6.76 Check that the selected region is on the target track. The target track icon is highlighted in yellow.

Figure 6.77 Choose Mark > Mark Selection.

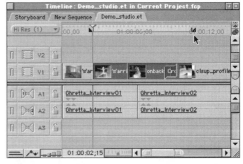

Figure 6.78 Sequence In and Out points are set to match the boundaries of the selected region.

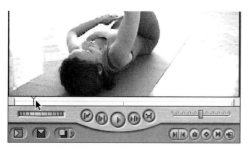

Figure 6.79 Park the Canvas playhead on the frame that you want to match in the source clip.

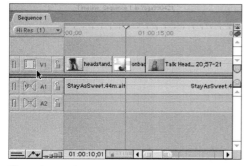

Figure 6.80 In the Timeline, make the selected clip's track the target track. The target track icon is highlighted in yellow.

Figure 6.81 Click the Match Frame button in the Canvas.

Locating a Match Frame

The Match Frame command opens a copy of the source clip for the frame at the play-head position on the target track. This is a convenient way to locate the source video for a clip.

To find a particular frame of video in a clip in the sequence:

1. In the Canvas or Timeline, park the play-head on the frame for which you want to locate the source clip (**Figure 6.79**).

2. Set the target track to the track that con-tains the desired frame (**Figure 6.80**).

3. Click the Match Frame button in the Canvas (**Figure 6.81**); or press F.

   The source clip opens in the Viewer with the In and Out points set. The current frame in the Viewer matches the current frame on the target track in the Canvas (**Figure 6.82**).

Figure 6.82 The source clip that matches the sequence clip opens in the Viewer. The frame displayed in the Viewer matches the current frame displayed in the target track in the Canvas.

USING THE
TIMELINE AND
THE CANVAS

The previous chapter introduced basic editing procedures in Final Cut Pro; this chapter outlines your display, navigation, and editing options in the Timeline and Canvas windows. You'll also learn about the Tool palette, a deceptively tiny floating toolbar that's packed with editing, selection, and display tools. The Tool palette is key to efficient workflow in the Timeline.

The Timeline and the Canvas program windows work together, but they present two different views of your edited sequence. The Timeline displays a chronological diagram view of all the clips in your sequence; the Canvas is a monitor where you view playback of your edited sequence. That's why the Canvas and Timeline playheads are locked together. The Canvas always displays the frame at the current position of the Timeline's playhead.

When you open a sequence, it appears simultaneously in the Timeline and the Canvas. Any changes you make to the sequence in the Timeline are reflected in the Canvas playback, and any changes you make in the Canvas are reflected in the Timeline display.

You can double-click a sequence clip in the Timeline to open a Viewer window for it. Sequence clips are identified in the Viewer by two lines of dots in the Viewer Scrubber bar. Why the distinction? Remember that when you insert a clip into a sequence, you are inserting a copy of the clip in the Browser. If you change the sequence version of the clip, your changes will be reflected in the sequence only. Opening the same clip directly from the Browser in a Viewer window opens a different copy of the clip. If you make changes to the Browser copy (for example, by making audio level adjustments or adding motion effects), these changes will not affect the clip in the sequence. It's important to understand the difference between working with clips that have been opened from the Browser and clips that have been opened from the Timeline. (For more information, see "FCP Protocol: Clips and Sequences," in Chapter 4.)

Anatomy of the Canvas

The Canvas window (**Figure 7.1**) looks like the Viewer and has many of the same controls. You can use the controls in the Canvas window to play edited sequences, mark sequence In and Out points, add sequence markers, and set keyframes. In addition to the Viewer-like marking controls, the Canvas has two areas where you can perform various types of drag-and-drop edits. The Canvas edit buttons are arrayed in the lower-left corner of the window. The Canvas edit overlay appears when you drag a clip from the Viewer to the Canvas.

You can also use the Canvas window to plot out effects. Learn about applying filters and effects in Chapter 13, "Compositing and Special Effects."

✔ Tips

■ You can use the ToolTips feature to identify most of the control buttons in the window. Rest the cursor over the button and then wait a second, and a name label will appear. (Switch on ToolTips in the Preferences window.)

■ Two playback options don't have interface controls: Play Every Frame (Option-P) and Loop Playback (Control-L).

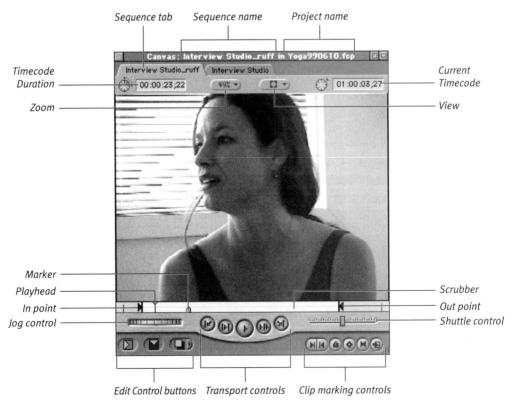

Figure 7.1 An overview of the Canvas window. Use the Canvas to play sequences, perform edits, and set keyframes.

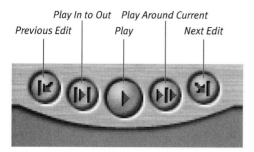

Figure 7.2 The Canvas's transport control buttons.

Figure 7.3 The Shuttle control.

Onscreen controls and displays

The Canvas controls include transport controls, Canvas display options, and editing controls.

Note that all of the Canvas controls listed here (except the edit buttons and overlay) appear in the Viewer window as well and operate in the same way.

The following paragraphs provide a rundown of the onscreen controls you will encounter in the Canvas.

Transport controls:

The Canvas's transport control buttons are shown in **Figure 7.2**.

◆ **Previous Edit:** Click to jump the playhead back to the previous edit, the In point, or the Out point.

◆ **Play In to Out:** Click to play the clip from the In point to the Out point.

◆ **Play:** Click to play the clip from the current position of the playhead. Click again to stop playback.

◆ **Play Around Current:** Click to play the part of the clip immediately before and after the current position of the playhead. The Pre-roll and Post-roll settings (in Preferences) determine the duration of the playback.

◆ **Next Edit:** Click to move the playhead to the next edit, the In point, or the Out point.

◆ **Shuttle control:** Drag the control tab away from the center to fast forward or rewind. Speeds can vary depending on the tab's distance from the center. A green control tab indicates normal playback speed (**Figure 7.3**).

continues on next page

ANATOMY OF THE CANVAS

- **Jog control:** Click and drag your mouse to the left or right to step through your sequence one frame at a time (**Figure 7.4**).

- **Scrubber** and **playhead:** The Scrubber is the strip immediately below the image window. Move through the sequence by dragging the playhead, or click the Scrubber to jump the playhead to a new location (**Figure 7.5**).

Marking controls:

All of the onscreen controls you use to mark clips are grouped in the lower-right corner of the Canvas (**Figure 7.6**):

- **Match Frame:** Click to display in the Viewer the frame currently showing in the Canvas. This control is useful for synchronizing action.

- **Mark Clip:** Click to set the sequence In and Out points at the outer boundaries of the clip at the position of the playhead in the target track.

- **Add Keyframe:** Click to add a keyframe to the sequence clip at the current playhead position.

- **Add Marker:** Click to add a marker to the sequence at the current playhead position.

- **Mark In** (left) and **Mark Out** (right): Click to set the In point or the Out point for the sequence at the current playhead position.

View selectors:

- **Zoom:** Adjust the Canvas's image display size (**Figure 7.7**). (This pop-up selector does not affect the actual frame size of the image.)

- **View:** Select a viewing format. Title Safe and Wireframe modes are accessible from this pop-up menu (**Figure 7.8**).

Figure 7.4 The Jog control.

Figure 7.5 The Scrubber and playhead.

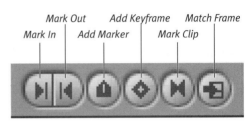

Figure 7.6 The Canvas's clip marking control buttons.

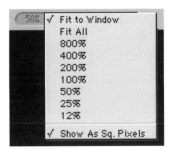

Figure 7.7 The Zoom pop-up selector.

Figure 7.8 The View pop-up selector.

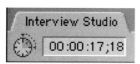

Figure 7.9
The Timecode
Duration display.

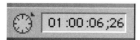

Figure 7.10 The Current Timecode display.

Figure 7.11 The
Current Timecode
pop-up menu. Select a
sequence marker from
the list to jump to that
marker's location.

Timecode navigation and display

There are two timecode displays in the upper corners of the Canvas window. They are useful for precision navigating to specific timecode locations.

◆ **Timecode Duration:** This display shows the elapsed time between the In and Out points of a clip. If no edit points are set, the beginning and end of the sequence serve as the In and Out points (**Figure 7.9**).

◆ **Current Timecode:** This display shows the timecode at the current position of the playhead. You can enter a timecode in this display to jump the playhead to that point in the sequence (**Figure 7.10**).

✔ Tips

■ Control-click the Current Timecode field to see a pop-up selector of sequence markers in the current sequence. Select one to jump the playhead to that marker's location (**Figure 7.11**). The same list of sequence markers is available from the Timeline ruler's shortcut menu.

■ You can use keyboard shortcuts to step through both sequence and clip markers in the Timeline, but you need to open a clip in the Viewer to make changes to that clip's marker. For details, see "About Markers in the Timeline and Canvas" later in this chapter.

Editing controls

Seven buttons in the lower-left corner of the Canvas (**Figure 7.12**) allow you to perform drag-and-drop edits from the Viewer or the Browser. You can also insert a clip displayed in the Viewer into your sequence by clicking the appropriate editing control button.

All of the edit types available in the Canvas edit overlay (**Figure 7.13**) are also available as editing control buttons. The Canvas edit overlay and Final Cut Pro edit procedure are detailed in Chapter 6, "Editing in Final Cut Pro."

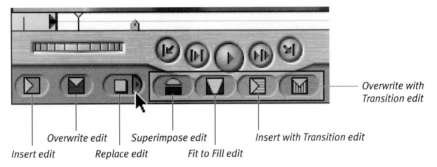

Overwrite with
Transition edit

Overwrite edit   Superimpose edit   Insert with Transition edit

Insert edit   Replace edit   Fit to Fill edit

Figure 7.12 The Canvas edit buttons with the pop-up selector fully expanded.

Edit types:

◆ **Insert edit:** This type of edit inserts a source clip into a sequence by pushing back the part of the sequence that's past the sequence In point, making room for the new source clip.

◆ **Overwrite edit:** The source clip overwrites sequence clips past the sequence In point. Overwrite uses the source In and Out points to calculate the edit duration. The sequence material is replaced by the incoming source clip; there is no time shift in the existing sequence.

◆ **Replace edit:** This edit type replaces the contents of a sequence clip with the source clip material. It allows specified single frames in the source clip and sequence to be aligned. The material between the sequence In and Out points is replaced by corresponding material from the source clip on either side of the frame that was matched.

◆ **Fit to Fill edit:** The speed of the source clip will be modified to fill the duration specified by the sequence In and Out points; the clip must be rendered before the edit can be played back.

◆ **Superimpose edit:** The source clip is placed on a new track above the target track, starting at the sequence In point. The target track is not changed. If the clip has audio, the source audio is added to new tracks below the target audio track.

◆ **Transition edit:** The source clip is inserted into the sequence with the default transition at the source clip's head.

◆ **Target track indicators:** These show which tracks have been targeted for this edit.

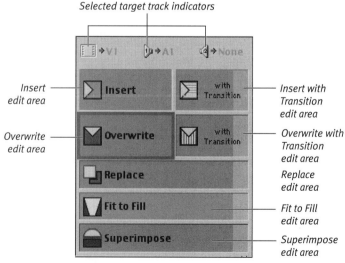

Selected target track indicators

Insert edit area

Overwrite edit area

Insert with Transition edit area

Overwrite with Transition edit area

Replace edit area

Fit to Fill edit area

Superimpose edit area

Figure 7.13 The Canvas edit overlay allows drag-and-drop editing for seven types of edits.

Using the Canvas Window

The Canvas and Viewer windows operate in much the same way. If you review the sections in Chapter 5, "Introducing the Viewer," that detail the Viewer window operation, you'll know how to use the Canvas window as well.

Editing in the Canvas is detailed in Chapter 6, "Editing in Final Cut Pro."

So what does that leave for this section? Just a few odds and ends.

To open a sequence in the Canvas:

◆ Start in the Browser. Double-click the sequence icon. The sequence opens in the Canvas and Timeline.

To composite or add effects to a sequence in the Canvas:

1. Start in the Canvas with your sequence cued to the location to which you want to add effects.

2. Choose Wireframe or Image+Wireframe from the View selector in the Canvas (**Figure 7.14**).

   The Canvas acts as your monitor as you compose and review effects or create motion paths (**Figure 7.15**). Learn more about creating effects in Chapter 13, "Compositing and Special Effects."

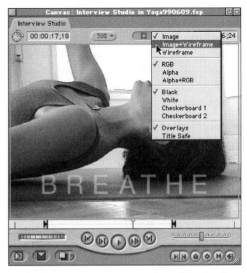

Figure 7.14 Selecting Image+Wireframe from the View pop-up selector.

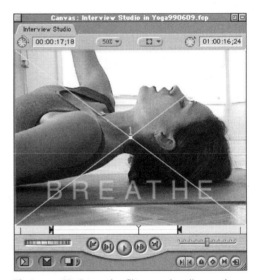

Figure 7.15 Motion paths, filters, and scaling can be applied directly in the Canvas window.

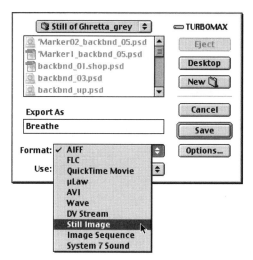

Figure 7.16 Select Still Image from the Format pull-down menu.

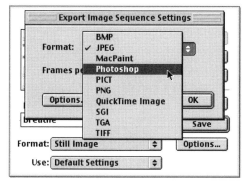

Figure 7.17 Select an export format for your still image from the pull-down menu.

Creating and exporting still frames

It's easy to turn any single video frame into a freeze-frame image and use it in a sequence. If you want to convert this image into a graphic file and work with it outside of FCP, you'll need to export it using the Export command on the File menu.

To create a still image from a Canvas frame:

1. In the Canvas, position the playhead on the desired frame.

2. Choose Modify > Make Freeze Frame.

   The new freeze-frame image opens in the Viewer window as a clip. It has the default duration as specified on the General tab of the Preferences window for stills. You can modify the freeze-frame clip's duration by setting In and Out points and edit it into your sequence.

To export a still image from a Canvas frame:

1. In the Canvas, position the playhead on the desired frame.

2. Choose File > Export > QuickTime.

3. In the dialog box, type a new name for your exported still image in the Export As field.

4. Select a destination folder from the pull-down menu at the top of the dialog box.

5. Select Still Image from the Format pull-down menu (**Figure 7.16**).

6. To set export format options, click Options.

7. In the Export Image Sequence Settings dialog box, select an export format from the pull-down menu at the top (**Figure 7.17**); then click OK. You can ignore the frame rate settings because you are exporting a single frame.

8. Back in the first dialog box, click Save.

To set the time display view:

◆ In the Canvas, Control-click either time-code display field; then select a time display option from the shortcut menu (**Figure 7.18**).

✔ Tips

■ Check the time display mode to quickly determine which type of timecode is currently specified in your sequence settings. The timecode type specified in your sequence settings appears in bold.

■ Changing the timecode display in the Canvas won't alter your sequence's timecode settings. That's why the timecode display short menu reads "View As."

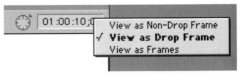

Figure 7.18 Select a time display option from the shortcut menu in the Canvas' Current Timecode display.

Adjusting the Canvas Display

You can set up the Canvas to show your clips in a variety of display formats and magnifications. Final Cut Pro also lets you overlay an array of useful information on your clip image, or you can turn off everything.

Display options operate the same way in the Canvas and the Viewer. Learn more about Canvas display options by reading these sections in Chapter 5, "Introducing the Viewer":

◆ "Changing magnification and window size in the Viewer or Canvas window"

◆ "Viewing Title and Action Safe boundaries"

◆ "Viewing overlays"

◆ "Viewing with different backgrounds"

Figure 7.19 The Tool palette as a compact floating toolbar.

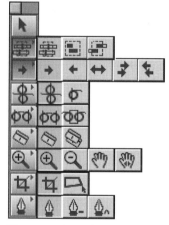

Figure 7.20 The Tool palette with every pop-up selector displayed. You'll see only one of these bars at a time, when you select a tool.

Anatomy of the Tool Palette

The Tool palette contains tools for selecting and manipulating items in the Timeline, Canvas, and Viewer. As you work in the Timeline with an assembly of clips in a rough sequence, you use the tools in the palette to do the following:

◆ Select anything, from a sliver of a single clip to all of the tracks in your sequence.

◆ Select and adjust edit points in your sequence.

◆ Adjust the scale of the Timeline so you can see what you are doing.

◆ Crop or distort an image.

◆ Add and edit keyframes in the Timeline.

Figure 7.19 shows the Tool palette as it appears in the program.

Figure 7.20 shows the Tool palette with all of its pop-up selectors fully extended. When you actually use the Tool palette to select a tool, you will see only one of these selectors at a time, but they are assembled in this illustration to give you an overview of the location of every available tool.

continues on next page

ANATOMY OF THE TOOL PALETTE

The following paragraphs describe the tools in the Tool palette.

Selection tools:

 Selection: Selects individual items.

 Edit Selection: Selects just the edit points inside your selection.

 Group Selection: Selects whole clips or groups of whole clips.

 Range Selection: Selects the area inside the selection marquee you draw. Select partial clips with this tool.

 Select Track Forward: Selects all of the contents of the track after the selection point.

 Select Track Backward: Selects all of the contents of the track before the selection point.

 Track Selection: Selects the entire contents of a single track.

 Select All Tracks Forward: Selects the contents of all tracks after the selection point.

 Select All Tracks Backward: Selects the contents of all tracks before the selection point.

Edit tools:

 Roll: Rolls edit points.

 Ripple: Ripples edit points.

 Slip: Slips a clip's In and Out points.

 Slide: Slides a clip in a sequence.

 Razor Blade: Cuts a single clip into two sections.

 Razor Blade All: Cuts clips on all tracks at the selection point into two sections.

Learn more about performing these edits in Chapter 8, "Fine Cut: Trimming Edits."

View tools:

 Zoom In: Zooms in on an image or within the Timeline.

 Zoom Out: Zooms out from an image or within the Timeline.

 Hand: Moves the Timeline or image view from side to side.

 Video Scrub Hand: Scrubs the thumbnail image displayed on Timeline clips.

Image modifiers:

 Crop: Crops the edges of an image in the Viewer or Canvas (in Wireframe mode).

 Distort: Distorts a selection by click-dragging corner points.

Keyframe tools:

 Pen: Adds a keyframe.

 Pen Delete: Deletes a keyframe.

 Pen Smooth: Smoothes a curve by adding Bézier handles to the selected keyframe.

You can use the Pen tools in keyframe graphs in the Viewer effects tabs, in keyframe overlays in the Timeline, and on a motion path in the Canvas or Viewer.

Figure 7.21 Click a tool to select it from the Tool palette.

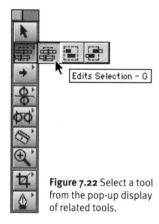

Figure 7.22 Select a tool from the pop-up display of related tools.

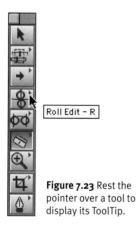

Figure 7.23 Rest the pointer over a tool to display its ToolTip.

Using the Tool palette

When you click and hold the mouse on a tool in the palette, the Tool palette extends to display multiple tools on pop-up selectors. The pop-ups display all of the tools available from that palette button. After you've made a selection from the pop-up, your selected tool will be displayed on the palette.

✔ Tip

■ See Appendix B for a complete list of keyboard shortcuts for tool selection, Shortcuts are also listed in ToolTips and on FCP menus.

To select a tool from the palette:

Do one of the following:

◆ Click the tool to select it (**Figure 7.21**).

◆ Click and hold on the tool icon; then make a selection from the pop-up display of related tools (**Figure 7.22**).

◆ Rest the pointer over the tool icon in the palette. A ToolTip displaying the name of the tool and its keyboard shortcut will appear (**Figure 7.23**).

New in 2: Timeline Features

New Interface Features:

Final Cut Pro 2's changes to the Timeline interface are subtle, but very useful. More bits of useful information appear out in the open in the main program windows.

Here's a rundown:

◆ **New render status bars:** Two render status bars have replaced the single red-and-gray status bar in the Timeline; the upper one is for video, and the lower one is for audio.

On non-real-time FCP systems, you'll see the familiar red and gray status codes, plus a new blue-gray color code indicating material that has already been rendered (it's hard to distinguish from the gray render bar—Apple must have wanted to save the fiesta colors for real-time codes).

◆ **Red:** Needs to be rendered.

◆ **Gray:** No rendering is required.

◆ **Blue-gray:** The material has already been rendered.

Real-time systems add two more color codes to the render status bars:

◆ **Green:** Does not need rendering and can be played in real time.

◆ **Yellow:** Proxy real-time material.

When you play back, Final Cut Pro shows a real-time approximation of the final effect. To get the true final effect, you'll still need to render the material. You'll also see the final effect when play is stopped or when scrubbing.

◆ **Linked Selection control:** The Linked Selection indicator controls whether linked selection is active or disabled.

◆ **Snapping control:** Use this control to toggle snapping and check snapping status.

◆ **Clip labels:** You can add colored, customizable labels to Timeline clips. Now you have more ways to organize your clips—and a more festive Timeline!

◆ **Speed change:** If you modify a clip's playback speed, the new speed setting appears next to the clip's name in the Timeline.

New Timeline Features:

◆ **Multiple-clip level control for audio:** This feature is nice. You don't need to nest your audio to set levels on multiple audio clips. Select the clips in the Timeline (you can select all of the audio tracks in your sequence if you like) and use the new Modify > Levels menu command.

◆ **Opacity-level control for multiple clips:** This works like the multiple-clip audio level command. You can adjust opacity by a relative or absolute percentage.

◆ **Video Scrub Hand tool:** Select the Video Scrub Hand tool and drag across the Timeline clip's thumbnail image. The tiny thumbnail image plays as moving video.

Anatomy of the Timeline

The Timeline displays multiple video and audio tracks along a time axis (**Figure 7.24**). The base layers of video (V1) and audio (A1 and A2) appear toward the center of the Timeline window. Additional audio tracks extend below the base layer; additional video tracks stack above the base layer.

If you have multiple sequences open, the Timeline and Canvas will display a tab for each sequence.

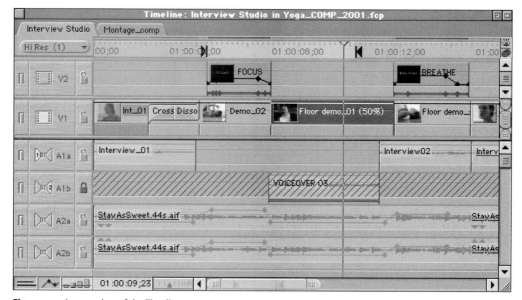

Figure 7.24 An overview of the Timeline.

Onscreen controls and displays

Use the controls in the Timeline window to move the playhead, view the tracks in your edited sequence, and perform edits and keyframe adjustments. Timeline controls and displays include track icons, sequence edit points, and clip and sequence markers (**Figures 7.25, 7.26, and 7.27**).

◆ **Sequence tabs:** There is one sequence tab for each open sequence in the Timeline. To make a sequence active, click its tab.

◆ **Render Quality pop-up menu:** Switch between available render quality settings or edit the render qualities.

◆ **Track Visibility control:** Click to make a track invisible. When the track is invisible, the contents remain in the Timeline but are not played or rendered with the sequence. Invisible tracks appear dimmed in the Timeline. Caution: Render cache files are deleted if the track is made invisible.

◆ **Target Track control:** Click to select the target tracks (one video track and up to two audio tracks) before performing an edit.

◆ **Lock Track control:** Lock a track to prevent any changes to its contents. Locked tracks are cross-hatched in the Timeline.

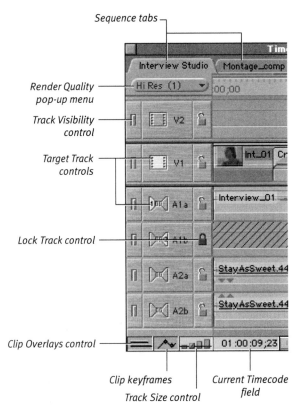

Figure 7.25 Detail of the left side of the Timeline.

ANATOMY OF THE TIMELINE

◆ **Clip Overlays control:** Click to toggle the display of Audio Level line graphs over audio clips and Opacity Level line graphs in video clips.

◆ **Clip keyframes:** Click to toggle the display of filter (green) bars and motion (blue) bars underneath tracks. The bars display keyframe locations.

◆ **Track Size control:** Click to switch among the four track display sizes in the Timeline.

◆ **Current Timecode field:** This field displays the timecode at the current position of the playhead. You can enter a time in the display to jump the playhead to that point in the clip. This display/control

operates like the Current Timecode boxes in the Viewer and Canvas.

◆ **Render status bars:** Two render status bars indicate which parts of the sequence have been rendered in the current (selected) render quality setting. The upper bar is for video tracks, and the lower bar is for audio tracks. Red bars indicate material that requires rendering to be played back. Gray bars indicate material that does not require rendering. A blue-gray bar indicates material that has already been rendered. On real-time equipped systems, a green status bar indicates that the material can be played back in real time, and yellow indicates real-time play back with a proxy (lower-quality) version of the material.

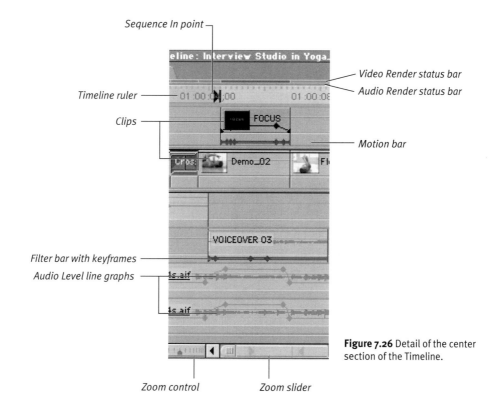

Sequence In point

Video Render status bar
Audio Render status bar

Timeline ruler

Clips

Motion bar

Filter bar with keyframes
Audio Level line graphs

Figure 7.26 Detail of the center section of the Timeline.

Zoom control   Zoom slider

◆ **Timeline ruler:** This displays the time-code for the current sequence and sequence In and Out points. Edit-point overlays are displayed along the ruler. Adjust the time scale with the Zoom slider or the Zoom control.

◆ **Clips:** You can display clips as solid bars or as video frames. Clips that have clip visibility turned off appear dimmed in the Timeline. Clips on locked tracks are cross-hatched in the Timeline. Clips with a speed change applied display the current speed setting.

◆ **Filter** and **Motion bar:** This bar displays keyframes for any filters or motion effects applied to a clip. Double-click the bar to open the settings in the Viewer window.

◆ **Zoom control:** Click to jump between different time scale views.

◆ **Zoom slider:** Use this slider to scroll through your sequence and to adjust the time scale of your view.

◆ **Playhead:** The playhead reflects the chronological position in the sequence of the frame displayed in the Canvas. The playhead in the Timeline always moves in tandem with the Canvas playhead.

◆ **Vertical scroll bars:** This two-part scroll bar allows the video and audio tracks to scroll independently. Adjust the thumb tabs between the scroll controls to create a static area in the center of the Timeline.

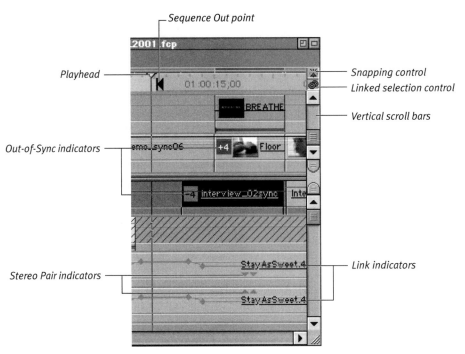

Figure 7.27 Detail of the right side of the Timeline.

Table 7.1

Color Coding in the Timeline	
COLOR	ITEM
Purple	Video sequences
Cyan	Video clips
Aquamarine	Video graphics
Green	Audio clip
Light green	Audio sequences
White	Offline video or audio clips

Table 7.2

Clip Labels and Colors	
COLOR	LABEL
Orange	Good Take
Red	Best Take
Blue	Alternate Shots
Purple	Interviews
Green	B-Roll

- **Out-of-Sync indicators:** This display indicates the number of frames by which a clip's video and audio tracks are out of sync.

- **Link indicators:** Linked clips are displayed in the Timeline with underlined names. When a linked clip is selected, moved, or trimmed, items linked to it are affected in the same way. Linked selections can be switched on and off as a sequence preference.

- **Stereo Pair indicators:** These indicators appear as two triangles. These two audio clips are linked as a stereo pair.

- **Linked Selection control:** The Linked Selection indicator controls whether linked selection is active or disabled. Note: This control toggles the Linked Selection feature, not Link/Unlink. One click on this tiny icon is not going to permanently unlink the linked clips in your sequence. You typically disable linked selection to select just the audio or video track of a linked A-V clip, to adjust a split edit in a sync sequence, for example.

- **Snapping control:** Click to toggle snapping on and off.

Color coding in the Timeline

Final Cut Pro uses two types of color coding.

- Final Cut Pro uses a color coding system to identify the various clip and sequence types found in the Timeline. **Table 7.1** lists the file types and their colors.

- Mac Finder-style labels provide an additional sorting option. Labeled clips appear in the Timeline with the clip's name highlighted in the label color. You can customize the label text; the default labels and label colors are listed in **Table 7.2**.

ANATOMY OF THE TIMELINE

Customizing Timeline Display Options

Timeline display options are customizable for each sequence. The Timeline Options tab of the Sequence Settings window is a central location for reviewing or modifying your Timeline display options. Your custom display settings will apply only to the currently open sequence. If you want the same customized Timeline display to appear every time you create a new sequence, you can specify your preferred Timeline display setup on the Timeline Options tab of the Preferences window. For Preferences setting details, see Chapter 2, "Welcome to Final Cut Pro."

To set clip display mode on video tracks for the current sequence:

1. Make the Timeline active; then choose Sequence > Settings.

2. When the Sequence Settings window appears, click the Timeline Options tab (**Figure 7.28**).

3. From the Thumbnail Display pop-up menu, select from three thumbnail display options (**Figure 7.29**):

   ▲ Name displays the name of the clip and no thumbnail images.

   ▲ Name Plus Thumbnail displays the first frame of every clip as a thumbnail image and then the name of the clip.

   ▲ Filmstrip displays as many thumbnail images as possible for the current zoom level of the Timeline.

4. Click OK.

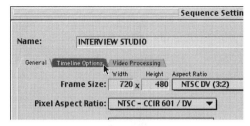

Figure 7.28 Click the Timeline Options tab in the Sequence Settings window.

Figure 7.29 Select a name display option from the Thumbnail Display pop-up menu.

✔ Tip

■ If you are editing a long program in multiple-sequence segments, you might want to set the starting timecode to reflect each sequence's start time in the master program. You can do that by entering the start time in the Starting Timecode field on the Timeline Options tab.

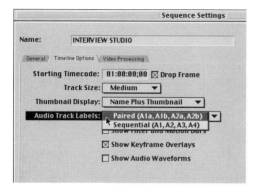

Figure 7.30 Select a track labeling display option from the Audio Track Labels pop-up menu.

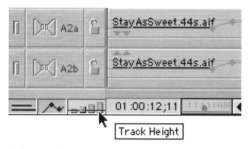

Figure 7.31 Select from the four track display sizes by clicking one of the icons in the Track Size control.

To modify audio track display settings for the current sequence:

1. Make the Timeline active; then choose Sequence > Settings.

    The Sequence Settings window appears.

2. Click the Timeline Options tab.

3. Click the Show Audio Waveforms check box to toggle the display of waveforms in the Timeline.

4. From the Audio Track Labels pop-up menu, select from two track labeling options (**Figure 7.30**):

    ▲ Paired (A1a, A1b, A2a, A2b): This is a good labeling scheme if you are working with stereo tracks.

    ▲ Sequential (A1, A2, A3, A4,): This is a good labeling scheme if you are working with a collection of single tracks—for instance, dialog tracks.

5. Click OK.

✔ Tip

■ The Timeline's audio waveform display is really useful for tweaking your audio edits, but Timeline display performance suffers when waveforms are displayed. Have it both ways: Command-Option-W is the keyboard shortcut for toggling audio waveform display in the Timeline.

To set the track display size:

◆ Click one of the four size option icons on the Track Size control located in the lower-left corner of the Timeline (**Figure 7.31**).

To customize your default Timeline display settings:

1. Choose Edit > Preferences. In the Preferences window, click the Timeline Options tab.

2. On the Timeline Options tab, set your preferred display options (**Figure 7.32**).

   Your custom Timeline display settings will be the defaults for subsequent new sequences.

Timeline scaling and scrolling

Final Cut Pro has state-of-the-art Zoom features and scroll bars. The time scale in the Timeline is continuously variable; you can transition smoothly from viewing several minutes of your sequence down to a single frame. The horizontal scroll bar—the Zoom slider—is a combination Zoom and scroll control. The Zoom control is handy—you can jump to any time scale with a single mouse click.

The vertical scroll bar allows you to set a static area in the center of the Timeline window, so your base tracks are always in view.

To adjust the time scale of the Timeline display:

Do one of the following:

- The thumb controls are the ribbed-looking ends of the Zoom slider. Click a thumb control and drag it to shrink the time scale and expose more of your sequence (**Figure 7.33**). Shift-click and drag to adjust both ends of your view simultaneously.

- Click the Zoom control to the left of the Zoom slider to jump to a different time scale (**Figure 7.34**).

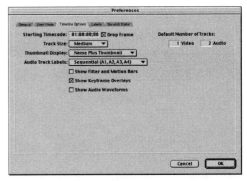

Figure 7.32 Set your preferred default Timeline display options on the Timeline Options tab of the Preferences window.

Figure 7.33 Click and drag a thumb control of the Zoom slider to adjust the scale of your Timeline view.

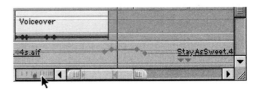

Figure 7.34 Click the Center Zoom control to jump to a new time scale.

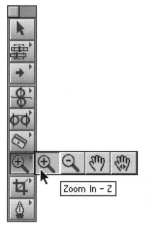

Figure 7.35 Click the Zoom In tool to select it from the Tool palette.

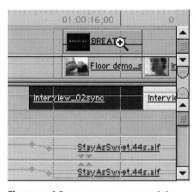

Figure 7.36 Drag a marquee around the section you want to zoom in on.

To zoom the view of the Timeline:

1. From the Tool palette, select the Zoom In or Zoom Out tool (**Figure 7.35**); or press Z.

2. Click in the Timeline or drag a marquee around the section you want to display (**Figure 7.36**).

   Or do one of the following:

   ▲ Use one of the keyboard shortcuts. (See the appendix for a complete list of shortcuts.)

   ▲ Choose View > Zoom In (or Zoom Out).

✔ Tips

■ When the Timeline is zoomed in or out to the maximum, the plus sign (+) or minus sign (–) disappears from the Zoom tool's pointer.

■ Pressing Option while using the Zoom In tool toggles it to Zoom Out.

Best Zoom Shortcuts

Final Cut Pro has a jillion ways to zoom and scroll program windows. Which shortcuts are most useful in the Timeline?

◆ Option-+ (plus) / Option- – (minus): This keyboard combo zooms the Timeline even if the Canvas or Viewer is currently selected, and it keeps the selected clip (or the playhead, if no clip is selected) centered in the Timeline as it scales. This shortcut is the best way to zoom in and out of the Timeline.

◆ Command-+ (plus) / Command- – (minus): This shortcut works like Option plus and minus, but it zooms the selected program window.

◆ Shift-Z: This key combination adjusts the time scale to fit the entire sequence in the Timeline window.

◆ Shift-Page Up / Shift-Page Down: This shortcut scrolls the Timeline one full length of the Timeline window at the current scale.

To scroll through your sequence:

◆ Drag the Zoom slider across the scroll bar.

To set up the vertical scroll bars:

1. In the Timeline, click and hold the upper-most thumb tab near the center of the vertical scroll bar. Drag the thumb tab up the scroll bar to create a static area for as many video tracks as you want to keep in constant view (**Figure 7.37**).

   You'll see an overlay indicating the size of the static area.

   You can use the upper scroll bar to scroll through higher video tracks in the upper portion of the Timeline window.

2. Click and hold the lowest thumb tab in the vertical scroll bar. Drag the thumb tab down the scroll bar, creating a static area for as many audio tracks as you want to keep in constant view (**Figure 7.38**).

   You can use the lower scroll bar to scroll through additional audio tracks in the lower portion of the Timeline window.

3. Once you have set up your static view area, use the center tab on the scroll bar to move the static area up or down in the window (**Figure 7.39**).

Figure 7.37 Drag the thumb tab up the scroll bar to create a static display area for a video track in the Timeline.

Figure 7.38 Drag the thumb tab down the scroll bar to create a static display area for an audio track in the Timeline.

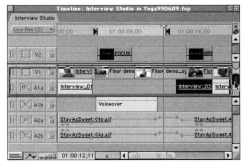

Figure 7.39 Use the center tab in the scroll bar to move the static display area up or down the Timeline display.

Figure 7.40 Drag the playhead along the Timeline ruler to scrub through your sequence.

Navigating in the Timeline

Many of the tasks described here can be accomplished with the help of keyboard shortcuts. Final Cut Pro has an army of key commands; many professional editors prefer a keyboard-intensive working style. This section demonstrates some other ways to approach the Timeline interface because, frankly, keystrokes don't make good illustrations. Check out the keyboard shortcuts in the appendix. You keyboard diehards, you might find something there you actually like.

✔ Tip

■ Use the "gear-down dragging" option to make precision adjustments to clips, levels, or edits in the Timeline. Hold down the Command key while dragging an item.

Positioning the playhead in a sequence

The playhead in the Timeline can be positioned by the same methods as the Canvas and Viewer playheads.

The playhead sits on the Timeline ruler and has a vertical locator line that extends down through the Timeline track display.

✔ Tip

■ You can use the locator line to help identify the exact timecode location of an item way down at the bottom of the Timeline window. Set the playhead's locator line on the point you want to identify, and the Current Timecode display will give you its exact timecode location.

To scrub through a sequence in the Timeline:

◆ Drag the playhead along the Timeline ruler (**Figure 7.40**).

To jump the playhead to a new location:

◆ Click the location on the Timeline ruler to move the playhead to that location (**Figure 7.41**).

Navigating with timecode in the Timeline

Just as in the Viewer, using timecode values to position the playhead in the Timeline and Canvas will result in frame-accurate positioning. Final Cut Pro's timecode input functionality is very flexible (see "FCP Protocol: Entering Timecode Numbers" in Chapter 5 for protocol and entry shortcuts).

To navigate using timecode values:

1. Start in the Timeline. Make sure all clips are deselected, or you'll move the selected clip and not the playhead.

2. Enter a new timecode number or use the shorthand methods detailed in Chapter 5. You don't need to click in the field to begin entering a new timecode; just type the numbers (**Figure 7.42**).

3. Press Enter.

   The playhead moves to the new timecode value, and the new timecode position is displayed in the Current Timecode field in the lower-left corner of the Timeline (**Figure 7.43**).

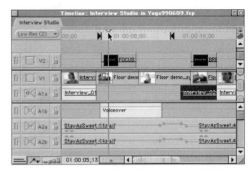

Figure 7.41 Click a point in the Timeline ruler to jump the playhead to that location.

Figure 7.42 Typing +4.00 to move the playhead 4 seconds later in the sequence.

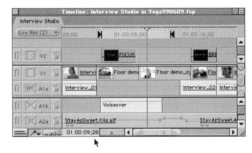

Figure 7.43 The playhead is repositioned 4 seconds later in the sequence.

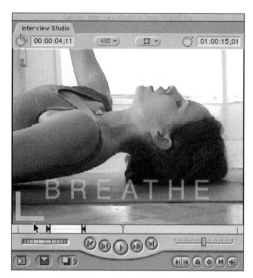

Figure 7.44 An L-shaped icon in the lower left of the Canvas indicates the first frame of a clip after an edit point.

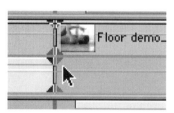

Figure 7.45 The Timeline with snapping turned on. The current position indicator displays arrows to show that it has snapped to an edit.

Figure 7.46 You can activate Timeline snapping by clicking the Snapping control on the right side of the Timeline. The control turns green when snapping is enabled.

To jump the playhead from edit to edit:

Do one of the following:

- Press the Up Arrow (previous) or Down Arrow (next) key on the keyboard.

- In the Canvas, click the Previous Edit or Next Edit button.

- Choose Mark > Previous (or Next) > Edit from the submenu.

- Press Option-E (for the previous edit) or Shift-E (for the next edit).

The playhead jumps to the first frame of the clip. If you've enabled Show Overlays on the View menu, an L-shaped icon appears in the lower left or right of the Canvas window, indicating that you are on the first or last frame of the sequence clip (**Figure 7.44**).

About snapping in the Timeline

Snapping is an interface state (or mood, if you will) that makes certain points in the Timeline "sticky." With snapping turned on, the edges of clips will snap together, or a clip will snap to an edit point on an adjacent track when dragged close to it. The playhead snaps to edits, clip and sequence markers, and keyframes (if displayed) on all visible tracks. If you drag the playhead across the Timeline ruler, it snaps to items in the Timeline when it encounters them. A small arrow appears above or below the edit, marker, or keyframe, showing you what the playhead has snapped to (**Figure 7.45**).

To turn snapping on or off:

Do one of the following:

- Choose View > Snapping. Choosing it again toggles snapping off.

- Click the Snapping control located on the upper-right side of the Timeline window (**Figure 7.46**).

To toggle snapping on and off on the fly:

◆ Press N; then drag the playhead, or your selected clip, to the new location (**Figure 7.47**).

Snapping remains in the toggled state until you press the N key again. Snapping can be toggled at any time, even in mid-edit.

About markers in the Timeline and Canvas

Final Cut Pro has two types of markers:

◆ Clip markers appear on individual clips in the Timeline.

◆ Sequence markers appear on the Timeline ruler.

If you open a Timeline clip in the Viewer, the clip markers will appear in the Viewer Scrubber bar. Sequence markers that fall within that clip will appear on the ruler of the clip's Filter and Motion tabs.

You can learn more about working with markers in Chapter 5, "Introducing the Viewer."

To set a sequence marker:

1. In the Timeline, position the playhead at the point where you want to set the marker. Make sure no clips are selected at the playhead's location.

2. Press M.

A sequence marker appears in the Canvas scrubber and on the Timeline ruler.

✔ Tips

■ You can set a sequence marker only if no clips are selected at the playhead position in the Timeline. With a selected Timeline clip under the playhead, your marker will be set as a clip marker on the selected clip.

■ You can delete sequence markers only if no clips are selected in the Timeline.

Figure 7.47 Snapping a clip to an edit point. You can toggle Timeline snapping even in mid-edit by pressing N at any time.

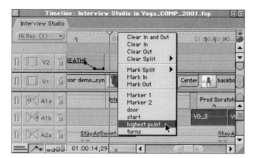

Figure 7.48 Choosing a marker from the Timeline ruler's shortcut menu.

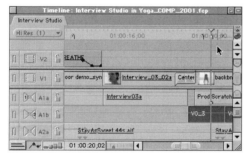

Figure 7.49 Selecting the marker jumps the playhead to that marker's location.

To position the playhead on a specific sequence marker:

◆ Control-click the Timeline ruler; then choose a marker from the list of sequence markers in the shortcut menu (**Figure 7.48**).

The playhead jumps to the selected marker's position (**Figure 7.49**).

To jump the playhead to the next or previous sequence marker:

Do one of the following:

◆ Choose Mark > Previous (or Next) > Marker.

◆ Press Option-M for the previous marker.

◆ Press Shift-M for the next marker.

These are the same commands you use to locate clip markers in the Viewer; when you use them in the Canvas or Timeline, they look for sequence markers only, unless you have selected a Timeline clip. With a Timeline clip selected, the Next/Previous Marker command will locate both clip and sequence markers in the selected clip.

NAVIGATING IN THE TIMELINE

271

To position the playhead on a specific Timeline clip marker:

◆ In the Timeline, Control-click the clip; then choose a marker from the list of clip markers in the shortcut menu (**Figure 7.50**).

The playhead jumps to the selected marker's position.

✔ Tip

■ Say you have a specific phrase in the middle of a narration track that you'd like to align with an action in your video track. You can place a clip marker in the audio track and a sequence marker in the video clip at key points and then grab the audio clip by its marker and drag it to align it to your video clip marker (**Figure 7.51**). This procedure works best with snapping enabled.

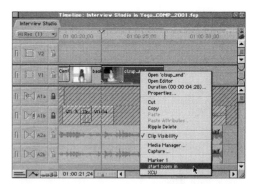

Figure 7.50 Selecting a clip marker from a Timeline clip's shortcut menu jumps the playhead to that marker's location.

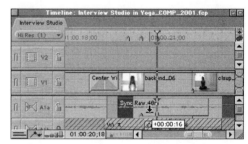

Figure 7.51 You can grab a Timeline clip by its marker and drag it to align it to another marker or to an edit point.

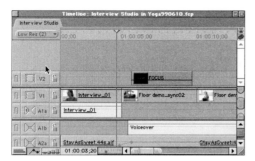

Figure 7.52 A sequence in the Timeline. Note the open space above the last video track.

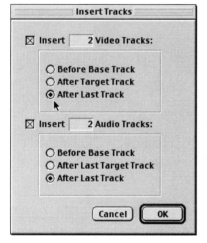

Figure 7.53 Adding two new video tracks and two new audio tracks to the sequence. The location specified is after the last track.

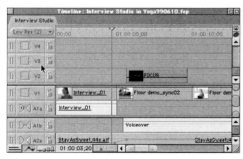

Figure 7.54 Two new video tracks (V3 and V4) have been added at the specified location above V2.

Working with Timeline Tracks

Editing operations in Final Cut Pro frequently involve configuring tracks. Timeline tracks can be locked, unlocked, targeted, added, deleted, and made visible or invisible. There is a difference between tracks and the contents of tracks. The procedures described in this section affect whole tracks. To learn about editing procedures that affect individual sequence clips, edit points, and keyframes, see "Working with Items in the Timeline" later in this chapter.

To add tracks to a sequence:

1. Open the sequence in the Timeline (**Figure 7.52**).

2. Choose Sequence > Insert Tracks.

3. In the Insert Tracks dialog box, enter the number of new tracks for either video or audio. Final Cut Pro supports up to 99 tracks for video and 99 tracks for audio.

4. Select from options for inserting tracks:

   ▲ Click the check box next to Video and/or Audio to select track types.

   ▲ Choose Before Base Track to insert your tracks before the first track in the Timeline.

   ▲ Choose After Target Track or After Last Target Track to insert your tracks after the current target track for video or after the last target track for audio in the Timeline.

   ▲ Choose After Last Track to insert your tracks after the last track in the Timeline (**Figure 7.53**).

5. Click OK to insert the tracks.

   The new tracks are added at the specified location (**Figure 7.54**).

To add a track to a sequence quickly:

Do one of the following:

◆ Drag a clip to the area above the top video track or below the bottom audio track (**Figure 7.55**).

A new track will be added to the sequence automatically (**Figure 7.56**).

◆ Control-click anywhere on the track header; then choose Add Track from the shortcut menu.

To delete a single track from a sequence:

◆ Control-click anywhere on the track header; then choose Delete Track from the shortcut menu (**Figure 7.57**).

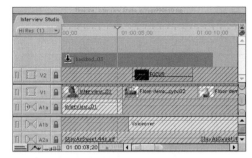

Figure 7.55 Drag and drop a clip in the area above the top video track.

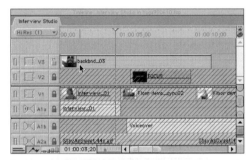

Figure 7.56 A new track is created automatically, and the clip is added to the sequence.

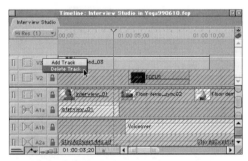

Figure 7.57 In the Timeline, delete a track by Control-clicking the track's header and then choosing Delete Track from the shortcut menu.

Figure 7.58 Specify the track you want to delete by making it the target track; then choose Sequence › Delete Tracks.

Figure 7.59 Select Current Target Track from the options in the Delete Tracks dialog box.

Figure 7.60 The target track is deleted from the sequence.

To delete multiple tracks from a sequence:

1. Open the sequence in the Timeline. To delete a specific track, make that track the target track (**Figure 7.58**).

2. Choose Sequence > Delete Tracks.

3. In the Delete Tracks dialog box, select from options for deleting tracks:

   ▲ Click the check box next to Video and/or Audio to select track types.

   ▲ Choose Current Target Track to delete the current target track in the Timeline (**Figure 7.59**).

   ▲ Choose All Empty Tracks to delete every empty track in the Timeline.

   ▲ Choose All Empty Tracks at End of Sequence to delete all empty tracks after the last track used in the Timeline.

4. Click OK to delete the tracks.

   The selected track is deleted from the sequence; remaining tracks are renumbered consecutively (**Figure 7.60**).

✔ Tip

■ Next time you are building a sequence involving multiple takes or a multicamera shoot, try loading your synchronized clips into tracks above and below the base layer (V1 and A1 to A2), keeping the base layer clear to assemble your cut. You can turn on single tracks for viewing and then copy and paste your selections into the base layers.

To lock a Timeline track:

Do one of the following:

◆ In the Timeline, click the Track Lock control on the left side of the track. Click again to unlock the track (**Figure 7.61**).

◆ To lock an audio track, press F4 + the track number of the track you are locking.

◆ To lock a video track, press F5 + the track number of the track you are locking.

To lock all Timeline video tracks:

◆ To lock all video tracks in the sequence, press Shift-F5.

To lock all Timeline audio tracks:

◆ To lock all audio tracks in the sequence, press Shift-F4.

✔ Tip

■ Option-click a Track Lock control to toggle locking on all other audio or video tracks except the selected track.

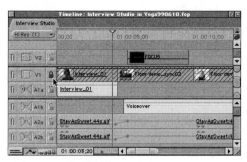

Figure 7.61 Lock a Timeline track by clicking the Track Lock control. Click again to unlock the track.

FCP Protocol: Lock vs. Target

One of the your tasks when learning a new program is getting in sync with the logic behind the program design. If you are coming to FCP from another editing system, there are probably a few things that FCP does differently. Getting the difference between locking and targeting is important to your editing happiness, so let's get this straight.

Locking a track keeps it from getting into trouble. So unless you're working on a particular track, you might as well keep it locked so that your editing operations don't have unforeseen consequences, like trimming or moving tracks that are stacked above or below the base layer, out of your Timeline view (spooky music here). You have to take the responsibility to lock your tracks because FCP defaults to unlocked tracks (unlike Avid, which disables tracks by default until you enable them).

Here are the keyboard shortcuts for locking tracks:

◆ Shift-F4 locks all video tracks.

◆ F4 plus the track number locks that video track.

◆ Shift-F5 locks all audio tracks.

◆ F5 plus the track number locks that audio track.

Lock 'em. Just do it. You're welcome.

Even if you've selected a specific edit on one track with the selection tool, any unlocked track is capable of responding to changes you make to that edit. If you have locked a track that you don't want cut or moved, this is a great thing. For example, you can make multitrack cuts, moves, and lifts to dialog tracks or multicamera sync setups and leave your locked music track right where it is.

Target tracks are a scheme for mapping which source track is going where on the record side. Even though you don't always need to specify a target track to perform an edit, it's a good habit to check your target assignments whenever you perform an edit.

FCP also uses targeting as way to specify the track when you perform a specific operation. For example, you target a track when you are getting ready to delete it.

Making a Timeline track invisible

You can temporarily hide a track by making it invisible so that the contents of that track do not appear in the sequence when you play it back. This is useful when you tweak multi-layered composited sequences.

You can also single out a track by making all of the other tracks in the sequence invisible. This allows you to focus on the contents of a single track temporarily. You can single out video and audio tracks independently.

Note that changing the visibility of a track will cause a loss of any render files associated with the track. A warning dialog box appears when you attempt to change visibility on a track.

If you've invested a lot of rendering in a sequence, you can use a couple of work-arounds to avoid re-rendering just because you turned a track off for a moment:

◆ You don't need to turn off the entire track. You can make individual clips invisible, by Control-clicking the clip in the Timeline and unchecking "Clip Visibility" in the clip's shortcut menu. If you are interested in a short section of your sequence, you can turn off just the clips you want to hide, and you'll sacrifice only the render file for that clip, preserving your render files for the rest of the sequence.

◆ Undo and Redo might work. FCP has many layers of undo, and if you haven't been messing around too much in the interim, you can revert to the state before the render file loss.

◆ You can try switching to another render quality, such as Cuts Only, to see what your composites look like with various tracks off, and then switch back to the render quality you used to for rendering everything. You will have to render again in any case if you made editing changes that require re-rendering.

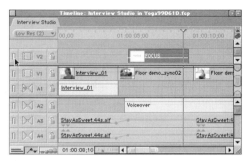

Figure 7.62 Click the Track Visibility control to make a track invisible.

Figure 7.63 If making a track invisible will cause a loss of render files, you'll see this warning.

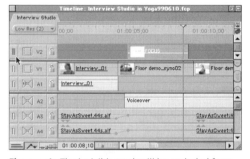

Figure 7.64 The invisible track will be excluded from playback.

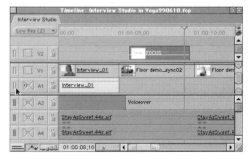

Figure 7.65 Audio track A1 will play back alone. All other audio tracks are muted.

To make a track invisible:

1. In the Timeline, click the Track Visibility control at the far left of the track you want to affect (**Figure 7.62**).

2. If the sequence has been rendered, a dialog box will appear warning you about impending loss of render files (**Figure 7.63**). If you don't need your render files in the current render quality, click Continue.

3. The track is made invisible. The Render status bar updates to show which sections of your sequence have been altered and may require re-rendering (**Figure 7.64**).

✔ Tip

- You can still edit invisible tracks. Lock invisible tracks if you don't want them to respond to edits.

To single out a track for visibility:

◆ Option-click the Track Visibility icon.

The contents of all of the video or audio tracks except the selected one are hidden from view in the Canvas (**Figure 7.65**).

Using the track selection tools

The track selection tools give you a variety of ways to select the contents of one or more tracks. Don't forget: If you are selecting an item that you've included in a linked selection, all of the items involved in that linked selection are going to be affected by whatever operation you're about to perform.

✔ Tip

- Deselect an individual Timeline item from a group selection by pressing Command and clicking the item.

To select all of the items on a single track:

◆ From the Tool palette, choose the Select Track tool and click anywhere in the track.

To select all items on a single track forward or backward from the selected point:

1. From the Tool palette, choose the Select Track Forward or Select Track Backward tool.

2. In the Timeline track, click the first clip to be included in the selection.

   That entire selected clip plus all of the items in front of it or behind it are selected (**Figure 7.66**).

✔ Tip

■ The Track Forward and Track Backward tools select entire clips only; they do not make range selections.

To select all items on all tracks forward or backward from the selected point:

1. From the Tool palette, choose the Select All Tracks Forward or Select All Tracks Backward tool.

2. In the Timeline, click the first clip on any track that should be included in the selection (**Figure 7.67**).

   All of the contents of all tracks from that point forward or backward are selected (**Figure 7.68**).

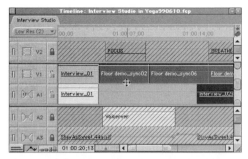

Figure 7.66 All tracks to the right of the selected clip are also selected, along with a linked audio clip on track A1.

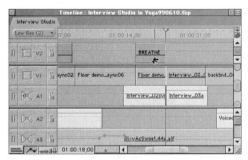

Figure 7.67 Using the Select Backward tool to click the first clip on any track to be included in the selection.

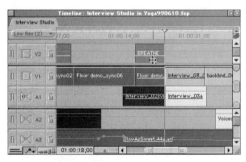

Figure 7.68 The contents of all tracks to the left of the selection point are selected. The music track on A3 is selected because it extends on both sides of the selection point.

Working with Items in the Timeline

This section covers Timeline editing procedures that affect individual sequence clips, edit points, and keyframes. Manipulation of Timeline items makes extensive use of the tools available in the Tool palette. If you haven't used the Tool palette yet, review "Anatomy of the Tool Palette" earlier in this chapter.

Selecting items in the Timeline

All of the selection tasks described here use tools from the Tool palette. There are some great selection tools available in Final Cut Pro but very few keyboard equivalents.

Here's a list of items you can select in the Timeline:

◆ Clips, including multiple clips or ranges of clips

◆ Transitions, which can then be trimmed or deleted

◆ Edits, which can then be modified in several ways

◆ Gaps, which can be closed or filled with media

Here are the items you cannot select in the Timeline:

◆ Filter and Motion bars and their keyframes: You can't select the keyframes, but you can move them by dragging them.

◆ Overlay keyframes: You can move these in the Timeline by dragging them.

◆ Tracks: You can't select a track, but the contents of tracks can be selected.

To select an entire clip:

1. From the Tool palette, choose the Arrow tool; or press A.

2. In the Timeline, use the Arrow tool to click the clip you want select.

   The Canvas indicates the selection by displaying a cyan border around the video of the selected clip.

To select part of a clip or a larger selection including partial clips:

1. From the Tool palette, choose the Range Selection tool (**Figure 7.69**).

2. In the Timeline, drag a marquee around the range to select it (**Figure 7.70**).

   A two-up display in the Canvas displays the first and last frames of your selection.

To select multiple whole clips:

1. From the Tool palette, choose the Group Selection tool (**Figure 7.71**).

2. In the Timeline, drag a marquee around all of the clips you want to select. You don't need to include the entire clip; any clip you touch will be included in its entirety.

To select multiple noncontiguous clips:

1. From the Tool palette, choose the appropriate selection tool.

2. In the Timeline, Command-click with the appropriate selection tool on the items you want to select (**Figure 7.72**). Command-click again on a selected item to deselect it.

Figure 7.69 Choose the Range Selection tool from the Tool palette.

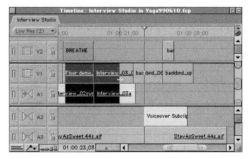

Figure 7.70 Drag a marquee around the range you want to select. You can select partial clips with this tool.

Figure 7.71 Choose the Group Selection tool from the Tool palette.

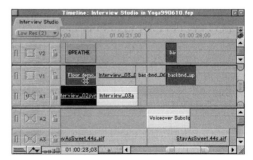

Figure 7.72 Command-click to select discontinuous clips in the Timeline or to deselect an individual clip from a group selection.

Figure 7.73 Setting a sequence Out point in the Canvas.

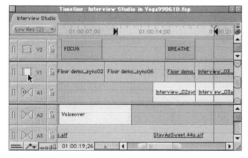

Figure 7.74 Click to turn on the Target Track control for the track where you want to make the selection.

Figure 7.75 The boundaries of your selection become the sequence In and Out points.

To select all items between the In and Out points:

1. Set the sequence In and Out points in the Canvas (**Figure 7.73**).

2. In the Timeline, specify the target tracks (**Figure 7.74**).

3. Choose Mark > Select In to Out; or press Option-A.

To set In and Out points around a selected part of a sequence:

1. From the Tool palette, choose the Range Selection tool. If your desired selection is composed of whole clips, use the Group Selection tool.

2. In the Timeline, drag a marquee around the range you want to select.

3. Choose Mark > Mark Selection; or press Shift-A.

   The bounds of the selection become the sequence In and Out points (**Figure 7.75**).

Linking clips is Final Cut Pro's scheme for grouping clips. When clips are linked, any action performed on one clip affects the other clips as well. Check out the sidebar "FCP Protocol: Linked Clips" later in this chapter for the rules governing linked clips and the operation of linked selection.

To link a group of unrelated clips:

1. In the Timeline, select the tracks you want to link (**Figure 7.76**).

   You can select one video and up to two audio clips from different tracks.

2. Choose Modify > Link; or press Command-L.

To permanently unlink a group of linked clips:

1. Select an item.

2. Choose Modify > Link; or press Command-L.

✔ Tip

■ When you're editing sync video with production audio that has been recorded separately, you can sync up your audio and video takes in FCP and use the Modify > Link command to create linked audio+video clips. You can select your newly linked Timeline clips and drag them back into the Browser, and you'll be able to assemble them into a sequence. The clips will load into the Viewer as if they were a single clip, and the audio and video will reference each other, keeping track of changes in sync.

Figure 7.76 Select the sequence clips you want to link in the Timeline.

FCP Protocol: Linked Clips

Here is how Final Cut Pro handles linked clips:

◆ Video and audio clips that originated from the same media file are linked automatically.

◆ You can set up multiple linked clip groups.

◆ You can switch linked selection on or off.

◆ When linked selection is turned on, FCP treats your linked items as a single entity for most operations.

◆ If you switch linked selection off, all of your linked items will be treated as if they were unlinked.

◆ Locking a track overrides a linked selection. If a linked item is on a locked track, it won't be modified, even if you modify an item it's linked to.

◆ Audio and video clips that were captured in sync continue to reference each other even when linked selection is disabled and will display out-of-sync indicators if moved out of sync with each other.

◆ Moving a linked clip's video to a higher track (for example, from track V1 to track V2), will automatically move the clip's audio to higher-numbered audio tracks (from tracks A1 and A2 to tracks A3 and A4).

Using linked selection

You can temporarily override the rules that govern a linked clip's selection. Editors frequently disable linked selection to select just the video (or just the audio) track of a linked clip, to create a split edit.

You can disable linked selection for the entire sequence or for a single selection operation.

To turn linked selection on or off:

Do one of the following:

◆ Click the Linked Selection control on the right side of the Timeline window. (**Figure 7.77**).

◆ Choose Sequence > Linked Selection.

◆ Press Shift -L to toggle linked selection on and off.

To select an item without selecting any items that are linked to it:

◆ Hold down the Option key when you select the item.

Figure 7.77 Activate linked selection by clicking the Linked Selection control. The control turns green when linked selection is enabled.

Moving Timeline clips

As with most things in Final Cut Pro, you have a choice of methods for moving clips within and between sequences. There are a variety of drag-and-drop methods, plus the timecode entry method, which offers greater precision and a little less flexibility.

✔ Tip

■ You can make copies of sequence clips by dragging them from the Timeline into the Browser. Drag multiple clips to make a copy of each clip. Remember that this clip copy will include any changes you have made to the clip in the sequence.

To drag a clip to a new position:

1. In the Timeline, select the clip and drag it to a new position (**Figure 7.78**).

2. In the new position, *do one of the following:*

   ▲ Drop the clip while holding the Option key to perform an Insert edit.

   ▲ Drop the clip to perform an Overwrite edit (**Figure 7.79**).

To shift a clip to another track at the same timecode location:

1. In the Timeline, select the clip you want to move.

2. Hold down the Shift key while dragging the clip vertically to another track (**Figure 7.80**).

   The clip will maintain its timecode position at the new track location.

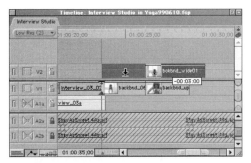

Figure 7.78 Dragging a clip to a new location. The pop-up indicator shows the offset from the clip's original location.

Figure 7.79 Dropping the clip performs an Overwrite edit in the new location.

Figure 7.80 Hold down the Shift key while dragging the clip from V2 to V3.

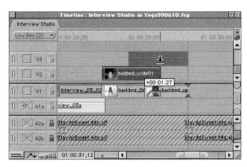

Figure 7.81 Hold down the Option key while dragging to copy the clip from V2 to V3.

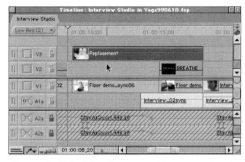

Figure 7.82 Select the clip you want to copy and paste.

Figure 7.83 Position the playhead where you want the pasted clip to start; then target the track you want to paste into.

To copy a clip to a new location:

1. In the Timeline, select the clip you want to move.

2. Hold down the Option key while dragging the clip to another location (**Figure 7.81**). A copy of the selected clip will be edited into the new location.

✔ Tips

- You can make copies of clips by dragging them from the Timeline into the Browser. Remember that this clip copy will include any changes you have made to the clip in the sequence.

- A quick way to make a Browser copy of every clip you've used in a sequence is to select the entire sequence in the Timeline (Command-A) and then drag the clips over to a Browser bin. Don't worry about wiping out your sequence—remember, you're making copies.

To copy and paste a clip into the Timeline:

1. In the Timeline, select the clip (**Figure 7.82**); or use the Group Selection tool from the Tool palette to select clips from multiple tracks.

2. Cut or copy the selected material to the clipboard.

3. Position the playhead where you want to paste the clip (**Figure 7.83**).

continues on next page

WORKING WITH ITEMS IN THE TIMELINE

4. Choose Edit > Paste; or press Command-V.

The pasted material overwrites the sequence clips, starting at the playhead location in the target track and extending for the duration of the pasted material (**Figure 7.84**).

✔ Tip

- Press Shift-V while pasting to insert edit the pasted material in the new sequence location.

To reposition an item in the Timeline by entering a timecode:

1. In the Timeline, select the clip you want to move.

2. Enter a new timecode number; or use the shorthand methods detailed in Chapter 5, "Introducing the Viewer."

As you type, a text entry window appears below the Timeline ruler (**Figure 7.85**).

3. Press Enter.

The clip is repositioned, if there is space at the new timecode location.

If an edit tool has been selected from the Tool palette before timecode entry, the edit is performed in the direction indicated by the timecode.

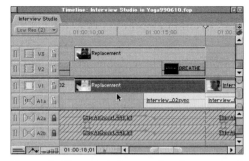

Figure 7.84 The pasted clip overwrites the contents of the target track.

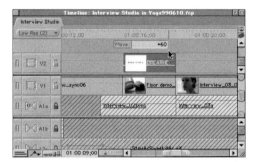

Figure 7.85 Type +60 and then press Enter to reposition the clip 60 frames (2 seconds) later in the sequence.

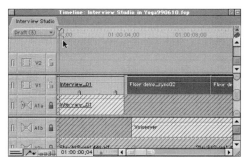

Figure 7.86 Pressing the Home key positions the playhead at the beginning of the sequence.

Figure 7.87 The playhead jumps to the start of the first gap found.

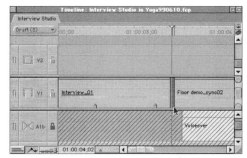

Figure 7.88 Position the playhead anywhere in the gap you want to close.

Finding and closing gaps

As you're assembling a sequence in Final Cut Pro, all that cutting and pasting and slipping and sliding may create gaps in your sequence tracks. Sometimes the gaps are so small you won't be able to see them in the Timeline, but a gap of even a single frame is easily detectable in Canvas playback.

This section contains a repertoire of techniques for detecting and closing gaps and explains FCP protocol for defining gaps.

To find gaps in a sequence:

1. Make the sequence active; then press the Home key to position the playhead at the beginning of the sequence (**Figure 7.86**).

2. Choose Mark > Next > Gap; or press Shift-G.

   The playhead moves to the beginning of the first gap found (**Figure 7.87**).

3. If you want to close the gap, use one of the procedures described in the next section, "To close a gap."

4. Repeat steps 2 and 3 until you reach the end of the sequence.

✔ Tip

- Press Option-G to jump the playhead back to the previous gap.

WORKING WITH ITEMS IN THE TIMELINE

To close a gap:

1. Make the sequence active; then position the playhead anywhere in the gap (**Figure 7.88**).

2. *Do one of the following:*

   ▲ Select the gap and press Delete.

   ▲ Control-click the gap; then select Close Gap from the shortcut menu (**Figure 7.89**).

   ▲ Choose Sequence > Close Gap.

   Clips to the right of the gap will shift left to close the gap. These clips adjust their timecode location to occur earlier, and the sequence duration may change (**Figure 7.90**).

Figure 7.89 Control-click the gap; then choose Close Gap from the shortcut menu.

Figure 7.90 Clips to the right of the gap shift left to close the gap.

WORKING WITH ITEMS IN THE TIMELINE

FCP Protocol: Gaps and Track Gaps

Final Cut Pro defines two classes of gaps: gaps and track gaps.

◆ A gap is any empty spot across all unlocked video or audio tracks. If you have a gap on one track, but have a clip bridging the gap on a higher or lower track, FCP defines that as a *track gap*.

◆ A track gap is any empty spot on an individual track in a sequence.

Some gap-closing techniques, such as Ripple Delete, work only with gaps, not track gaps. To close track gaps, lock all other tracks, leaving the gapped tracks as the only unlocked tracks in your sequence.

Streamlined procedures for closing track gaps by locking other sequence tracks are described in the section "Finding and closing gaps" earlier in this chapter.

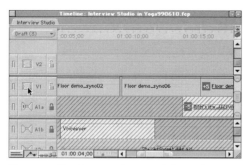

Figure 7.91 To select a track to search for track gaps, click to turn on the Target Track control.

Figure 7.92 The playhead jumps to the start of the first track gap found.

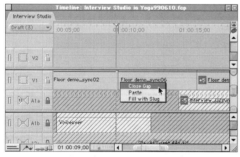

Figure 7.93 Control-click the gap; then choose Close Gap from the shortcut menu.

To find track gaps in a Timeline track:

1. In the Timeline, click the Target Track control of the track you want to search to make it the target track (**Figure 7.91**).

2. Press the Home key to position the playhead at the beginning of the sequence.

3. Choose Mark > Next > Gap.

   The playhead moves to the beginning of the first track gap found (**Figure 7.92**).

To close a track gap:

Do one of the following:

◆ Open the shortcut menu over the gap and choose Close Gap (**Figure 7.93**).

◆ Select the gap and press the Delete key.

◆ Position the playhead anywhere within the gap; then choose Sequence > Close Gap.

✔ Tip

■ Sometimes a gap can't be closed because clips don't have space to shift back. If the command can't be completed, the Close Gap command is dimmed. Try the track locking technique discussed next.

To close a track gap without affecting other tracks in sequence:

1. Press Shift-F4 to lock all video tracks in your sequence.

2. Press Shift-F5 to lock all audio tracks in your sequence.

3. Click the Track Lock control of the gapped track.

   Your selected track is now the only unlocked track in your sequence (**Figure 7.94**).

4. *Do one of the following:*

   ▲ Select the gap and press Delete.

   ▲ Control-click the gap; then select Close Gap from the shortcut menu (**Figure 7.95**).

   ▲ Choose Sequence > Close Gap.

   Clips to the right of the gap will shift left to close the gap. These clips adjust their timecode locations to occur earlier, and the sequence duration may change (**Figure 7.96**).

5. If you want to unlock your sequence tracks after closing the gap, press Shift-F4 and Shift-F5 again to toggle track locking off.

Figure 7.94 Locking every other track but the gapped track allows you to close this gap by shifting material on the unlocked track only.

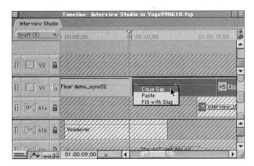

Figure 7.95 Control-click the gap; then choose Close Gap from the shortcut menu.

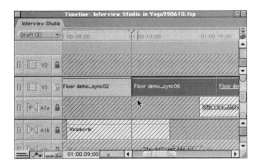

Figure 7.96 Clips to the right of the gap shift left to close the track gap. Clips on the locked tracks have not moved.

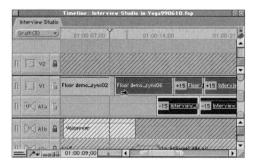

Figure 7.97 Use the Select Track Forward tool to click the first clip to the right of the track gap.

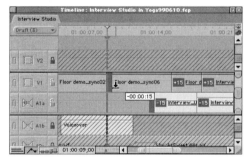

Figure 7.98 Drag the selected clips to the left until they snap to close the gap; then drop them as an Overwrite edit.

To close a track gap with the Select Forward tool:

1. Choose View > Snapping to make sure snapping is turned on.

2. From the Tool palette, choose the Select Track Forward tool; then click the first clip to the right of the track gap (**Figure 7.97**).

   The clips to the right of the sequence are selected, and the cursor changes to a four-headed arrow pointer.

3. Drag the selected clips to the left until they snap to close the gap; then drop them as an Overwrite edit (**Figure 7.98**).

To close a gap by extending an adjacent clip (an Extend edit):

◆ In some cases, you may prefer to close a gap in your sequence by extending the duration of a clip that's adjacent to the gap. One advantage of an Extend edit (that's what it's called) is that all of the clips in your sequence can stay put, and you won't develop sync problems. To learn how to perform an Extend edit, see Chapter 8, "Fine Cut: Trimming Edits."

✔ Tips

- When you are fine-tuning gaps in your sequences, take advantage of the Zoom tools to scale your view so you can see what you're doing. You may also find that turning on snapping will simplify selection and manipulation of gaps and track gaps.

- You can get a quick reading of the duration of a gap by Control-clicking the gap and then choosing Fill with Slug from the shortcut menu. Now you can Control-click the slug, and the duration will appear as one of the items in the shortcut menu. When you're done, just select the slug and press Delete—your gap's back, and you can decide what to do next.

- Here's another way to read a gap's duration: Select the gap in the Timeline, and then press Shift-A. The Mark Selection command sets sequence In and Out points, and your gaps' duration appears in the Timecode Duration field in the Canvas. Wow—it actually takes longer to describe it than to do it.

FCP Protocol: Deleting Items in the Timeline

You can delete items in the Timeline simply by selecting them and then pressing Delete. But if the Timeline window is active and you press Delete with no items selected in the Timeline, then FCP protocol dictates that all material between the Timeline and Canvas In and Out points is deleted on all unlocked tracks.

Learn more about performing Delete edits in Chapter 6, "Editing in Final Cut Pro."

Copying and pasting clip attributes

Clip attributes are all of the settings applied to a particular media file in Final Cut Pro. You can paste all of the attributes of one clip onto another clip, or you can select and paste some of the settings of a clip onto another clip without affecting other attributes. For example, you can apply just the filter settings from clip A to clip B without changing the video frames of clip B. Conversely, you can replace the video frames of clip B without disturbing the filters that have been applied to it by pasting only the video frames from another clip. If you just paste into a sequence without selecting a clip in the Timeline or Canvas, the clip's media contents are included in addition to the selected attributes.

These are the attributes you can transfer from one clip to another (**Figure 7.100**):

◆ **Scale Attribute Times:** Check this box to adjust the timing of the incoming keyframes to fit the duration of the clip inheriting the attributes. If this option is not selected, leftover keyframes will be cropped off the end.

◆ **Video Attributes:** Check this box if you want to paste any of the video attributes from the following list:

▲ **Content:** Paste the video frames only. If the receiving clip is a different length, incoming video frames are cropped or lengthened to match the duration of the receiving clip. The clip speed is not affected.

▲ **Basic Motion**, **Crop**, **Distort**, **Opacity**, **Drop Shadow**, **Motion Blur**, and **Filters:** You can pick and choose among these options to apply the parameter values and keyframes you have set for each attribute.

▲ **Speed:** Apply the same speed settings.

▲ **Clip Settings:** Paste all capture settings that are logged with a clip. (You can review these settings on the Clip Settings tab of the Log and Capture window.)

◆ **Audio Attributes:** Check this box if you want to paste any of the audio attributes from the following list:

▲ **Content:** Paste the audio waveform only. If the receiving clip is a different length, the incoming audio file is cropped or lengthened to match the duration of the receiving clip. The clip speed is not affected.

▲ **Levels** and **Filters:** Apply the parameter values and keyframes you have set for each attribute.

To paste the attributes of a copied clip into another clip:

1. In the Timeline or Browser, select a clip whose attributes you want to copy (**Figure 7.99**); then press Command-C to copy it to the clipboard.

2. Select the clip that will inherit the attributes; then choose Edit > Paste Attributes.

3. In the Paste Attributes dialog box, select the attributes that you want to transfer to the selected clip (Figure 7.100).

4. Click OK.

   The selected attributes will be pasted into the receiving clip (**Figure 7.101**).

✔ Tip

■ Pasting audio levels can be a quick way to add an audio element—say, another sound effects track—to a scene you have already mixed. You can "borrow" the mix levels from a track that has already been adjusted to match action and paste those levels onto your new effects track. You can apply the same idea to video compositing. Paste the motion path from one video layer to another that you want to track the same path. Or paste and then offset the timing of the motion path.

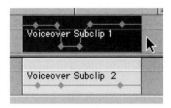

Figure 7.99 Select the clip whose attributes you want to copy; then press Command-C.

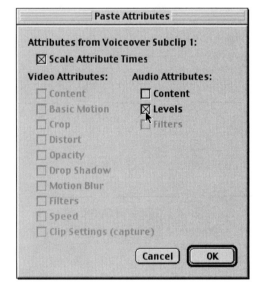

Figure 7.100 Selecting audio levels in the Paste Attributes dialog box.

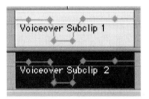

Figure 7.101 The audio levels from Voiceover Subclip 1 have been copied and pasted into Voiceover Subclip 2.

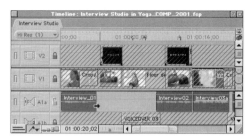

Figure 7.102 Selecting multiple audio clips with the Select Track Forward tool.

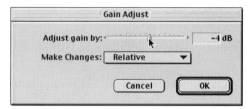

Figure 7.103 Adjusting the audio levels relative to their current levels.

Making multiclip adjustments

Two commands in the Modify menu allow adjustments on multiclip selections:

◆ Use Modify > Levels to adjust levels for a group of audio clips.

◆ Use Modify > Opacity to adjust opacity levels for a group of video clips.

To adjust audio levels for a group of clips:

1. In the Timeline, select a group of audio clips whose levels you want to adjust (**Figure 7.102**).

2. Choose Modify > Levels.

3. In the Gain Adjust dialog box, *do one of the following:*

   ▲ Choose Relative from the pop-up menu; then use the slider to adjust each clip's volume relative to its current level by the dB value indicated next to the slider (**Figure 7.103**).

   ▲ Choose Absolute from the pop-up menu; then use the slider to set each clip's volume to the dB value indicated next to the slider.

4. Click OK.

✔ Tip

■ Use FCP's audio level meters to check your audio level adjustments. Choose Window > Audio Meters to display the meters.

To adjust opacity levels on a group of clips:

1. In the Timeline, select a group of clips whose levels you want to adjust.

2. Choose Modify > Levels.

3. In the Opacity Adjust dialog box, *do one of the following:*

   ▲ Choose Relative from the pop-up menu; then use the slider to adjust each clip's opacity relative to its current level by the percentage value indicated next to the slider.

   ▲ Choose Absolute from the pop-up menu; then use the slider to set each clip's volume to the percentage value indicated next to the slider (**Figure 7.104**).

4. Click OK.

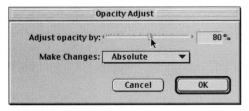

Figure 7.104 Setting opacity levels to 80 percent for all selected clips.

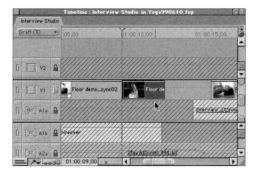

Figure 7.105 Select the clip in the Timeline.

Changing the playback speed of a clip

Changing the playback speed of a clip adjusts its duration by duplicating or skipping clip frames and creates either a slow-motion or fast-motion effect. For example, if you start with a 1-minute clip and set the playback speed to 50 percent, Final Cut Pro will duplicate each frame, doubling the clip length to 2 minutes. Your adjusted 2-minute clip will play back at half speed. If you start with the same 1-minute clip and increase the playback speed to 200 percent, the adjusted clip will skip every other frame and play back at double speed in 30 seconds. You can specify frame blending when modifying a clip's speed to smooth out your slow-motion or fast-motion effect. (Yes, adjusting the speed requires rendering before you can play back the clip.)

To change the playback speed of a clip:

1. Select the clip in the Timeline (**Figure 7.105**).

2. Choose Modify > Speed; or press Command-J.

3. Choose from the options in the Speed dialog box:

   ▲ You can modify the clip speed by a percentage or specify a duration for the adjusted clip. Changing the clip speed or duration automatically adjusts the other value.

   ▲ The Frame Blending option smoothes motion at slow or fast speeds.

   ▲ The Reverse check box renders the clip's frames in reverse order; the adjusted clip will play in reverse.

continues on next page

WORKING WITH ITEMS IN THE TIMELINE

4. Click OK (**Figure 7.106**).

The adjusted duration of the modified clip will be calculated based on the clip's original In and Out points (**Figure 7.107**).

✔ Tip

- If you want to apply speed effects to only a portion of a clip, first use the Razor Blade tool to break out that portion of the clip you want to process. Speed effects can be applied only to whole clips.

Using offline clips

An offline clip is defined as a placeholder for an actual media file. An offline clip could be:

- ◆ Logged but not yet captured

- ◆ A stand-in for the actual media file, which has been moved or deleted

- ◆ A stand-in for media that is not yet available

You can treat offline clips just like regular clips: You can set In and Out points, add transitions and filters, rename the clips, and so on. Later, you can replace an offline clip by recapturing it or reconnecting to the original source media.

Final Cut Pro is so advanced, you can edit media that doesn't even exist yet!

To create an offline clip:

- ◆ Choose File > New > Offline Clip.

  An offline clip is inserted into the Browser (**Figure 7.108**).

See "Reconnecting Offline Files" in Chapter 12, "Big Picture: Managing Complex Projects." for more information on offline clips.

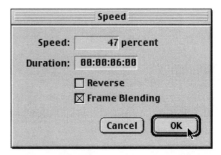

Figure 7.106 Modify your clip's speed by a percentage or specify a duration; then click OK.

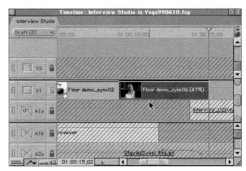

Figure 7.107 The size of the clip's icon increases to reflect the duration change caused by modifying the playback speed, and the adjusted speed appears next to the clip's name. You must render the clip to review the speed change.

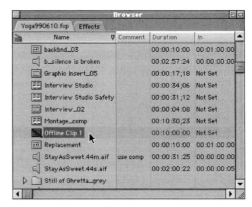

Figure 7.108 A new offline clip appears in the Browser. You can insert an offline clip into a sequence and edit it, but you will not see it.

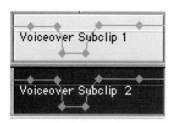

Figure 7.109 Keyframe overlays allow you to sculpt audio levels right in the Timeline.

Figure 7.110 Keyframes appear on the Filter and Motion bars in the Timeline, but it's easier to adjust these keyframes on the Viewer's Effects tab or in the Canvas.

Working with Keyframes in the Timeline

Keyframes indicate that effects parameters are changing over time. You can think of a keyframe as a kind of edit point: You stamp a keyframe at the point where you want to change the value of an effect's parameter. This section covers Timeline functions relating to keyframes.

Final Cut Pro has two types of keyframes that can be displayed in the Timeline:

◆ **Keyframe overlays** indicate clip opacity for video clips and volume level for audio clips. Keyframe overlays are displayed as line graphs right on top of the track display in the Timeline (**Figure 7.109**).

◆ **Keyframes appear** in the Filter and Motion bars beneath sequence clips that have filter and motion effects applied to them (**Figure 7.110**). Keyframes indicate where parameters change for filter and motion effects. You can select the parameter keyframes you want to display in a particular Filter or Motion bar.

The Timeline's Filter and Motion bars are good places to get a big-picture idea of the relationship between keyframes on different tracks, but the Timeline view is not ideal for adjusting keyframes on a detailed level.

For more precise control of keyframes, double-click the clip in the Timeline to open it in the Viewer; then select the Filter or Motion tab. Working with keyframes to create effects using the Filter and Motion tabs is covered in Chapter 13, "Compositing and Special Effects."

✔ Tip

■ The Pen tool selects only keyframes, so it's the best tool to use if you need to adjust a keyframe overlay near an edit point—for example, when you're fine-tuning a fade.

To display keyframes for individual effects parameters:

◆ In the Timeline, click the Clip Keyframes button (located in the lower-left corner) to display the Filter and Motion bars.

Keyframes are displayed in a clip's Filter and Motion bars (**Figure 7.111**).

To select the effects keyframes displayed in the Timeline:

1. In the Timeline, Control-click the Filter or Motion bar to access its shortcut menu (**Figure 7.112**).

2. From the list of all of the parameters for each filter currently applied to the clip:

   ▲ Select the name of a parameter to display its keyframes in the Timeline.

   ▲ Select the filter name to display all the parameters for that filter.

✔ Tips

■ After you've selected a filter in the Filter and Motion bars, double-click the bar to open that filter on the Viewer's Effects tab.

■ You can slide a whole set of keyframes in a clip's Filter and Motion bars. Use the Selection tool to click and drag on the bar, and the keyframes will slide to the left or right (**Figure 7.113**).

■ Any time you're working with the Selection tool, the fastest way to a Pen tool is to press the Option key. The Selection tool switches to Pen tool mode as long as you're holding down the Option key.

To display keyframe overlays in the Timeline:

◆ In the Timeline, click the Clip Overlays button in the lower-left corner (**Figure 7.114**).

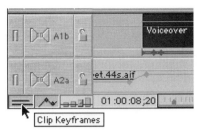

Figure 7.111 Click the Clip Keyframes control in the Timeline window to toggle the display of filter and motion keyframes.

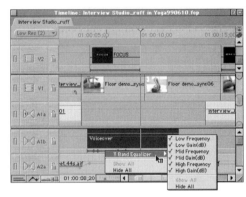

Figure 7.112 Control-click a clip's Filter or Motion bar to access and choose from a list of parameters to display.

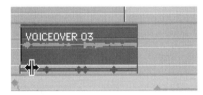

Figure 7.113 Use the Selection tool to click and drag the bar and slide the whole set of keyframes.

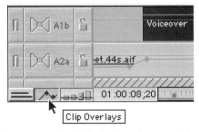

Figure 7.114 Click the Clip Overlays control in the Timeline window to toggle the display of keyframe overlays.

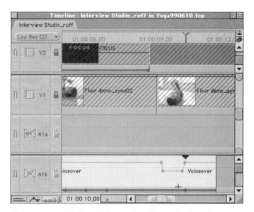

Figure 7.115 Click and drag a keyframe in the Filter and Motion bars to adjust its location.

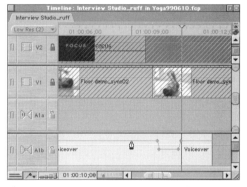

Figure 7.116 Use the Pen tool to add a keyframe to a clip's keyframe overlay graph.

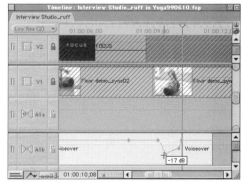

Figure 7.117 A ToolTip displaying the current audio level updates as you adjust the keyframe.

To move keyframes in the Timeline:

◆ In the sequence clip's Filter and Motion bars, click and drag the effect keyframe left or right to adjust its timecode location (**Figure 7.115**).

   If snapping is on, the keyframe snaps to other keyframes and markers to help you align keyframes to particular points in the sequence.

To add an overlay keyframe to a track:

1. From the Tool palette, select the Pen tool.

2. On the selected clip's overlay keyframe graph, click where you want to place the keyframe (**Figure 7.116**).

   A new keyframe will be added to the overlay.

To adjust the values of individual overlay keyframes:

Do one of the following:

◆ Click and drag overlay keyframes vertically to adjust their values. As you drag, a ToolTip appears, displaying the parameter's value (**Figure 7.117**).

◆ Shift-drag the graph line between two overlay keyframes to adjust its position.

To delete overlay keyframes:

◆ Drag keyframes off the track completely to delete them.

   The keyframes (except for the last one) are removed, and the keyframe path is adjusted to reflect the change.

Searching for Items in the Timeline

Final Cut Pro's search engine is built to search for other items beyond clips and sequences. Use FCP's Find command to search the Timeline for clip names, marker text, and clip timecodes. You can search for items forward or backward. You can also search for and close gaps in all tracks in a sequence or in individual tracks.

✔ Tip

- This might be a good time to mention that when you place a clip in a sequence, even though the two clips may have the same name, the sequence clip is a separate version of the clip from the one that stays in the Browser. So if you are searching for the *sequence version* of a clip, you need to search in that sequence.

To search for items in the sequence:

1. Open the sequence in the Timeline.

2. *Do one of the following:*

   ▲ To search the entire sequence, position the playhead at the start of the sequence.

   ▲ To search a selected portion of the sequence, set the sequence In and Out points to specify the search area; or position the playhead at the beginning of the section you want to search (**Figure 7.118**).

3. Choose Edit > Find; or press Command-F.

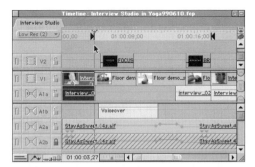

Figure 7.118 Position the playhead at the beginning of the section you want to search.

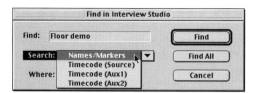

Figure 7.119 Specifying a search for clips or markers with "floor demo" in their names.

Figure 7.120 Specifying a search of the sequence from the sequence In to Out points.

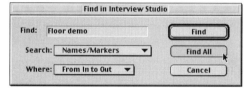

Figure 7.121 Specifying Find All will highlight all clips in the sequence that match the search criteria.

Figure 7.122 Three clips whose names contain the phrase "floor demo" are highlighted in the Timeline. Only the section between the sequence In and Out points has been searched.

4. From the Search pop-up list, choose the type of item to search for (**Figure 7.119**):

▲ **Names/Markers:** Search for the text in clip names, marker names, and marker comments.

▲ **Timecode Options:** Search for any source or auxiliary timecode in a clip.

5. Choose which tracks to search from the Where pop-up menu:

▲ **All Tracks:** Search all tracks in the sequence.

▲ **Target Tracks:** Search only the current target tracks.

▲ **From In to Out:** Search between the sequence In and Out points on all tracks (**Figure 7.120**).

6. To perform the search, *do one of the following:*

▲ Click Find to find the item.

▲ Click Find All to find all occurrences of clips that match the search criteria (**Figure 7.121**).

All clips that match the search criteria are selected in the Timeline (**Figure 7.122**). If the search returns a marker, the playhead is positioned on the marker.

To cycle through items in the Timeline that match the criteria:

◆ Follow the search procedure outlined in the preceding steps; then press F3.

To search for an item backward from the position of the playhead:

◆ Follow the search procedure outlined in the preceding steps, and then press Shift-F3.

SEARCHING FOR ITEMS IN THE TIMELINE

305

FINE CUT: TRIMMING EDITS

What's the difference between performing an edit and trimming an edit? An edit adds new material to a sequence; a trim is an adjustment to previously assembled sequence material. The development of nonlinear editing has expanded the repertoire of trim edit types. Some of these trim edit types (like Ripple and Roll) date back to the tape-to-tape days of video editing; others (like the Slide edit) could not have existed until the advent of nonlinear systems. Certainly none of these trim edits were implemented in the same way in older editing schemes. You can perform a Slip-edit cutting on film—but it's more like "strip-snip-snip-slip; hand me the glue."

In this chapter, you'll learn about the types of trim edits available in Final Cut Pro. Each type of trim edit can be performed in a variety of ways (with tools, with timecode entry, or with keystrokes) and in a few different locations (in the Timeline, the Trim Edit window, and the Viewer), so you'll learn how and where you can perform each type. This chapter also introduces the Trim Edit window, a specialized work environment for making fine adjustments to your edits.

Types of Trimming Operations

Each of the trim edit types can solve a particular editing problem, so it's a good idea to familiarize yourself with the whole palette—maybe even try them all in advance. If you would like to review the list of FCP's basic editing types, return to Chapter 6, "Editing in Final Cut Pro."

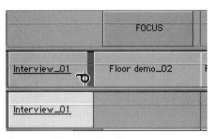

Figure 8.1 A Ripple Left edit, as performed in the Timeline.

◆ **Ripple:** A Ripple edit adjusts the length of one clip in a sequence by changing either the In or the Out point of that clip. A Ripple edit is designed to accommodate the change by rippling (or shifting) the timecode location of the clips that come after the adjusted edit without affecting their duration. Use a Ripple edit if you want to adjust the length of a clip in a sequence without losing sync or creating a gap. Locked tracks will not be rippled. The Close Gap command in the Timeline performs a Ripple Delete edit.

Figure 8.1 shows a Ripple Left edit, in contrast to **Figure 8.2**, which shows a Ripple Right edit, as performed in the Timeline. Note the differences in the cursor and in the selected edit points.

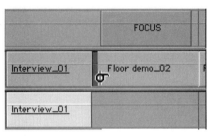

Figure 8.2 A Ripple Right edit, as performed in the Timeline.

◆ **Roll:** A Roll edit (**Figure 8.3**) adjusts the location of an edit point shared by two clips. A rolling edit is designed to accommodate the change by subtracting frames from clip A on one side of the edit to compensate for the frames added to clip B on the other side of the edit. The overall duration of the sequence is unchanged, but the location of the edit in the sequence is changed.

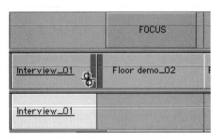

Figure 8.3 A Roll edit, as performed in the Timeline.

◆ **Slip:** A Slip edit (**Figure 8.4**) is an adjustment made within a single clip. When you slip a clip, you are selecting a different part of that clip to include in the sequence, while maintaining clip duration and

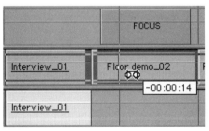

Figure 8.4 A Slip edit, as performed in the Timeline. The selected portion of the clip has shifted –14 frames.

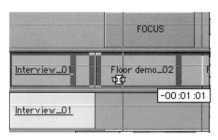

Figure 8.5 A Slide edit, as performed in the Timeline. The selected clip has slid 1 second, 1 frame earlier in the sequence.

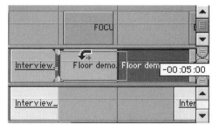

Figure 8.6 A Swap edit, as performed in the Timeline. The two Floor demo clips will swap positions.

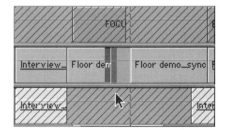

Figure 8.7 An Extend edit. Select the edit point of the clip you want to extend to the playhead position.

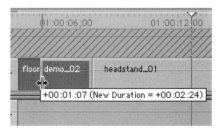

Figure 8.8 Resizing a clip in the Timeline. Drag an edit point with the Selection tool to adjust clip duration.

timecode location in the sequence. Surrounding clips are not affected, and the sequence duration does not change.

◆ **Slide:** A Slide edit (**Figure 8.5**) moves a single clip in relation to those before and after it, so that the durations of the clips on either side are changed, but the In and Out points of the clip you're sliding remain the same. The clips immediately adjacent to the sliding clip accommodate the change; the overall sequence duration does not change.

◆ **Swap:** A Swap edit (**Figure 8.6**) makes no changes to any sequence clips but changes the order in which they appear in the sequence. Perform a Swap edit in the Timeline by selecting a clip, dragging it to a new location, and Insert editing it into the sequence.

◆ **Extend:** An Extend edit (**Figure 8.7**) moves a selected edit point to the playhead position by extending the clip's duration, rolling over any gaps or clips that are encountered. You can extend an edit only to the maximum length of that clip's media. An Extend edit is a useful way to fill sequence gaps without affecting the sequence duration.

◆ **Resize:** The Selection (or Arrow) tool can be used to resize a clip in the Timeline by dragging an edit point. You can drag the edit point to create a gap (by making the duration of the clip smaller, **Figure 8.8**) or to cover an existing gap.

✔ Tip

■ Press the Command key to "gear down" the onscreen tools while performing fine adjustments to a trim. With the Command key engaged, your manipulation of the onscreen trim tools will result in much smaller adjustments to your edit points.

Selecting an Edit for Trimming

The first step in trimming an edit in the Trim Edit window or the Timeline is selecting the edit. If you use a trimming tool from the Tool palette to select the edit, you can select and define the type of trim to perform at the same time. You can select only one edit per track.

If an edit point you select for trimming has been linked to others, the edit points of the linked items are also selected. Any adjustments you make will be applied to all of the clips in the linked selection, so if you find that you can't trim an edit point, the conflict may be with one of the linked items. You can toggle linked selection off by holding down the Option key as you select the edit.

With snapping turned on, edit points will snap to markers, keyframes, the playhead, and edit points on other tracks. Snapping can simplify alignment of edits in the Timeline. To toggle snapping on and off on the fly, press the N key while dragging edit points.

✔ Tips

■ Many trim operations will ripple all of your unlocked tracks as part of the trim process. If you don't want your tracks taking unplanned trips when you are trimming, lock all tracks except the ones you want to adjust.

■ If FCP refuses to execute a trim edit that would ripple your unlocked tracks backward, you might check to see if clips on other tracks in your sequence can't move back in time without bumping into other clips.

Tips on Tools

FCP's edit tools get a heavy workout when you transform your rough assembly into a fine cut. You can review the contents of the Tool palette's selection and edit tools in "Anatomy of the Tool Palette" in Chapter 7, but here are some other ideas for making efficient use of these tools:

◆ Use the keyboard shortcuts for calling up an edit tool. See **Table 8.1** for a list of basic selection shortcuts. Check out Appendix B for more shortcuts.

◆ Once you've selected an edit tool, Press U to cycle through the three principal trim types: Roll, Ripple Left, and Ripple Right.

◆ You can use the Ripple and Roll tools to directly select the edit you're adjusting. One click, and you've selected the edit and specified the edit type.

◆ Pressing the Option key to override linked selection works on all of the edit tools, not just the Selection arrow.

◆ Pressing the Command key when you're dragging an edit tool on a selected edit in the Timeline will gear down the tool and allow you to make fine adjustments.

◆ Turn Snapping off when you are trying to make fine adjustments that don't align with an existing edit point, marker, or clip boundary.

◆ Turn on snapping when you're trying to align an edit to another existing edit point or marker.

Figure 8.9 Choose the Edits Selection tool from the Tool palette. This tool is designed to detect and select edits only.

Table 8.1

Tool Selection Shortcuts

Tool	Shortcut
Roll Edit	R
Ripple Edit	R+R
Slip Item	S
Slide Item	S+S
Razor Blade	B
Razor Blade All	B+B
Selection	A
Edit Selection	G

Quick Navigation Keys

Option and Shift modifier keys are used throughout FCP's keyboard shortcuts for navigation. Here's a set of keyboard shortcuts to help you motor through your sequence when you're fine-tuning your edit.

Key	Shift + key	Option + key	No modifier
I	Go to In	Clear In	Set In
O	Go to Out	Clear Out	Set Out
M	Next Marker	Previous Marker	Set Marker
E	Next Edit	Previous Edit	Extend Edit
G	Next Gap	Previous Gap	
K	Next Keyframe	Previous Keyframe	

To select an edit in the Timeline:

Do one of the following:

- From the Tool palette, choose the Edits Selection tool (**Figure 8.9**); or press G; then click an edit point in the Timeline.

   The Trim Edit window opens as you release the mouse button.

- From the Tool palette, choose the Selection tool; then click the edge of the clip in the Timeline. Double-click the edit if you want the Trim Edit window to open as well.

- From the Tool palette, choose the Ripple tool or Roll tool; then click the edge of the clip in the Timeline.

✔ Tips

- If you are having trouble selecting Timeline edit points, use the Zoom slider to magnify your view, or try again with the Ripple tool or the Roll tool; they're designed to select edit points only, so you can't accidentally select a clip.

- Using the Option key to override linked selection works with any edit tool, just as it does with the Selection arrow.

- Here's a keyboard shortcut to speed edit selection in the Timeline: press V to select the edit point nearest the play head's location.

To select multiple edits in the Timeline:

Do one of the following:

◆ From the Tool palette, choose the Edits Selection tool, then draw a marquee around the edit points of one or more Timeline tracks (**Figure 8.10**). You can select one edit per track; the selected edits don't have to be aligned in time.

The Trim Edit window opens as you release the mouse button.

◆ From the Tool palette, choose the Selection tool; then Command-click the edge of the clips in the Timeline. Double-click any selected edit if you want the Trim Edit window to open as well.

◆ From the Tool palette, choose the Ripple tool or Roll tool; then Command-click the edge of the clips in the Timeline.

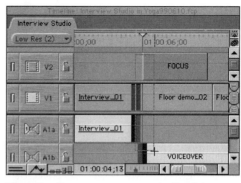

Figure 8.10 Draw a marquee around edit points you want to select.

All Keys: Mouse-less Trimming in FCP

You can work your way through your edit without touching the mouse. Here's one possible scenario:

1. Press Shift-E to jump the playhead to the next edit in the Timeline.

2. Press V to select the nearest edit.

3. Press \ (backslash) to play the sequence before and after the selected edit point.

4. Press R to select the Roll tool.

5. Press + (plus) or – (minus) and then enter a number of frames to roll the edit.

So many keyboard shortcuts in FCP, and so many ways to speed your work while you give your mouse hand a rest. Check out the Keyboard shortcuts in Appendix B.

Anatomy of the Trim Edit Window

The Trim Edit window is a work environment optimized for making fine adjustments to a single edit point. You can trim the selected edit by one frame or several frames, quickly switch between Ripple and Roll edits, and play the edit back to review your trim adjustments. The Play Around Edit button is designed to loop playback of your edit while you're fine-tuning it. The looping is not seamless; there is a slight interruption in the playback when you nudge the edit point.

Figure 8.11 shows an overview of the Trim Edit window.

◆ **Outgoing clip name:** Displays the name of the outgoing clip.

◆ **Outgoing clip duration:** Displays the elapsed time between the In and Out points of the outgoing clip. This value updates to reflect trim adjustments.

◆ **Outgoing clip current timecode:** Displays the clip's source timecode at the current position of the playhead.

◆ **Track pop-up menu:** Displays a list if multiple edits have been selected. Select the track you want to edit in the Trim Edit window.

◆ **Current sequence timecode:** Displays the sequence timecode location of the edit point. Enter + or – and a duration to roll the edit point. You don't need to click the field; just start typing.

◆ **Incoming clip current timecode:** Displays the clip's source timecode at the current position of the playhead.

continues on next page

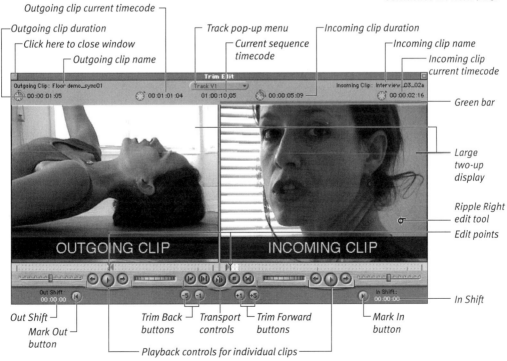

Figure 8.11 Use the Trim Edit window to make fine adjustments to a selected edit point.

ANATOMY OF THE TRIM EDIT WINDOW

◆ **Incoming clip duration:** Displays the elapsed time between the In and Out points of the incoming clip. This value updates to reflect trim adjustments.

◆ **Incoming clip name:** Displays the name of the incoming clip.

◆ **Large two-up display:** The left screen displays the last frame before the edit. The right screen displays the first frame after the edit.

◆ **Green bar:** Indicates which side of the edit you are trimming.

◆ **Edit points:** Indicates the current Out and In points for the two clips in the Trim edit window. You can trim by dragging the outgoing clip's Out point or the incoming clip's In point with an edit tool.

◆ **Playback controls for individual clips:** The outgoing and incoming clips have separate playback controls. Use these controls to play only that clip without changing the current edit point location.

◆ **Out Shift:** Indicates the number of frames that the Out point has been adjusted.

◆ **Mark Out button:** Click to set a new Out point for the outgoing clip at the current playhead position.

◆ **Trim Back buttons:** Nudge the selected edit point to the left. Trim by single-frame increments or by another frame increment you specify on the General tab in the Preferences window.

◆ **Trim Forward buttons:** Nudge the selected edit point to the right.

◆ **Mark In button:** Click to set a new In point for the incoming clip at the current playhead position.

◆ **In Shift:** Indicates the number of frames that the In point has been adjusted.

Figure 8.12 shows a detail of the Trim Edit window's transport control buttons.

◆ **Previous Edit button:** Click to move the previous edit into the active area of the Trim Edit window.

◆ **Play In to Out button:** Click to play from the start of the first clip to the end of the second clip.

◆ **Play Around Edit Loop button:** Click to loop playback of the edit point plus the specified pre-roll and post-roll. Playback loops until you click Stop. You can continue trimming the edit while playback is looping.

◆ **Stop button:** Click to stop playback and position the playhead on the edit point.

◆ **Next Edit button:** Click to move the next edit into the active area of the Trim Edit window.

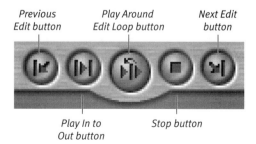

Previous Edit button *Play Around Edit Loop button* *Next Edit button*

Play In to Out button *Stop button*

Figure 8.12 Trim Edit window transport controls detail.

FCP Protocol: Trimming Error Messages

When you attempt a trim operation that can't be executed, Final Cut Pro will warn you by displaying one of the following error messages:

◆ You cannot set the In point later than a disabled Out point: When you're adjusting an In or Out point in the Trim Edit window, you can't position your clip's In point later than its Out point. Likewise, Out points cannot be placed before an In point.

The word *disabled* in the message refers to Trim Edit window protocol. Only the outgoing clip's Out point and the incoming clip's In point are active while you're in the Trim Edit window.

The next three messages specify the track number where the error occurred:

◆ **Clip collision:** A trimming operation would cause clips to collide or one clip to overwrite another.

◆ **Transition conflict:** A transition duration adjustment would be required to accommodate the trimming change.

◆ **Media limit:** There is insufficient media in the source clip to complete the edit as specified.

◆ **Insufficient content:** The same as Media Limit; there is insufficient media in the source clip to complete the edit.

Using the Trim Edit Window

The Trim Edit window offers plenty of flexibility to accommodate your editing style; you can mix and match trimming methods in a single trim operation. This window features two good-sized screens displaying the clips on either side of the edit you are adjusting, as well as Duration and Current Timecode displays for each side.

✔ Tips

■ If you're using Timecode entry in the Trim edit window, you can cancel an edit by pressing the Esc key while the Timecode field is still active. You can also undo an edit at any time by pressing Command-Z.

■ All of the plus and minus adjustments you are making in the Trim Edit window are referring to the location of the edit point, not the duration of either clip. That's especially important to remember when you're making adjustments on the right side of the edit point.

To open the Trim Edit window:

Do one of the following:

◆ Press Command-7.

The playhead jumps to the closest edit on the target track, and the Trim Edit window opens with a Roll edit selected.

◆ In the Timeline, click an edit with the Edits Selection tool (**Figure 8.13**).

The edit is selected, and the Trim Edit window opens automatically (**Figure 8.14**).

◆ Choose Sequence > Trim Edit.

◆ In the Timeline, double-click an edit.

To close the Trim Edit window:

Do one of the following:

◆ Move the Timeline or Canvas playhead away from the edit.

◆ Click anywhere in the Timeline away from an edit to deselect all edits in the Timeline.

◆ Click in the upper-left corner of the Trim Edit window (**Figure 8.15**).

To trim an edit in the Trim Edit window:

1. Select one or more edit points to trim, using any of the methods described earlier in this section. Then, if the Trim Edit window has not opened automatically, press Command-7 to open the Trim Edit window.

2. In the Trim Edit window, use the cursor to select the type of trim operation. The pointer changes to indicate whether you've selected Ripple Left, Roll, or Ripple Right.

   ▲ Click the left image to trim the outgoing clip with a Ripple Left edit.

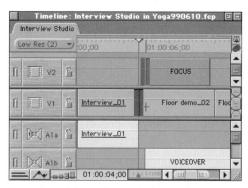

Figure 8.13 Click an edit point in the Timeline with the Edits Selection tool.

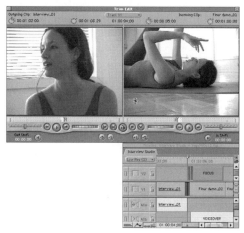

Figure 8.14 The Trim Edit window opens automatically.

Figure 8.15 Close the Trim Edit window by clicking the upper-left corner.

Figure 8.16 Click the image on the right in the Trim Edit window to select a Ripple Right edit.

Figure 8.17 Clicking this Trim Forward button moves the edit point to the right by single-frame increments.

▲ Click the right image to trim the incoming clip with a Ripple Right edit (**Figure 8.16**).

▲ Click the area between the images to select a Roll edit.

A green bar appears above the clip image, indicating that that side of the edit is selected for trimming.

3. Trim the edit using any of the following methods:

▲ Use the trim buttons to move the edit point to the left or right by frame increments (**Figure 8.17**).

▲ Trim the edit point by typing + or – and a duration to add or subtract. You don't need to click the field—just start typing and then press Enter. The type of trim performed depends on the edit selection you made in step 2.

▲ Click and drag an edit point in the Scrubber bar.

▲ Use the individual playback controls under either clip to play the clip; then mark a new Out point for the outgoing clip or a new In point for the incoming clip.

The In Shift and Out Shift fields update to show the total cumulative shift in the edit point. These fields will track the shift, even if you perform the trim as several small adjustments. The Timeline display updates to reflect your trim.

4. Use the transport controls to review your edit.

▲ Click the Play In to Out button to play from the start of the first clip to the end of the second clip.

continues on next page

USING THE TRIM EDIT WINDOW

▲ Click the Play Around Edit Loop button to loop playback of the edit point plus the specified pre-roll and post-roll (**Figure 8.18**).

▲ Click the Stop button to stop playback and position the playhead on the edit point.

5. When you are finished trimming, close the Trim Edit window.

✔ Tips

■ You can use the Previous Edit and Next Edit buttons in the Trim Edit window to move to the next edit on the current track without leaving the Trim Edit window.

■ If you have selected multiple edits to trim, use the Track pop-up menu to select the track to view in the Trim Edit window.

To slip an edit in the Trim Edit window:

1. Select an edit in the Timeline (**Figure 8.19**).

2. Press Command-7 to open the Trim Edit window.

3. In the Trim Edit window, Shift-drag the active edit point on either Scrubber bar to slip that clip (**Figure 8.20**); or drag the edit point with the Slip tool.

   The Current Time display switches to show the adjusted timecode location for the edit point you are slipping.

4. Release the mouse button to complete the Slip edit.

   The Current Time display reverts to displaying the timecode location at the clip's current playhead position.

5. When you are finished trimming, close the Trim Edit window by clicking the upper-left corner of the window.

Figure 8.18 Click the Play Around Edit Loop button to loop playback of your edit point plus the specified pre-roll and post-roll.

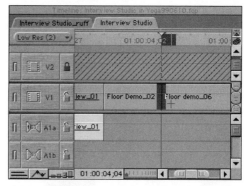

Figure 8.19 Click an edit point in the Timeline with the Edits Selection tool, and the Trim Edit window will open automatically.

Figure 8.20 Shift-dragging an active edit point in the Trim Edit window slips the selected clip. During the slip, the display changes to show the new In and Out points.

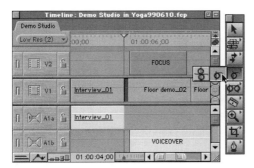

Figure 8.21 Choose the Ripple tool from the Tool palette.

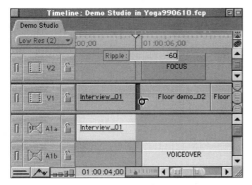

Figure 8.22 After selecting the edit you want to ripple, type + or – followed by the number of frames to add or subtract from the edit point.

Trimming Edits in the Timeline

The Timeline can be a good place to trim your sequence if you need to keep tabs on multiple tracks in relation to one another. You can perform all types of trim edits in the Timeline: Ripple, Roll, Slip, Slide, Extend, Swap, and Resize.

✔ Tip

■ Set up your Timeline display to optimize the efficiency of your trim operation. Things to check include the time scale, track size, snapping, and vertical scroll bar setup. You'll find details on Timeline display options in Chapter 7, "Using the Timeline and the Canvas."

To perform a Ripple edit in the Timeline:

1. From the Tool palette, choose the Ripple tool (**Figure 8.21**).

2. In the Timeline, select the edit by clicking near the edge of the clip.

   The selected side of the edit will be highlighted.

3. Ripple the edit using *one of the following* methods:

   ▲ Click and drag the edit to adjust the duration of the clip in the sequence.

   ▲ Type + or – followed by the number of frames to add or subtract from the current edit point (**Figure 8.22**); then press Enter.

To ripple on multiple tracks simultaneously:

◆ Command-click to select multiple edit points; then use the Ripple tool to perform the Ripple edit across all of the tracks (**Figure 8.23**).

✔ Tip

■ Holding down the Shift key while you are performing a trim toggles the cursor between the Ripple and Roll tools.

To perform a Roll edit in the Timeline:

1. From the Tool palette, choose the Roll tool (**Figure 8.24**).

2. In the Timeline, select the edit point.

3. Roll the edit using *one of the following* methods:

   ▲ Click and drag in either direction. As you drag, the Canvas display changes to two smaller screens showing the Out point of the outgoing clip on the left and the In point of the incoming clip on the right (**Figure 8.25**).

   ▲ Type + or – followed by the number of frames to add or subtract from the current edit point; then press Enter.

Figure 8.23 Performing a Ripple edit on multiple tracks in the Timeline.

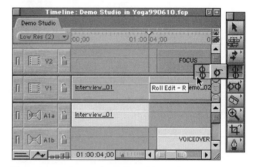

Figure 8.24 Choose the Roll tool from the Tool palette.

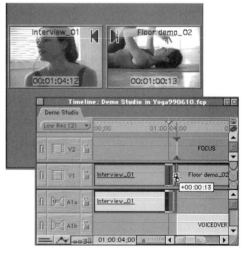

Figure 8.25 During a Roll edit, the Canvas window converts to dual-screen mode, displaying the outgoing Out point on the left and the incoming In point on the right.

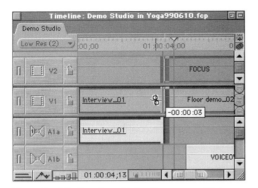

Figure 8.26 Performing a Roll edit across multiple tracks in the Timeline.

Figure 8.27 Choose the Slip tool from the Tool palette.

Figure 8.28 During the Slip edit, the Canvas window converts to dual-screen mode, displaying the In point frame on the left and the Out point frame on the right.

To roll multiple tracks simultaneously:

◆ Command-click to select multiple edit points; then use the Roll tool to perform the Roll edit across all of the tracks (**Figure 8.26**).

✔ Tip

■ If you're still dragging but your Roll edit stops rolling, your clip has reached the end of the media.

To slip a clip in the Timeline:

1. In the Tool palette, choose the Slip tool (**Figure 8.27**).

2. In the Timeline, select the clip and drag it left or right. As you drag:
   ▲ An outline of the complete clip appears, indicating the amount of media available.
   ▲ The Canvas display changes to two smaller screens showing the In point frame on the left and the Out point frame on the right (**Figure 8.28**).

3. Release the mouse when you have positioned the clip at its new location.

✔ Tip

■ Try turning off snapping in the Timeline before you slip your clip. Your clip will slip more smoothly.

To slip a clip in the Timeline using numerical timecode entry:

1. Select the clip in the Timeline.

2. In the Tool palette, choose the Slip tool.

3. Type + or – and the number of frames to slip; then press Enter.

To slide a clip in the Timeline:

1. In the Tool palette, choose the Slide tool.

2. In the Timeline, select the entire clip (**Figure 8.29**) and drag it left or right.

   As you drag:

   ▲ An outline of the complete clip appears, indicating the amount of media available (**Figure 8.30**).

   ▲ The Canvas display changes to two smaller screens showing the Out point frame of the clip to the left of the sliding clip and the In point frame of the clip to the right of the sliding clip.

3. Release the mouse when you have positioned the clip at its new location (**Figure 8.31**).

To slide a clip in the Timeline using numerical timecode entry:

1. In the Tool palette, choose the Slide tool.

2. Select the clip in the Timeline.

3. Type + or – and the number of frames to slide; then press Enter.

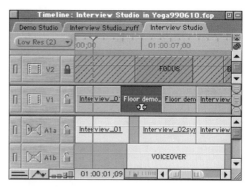

Figure 8.29 Select the clip with the Slide tool.

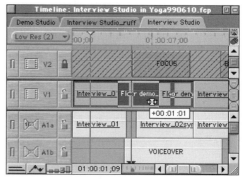

Figure 8.30 During the Slide edit, an outline of the complete clip appears in the Timeline, indicating the amount of media available outside the clip's edit points.

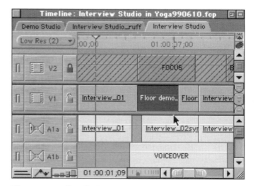

Figure 8.31 The clip in its new sequence location.

To perform a Swap edit in the Timeline:

1. In the Timeline, select the clip you want to move.

2. Drag the clip out of the Timeline track (**Figure 8.32**).

3. Align the head of the selected clip with the head of the clip in the Timeline at the insert location (**Figure 8.33**); then press Option without releasing the mouse. The pointer becomes a curved arrow.

4. Drop the selected clip in at the insert point you selected (**Figure 8.34**).

The inserted clip swaps out with the sequence clip's position; no sequence clip durations are altered (**Figure 8.35**), but the order in which they appear has changed.

✔ Tips

■ The Swap edit is one way to go if you want to preserve render files you've already created. The swapped clips don't change duration, and they maintain the linkage to their previously rendered files.

■ You can perform swap edits only with single clips.

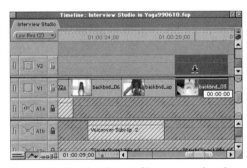

Figure 8.32 Drag the clip out of its sequence location.

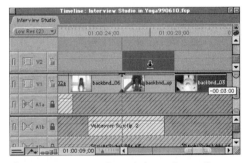

Figure 8.33 Use snapping to help you line up the head of the clip you are moving with the edit point where you want to insert the clip.

Figure 8.34 As you drop the clip into the Timeline, the cursor changes to a curved arrow icon. Drop the clip at the insertion point.

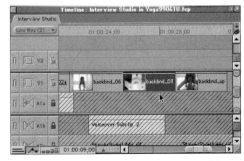

Figure 8.35 The inserted clip pushes the rest of the sequence clips down without altering any sequence durations.

To extend the duration of a clip in the Timeline:

1. Check the Snapping control to make sure snapping is turned on.

   (This procedure is a little easier with snapping turned on.)

2. From the Tool palette, choose the Edits Selection tool (**Figure 8.36**).

3. In the Timeline, click the edit of the clip you want to extend (**Figure 8.37**).

4. Move the playhead to the position that the edit will extend to; then press E on your keyboard (**Figure 8.38**).

   The clip with the selected edit extends to the playhead position. An Extend edit will overwrite any gaps or clips that are encountered, up to the position of the playhead (**Figure 8.39**).

   If there is not enough media to reach your selected playhead position, an "insufficient content for edit" error message appears, and the edit is canceled.

✔ Tip

- Use an Extend edit to create a split edit on the fly. In the Timeline, Option-select the edit you want to adjust, play back your sequence, and press the E key when you see your new edit location. The edit point will move to the playhead's position at the moment you pressed E—if you have enough media in your clip to extend it to that point.

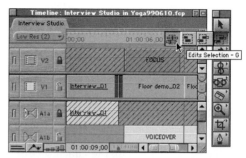

Figure 8.36 Choose the Edits Selection tool from the Tool palette.

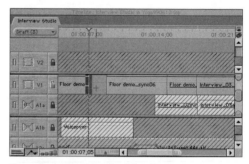

Figure 8.37 Click the edit of the clip you want to extend.

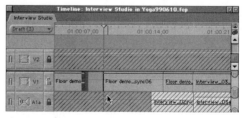

Figure 8.38 Position the playhead at the edit point on the other edge of the gap; then press E.

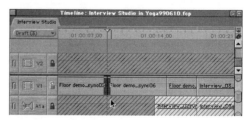

Figure 8.39 The clip on the left lengthens, extending to the playhead position and filling the gap.

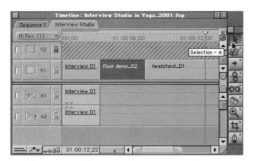

Figure 8.40 Choose the Selection tool from the Tool palette. The Selection arrow changes to a Resize cursor when you position it near an edit point.

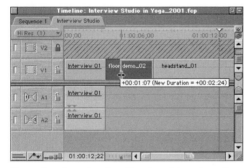

Figure 8.41 Dragging the edit point of the selected clip in the Timeline resizes the clip.

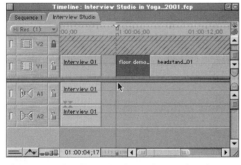

Figure 8.42 The clip, resized to a shorter duration, leaves a gap in its Timeline track.

To resize the duration of a clip in the Timeline:

1. In the Tool palette, choose the Selection tool (**Figure 8.40**).

2. In the Timeline, select an edit point and drag it (**Figure 8.41**).

   You can drag the edit point to create a gap (by making the duration of the clip shorter; **Figure 8.42**) or cover an existing gap (by making the duration of the clip longer).

To divide (razor-blade) a clip in the Timeline:

1. Set your target track to the track that contains the clip you want to divide (**Figure 8.43**).

2. In the Timeline, position the playhead at the point where you want to divide the clip (**Figure 8.44**); then press Control-V on your keyboard to add an edit point.

   The added edit point will create an additional clip that starts at the playhead position (**Figure 8.45**).

   Or do this:

   Press B to select the Razor Blade tool; then click at the point where you want to divide the clip.

✔ Tips

- Both halves of a divided clip will have the same name as the original, so if you plan on keeping both of them around, you may want to give them new names that reflect their history as two halves of a bladed clip—for instance, (*Clip name*_1).1 and (*Clip name*_1).2.

- Use the Razor Blade All tool to divide clips on all Timeline tracks at the same point.

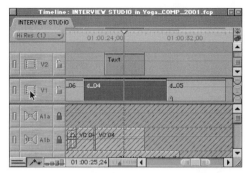

Figure 8.43 Target the track that contains the clip before you select its division point.

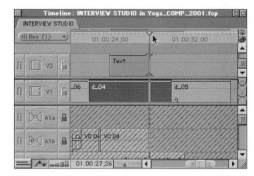

Figure 8.44 Position the playhead at the point where you want to divide the clip.

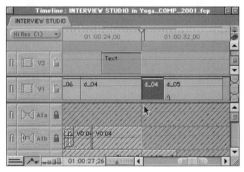

Figure 8.45 The clip divides at the playhead position.

TRIMMING EDITS IN THE TIMELINE

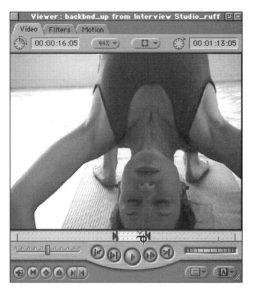

Figure 8.46 Dragging the Out point with the Ripple tool. The edit point will be rippled to the left.

Trimming Edits in the Viewer

You can perform four types of trim operations in the Viewer: Ripple, Roll, Slip, and Resize. Remember that you can perform trim operations only on sequence clips, so all of these trim operations require you to open the sequence clip in the Viewer by double-clicking it in the Timeline.

To perform a Ripple edit in the Viewer:

1. From the Tool palette, choose the Ripple tool.

2. In the Timeline, double-click the clip to open it in the Viewer.

3. In the Viewer's Scrubber bar, drag the In or Out point to ripple the clip (**Figure 8.46**).

To perform a Roll edit in the Viewer:

1. From the Tool palette, choose the Roll tool.

2. In the Timeline, double-click the clip to open it in the Viewer.

3. In the Viewer's Scrubber bar, drag the In or Out point to roll the edit.

   If you run out of media to accommodate the shift in your edit point, an overlay appears on the image in the Viewer warning you of a "media limit" on the track that's run out of frames.

To slip a clip in the Viewer:

1. From the Tool palette, choose the Slip tool.

2. In the Timeline, double-click the clip to open it in the Viewer.

3. In the Viewer's Scrubber bar, drag the In or Out point to slip the clip.

   As you slip, the Viewer displays the first frame of the clip; the Canvas displays the last frame of the clip (**Figure 8.47**).

✔ Tip

- You can also slip a clip in the Viewer by Shift-dragging the In or Out point with the Selection tool.

To resize a clip in the Viewer:

1. In the Tool palette, choose the Selection tool.

2. In the Timeline, double-click the clip to open it in the Viewer.

3. In the Viewer's Scrubber bar, drag the In or Out point to resize the clip (**Figure 8.48**).

   You can drag the edit point to create a gap (by making the duration of the clip shorter) or cover an existing gap (by making the duration of the clip longer).

Figure 8.47 As you slip the edit, the Viewer displays the first frame of the clip, and the Canvas displays the last frame.

Figure 8.48 Dragging the edit point in the Viewer's Scrubber bar resizes the selected clip.

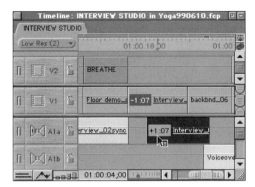

Figure 8.49 Control-click the clip's out-of-sync indicator to access the shortcut menu.

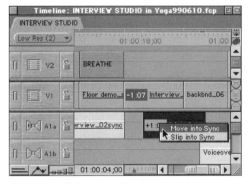

Figure 8.50 Choose Move into Sync from the shortcut menu.

Correcting Out-of-Sync Clips

When you insert a sync clip into a sequence, the audio and video are automatically linked. That means you'll have to go out of your way to knock them out of sync, because linked items are selected and moved together. However, if you have turned linked selection off, it's possible to knock a sync clip out of sync.

Boxes appear on the clips that are out of sync. These indicators display the number of frames the clips are out of sync in relation to each other.

Final Cut Pro offers two options for correcting a sync problem:

◆ You can move a clip into sync, which repositions the clip so that the sync is corrected.

◆ You can slip a clip into sync, which corrects the sync problem by performing a Slip edit on the clip (keeping the clip in the same position and shifting the contents of the clip).

There are plenty of good reasons to take a clip out of sync intentionally, such as when you are hoping to salvage your best-looking take (you know—the one with the sound problem) by substituting the dialogue from another take. If your save works, you will want to mark the video and the substitute audio as being in sync. In that case, you can mark a clip as in sync if the sync does not need to be corrected and you don't want to be warned of a sync problem.

To move a clip into sync:

◆ In the Timeline, control-click the out-of-sync indicator (the red box on the clip; **Figure 8.49**); then choose Move into Sync from the shortcut menu (**Figure 8.50**).

continues on next page

Note that you can move a clip into sync only if there is a gap in the track to accommodate the move.

To slip a clip into sync:

◆ In the Timeline, control-click the out-of-sync indicator (the red box on the clip); then choose Slip into Sync from the shortcut menu (**Figure 8.51**).

To mark a clip as in sync:

◆ In the Timeline, select the audio and video clips you want to mark as in sync (**Figure 8.52**); then choose Modify > Mark in Sync.

The two selected clips are marked as in sync, without shifting their positions in the Timeline (**Figure 8.53**).

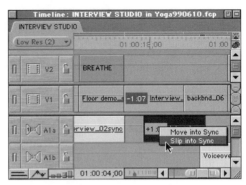

Figure 8.51 Choose Slip into Sync from the shortcut menu.

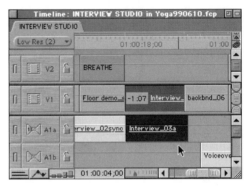

Figure 8.52 Select the audio and video clips you want to mark as in sync.

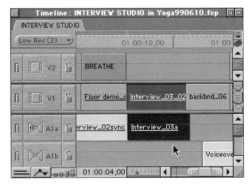

Figure 8.53 The clips do not shift position, but are marked as in sync.

CREATING
TRANSITIONS

Fancy-schmancy transitions have been with us since the earliest days of movie making. Over the years, transitions have developed an important role in film story language. Filmmakers rely on the audience's knowledge of the transition "code." This grammar of transitions and what they signify in movie language has grown up with the movies. These days, you are hardly aware of the translations that you make in film: a fade-out/fade-in means the passage of time, a ripple dissolve means "it was all a dream," and a heart-shaped iris wipe means you're watching reruns of "Love: American Style."

Final Cut Pro offers a library of more than 50 transition effects, which range from simple dissolves to complex 3D transitions. This chapter introduces the procedures for working with transitions in an editing context. For information on modifying effects settings to sculpt your transition, see Chapter 13, "Compositing and Special Effects."

Adding Transition Effects

You can add transitions along with clips as you assemble your sequence by performing a Transition edit, or you can apply transitions to edit points in your sequence after you have assembled your sequence. Once you have applied transitions to your sequence, you can go back and modify them as you refine your cut.

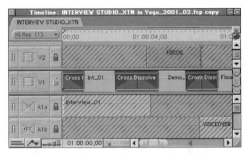

Figure 9.1 Transitions appear as overlays within a single Timeline track. The darker gray diagonal shading on the transition's Timeline icon indicates the direction, alignment, and speed of the transition.

Final Cut Pro displays transitions as overlays within a single Timeline track—an efficient use of screen real estate (**Figure 9.1**). You can make adjustments to a transition directly in the Timeline window, or you can make more complex adjustments to a transition in the Transition Editor. All of the following procedures for adding a transition to a sequence are performed in the Timeline.

FCP Protocol: Transitions

◆ Because transitions are created by overlapping material from two adjacent clips, each source clip will need additional frames equal to half of the transition's duration for Final Cut Pro to create the effect. If a source clip is too short to create the transition at your specified duration, Final Cut Pro will calculate and apply the transition with a shorter duration, or not apply it at all if you have no additional frames.

◆ You can add transition effects as you edit a clip into a sequence, or you can add transitions to a previously edited sequence.

◆ You can place a transition so that it is centered on the cut, starts at the cut, or ends at the cut.

◆ A transition edit will always place the transition centered on the cut between the two clips. If you want to add a transition that either starts or ends at the cut, add the transition after the clips are placed in the sequence.

◆ If you are planning on exporting an EDL from your FCP project so that you can finish the project on another editing system, you should keep in mind that EDL formats don't support transitions in any tracks other than V1. Transitions in other tracks won't appear in the EDL. Cross-dissolves and simple wipes are supported, but it's probably best to apply more complex transition effects after you've migrated to your destination system. See Chapter 11, "At Last: Creating Final Output," for more information on EDLs and FCP.

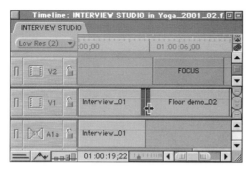

Figure 9.2 Selecting an edit point in the Timeline.

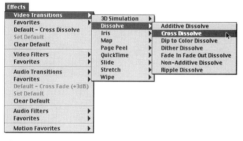

Figure 9.3 Choosing a Cross Dissolve from the Effects menu.

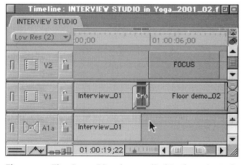

Figure 9.4 The Cross Dissolve applied to the selected edit point in the Timeline.

To add a transition effect that's centered on a cut:

1. In the Timeline, select the edit point between two clips on the same Timeline track (**Figure 9.2**).

2. To add the transition effect, *do one of the following:*

   ▲ Choose Effects > Video Transitions; then make a selection from the submenu's list of effects (**Figure 9.3**).

   ▲ Drag a transition effect from the Effects tab in the Browser onto the cut, centering it over the cut.

   ▲ To add the default transition, Control-click the edit point; then choose Add Transition from the shortcut menu.

   The transition is applied to the selected edit point (**Figure 9.4**).

✔ Tip

■ You can change the alignment of an existing transition by Control-clicking the selected transition in the Timeline, and then choosing a different alignment from the shortcut menu.

ADDING TRANSITION EFFECTS

To add a transition effect that starts or ends at a cut:

◆ Drag a transition effect from the Effects tab in the Browser onto the edit point in the Timeline, aligning it so that it starts or ends at the cut (**Figure 9.5**).

✔ Tips

■ Create a fade-to-black transition by dragging the Cross Dissolve transition from the Effects tab of the Browser to the final clip in your sequence, aligning it so that it ends at the cut.

■ To fade up from black, drag the Cross Dissolve transition onto the beginning of the first clip in your sequence, aligning it to start at the first frame of the sequence.

To delete a transition from a sequence:

◆ In the Timeline, select the transition; then press the Delete key.

Figure 9.5 Dragging the transition from the Effects tab of the Browser to the edit point in the Timeline. This Cross Dissolve is aligned to start at the cut, creating a fade up from black.

FCP Protocol: Saving Changes to Modified Transitions

When it comes time to save changes you've made to a transition, remember that transitions follow the same protocols as clips and sequences. (For more information, review "FCP Protocol: Clips and Sequences" in Chapter 4.) Here's a summary of the main points:

◆ When you add a transition to a sequence by dragging it from the Browser to the Timeline, a copy of the transition is inserted into the sequence.

◆ You can open a transition from the Browser (outside a sequence) or from the Timeline (within a sequence).

◆ If you make changes to a transition from the Browser before you insert the transition into a sequence, the transition that is placed in the sequence includes the changes that have been made in the Browser.

◆ Any changes you make to a transition from within a sequence are not made to the transition in the Browser. If you want to reuse a transition you've designed within a sequence, you'll need to drag a copy of your revised transition from the Timeline back to the Browser.

ADDING TRANSITION EFFECTS

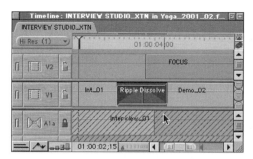

Figure 9.6 Select the transition you want to replace.

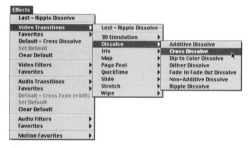

Figure 9.7 Choose a replacement transition from the Effects menu.

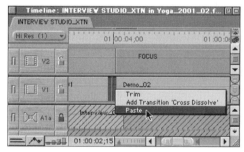

Figure 9.8 Control-click the edit point; then choose Paste from the shortcut menu.

To replace one transition with another:

1. In the Timeline, select the transition you are replacing (**Figure 9.6**).

2. Choose Effects > Video (or Audio) Transitions; then select a replacement transition from one of the submenus (**Figure 9.7**).

To copy a transition and paste it in another location:

1. In the Timeline, select the transition you want to copy; then press Command-C.

2. Control-click the edit point where you want to paste the transition; then choose Paste from the shortcut menu (**Figure 9.8**).

✔ Tip

■ You can copy and apply a transition to another edit point in one stylish move. Select, then Option-drag your desired transition to another edit point in the Timeline. This technique works with clips, too.

Working with Default and Favorite Transitions

You can specify one video and one audio transition to be used as the default transitions. The default transitions are available from the Effects menu, the edit point's shortcut menu, and as keyboard commands. Transition edits, available in the Canvas edit overlay, will automatically include your default transitions at the time you perform the edit. A default transition can be a transition you have already modified within a sequence.

You can also designate a transition (or any other type of effect) as a Favorite. Favorite effects will be placed in the Favorites bin on the Effects tab in the Browser and are available from the Effects menu. Using Favorites is an easy way to save a transition's settings so you can reproduce the effect later. You can build up a small group of favorite transitions for a particular project. When you're ready to bang out a string of identical transitions, you can promote one of your favorites to a default transition and get busy.

Defaults and favorites can speed up the work of constructing those quick-cut montages your producer is so fond of.

To set the default transition:

- On the Effects tab of the Browser, Control-click the effect you want to designate as your default transition; then choose Set Default Transition from the shortcut menu (**Figure 9.9**).

  The default transition appears on the Effects tab with a line under its name (**Figure 9.10**).

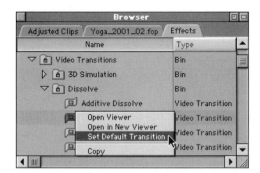

Figure 9.9 On the Effects tab of the Browser, Control-click the effect; then choose Set Default Transition from the shortcut menu.

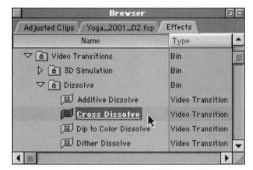

Figure 9.10 The default transition appears underlined on the Effects tab of the Browser.

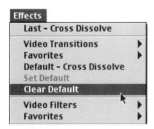

Figure 9.11 Choose Effects ›
Clear Default.

Figure 9.12 Control-click the edit point; then choose
Add Transition from the shortcut menu.

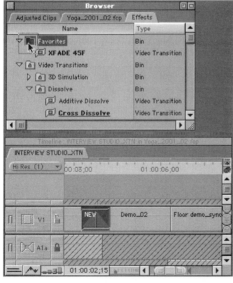

Figure 9.13 Dragging a modified transition from the
Timeline to the Favorites bin, located on the Effects
tab of the Browser.

To clear the default transition:

◆ Choose Effects > Clear Default
(**Figure 9.11**).

To apply the default transition:

Do one of the following:

◆ Select the edit point where you want to
place the transition; then choose Effects >
Default (the name of current default transition appears here).

◆ Control-click the edit point; then choose
Add Transition from the shortcut menu
(**Figure 9.12**).

◆ Select the edit point; then press
Command-T.

To create a favorite transition by saving its settings:

◆ In the Transition Editor or the Timeline,
click and drag the transition icon to the
Favorites folder on the Effects tab in the
Browser (**Figure 9.13**).

Or do the following:

1. In the Timeline, double-click the transition you want to make a favorite.

The transition opens in the Transition
Editor window.

2. Choose Modify > Make Favorite Effect.

To create a favorite transition before changing its settings:

1. On the Effects tab in the Browser, select the transition and drag it to the Favorites bin (**Figure 9.14**).

2. Open the Favorites bin; then double-click the transition.

   The transition opens in the Transition Editor.

3. Adjust the transition's settings (**Figure 9.15**); then close the Transition Editor.

4. In the Favorites bin, rename the new transition (**Figure 9.16**).

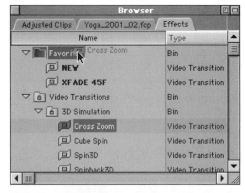

Figure 9.14 Dragging this Cross Zoom transition from the Video Transitions bin and dropping it in the Favorites bin places a copy of the transition in the Favorites bin.

Figure 9.15 Adjusting the Cross Zoom transition settings in the Transition Editor.

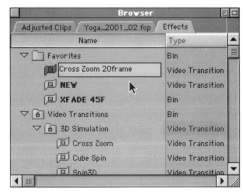

Figure 9.16 Rename your modified transition in the Favorites bin.

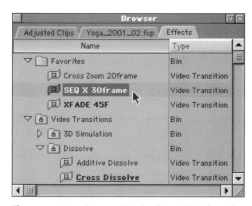

Figure 9.17 Dragging a customized transition from the Timeline to the Favorites bin places a copy of the transition in the Favorites bin.

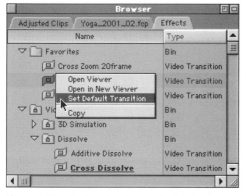

Figure 9.18 In the Favorites bin, Control-click your customized transition; then choose Set Default Transition from the shortcut menu.

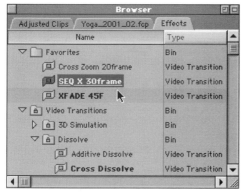

Figure 9.19 Your new default transition appears with an underlined name.

To set a customized sequence transition as the default transition:

1. In the Timeline, select and drag your customized transition into the Favorites bin on the Effects tab in the Browser.

   A copy of your customized transition will be placed in the Favorites bin (**Figure 9.17**).

2. In the Favorites bin, Control-click your customized transition; then choose Set Default Transition from the shortcut menu (**Figure 9.18**). Your new default transition appears with an underlined name (**Figure 9.19**).

✔ Tip

- You can also select a transition in the Browser and choose Duplicate from the Edit menu. A copy of the transition appears in the Favorites submenu of the Effects menu.

To delete a favorite transition from the Favorites folder:

1. In the Favorites bin, select the transition you want to delete.

2. Choose Edit > Clear.

About transition edits

There are two types of transition edits: Insert with Transition and Overwrite with Transition. A transition edit automatically places your default transition at the head of the edit. When using either of the transition edit types, you'll need enough footage in your source clip to create the transition. Each source clip will need additional frames equal to half of the transition's duration.

To perform a transition edit:

1. Set the sequence In point by positioning the Timeline playhead where you want the edit to occur (**Figure 9.20**).

2. In the Viewer, set source In and Out points to define the part of the source clip you want to add to the sequence (**Figure 9.21**).

3. Drag the clip from the Viewer to either the Insert with Transition or the Overwrite with Transition edit overlay in the Canvas (**Figure 9.22**).

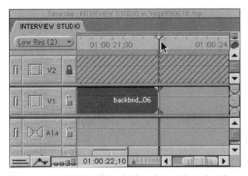

Figure 9.20 The Timeline playhead, positioned at the selected edit point; the playhead position will be used as the sequence In point.

Figure 9.21 Setting the source Out point in the Viewer.

Figure 9.22 Drag the source clip from the Viewer to the Canvas edit overlay; then drop the clip on the Overwrite with Transition edit area.

Editing Video Transitions

You can make dramatic changes to a video transition even after you have added it to your sequence. You can adjust duration and placement and customize its appearance. Opening your transition in the Transition Editor will give you maximum access to the transition's settings, but you can perform many adjustments directly in the Timeline.

Figure 9.23 shows an overview of the Transition Editor interface.

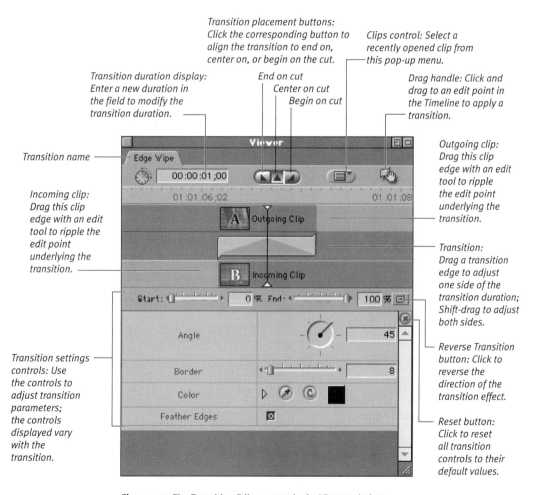

Transition placement buttons: Click the corresponding button to align the transition to end on, center on, or begin on the cut.

Clips control: Select a recently opened clip from this pop-up menu.

Transition duration display: Enter a new duration in the field to modify the transition duration.

End on cut
Center on cut
Begin on cut

Drag handle: Click and drag to an edit point in the Timeline to apply a transition.

Transition name

Incoming clip: Drag this clip edge with an edit tool to ripple the edit point underlying the transition.

Outgoing clip: Drag this clip edge with an edit tool to ripple the edit point underlying the transition.

Transition: Drag a transition edge to adjust one side of the transition duration; Shift-drag to adjust both sides.

Transition settings controls: Use the controls to adjust transition parameters; the controls displayed vary with the transition.

Reverse Transition button: Click to reverse the direction of the transition effect.

Reset button: Click to reset all transition controls to their default values.

Figure 9.23 The Transition Editor opens in the Viewer window.

Using the Transition Editor

The Transition Editor (sometimes known as the Transition Viewer) is a special version of the Viewer window that you use to make detailed adjustments to transition settings. Use the Transition Editor to do the following:

◆ Adjust the duration of the transition.

◆ Reverse the direction of the transition.

◆ Trim the edit point underlying the transition.

◆ Adjust the placement of the transition relative to the edit point. You can set a transition to end on the cut, center on the cut, begin on the cut, or occur anywhere in between.

◆ Adjust the starting and ending effect percentages. A simple cross-dissolve would start at 0 and end at 100 percent; these are the default settings for effect percentages. However, in a transition effect that incorporates a motion path, effect percentages will specify the portion of the full path that will be included in the transition.

The Timeline's Thumbnail Display option controls the way clips appear in the Transition Editor (**Figure 9.24**). You can adjust the thumbnail display on the Timeline Options tab of the Sequence Settings window.

To open a transition in the Transition Editor:

Do one of the following:

◆ Control-click the transition; then choose Open (name of transition) from the shortcut menu (**Figure 9.25**).

◆ In the Timeline, double-click the transition to open it in the Transition Editor.

◆ Select the transition's icon in the Timeline; then choose View > Transition Editor.

Figure 9.24 The Transition Editor display with Thumbnail Display set to Filmstrip.

Figure 9.25 Control-click the transition; then choose Open from the shortcut menu.

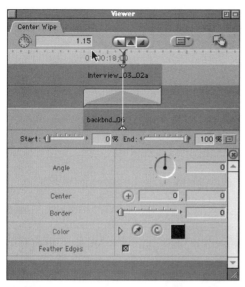

Figure 9.26 Type a new duration in the Duration field of the Transition Editor.

To change the duration of a transition in the Transition Editor:

Do one of the following:

◆ Type a new duration in the Duration field; then press Enter (**Figure 9.26**).

The change in duration is applied equally to both sides of the transition.

◆ Click and drag either end of the transition to adjust only the selected end (**Figure 9.27**).

The change in duration is applied to the selected end of the transition.

◆ Shift-drag to move both ends of the transition simultaneously.

Figure 9.27 Dragging the edge of a transition to adjust just its start point; dragging the other edge would adjust just the end point.

To perform a Ripple edit on a transition in the Transition Editor:

1. Position the cursor on the edit point you want to trim (**Figure 9.28**).

   In the Transition Editor, the edit points appear on the clip icons displayed in the tracks above and below the transition icon.

   The cursor changes to the Ripple tool.

2. Click and drag the edit point (**Figure 9.29**).

   A Ripple edit is performed on the edit point underlying the transition as the Canvas display changes to show your new In point.

To perform a Roll edit on a transition in the Transition Editor:

◆ Place the pointer anywhere on the transition. When the pointer changes to the Roll tool, drag the Rool tool on the transition to perform a Roll edit on the edit point underlying the transition. (**Figure 9.30**).

   A Roll edit is performed on the edit point underlying the transition. The Canvas display changes to show your new In point.

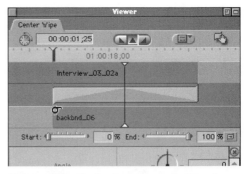

Figure 9.28 Positioning the cursor on the incoming clip's In point in the Transition Editor.

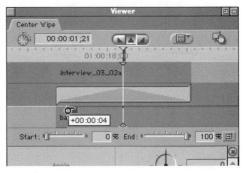

Figure 9.29 Performing a Ripple edit on the incoming clip's In point. Drag the edge of the clip to perform a Ripple edit on the edit point underlying the transition.

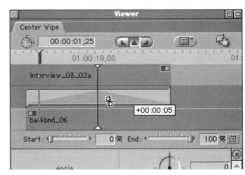

Figure 9.30 Drag the Roll tool on the transition to perform a Roll edit on the edit point underlying the transition.

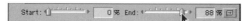

Figure 9.31 Using the slider to adjust end position settings for a wipe transition.

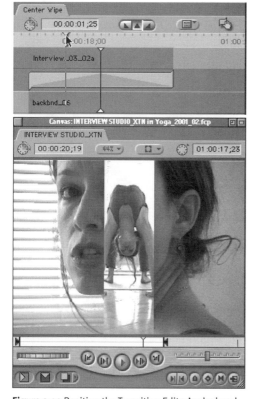

Figure 9.32 Position the Transition Editor's playhead at any point in the transition. The Canvas displays a preview of the transition at the selected playhead location.

To change the settings for a transition:

Do one or more of the following:

◆ To change the starting and ending effect percentages, drag the Start and End sliders (**Figure 9.31**) or type a percentage in the text boxes.

◆ To change the direction of the effect, click the Reverse button.

◆ To have the transition center on, begin on, or end on the edit, click the corresponding placement button at the top center of the Transition Editor. Once you've changed the center point of a transition, these controls won't remember the original edit point.

◆ Make other settings as desired for the transition. For more information, see Chapter 13, "Compositing and Special Effects."

To preview a transition in the Canvas:

1. Open the transition in the Transition Editor.

2. Position the Transition Editor's playhead at any point in the transition (**Figure 9.32**).

continues on next page

3. Adjust the transition settings.

The Canvas display updates to reflect any adjustments made to the transition settings (**Figure 9.33**).

4. To preview a frame at another point in the transition, reposition the Transition Editor playhead (**Figure 9.34**).

✔ Tip

- Hold down the Option key as you scrub the Canvas' Scrubber bar to preview your transition. You can also step through a transition one frame at a time by pressing the right arrow key to advance the transition by single frames. Press the left arrow key to step backward. A slow-motion view of the transition appears in the Canvas.

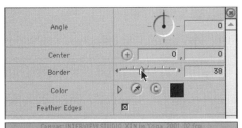

Figure 9.33 The Canvas display updates to reflect an adjustment to the transition's border width settings.

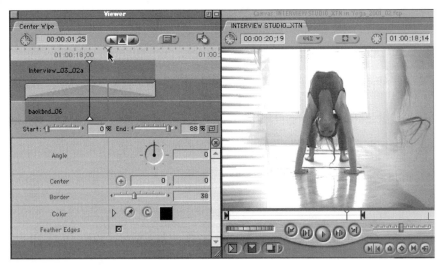

Figure 9.34 Reposition the Transition Editor's playhead, and the Canvas displays a preview of a frame later in the transition.

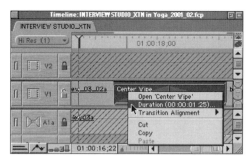

Figure 9.35 Control-click the transition; then choose Duration from the shortcut menu.

Figure 9.36 Enter a new duration for your transition.

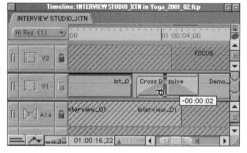

Figure 9.37 Trim an edit point underlying a transition by dragging the edit point with an edit tool. This Ripple edit will trim two frames off the outgoing clip's Out point.

Editing transitions in the Timeline

You can streamline transition editing in the Timeline by using the shortcut menus. One shortcut menu is accessed by selecting and Control-clicking the transition itself. A different shortcut menu is available for the edit point underlying the transition. Edit points that have transitions applied to them can still be trimmed in the same way as other edits; you can use the Trim Edit or Viewer windows or click and drag directly in the Timeline. For more information on trimming operations, see Chapter 8, "Fine Cut: Trimming Edits."

To adjust the duration of a transition in the Timeline:

◆ With the Selection tool, click and drag one edge of the transition to adjust its length.

Or do this:

1. Control-click the transition; then choose Duration from the shortcut menu (**Figure 9.35**).

2. In the Duration dialog box, enter a new duration (**Figure 9.36**).

3. Click OK.

✔ Tip

■ Control D is the keyboard shortcut to open the Duration dialog box for a selected clip or transition.

To trim an edit point underlying a transition:

Do one of the following:

◆ From the Tool palette, select the appropriate edit tool; then click and drag the edit point underlying the transition (**Figure 9.37**).

◆ With the Selection tool, double-click an edit point to open the Trim Edit window.

347

EDITING VIDEO TRANSITIONS

Modifying audio transitions

Final Cut Pro has only two audio transitions to choose from, but they're very useful. One is a 0-decibel cross-fade. The other is a +3-decibel cross-fade. How do you decide which one works best to finesse your audio edit? Try them out and trust your ears.

To modify the duration of an audio transition:

◆ With the Selection tool, click and drag one edge of the transition to adjust its length (**Figure 9.38**).

Or do this:

1. Control-click the transition; then choose Duration from the shortcut menu.

2. In the Duration dialog box, enter a new duration.

3. Click OK.

✔ Tip

■ Duration is the only adjustable parameter for the audio cross-fade transitions in Final Cut Pro, but you can build your own cross-fades. Set up the audio clips you want to transition between on adjacent tracks. You can adjust the clips' overlap and then set Level keyframes and sculpt your special-purpose cross-fade.

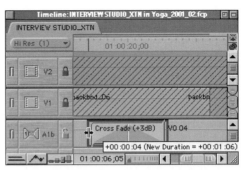

Figure 9.38 Adjusting the start point of an audio transition in the Timeline. Dragging a transition's edge affects the length of the transition effect but does not alter any underlying edit points.

FCP Protocol: r u YUV?

When you use a transition between two shots, you're likely to be looking for a way to blend the two shots together more seamlessly. Because you're trying to create that seamless illusion, rendered transitions are where most people notice the effects of RGB color space versus YUV (a.k.a. YCrCb) color space. Most computers store image data in RGB color space, but many digital video formats (including DV) use the YUV color space, If you render your transition and then notice color and luminance shifts during the rendered transition, you probably haven't selected the correct color space to render in. See "RGB or YCrCb: Choosing a Color Space" in Chapter 10 for information on how to select the correct color space for your project format.

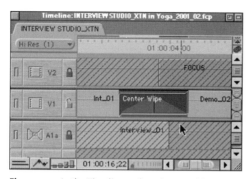

Figure 9.39 In the Timeline, select the transition you want to render.

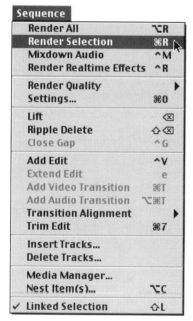

Figure 9.40 Choose Sequence > Render Selection.

Rendering transitions

Unless you are using a real-time system, You must render transitions before you can play them back. Consider using draft-quality rendering as a time-saver when you are designing a complex transition.

To render a transition:

1. Select the transition (**Figure 9.39**).

2. Choose Sequence > Render Selection (**Figure 9.40**).

EDITING VIDEO TRANSITIONS

Real-Time Transitions

If your Final Cut Pro system is equipped to support real-time effects, you'll be able to play certain transitions without rendering them first. The real-time transitions that are available on your particular system appear in bold type in the Effects menu and on the Browser's Effects tab (**Figure 9.41**). For more information on real-time systems and rendering, see Chapter 10, Rendering."

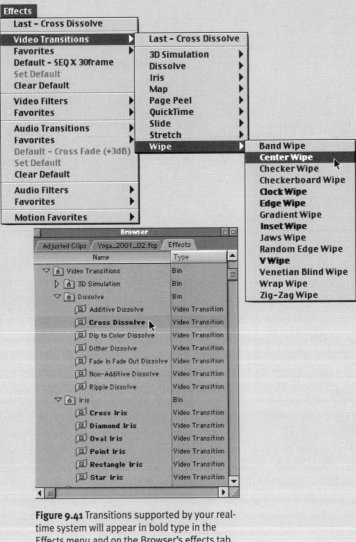

Figure 9.41 Transitions supported by your real-time system will appear in bold type in the Effects menu and on the Browser's effects tab.

10

RENDERING

Rendering is the process of combining your raw clip media with filters, transitions, and other adjustments to produce a new file. This new file, called the render file, can be played back in real time.

Final Cut Pro offers many, many ways to manipulate your raw media—a wild world of complex effects. Someday soon (we all hope), computer processing will speed up enough to dispense with the need to render in Final Cut Pro. But until then, you'll need to render clips with effects before you can play back your final result. Most Final Cut Pro sequences (containing transitions, motion, and filters) need to be rendered before they can be played in real time.

Final Cut Pro 2 introduces built-in support for the first generation of hardware-assisted "real-time" systems. Real-time systems use the additional power of specialized video cards to process added effects on the fly, allowing you to play them back without rendering them first. For editors (and their clients) who work extensively with effects, these systems can dramatically improve efficiency and creativity.

This is a chapter with more protocol than most. Understanding rendering protocols can be a big factor in making your post-production work efficient while producing high-quality results. This chapter lays out the rules governing video and audio render files, explains your options in setting up render qualities, and lays out some strategies for minimizing render time.

Rendering Protocols

Here are some general guidelines to help you understand Final Cut Pro's rendering protocols.

What needs to be rendered

In general, you need to render any transitions, effects, and composited layers to play a sequence smoothly.

Also, before your sequence can be exported or printed to video, you need to render any source media with frame rate, frame size, or video or audio compression settings that differ from those settings in your sequence.

Audio tracks with transitions or filters, as well as multiple audio tracks over your real-time playback limit, need to be rendered before playback.

Clips whose speed has been changed must also be rendered before playback.

What doesn't need to be rendered

Final Cut Pro sequences consisting of cuts only can be played back in real time without rendering, as long as the sequence size and frame rate match those of the original source material.

Multiple tracks of audio can be played back in real time without rendering. (See Table 10.1, "Final Cut Pro Audio Track Costs," later in this chapter for more information.)

Rendering order

Video frames in sequences are rendered in the following order:

◆ Effects applied within individual tracks are processed first. Speed changes, filters, motion, motion blur, opacity, and transitions, are processed next, in that order.

◆ After all the individual tracks have completed processing, the processed tracks are composited, starting with the top layer of video (the highest-numbered track), which is composited onto the track below it.

It is possible to change the order of rendering by using nested sequences. For more information on working with nested sequences, see "Creating Nested Sequences" in Chapter 12.

New in 2: Rendering

Hardware-assisted real time: Final Cut Pro 2 has been redesigned to work with real-time systems developed and sold by third-party developers like Matrox and Pinnacle. The new version takes advantage of any FCP-compatible real-time hardware you've added to your FCP system. If you're running Final Cut Pro without the hardware assist, it works just the same except for the absence of real-time playback of added effects.

Here are some of the differences you'll notice in the version 2 interface:

◆ **Render indicators:** Two render status bars have replaced the single red-and-gray status bar in the Timeline; the upper one is for video, and the lower one is for audio.

◆ **Time/Date-stamped Render files:** The Render Manager (called the Cache Manager in FCP 1) offers a new and welcome feature: render files can be sorted by date and time.

◆ **Reconnectable render files:** The Reconnect Media feature (called the Relink Media command in FCP 1) now allows you to reconnect a sequence and its render files.

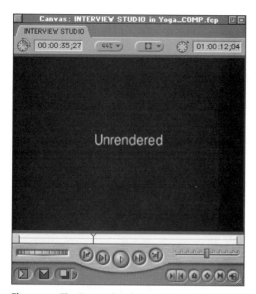

Figure 10.1 The "Unrendered" screen appears in the Viewer or Canvas when you try to play back video that cannot be played back in real time without rendering.

Figure 10.2 The rendering indicator is located above the Timeline ruler. The upper bar indicates the render status of video tracks. The lower bar shows the audio track status.

Rendering indicators

As you build your sequence, you'll encounter the following indicators:

◆ When you try to play video material that requires rendering in the Viewer or Canvas, a blue background with the word "Unrendered" appears (**Figure 10.1**), indicating that the video can't play in real time. If the Play Base Layer Only option is enabled for the current render quality, the base tracks play, but without any transitions or other special effects.

◆ When you try to play audio material that requires rendering in the Viewer or Canvas, you'll hear a steady beeping sound, indicating that the audio can't play in real time.

◆ In the Timeline, the rendering indicators above the ruler (**Figure 10.2**) indicate which sections of the sequence currently require rendering to play back smoothly in the selected render quality. This render status indicator consists of two thin bars. The upper bar indicates the render status of video tracks; the lower bar shows the audio track status.

Non-real-time FCP systems use the following status codes in the rendering indicators:

◆ **Red:** The material needs to be rendered.

◆ **Gray:** No rendering is required.

◆ **Blue-gray:** The material has already been rendered.

Real-time systems add two more color codes to the render status indicator:

◆ **Green:** Material does not need rendering and can be played in real time.

◆ **Yellow:** A real-time approximation of the final effect. To get the true final effect, you'll still need to render the material. You'll see the final effect when play is stopped or when scrubbing.

RGB or YCrCb: Choosing a Color Space

When you choose RGB or YCrCb (also known as YUV) color space on the Video Processing tab of the Sequence Settings window, you are specifying the color space in which the rendered sections of your sequence will be processed.

Rendered material is frequently intercut with unprocessed footage, so if you want your rendered footage to blend seamlessly with the unprocessed sections, it's critical that you understand how the choice of RGB or YCrCb color space in your sequence settings can affect the image quality of your rendered material.

DV video and computers use different schemes for interpreting image data, and this can cause headaches for the FCP user.

YCrCb (the color space used by DV video) organizes stored image data into three values for each pixel: one for luminance (Y) and two for color information (Cr and Cb).

RGB (the color space used by computers) also stores three values for each pixel, but all three represent color data: one each for the red, green, and blue components of the image.

Older versions of QuickTime used DV codecs that required the conversion of YCrCb (the color space used by DV video) to RGB (the color space used by computers) whenever rendering was required.

Because RGB allows a wider range of color and luminance values (0 through 255) than YCrCb, which usually has a more restricted range (16 through 235), the most intense RGB colors (including blacks and whites at the far ends of the luminance scale) can get clipped when you convert them back to the YCrCb video color space. The result: "chroma clamping," when RGB colors lose their saturation, and "luma clamping," when an RGB white value greater than 235 is clipped back to the 235 maximum on conversion back to YCrCb.

Since QuickTime has added support for rendering in YCrCb color space, you have a choice. The settings on the Video Processing tab allow you to specify how FCP will interpret color space when rendering clips used in sequences created with this sequence preset. For more information on your options, see "Specifying Video Processing Settings" in Chapter 2.

About Render-Quality Levels

You should pay attention to render quality levels for two important reasons: First, the render quality level you select for the final version of your project needs to produce rendered footage that looks as good as the rest of your program in your final distribution format and blends seamlessly with unprocessed footage. Second, strategic use of your "draft" render qualities can speed post-production in many ways. (For more information, see "Rendering Strategies" later in this chapter.)

Render-quality settings are applied only to the rendered output of your project, so ensuring a match between processed and unprocessed footage is up to you. When you're preparing a show for final output, you should select the render quality that matches the sequence settings of your project.

Don't forget that your choice of RGB or YCrCb color space on the Video Processing tab of the Sequence Preset Editor determines how color and luminance values in your footage are processed in a render operation.

Final Cut Pro provides four default render quality levels. All render quality levels offer the same set of options, but each default render quality level has a different set of the

available options preselected. You can customize the settings of each render quality in the Render Quality Editor. The settings you specify for each will affect the time it takes to render the file, the quality of the output, and the size of the render file.

Each render quality level has a number assigned to it. Render quality levels are referred to by number only (for example, RQ1, RQ1-4) in the Batch Export window. Here are the default render quality levels:

◆ **Hi Res (1)** (**Figure 10.3**): Rendering in Hi Res mode will produce a file that has the same frame rate and resolution as your sequence settings. All the final processing steps that produce the highest image and motion quality are enabled: field rendering, frame blending, and motion blur. All filters are enabled. Use Hi Res when you're ready to produce the final version of your effects sequence or to check image quality in selected areas.

◆ **Lo Res (2)** (**Figure 10.4**): Rendering in Lo Res mode produces a file that has the same frame rate as, but half the resolution of, your sequence settings. Any filters you have applied will be included, but field rendering, frame blending, and motion blur are disabled.

continues on next page

Figure 10.3 The default settings for Hi Res render-quality mode as they appear in the Render Quality Editor.

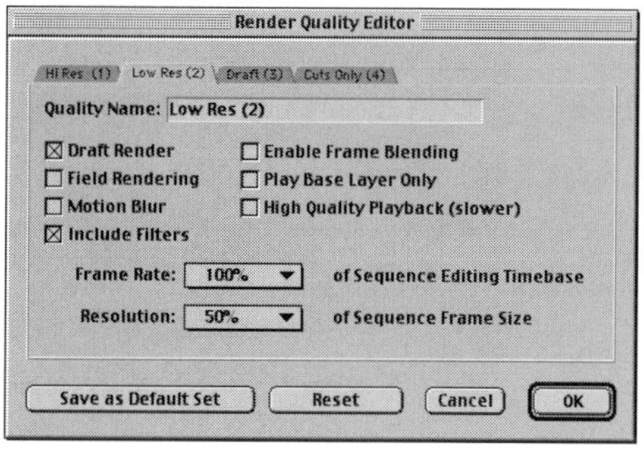

Figure 10.4 The default settings for Lo Res render-quality mode.

- **Draft (3)** (**Figure 10.5**): Rendering in Draft mode produces a file that has half the frame rate and half the resolution of your sequence settings. Any filters you have applied will be included, but field rendering, frame blending, and motion blur are disabled.

- **Cuts Only (4)** (**Figure 10.6**): Cuts Only mode is a high-resolution render mode, with the Play Base Layer Only option selected (see the description of this option later in this section).

The files for each render quality are stored in separate folders in the render storage locations specified on the Scratch Disks tab of the Preferences window (**Figure 10.7**). You can switch between render qualities as you work in Final Cut Pro without losing the render files you've processed at another render quality. As you switch render qualities, the rendering indicator (**Figures 10.8** and **10.9**) will update to show what areas still require rendering in your currently selected render quality. If you make changes to your sequence that invalidate your rendered files, all render qualities will require re-rendering in that area.

Figure 10.5 The default settings for Draft render-quality mode.

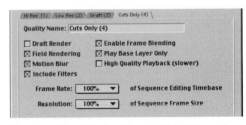

Figure 10.6 The default settings for Cuts Only render-quality mode.

Figure 10.7 Specify audio and video render file locations on the Scratch Disks tab of the Preferences window.

Figure 10.8 These two ripple dissolves have been rendered in Lo-Res quality. Note the blue-gray rendering indicator.

Figure 10.9 The same sequence in Hi Res quality. The rendering indicator shows that the two cross-dissolves have not yet been rendered in Hi Res quality.

Render quality settings

In the Render Quality Editor window (**Figure 10.10**), you can customize each of the four render quality levels in a variety of ways. Most of the choices you will make relate to balancing the quality of the render file with the speed of the rendering process.

Following are the Render quality settings:

◆ **Quality Name:** This field displays the name of the current quality-level settings. Names can be edited; edited names will appear everywhere within the current project.

◆ **Draft Render:** Check this box to render filters at the lowest possible quality. This is useful to speed up previewing but should be left unchecked before final rendering and export. Draft Render quality works with third-party filters only; FCP and QuickTime filters don't offer a Draft mode option.

◆ **Field Rendering:** Check this box to enable field rendering. Motion effects rendered with field rendering enabled will appear smoother during playback but will take longer to compute.

◆ **Motion Blur:** Check this box to include motion blur when rendering. Motion blur will be applied only to clips you have specified. Excluding motion blur from a render-quality setting will speed up rendering.

◆ **Include Filters:** Check this box to include filters when rendering. Filters will be applied only to clips you have specified. Excluding filters from a render-quality setting is another way to speed up rendering.

◆ **Enable Frame Blending:** Check this box to enable any motion smoothing effects you have previously applied to speed-modified clips.

continues on next page

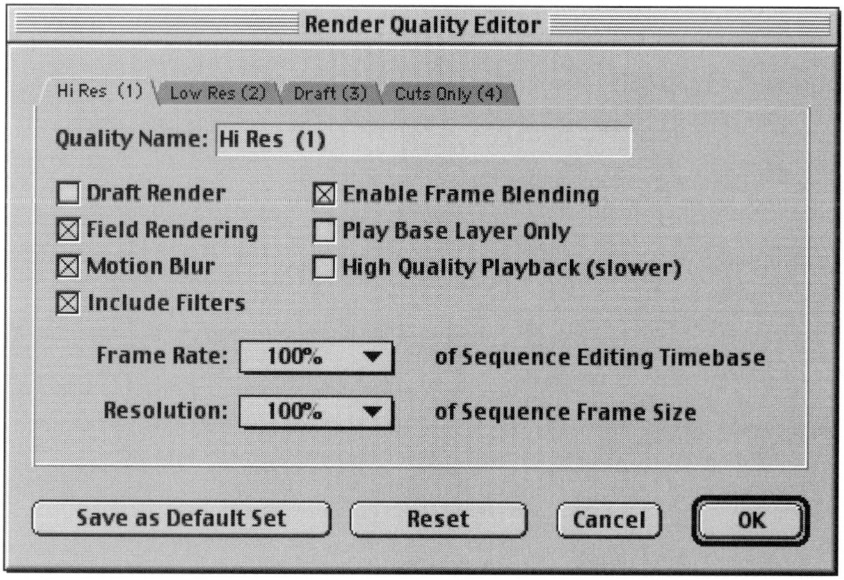

Figure 10.10 Review and customize render quality settings in the Render Quality Editor window.

- **Play Base Layer Only:** Check this box to play the base tracks (V1 and all audio tracks up to the Real Time Audio mixing track limit you set in General preferences) and cuts only. Cuts will be substituted for nonrendered or non–real-time transitions. Motion will not be applied to clips or sequences when played back in the Viewer. Play Base Layer Only is optimized to allow playback with minimal rendering. Unrendered sections will display the red render-status indicator.

- **High Quality Playback:** Check this box to use DV high-quality mode for playback, making visual quality a priority over frame rate on the computer monitor only. This does not affect the quality or speed of playback to the camcorder or deck. Use high-quality playback for checking the image quality of filtered or composited clips. Individual frames always appear in High Quality when play is paused.

- **Frame Rate:** Select an option from this pop-up menu to set the frame rate for the render quality to 25%, 33% 50%, or 100% of the sequence editing timebase.

- **Resolution:** Select an option from this pop-up menu to set the resolution (frame size) for the render quality to 25%, 33% 50%, or 100% of the resolution set for the sequence.

- **Save as Default Set:** Click this button to specify that any new project you create will use these render quality settings.

- **Reset:** Click this button to reload the saved render quality settings.

Figure 10.11 Click the Render Quality pop-up menu and then choose Edit Render Quality.

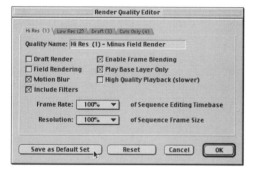

Figure 10.12 Click Save As Default Set to make your customized render quality settings the default for all new projects and sequences.

✔ Tips

- If you create a set of customized render quality settings you want to use, you can preserve them by creating a template project file containing your customized settings. If you should lose your FCP preference settings, you can restore your custom settings by opening the template project.

- If you've replaced Final Cut Pro's original default render quality settings with your own customized settings, you can restore the stock default settings by deleting your preferences file. See "How to 'Trash Your Prefs'" in Chapter 2.

To edit render qualities:

1. *Do one of the following:*

   ▲ Choose Sequence > Render Quality > Edit Render Qualities.

   ▲ Choose Edit > Project Properties and then click the Edit Render Qualities button.

   ▲ Open the Render Quality pop-up menu on the Sequence tab in the Timeline and choose Edit Render Quality (**Figure 10.11**).

2. Specify the settings for each render quality and then click OK.

✔ Tips

- It's probably a good idea to rename your customized render quality to remind you that you've altered the default settings.

- Press Y to switch between different render qualities in the Timeline. Press Shift-Y to automatically open the Render Quality Editor.

To save edited render qualities as the default:

1. Edit the render quality setting as specified in the previous section.

2. Click Save as Default Set (**Figure 10.12**) and then click OK.

   The customized render quality settings will be saved with your Final Cut Pro preferences and will be used on all new projects and sequences.

To restore default render qualities:

◆ In the Render Quality Editor window, click Reset to restore the render quality settings to the default values you've saved.

Rendering

The Render All command (in the Sequence menu) creates render files for all audio and video tracks in the current sequence.

The Render Selection command processes only the material you select in the Timeline.

You can also choose to render audio only or real-time effects only. See "Rendering Audio" and "Rendering Real-Time Effects" later in this chapter.

To render an entire sequence:

1. Open the sequence that you want to render in the Timeline.

2. In the Render Quality pop-up menu, confirm your selected render quality (**Figure 10.13**) or select a different render quality.

3. Choose Sequence > Render All (**Figure 10.14**).

    You'll see a progress bar displaying the percentage of completed processing while the sequence is being rendered (**Figure 10.15**). Click Cancel if you want to stop rendering. Final Cut Pro saves all the rendered frames it has processed, even if you cancel rendering.

✔ Tips

- To render just the audio in your sequence, choose Sequence > Mixdown Audio.

- If your project involves multiple sequences and lots of rendering, you can consolidate your rendering chores into a single operation. Check out the batch render feature discussed later in this section.

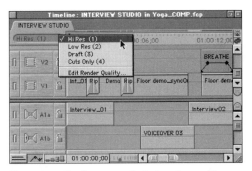

Figure 10.13 Confirm your selected render quality or select a different render quality.

Figure 10.14 Choose Sequence > Render All.

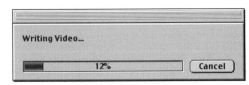

Figure 10.15 A progress bar tracks the speed of the rendering process. More complex effects will take more time to render than simple effects or audio processing.

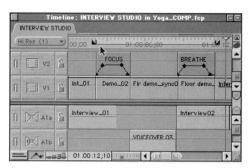

Figure 10.16 Set the Sequence In and Out points to select the area you want to render. (This figure shows split edit points, marking Video In and Video Out.)

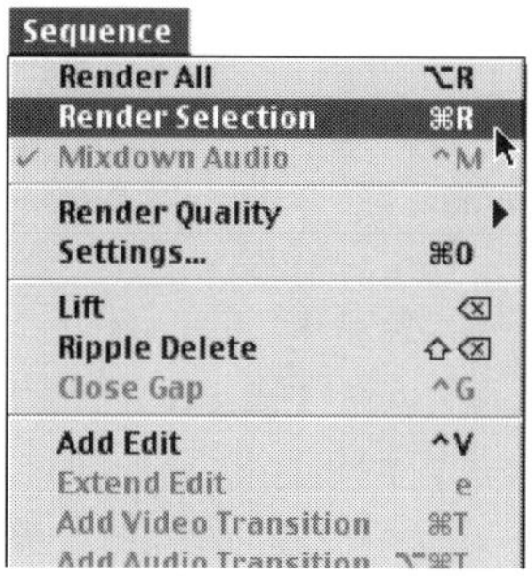

Figure 10.17
Choose Sequence > Render Selection.

Quick Preview Tips

The "instant-preview" techniques listed here can show you a quick, temporary preview of an effect or transition before you commit to rendering it. Place the Timeline playhead at the section you want to preview and then use one of these methods:

◆ Press Option-P (the Play Every Frame command) to force a frame-by-frame preview of your unrendered material. FCP will display the frames as fast as they can be processed.

◆ Use the Left and Right Arrow keys to step through your footage a frame at a time.

◆ Scrub the playhead across the Scrubber bar in the Canvas or the Timeline's ruler.

To render a section of a sequence:

1. *Do one of the following:*

   ▲ In the Timeline, select a portion of a clip or one or more clips or transitions.

   ▲ In the Timeline or Canvas window, set the sequence In and Out points to mark the area that you want to render (**Figure 10.16**).

2. *Do one of the following:*

   ▲ Choose Sequence > Render Selection (**Figure 10.17**); or press Command-R to render both video and audio in the selected area.

   ▲ Press Control-Option-R to render just the audio in the selected area.

   A progress bar displays the percentage of completed processing while the selected area is being rendered.

3. Click Cancel if you want to stop rendering. Final Cut Pro saves all the rendered frames it has processed, even if you cancel rendering.

Batch rendering

Batch rendering is a lifesaver for projects with multiple sequences that require rendering.

You can select multiple sequences from multiple projects and kick off a batch render that processes overnight (or while you're at your day job). Final Cut Pro will queue the sequences you select and render them sequentially.

To batch render multiple sequences:

1. Select the sequences in the Browser (**Figure 10.18**).

2. Choose Render All (**Figure 10.19**).

    You'll see a progress bar displaying the percentage of completed processing for the sequence that's currently processing.

3. Click Cancel if you want to stop rendering.

    You'll have to cancel each render operation in the batch separately. Final Cut Pro saves all the rendered frames it has processed, even if you cancel rendering.

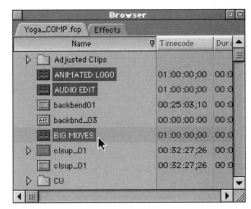

Figure 10.18 Select the sequences that you want to batch render in the Browser.

Figure 10.19 Choose Sequence > Render All to batch render the selected sequences sequentially.

FCP Protocol: Estimating Render Processing Time

Render processing times can range from a couple of seconds to many hours. How do you know whether you've got just enough time for a quick break or enough time for a two-hour lunch? Read on.

◆ Final Cut Pro expresses the progress of your rendering operation as a percentage, not as estimated time remaining. Watch the progress bar for a few minutes and make a guess, based on the speed of the progress bar and your knowledge of the sequence.

◆ Progress-bar feedback is based on how long the current frame takes times the number of remaining frames, so if your effects differ drastically in complexity, predicting the time required to render is difficult.

◆ After rendering, or whenever you move a large number of clips, Final Cut Pro rebuilds the QuickTime movie used for computer playback of your sequence, so it will be ready to play—wherever you put your playhead. While it's rebuilding, you may see a dialog box that says "Preparing Video for display."

RENDERING

Table 10.1

Final Cut Pro Audio Track Costs

ITEM	TYPE	TRACK COST
Each mono track	Track	1
Each mono track with transitions applied	Transition	2
Pair of stereo tracks	Track	2
Sub-sequence containing one stereo track	Track	4
Each track referencing a sub-sequence	Track	Number of audio tracks in sub-sequence
Compressor/limiter	Filter	6
Expander/gate	Filter	6
Vocal de-esser	Filter	6
Vocal de-popper	Filter	6
Reverb/echo	Filter	Must be rendered
All other filters	Filter	3?

Rendering audio

Although real-time video playback in Final Cut Pro is usually limited to a single, cuts-only track, FCP can mix and play back up to eight tracks of audio in real time, so audio rendering is not always necessary.

The number of tracks you specify in the Real-Time Audio Mixing preference (located in the General Preferences window) determines how many tracks Final Cut Pro will attempt to play back before it asks for audio rendering.

There's an additional factor that determines whether you have maxed out your real-time audio playback capabilities: All audio tracks are not created equal. When you apply filters or transitions to an audio track, Final Cut Pro must allocate processing power to calculate those effects on the fly in order to play the result back in real time—which brings us to track costs. (See the sidebar "FCP Protocol: Track Costs" and **Table 10.1**.)

FCP Protocol: Track Costs

Final Cut Pro uses the concept of track equivalent costs, or track costs, to calculate the total processing power needed to play back multiple channels of audio. Under certain conditions, you may be able to play back audio tracks with filters or transitions applied.

You can calculate the real-time audio capabilities available in your sequence by adding up the audio track costs. Track costs can accumulate quickly when even a couple of unmixed tracks are combined, if you have used filters and transitions. If you exceed your real-time playback capability, you'll hear beeps instead of your audio when you attempt playback. You'll need to render before you can play back by selecting the Mixdown Audio command from the Sequence menu.

To render a single audio sequence clip:

1. In the Timeline, select the audio clip that you want to render (**Figure 10.20**).

2. Choose Sequence > Render Selection (**Figure 10.21**); or press Command-R.

   All the audio tracks at your audio clip's location, along with any filters, levels, and transitions you have applied, are processed into a render file.

✔ Tip

■ If you want to exclude tracks from the processed audio file, turn off track or clip visibility before you render. For more information on toggling track and clip visibility, see "Making a Timeline track invisible" in Chapter 7.

To render just the audio in a sequence:

◆ Choose Sequence > Mixdown Audio.

   Your audio tracks, along with all applied filters, levels, and transitions, are processed into a render file. The Mixdown Audio menu item is dimmed, and a check mark indicates that the sequence audio has been mixed (**Figure 10.22**). The Mixdown Audio command remains dimmed until you modify the audio tracks.

✔ Tips

■ The Mixdown Audio command produces a render file with a computed mix. The bad news: You'll have to mix down separately in each render quality. The good news: You still have individual control over all your audio tracks. Think of Mixdown Audio as a "temp mix" you can use while you're working.

■ Rendered audio behaves differently than rendered video in one crucial way: If you reposition an audio clip that's been rendered, you lose the render file. Workarounds are available to deal with this small wrinkle. For more information, see "Preserving Render Files" later in this chapter.

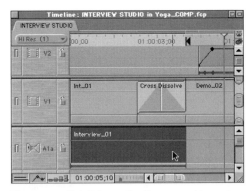

Figure 10.20 Select the audio clip you want to render.

Figure 10.21 Choose Sequence › Render Selection.

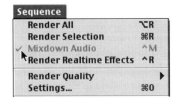

Figure 10.22 The Mixdown Audio menu item is dimmed, and a check mark indicates that the sequence audio has been mixed.

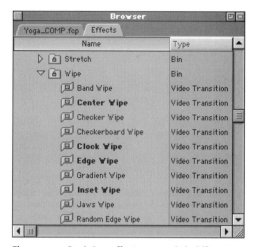

Figure 10.23 Real-time effects appear in boldface type on the Browser's Effects tab.

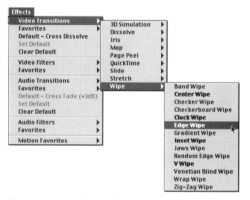

Figure 10.24 Real-time effects also appear in boldface in the Effects menu.

About Real-Time Effects

Final Cut Pro 2 has added built-in support for hardware-assisted video effects that are processed and played back in real time. FCP's program design allows video card developers to pick and choose which individual effects their real-time system will support. Effects that aren't programmed into that system's hardware are handled by Final Cut Pro's software, but they don't play back without rendering.

If you have a real-time card installed in your Mac's PCI slot, Final Cut Pro identifies that card and indicates which effects the card supports by displaying the available real-time effects in boldface type. You'll see the boldface indicators both on the Browser's Effects tab (**Figure 10.23**), and in the Effects menu (**Figure 10.24**).

The display will indicate available real-time effects for the current sequence preset. Different sequence settings may not support real-time playback of the same set of effects.

The Timeline's render indicator bars are color coded to let you know which sections of your sequence will play back in real time, and which sections still require rendering before you can play them.

A list of the color codes for the render status indicators appears near the beginning of this chapter.

Rendering real-time effects

Many real-time systems don't write permanent, usable render files as they process and play back the real-time effects they do support. You'll usually need to render everything in your sequence before you output the final version of your program.

To render real-time effects only:

1. *Do one of the following:*

   ▲ In the Timeline, select the clips or transitions that you want to render (**Figure 10.25**).

   ▲ In the Timeline or Canvas window, set sequence In and Out points to mark the area that you want to render.

   ▲ Leave the entire sequence unselected, and Final Cut Pro will render all real-time effects in the entire sequence.

2. In the Render Quality pop-up menu, confirm your selected render quality, or select a different render quality.

3. Choose Sequence > Render Realtime Effects (**Figure 10.26**) to render only the real time effects in the selected area.

   You'll see a progress bar displaying the percentage of completed processing while the sequence is being rendered. Click Cancel if you want to stop rendering. Final Cut Pro saves all the rendered frames it has processed, even if you cancel rendering.

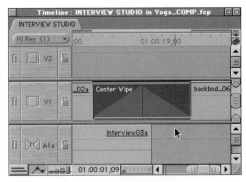

Figure 10.25 Select the real-time effect clip or transition in the Timeline. This Center Wipe transition can play back in real time only as a reduced-resolution proxy effect and must be rendered to play back the final version of the effect.

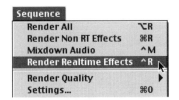

Figure 10.26 Choose Sequence > Render Realtime Effects to render the real-time effects in the area you selected.

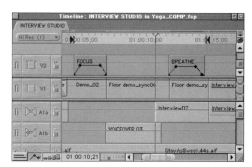

Figure 10.27 In the Timeline, set sequence In and Out points to mark the area that you want to render.

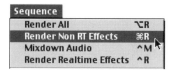

Figure 10.28 Choose Sequence > Render Non-RT Effects to render only the sections in your sequence marked with a red render status indicator and leave the real-time sections unrendered.

To render non-real-time effects only:

1. *Do one of the following:*

▲ In the Timeline, select the clips or transitions that you want to render.

▲ In the Timeline or Canvas window, set sequence In and Out points to mark the area that you want to render (**Figure 10.27**).

▲ Leave the entire sequence unselected, and Final Cut Pro will render all non-real-time effects in the entire sequence.

2. In the Render Quality pop-up menu, confirm your selected render quality or select a different render quality.

3. Choose Sequence > Render Non RT Effects to render only the non-real-time effects in the selected area (**Figure 10.28**). You'll see a progress bar displaying the percentage of completed processing while the sequence is being rendered.

FCP Protocol: Real-time Rendering Options

◆ The Sequence > Render All command renders all real-time and non-real-time effects.

◆ The Sequence > Render Selection command renders real-time and non-real-time effects for clips you select in the Timeline.

◆ If you've set sequence In and Out points to mark a section of your sequence, but haven't selected any Timeline clips:

   ▲ Choose Sequence > Render Non RT Effects to render non-real-time effects only.

   ▲ Choose Sequence > Render Realtime Effects to render just the real-time effects.

   ▲ Choose Sequence > Render All to render all real-time and non-real-time effects.

ABOUT REAL-TIME EFFECTS

Managing Render Files

Render files are valuable media elements. You can invest considerable time in a single complex rendering process. Rendering produces actual media files on your hard disk, like your original captured media files. Final Cut Pro names the render files according to its own internal naming protocols. You will not be able to identify individual render files by their file names, so it's important for you to plan your render file management strategy as a critical part of your post-production work.

Specifying storage locations for render files

You can specify multiple disk locations for storing render files. You can specify up to five disks for storing captured video, captured audio, or render files. As you create render files, Final Cut Pro will store them on the disk with the most available space. If you don't specify disk locations, Final Cut Pro saves video and audio render files in separate folders (called Render Files and Audio Render Files), which are located, along with your Capture Scratch folder, in the Final Cut Pro Documents folder (**Figure 10.29**). Render files are media files, and should be stored on the same media drives as your captured media.

Specify storage locations for your render files on the Scratch Disks tab in the General Preferences window. For more information on setting scratch disk preferences, see Chapter 2, Welcome to Final Cut Pro."

Figure 10.29 Render files are stored in the Final Cut Pro Documents folder, along with your Capture Scratch folder.

Using the Render Manager to manage rendered files

When you are working on multiple projects, each with multiple sequences, render files can build up quickly. You can use the Render Manager to delete render files for deleted or obsolete projects or to remove obsolete render files from your current projects. The Render Manager finds and lists files from unopened projects as well as open projects.

In the Render Manager window, files are organized by project and sequence. The Last Modified column indicates the last time each render file was rewritten.

Freeing up disk space by dumping old render files is an attractive proposition, but use caution if you are deleting render files for your current projects. Final Cut Pro uses render file names that are useful to the program but unintelligible to you.

A word of caution: You should not dispose of render files by deleting them in the Finder. Use the Render Manager window instead, so that FCP can track the status of the deleted files and update the affected projects and sequences.

✔ Tip

■ If you run out of disk space while working in Final Cut Pro, the Render Manager opens automatically, prompting you to recapture disk space by deleting old render files.

FCP Protocol: Render Manager File Tracking

There are a couple of limitations to the Render Manager's ability to track render files in multiple FCP projects:

◆ The Render Manager will only track render files you have stored in folder locations currently specified for render file storage on the Scratch Disks tab. If you have other render files stashed in scratch disk locations not currently selected on the Scratch Disks tab, they won't appear in the Render Manager list. To be able to use the Render Manager to track (and manage) all your render files, simply include all render file folder locations when you specify storage locations for your render files on the Scratch Disks tab in the General Preferences window. For more information on setting scratch disk preferences, see Chapter 2, Welcome to Final Cut Pro."

◆ The Render Manager can only display time and date information for render files in open projects. Time and date information for render files in closed projects is listed as "unknown."

To view or delete render files:

1. Choose Tools > Render Manager (**Figure 10.30**).

   The Render Manager displays a list of all of the Final Cut Pro render files on your designated scratch disks (**Figure 10.31**).

2. In the Remove column of the Render Manager, click next to the names of render files you want to delete (**Figure 10.32**).

   A check mark appears in the column to indicate each selection.

3. Click OK.

4. A dialog box appears, warning you that deleting your render files will "flush your undo queue," meaning that you won't be able to undo this operation (**Figure 10.33**). If that's all right, click OK.

   All selected render files are deleted from your hard disk.

Figure 10.30 Choose Tools > Render Manager.

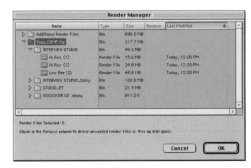

Figure 10.31 The Render Manager displays a list of folders containing all render files currently on your designated scratch disks.

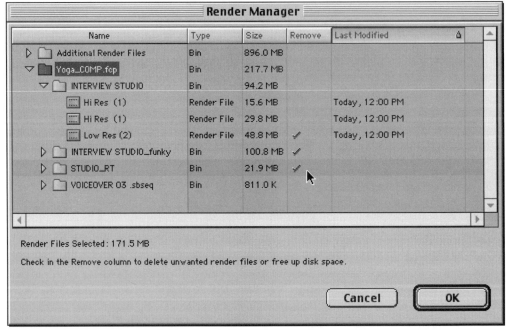

Figure 10.32 Click to place a check mark next to a folder or render file you want to delete. Render files are named according to a program protocol; you cannot name them.

MANAGING RENDER FILES

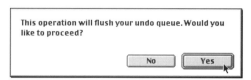

Figure 10.33 This dialog box is warning you that once you delete your render files, you won't be able to undo this operation.

Figure 10.34 This clip looks normal when opened from the Browser.

Figure 10.35 The same clip as it appears in the Canvas. The mismatched sequence settings override the clip settings, causing the clip to appear distorted and to play back poorly.

Rendering Strategies

To get the full advantage and use of the media manipulation techniques that are possible with Final Cut Pro, you will need to render to produce your finished results, but you'll also need to render to review your sequence and evaluate any effects you've created. The rendering strategies in this section fall into three basic categories:

◆ Tips for avoiding unnecessary rendering

◆ Techniques to speed up render times

◆ Schemes for preserving render files

Avoiding unnecessary rendering

Final Cut Pro will allow you to add to your sequence source material whose frame rate and compression setting do not match your sequence settings. However, if the frame rate, frame size, or video or audio compression settings in your source media are different from those settings in your sequence, those frames need to be rendered before the sequence can be exported or printed to video.

If a particular group of source clips looks normal when you open it from the Browser window (**Figure 10.34**), but it requires rendering or it changes size or shape when you add it to a sequence and view it in the Canvas window (**Figure 10.35**), you probably have a settings mismatch between your source clips and your sequence settings.

Important: To avoid rendering when creating a sequence with cuts only, make sure that the sequence's editing timebase, frame rate, and compression settings are the same as the frame rate, frame size, and compression settings of your source media.

How do you compare source clip and
sequence settings? Follow the instructions
here for viewing settings for both source clip
settings and sequence settings. To learn
more about specifying source clip settings,
see Chapter 3, "Input: Getting Digital with
your Video." For information on specifying
sequence settings, see Chapter 2, "Welcome
to Final Cut Pro."

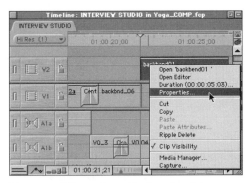

Figure 10.36 Choose Properties from the clip's
shortcut menu.

To view settings for a clip:

1. Control-click the clip in the Browser or
   Timeline and then choose Properties
   from the shortcut menu (**Figure 10.36**).
   The Item Properties window appears.

2. In the Item Properties window, note
   the clip's video rate, frame rate, frame
   size, and compression settings
   (**Figure 10.37**).

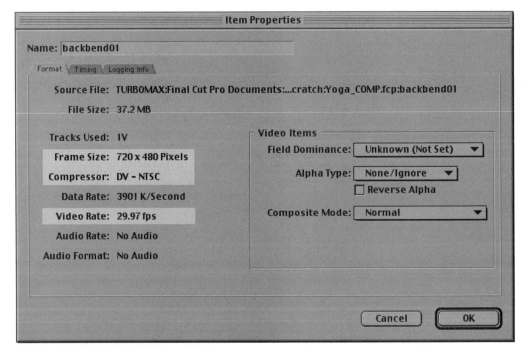

Figure 10.37 In the Item Properties window, check the clip's video rate, frame rate, frame size, and compression
settings. Highlighted settings must match sequence settings for the sequence to play in real time.

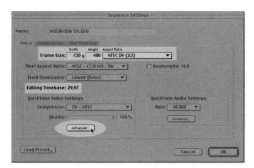

Figure 10.38 In the Sequence Settings window, check the sequence's frame size and editing timebase settings; the editing timebase should match the clip's video rate. Click the Advanced button in the QuickTime Video Settings section to access the compression settings. Highlighted settings must match the clip settings for the sequence to play in real time.

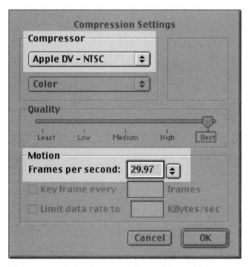

Figure 10.39 In the Compression Settings window, check the selected compression codec and the frame rate. Highlighted settings must match the clip settings for the sequence to play in real time.

To view settings for a sequence:

1. Select the sequence in the Browser or Timeline (for a nested sub-sequence).

2. Choose Sequence > Settings.
   The Sequence Settings window appears.

3. Note the sequence's frame size and editing timebase settings; the editing timebase should match the clip's video rate. Then click the Advanced button in the QuickTime Video Settings section to access the compression settings (**Figure 10.38**).

4. In the Compression Settings window, check the sequence's frame rate and compression settings (**Figure 10.39**).

Disabling rendering

There are two ways to delay rendering your sequence until you have completed your desired adjustments: You can enable the Play Base Layer Only option in your current render quality setting, or you can press the Caps Lock key to temporarily disable rendering.

The Play Base Layer Only option is optimized to allow playback with minimal rendering. With Play Base Layer Only enabled, Final Cut Pro will play the lowest opaque track in the sequence and all audio tracks rather than displaying the "Unrendered" message in areas that still require rendering. Cuts will be substituted for nonrendered transitions. Motion will not be applied to clips or sequences when played back in the Viewer.

Pressing the Caps Lock key temporarily disables rendering.

Reducing Rendering Time

Following are a few strategies that can help you minimize your rendering time. Using a lower-resolution draft quality saves disk space, as well as time, because lower-resolution render files are smaller.

Use draft mode

Use draft and low-resolution render qualities to perfect your element positioning, motion paths, scaling, and other basic design decisions. After you are satisfied with the timing and movement of your effects sequence, start including your most calculation-intensive effects. Render short test sections first and then review them to evaluate your final image quality. If you are set up to use an external NTSC or PAL monitor, you'll want to check your output on the monitor to see that your render quality is sufficient.

Render in stages

If you are building a highly complex effects sequence, you may want to render your elements in stages. For example, you might perfect just the motion paths and interactions of your composited layers and then render just that portion of your sequence in high quality by exporting and re-importing your rendered elements. The export process will create a new piece of source media, and you can continue to sculpt your sequence using the new composited clip as a fully rendered base track. Exporting to preserve a render file is described later in this chapter.

Batch render

Use the batch-render feature to render all your projects while you're busy elsewhere.

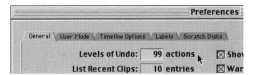

Figure 10.40 You can specify up to 99 levels of undo in Final Cut Pro.

Preserving Render Files

You can spend days creating a polished effects or title sequence in Final Cut Pro and then wait hours for your final product to be rendered. How can you protect your investment?

Following are a few strategies to help you hold on to your render files.

✔ Tip

■ Final Cut Pro allows multiple undos (**Figure 10.40**). If you just want to try out a new idea on material you've already rendered, when you're done, you can undo (Command-Z) your experiment until you have reverted to your previously rendered file. Careful use of the undo function can give you the freedom to experiment without risking rendered sequence material.

Using nested sequences to preserve render files

You can select a group of sequence clips or a portion of a Final Cut Pro sequence and, by using a command called Nest Items, convert that selection into a self-contained sub-sequence. As a sub-sequence inside a parent sequence, nested sequences are treated the same as other clips in a sequence. But unlike clips, nested sequences are actually pointers, or references to, the original sequence, not copies.

continues on next page

FCP Protocol: Salvaging Renders with Undo

FCP protocol dictates that when you invalidate a render file by making changes to a sequence, the invalid render file will become unrecoverable either when you next save the project, or when you are past the point where you can use Undo to make the render file valid again, whichever is later.

Nested sequences can help preserve your render files, because even though they can be edited into another sequence in pieces just like a clip, the render files associated with the nested sequence are preserved within the nested sequence. Even if you make a change in the parent sequence that requires the nested sequence to rerender, when you open the nested sequence, your original render files created within the nested sequence will still be available.

However, like everything else associated with rendering, you need to be aware of particular protocols governing the preservation of render files when a sequence is nested as a sub-sequence in another, parent sequence.

To learn how to create nested sequences, see Chapter 12, "Big Picture: Managing Complex Projects."

✔ Tips

■ Before rendering a sequence that you intend to nest in a parent sequence, make sure that the nested sequence has the same render settings (frame rate, frame size, and compression settings) as the parent sequence to avoid rendering the nested sequence again. (See Chapter 12 for more information on nesting.)

■ Final Cut Pro cannot reliably track down all nested sub-sequence material that requires rendering when performing a Render All process. Try rendering at least one element in each nested sequence to help FCP track down the nested rendering required. If you have built multiple levels of nested, unrendered sub-sequences into your project, this tip's for you. Double-check your rendered sequences before you invite your client in for a screening.

FCP Protocol: Nested Sequences and Rendering

When you nest, or place a sequence inside another sequence, the nested sequence will switch to the render quality of the main, or parent, sequence. If render files already exist for the nested sequence at that render quality, then those render files will be used. If the nested sequence does not yet have render files at that quality, render files that match the current render quality settings of the parent sequence will be created when the parent sequence is rendered. Render files for the nested sequence will be saved separately, with the nested sequence.

Nested sequences may require separate rendering in a parent sequence in the following circumstances:

♦ If a parent sequence modifies a nested sequence, the nested sequence must be re-rendered. Modifications include any compositing, filters, transitions, speed changes, and so on.

♦ If movement, such as rotation, has been applied to a sequence and then rendered, the sequence needs to be re-rendered if it is nested inside another sequence.

♦ If a nested sequence is placed inside a parent sequence, its alpha channel type is set to Straight. If you set the alpha channel for that nested sequence to None, the clips it contains won't need to be re-rendered. Its rendered files will be retained as long as they do not need to be combined with other tracks in the sequence, but because you've turned off the alpha channel the clip will be opaque.

Figure 10.41 In the Timeline, select the audio clips to be rendered.

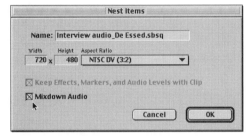

Figure 10.42 In the Nest Items dialog box, check Mixdown Audio.

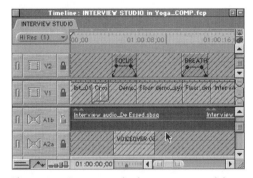

Figure 10.43 A new nested sub-sequence containing the rendered audio clip appears in the Timeline at the clip's former location.

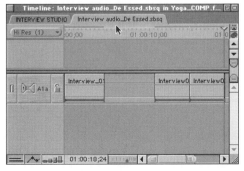

Figure 10.44 Open the nested sub-sequence to perform further adjustments to your nested audio.

Using nested sequences to preserve audio render files

Unlike video clips, which can be moved and retain the linkage to their render files, if you change the location of audio clips in your sequence, the clips that you have moved will lose the linkage to their existing render files and will require re-rendering. This section contains some workarounds for this problem.

When you nest an audio clip, you've redefined it as a new sub-sequence within your main sequence. Audio contained within its own sub-sequence can be moved and retain its render files.

To preserve a rendered audio track:

1. In the Timeline, select the audio clips that will require rendering (**Figure 10.41**).

2. Choose Sequence> Nest Items.
   The Nest Items dialog box appears.

3. In the Nest Items dialog box, check Mixdown Audio (**Figure 10.42**).
   The selected audio will render and then will be nested in a new sub-sequence, which appears at the clip's former location in the Timeline (**Figure 10.43**).

4. If you need to make further adjustments to your rendered audio, double-click the new sub-sequence in the Timeline to open the nested sub-sequence that contains just the audio to perform those adjustments (**Figure 10.44**).

5. Re-render the nested sequence.

✔ Tip

■ You can also use this nesting technique to mix down all the audio in your sequence into one render file. Select all the audio tracks in your sequence before you use the Nest Items command.

To process a raw audio track before editing:

1. In the Browser, press Command-N.

   A new, untitled sequence appears (**Figure 10.45**).

2. Double-click the new sequence to open it in the Timeline.

3. Drag the complete, unedited audio track from the Browser to your new sequence (**Figure 10.46**).

4. Double-click the audio track in the Timeline to open it in the Viewer, and then apply and adjust your selected filters (**Figure 10.47**).

5. In the Timeline, select your entire, filtered audio clip; then choose Sequence > Render All to render your filtered audio track.

6. In the Timeline, select the audio clip you just rendered and then Choose Sequence > Nest Item(s).

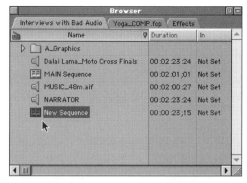

Figure 10.45 The new sequence in the Browser.

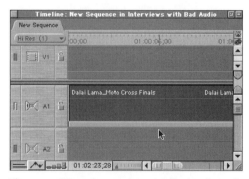

Figure 10.46 Drag the complete, unedited audio track into your new sequence.

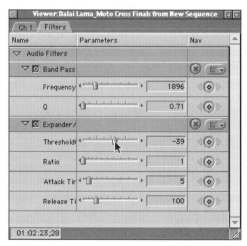

Figure 10.47 Open the audio track in the Viewer; then apply and adjust the appropriate filters.

7. In the Nest Items dialog box, name your new, nested audio sub-sequence and then click OK (**Figure 10.48**).

A new nested sub-sequence containing your processed audio clip appears at the filtered clip's location in the Timeline.

8. Control-click the nested sub-sequence and then choose Open Viewer from the shortcut menu (**Figure 10.49**).

Your processed audio, contained in the nested sub-sequence, opens in the Viewer.

9. In the Browser, double-click the icon of the main sequence into which you want to edit your processed audio.

The main sequence opens as the front tab of the Timeline (**Figure 10.50**). (The sequence containing the nested sub-sequence containing your audio is still open on the rear tab.)

10. Edit your processed audio track into your main sequence as you would any other clip (**Figure 10.51**).

The processed audio track's render files are protected from loss.

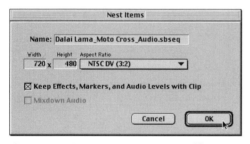

Figure 10.48 Choose Sequence > Nest Item(s) and name your new nested audio sub-sequence; then click OK.

Figure 10.50 The main sequence opens on the front tab of the Timeline.

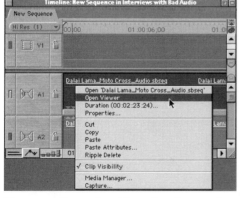

Figure 10.49 Choose Open Viewer from the nested sub-sequence's shortcut menu.

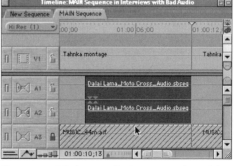

Figure 10.51 Edit the nested sub-sequence (containing your processed audio track) into the main sequence, just as you would a clip.

Export to preserve render files

Exporting creates a physical copy of your rendered file on your hard disk. Exporting is the safest way to preserve rendered material. Once you have exported them, you can re-import render files and use them just as you would raw captured media. For your render file to be exported without re-rendering, the export settings must match the render file's settings. If you wish, you can archive an effects sequence by re-rendering it as you export; your selection of export settings and render quality will determine the quality of your exported copy.

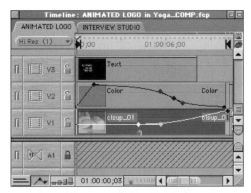

Figure 10.52 A portion of a sequence, selected for exporting. The sequence In and Out points form the boundaries of the selection.

To export an existing render file without re-rendering:

1. In the Timeline, select the sequence or portion of a sequence for which you want to export the render file (**Figure 10.52**).

2. Choose File > Export > Final Cut Pro Movie.

3. In the Export dialog box, select a destination for your exported render file from the pop-up menu at the top of the window (**Figure 10.53**).

4. Type a name for your exported render file in the Export As field.

5. From the Settings pop-up menu, choose Current Settings.

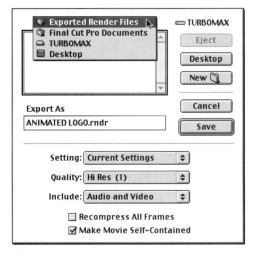

Figure 10.53 In the Export dialog box, select a destination for your exported file.

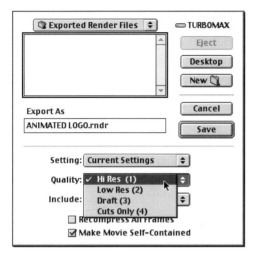

Figure 10.54 Make sure the export render quality matches the quality mode of the render file you are exporting.

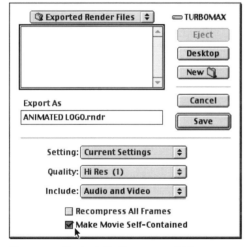

Figure 10.55 Uncheck the Recompress All Frames check box and check Make Movie Self-Contained to export your render file as a copy.

6. From the Quality pop-up menu, select the render quality that matches the quality mode of the render file you are exporting (**Figure 10.54**).

7. Uncheck the Recompress All Frames check box and check Make Movie Self-Contained (**Figure 10.55**).

8. Click Save.

With Recompress All Frames left unchecked, your render file will be copied into the selected location. In most cases, copying is much faster than re-rendering.

Switching render qualities to preserve render files

Final Cut Pro stores and tracks files for each render quality mode separately. If you have built and rendered an effect, title, or transition and you would like to preserve that rendered version while you toggle the track visibility for one of your tracks, you can save your render files.

Ordinarily, turning off a track will trigger the loss of your render files. However, if you switch to another render quality before disabling the track, your previously rendered file will be preserved (you created it in the previously selected render quality). After you are done viewing the sequence, switch back to the previous render quality, and your original render files will still be intact—unless, of course, you make any edits that would force re-rendering. (For more information on toggling track visibility, see Chapter 7, "Using the Timeline and the Canvas.")

At Last: Creating Final Output

You've gotten this far. Now it's time to send your masterpiece out into the world.

Final Cut Pro has a variety of output options. How do you choose the right one? The best output format for your Final Cut Pro project depends on where you plan to take it next.

- Are you going to distribute it on VHS?

- Do you need a broadcast-quality master?

- Will you distribute your program as a DVD?

- Are you preparing a Webcast?

- Will you be re-creating your edited show on another system—do you need an Edit Decision List?

- How about "all of the above"?

This chapter will walk you through Final Cut Pro's output options and help you decide which one will deliver what you need.

In the first part of this chapter, you'll learn about options for outputting your project to tape: recording Timeline playback, printing to video, and editing to tape.

The second part of the chapter is devoted to Final Cut Pro's file export options. You can export just the editing and clip information from a sequence as a formatted text file. You can also use the file export options to convert your FCP sequence or clip to another digital format for use in computer-based media.

One of the beautiful things about digital video is the wide variety of output options available to you—without having to leave your desktop.

Using Tape Output Modes

Final Cut Pro is designed to support external video monitoring at any time using your deck or camcorder, so you can always record FCP's output. You don't need to process your FCP material unless you are exporting your sequence as a computer-compatible format.

Here's a rundown of Final Cut Pro's tape output modes:

◆ **Recording Timeline playback:** One of the easiest ways to record Final Cut Pro's output to videotape is simply to start recording on your video deck or camcorder and play your sequence in the Timeline. For more information, see "Recording Timeline Playback" later in this chapter.

◆ **Print to Video:** Use Print to Video to output a Final Cut Pro sequence or clip to videotape. The Print to Video function lets you configure pre-and post-program elements such as color bars and a 1-kHz tone, leader, slate, and countdown. Print to Video's loop feature allows you to print your sequence multiple times automatically.

You don't need device control to use Print to Video. Use Print to Video if you want to make a videotape copy of your FCP sequence that includes customized pre-program elements, or if you want to loop your sequence.

◆ **Edit to Tape:** If your external video hardware supports device control, you can use the Edit to Tape window to perform frame-accurate Insert and Assemble edits to videotape, using Final Cut Pro's output as source material.

The editing functionality available in the Edit to Tape window depends entirely on the capabilities of your video hardware. The DV format has some significant limitations when it comes to editing to tape, so it's smart to investigate your equipment's capabilities before you make plans.

If you are using Final Cut Pro with a DV system, you can use Edit to Tape to assemble multiple sequences onto tape as a single, longer program or to place your sequence to start at a specific timecode, such as 01:00:00;00.

New in 2: Export Options

Audio export to OMF: FCP 2.0 can export your audio tracks as OMF-format files. That means you can export your audio tracks with track separations, edit points, cross-fades, and video sync intact. You can add handles, too—if there's enough audio in your source file. Most audio post-production facilities use OMF-compatible digital audio workstations (DAWs), such as ProTools.

Cutting film on FCP: Apple has just acquired Filmlogic, a software application, from Focal Point Systems. Filmlogic blazed the trail for projects shot on film, edited in Final Cut Pro, and finished on film. You can use Filmlogic to track the conversion of your film's edge code numbers through conversion to timecode for a video post-production process. After you export an EDL of your finished FCP edit, Filmlogic can reconvert that EDL back to a cut list (that's an EDL for film negative cutters) based on your film negative's edge code numbers. Now that this post production path has been cleared, expect more and more films to be edited in Final Cut Pro. Your best source of up-to-date information on using FCP for 24-frame editing is DigitalFilmTree (http://www.digitalfilmtree.com), pioneers of FCP 24-frame post-production.

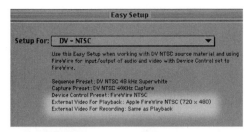

Figure 11.1 Check the external video settings for your current Easy Setup.

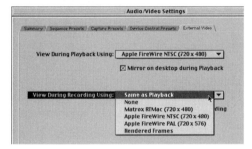

Figure 11.2 You can examine your external video settings in more detail on the External Video tab of the Audio/Video Settings window.

Figure 11.3 Select the render quality you want to record to tape from the pop-up menu in the Timeline.

Setting up for recording to tape

Before you record FCP's output on videotape, you need to make sure that your recording device is connected and receiving Final Cut Pro's output, and that the sequence or clip you're outputting is set up correctly.

Use this setup checklist for all three tape output modes:

◆ Make sure your video deck or camcorder is set to VTR (or VCR) mode. Final Cut Pro can't record to devices set to Camera mode.

◆ Make sure your video deck or camcorder is receiving Final Cut Pro's output. Check the external video settings for your current Easy Setup. Your external video setting should send FCP's video signal out to the external video device you want to record to (**Figure 11.1**).

If you want to examine your external video settings in more detail, check the External Video tab of the Audio/Video Settings window (**Figure 11.2**), particularly the View During Recording Using setting. That's where you choose which video output routing to use when you're using Print to Video or Edit to Tape.

For more information, see "Controlling Video Devices with Final Cut Pro" in Chapter 1 and "Using External Video Settings" in Chapter 2.

◆ All of FCP's tape output modes print your selected sequence or clip to tape at the currently selected render quality. Open your selected sequence in the Timeline and check to see which render quality is currently selected in the Render Qualities pop-up menu before you kick off the recording process. If you want to output a different render quality, select a different render quality from the pop-up menu (**Figure 11.3**). For more information, see "About Render-Quality Levels" in Chapter 10.

continues on next page

USING TAPE OUTPUT MODES

- If you want to print only a selected portion of a sequence or clip, open the clip or sequence and then set In and Out points to specify the portion you want to record (**Figure 11.4**).

- You should enable the Report Dropped Frames During Playback preference on the General tab of the Preferences window. Feedback on dropped frames is especially critical during final output.

  If you enable dropped frames reporting and find you're dropping frames in your external output during playback, you might try this first: disable the Mirror on Desktop During Recording option on the External Video tab of the Audio/Video settings window. You'll immediately free up some performance power for the Print to Video or Edit to Tape functions.

  See "Optimizing Performance" in Chapter 1 and "Is Your System Capture-Ready?" in Chapter 3 for more tips on eliminating dropped frames by improving FCP's performance.

- Test your setup by recording a section of your show to tape. Play back the test recording and scrutinize the results in your external monitoring setup. Do the rendered sections of the program match quality with the rest of the footage? Are your titles crisp? Are your video levels within the recommended IRE range for your output format, or has your video image developed hot spots? Is the audio playback level healthy, but not overmodulated? Are both stereo tracks properly balanced and panned correctly? A little extra care and patience now, when you're producing your final product, will protect all the care and patience you've lavished on your project up until now.

Figure 11.4 Set In and Out points to specify the portion you want to record.

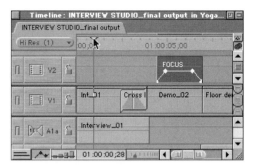

Figure 11.5 Cue your sequence in the Timeline and then select a render quality from the Timeline's Render Quality pop-up menu.

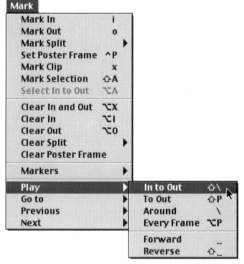

Figure 11.6 Choose Mark > Play and then select a play option from the submenu. In to Out plays only the portion of your sequence between the In and Out points.

Recording Timeline Playback

If you are receiving Final Cut Pro's output in your video deck or camcorder, you don't need to use Print to Video or Edit to Tape to record your FCP sequence to tape. Print to Video and Edit to Tape provide mastering options (Color Bars, Slate, and so on). Edit to Tape also allows you to start your recording at a specified timecode location. Otherwise, recording Timeline playback directly provides exactly the same output quality, and you may find it more convenient.

To record Timeline playback onto tape:

1. Cue your videotape to the point where you want to start recording.

2. Cue your sequence in the Timeline (**Figure 11.5**) and select the render quality you want to use for the recording.

3. Render any unrendered sections of your sequence. Unrendered material will appear as blue unrendered graphics when you record Timeline playback to tape.

4. Start recording on your video deck.

5. Choose Mark > Play and then select a play option from the submenu (**Figure 11.6**).

   Final Cut Pro plays the contents of the Timeline as you specified and then holds on the final Timeline frame marked for playback. A freeze frame is recorded on your tape until you stop recording.

6. Stop recording on your deck when Timeline playback is done.

Touching Up Your Timeline Playback

Recording your Timeline playback can be a real timesaver, but because you are making a live recording of Final Cut Pro's output, you need to do a few things differently to get smooth-looking results. Here are a few pointers:

◆ You don't have use Print to Video just because you want to add pre-program elements to your tape output. Black leader, color bars, and audio reference tone are available in the Viewer's Generator pop-up menu. You can edit your pre-program elements into the Timeline. For more information, see "Using Generators" in Chapter 13.

◆ When you record Timeline playback, your video deck or camcorder will record whatever is being sent to Final Cut Pro's external video output from the instant you press your deck's to Record/Play button. If the Viewer or Canvas is active, you'll record whatever is currently displayed until you start playback of your Final Cut Pro sequence. Even if you have positioned the Timeline playhead at the start of your sequence, you'll record a freeze frame of the first frame of the sequence until you start Timeline playback. Make sure your external video output is displaying black by inserting a frame of black before the first frame in your sequence. Now the freeze frame will appear as a solid black leader at the start of your recording.

◆ Place another frame of black at the end of your sequence, so when FCP reaches the end of the Timeline and freezes the final frame, that frame is black as well.

◆ Wait for a couple of seconds after you start recording before you start the Timeline playback. You'll give your videotape time to get up to speed, and your picture will be rock solid from the first frame of your sequence.

Print to Video: Rendering Tips

◆ The quality of the render settings you specify before you use Print to Video is reflected in the quality and size of the playback window you see on your computer screen and on your videotape copy. In other words, what you see is what you get.

◆ If you have multiple layers of sub-sequences in your sequence, (sub-sequences within sub-sequences inside the master sequence), it's a good idea to render things in the nested items at the lowest root, or sub-sequence, level first—at least for the very first render. Subsequent adjustments and re-renders can be processed at the parent level, and Final Cut Pro will more reliably find all the nested sub-sequence material that requires re-rendering.

◆ The pre-program elements discussed in the section "Print to Video settings checklist" must be rendered before you can print to video.

◆ If you use the same pre-program sequence frequently, you might want to use the Print to Video function to assemble your color bars, leader, slate, and countdown in advance. After your pre-program sequence has been rendered, print it to video and then capture it as a clip. You can drop your prepared pre-program clip into sequences before you print, speeding up the final output process.

Printing to Video

The Print to Video command is the correct choice when you want to make a videotape copy of a Final Cut Pro sequence or clip that includes pre-program elements, such as color bars, slate, and countdown. Print to Video is also your best choice if you want to loop playback and print multiple passes of your sequence on the same tape. You need to have your videotape deck or camera already hooked up to your Macintosh to do this, but you don't need a deck that supports device control to use Print to Video. For information on hardware setup, see Chapter 1, "Before You Begin."

If you don't need customized pre-program elements at the beginning of your videotape dub, playing your sequence in the Timeline and recording the output directly may give you satisfactory results and save you some time as well. See "Recording Timeline Playback" earlier in this chapter.

Print to Video settings checklist

The Print to Video dialog box (**Figure 11.7**) displays a list of formatting options. Select the elements you want to include in your videotape copy. You can specify durations for all options.

◆ **Leader:** Select the pre-program elements you want to include in your videotape copy. Your pre-program sequence will be assembled in the same order that the elements are listed in the dialog box, which is why there are two separate Black options. Check the elements you want to include and then specify a duration (in whole seconds) for each option in the field next to the option. These elements must be rendered before printing to video can begin.

▲ **Color Bars:** Check this box to include color bars and a 1-kHz tone, preset to –12 dB, before the beginning of the sequence or clip.

▲ **Tone Level:** If necessary, adjust this slider to change the level of the preset –12 dB 1-kHz audio reference tone. Note that this slider does not adjust the output level of your audio track, just the level of the reference tone.

▲ **Black:** Check this box to add black frames between the color bars and slate.

▲ **Slate:** Check this box to include the slate information specified in the Slate Source pop-up menu in the adjoining field.

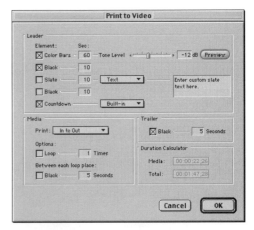

Figure 11.7 Select the pre-program elements you want to include in your videotape copy from the Print to Video dialog box.

Figure 11.8 Final Cut Pro's countdown screen.

▲ **Slate Source pop-up menu:** Select a source for the information that will appear on your slate from this pop-up menu. You can specify the sequence or clip name, a file on disk, or multiple lines of custom text.

▲ **Black:** Check this box to include black frames between a slate and countdown (or before the beginning of the sequence or clip, if you aren't adding a slate and countdown).

▲ **Countdown:** Check this box to add a 10-second countdown before the sequence or clip (**Figure 11.8**). Choose FCP's built-in 10-second SMPTE standard countdown or use the File pop-up menu and Browse button to specify your own custom countdown file.

◆ **Media:** Specify the material you want to include in the program section of your tape copy. You can print an entire sequence or clip or only a marked portion. You can also loop the sequence or clip selection and insert black at the end of each loop.

▲ **Print pop-up menu:** Choose Entire Media if you want to print the entire sequence or clip. Choose In to Out if you want to print a portion of the

selected item. Specify the portion to be printed by setting In and Out points in the sequence or clip.

▲ **Loop:** Check this box to print your selection multiple times.

▲ **Times:** Specify the number of repetitions for Loop.

▲ **Black:** Check this box to insert black frames between repetitions for the duration specified in the Black field.

◆ **Trailer:** Check the Black box to add a black trailer at the end of the printed sequence or clip; then specify the duration in the Seconds field. If you are looping the sequence or clip, the trailer appears after the last repetition.

◆ **Duration Calculator:** These fields display the total duration of all the media you selected to print, as you have specified it.

✔ Tip

■ Be sure your tape is of sufficient length to record the entire program running time as calculated by the Duration Calculator. Most tape stock has a little extra capacity over the program length printed on the packaging, but it's a good idea to respect the official program length capacity.

To print a sequence or clip to video:

1. Read and follow the setup process described earlier in "Setting up for recording to tape."

2. *Do one of the following:*

   In the Browser, select the sequence or clip you want to print (**Figure 11.9**). Open the sequence and make the Timeline active.

3. Choose File > Print to Video.

   The Print to Video dialog box will appear.

4. Select the program elements you want to include in your program. Refer to the "Print to Video settings checklist" earlier in the chapter for explanations of your options. If you need to change any of the settings, do so now.

5. Click OK (**Figure 11.10**).

   If the sequence you select needs to be rendered before it can be printed, Final Cut Pro automatically renders any unrendered sequence material, plus any additional program elements you've specified. When the rendering is complete, FCP will display a dialog box telling you to go ahead and start recording on your video deck (**Figure 11.11**).

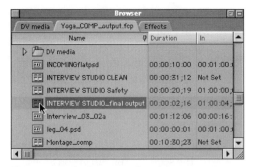

Figure 11.9 In the Browser, select the sequence you want to print to video.

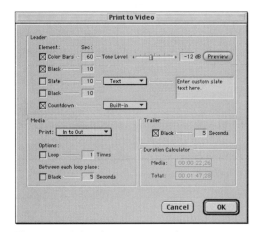

Figure 11.10 Select the pre-program elements you want to include in your videotape copy and then click OK.

Figure 11.11 Click OK to start playback of your Final Cut Pro sequence.

6. Start recording on your video deck and, when your video deck is up to speed, click OK to start playback of your Final Cut Pro sequence.

7. When your program material has finished printing, stop recording on your deck or camcorder. Final Cut Pro doesn't provide any end-of-process beep (the large black box disappears from the screen, and the interface returns), so check in at the scheduled end-of-program if you plan on recording unattended.

✔ Tips

- If you don't specify any post-program black trailer, Final Cut Pro will hold on the last frame of your sequence, creating a freeze-frame that will be recorded onto your tape until you stop recording.

- Once the Print to Video process is complete, you'll have access to the render files created for Print to Video in your regular Timeline version of the sequence.

- If the Mirror on Desktop During Recording option is enabled (on the External Video tab of the Audio/Video Settings window), some frames may be dropped in your output to tape. You can disable mirroring by unchecking the box next to this setting.

Editing to Tape

Use the Edit to Tape window to perform frame accurate Insert and Assemble edits to videotape using Final Cut Pro's output as source material.

You must have device control over your video deck or camcorder to use Edit to Tape. The editing functions available to you depend on the capabilities of your external video hardware. If Final Cut Pro finds that your deck or camcorder is unable to perform certain functions, the Edit to Tape window will appear with those buttons or functions dimmed (**Figure 11.12**).

Edit to Tape offers three edit modes:

◆ **Insert edit:** An Insert edit overwrites media on the tape with the item you drag, using three-point editing rules. An Insert edit won't disturb the control track or timecode track. Insert edit is the default edit type, if it is available on your deck. Note that Insert editing is not available for DV decks.

◆ **Assemble edit:** An Assemble edit overwrites media on the tape, including the control and timecode tracks; this may cause a glitch at the beginning and end of the material being recorded. Note that Assemble editing is the only edit type available for DV decks.

◆ **Preview edit:** A Preview edit simulates an Insert edit without actually recording to tape. The preview includes all selected mastering options and plays back on your external monitor, if you have one. Note that Preview editing is not available for DV decks.

Figure 11.12 If your deck or camcorder is not equipped to perform Insert or Preview edits, the Edit to Tape window will appear with the Insert and Preview buttons dimmed.

Insert versus Assemble Editing

Insert edits allow you to select which elements to include in the edit: video or audio, or both. An Insert edit begins and ends exactly at the specified timecode and leaves the timecode on your recording tape untouched.

Assemble edits overwrite the entire contents of the tape: video, audio, and timecode information. Modern assemble-only DV video decks are pretty good at performing accurate Assemble edits, because they generally extend the Out point of an edit operation a few frames to ensure that the deck can pick up the existing timecode when it performs the next edit. This ensures a continuous timecode track, but it may not produce an Out point edit that's accurate enough to allow you to drop a shot into the middle of a finished program. Test the capabilities of your video equipment to see what kind of results you can expect.

EDITING TO TAPE

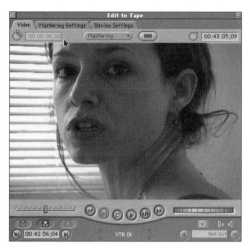

Figure 11.13 In Mastering mode, Duration and Out fields are dimmed since the mastering options you select will modify the overall duration of your edit.

Figure 11.14 Choose Tools › Edit to Tape to open the Edit to Tape window.

The Edit to Tape function has two modes:

◆ **Mastering:** Mastering mode offers the same selection of pre-program elements as the Print to Video function: color bars and tone, a slate, and a countdown. The Duration and Out fields are dimmed (**Figure 11.13**), since the mastering options you select will modify the overall duration. Use Mastering mode when you want to output a complete finished sequence to tape from a specific starting timecode.

◆ **Editing:** Editing mode offers the same device-controlled editing functions as Mastering mode but without the mastering options. In Editing mode, you can perform standard three-point edits directly onto tape. Use Editing mode if you want to string a series of shorter segments into one longer program or fix a mistake in a previously recorded program. If your deck supports Insert editing, you can choose to replace just the video, just the audio, or both.

To open the Edit to Tape window:

◆ Choose Tools > Edit to Tape (**Figure 11.14**).

Anatomy of the Edit to Tape Window

Just as you use the Canvas window to play back and then add new clips to your edited sequence, you use the Edit to Tape window interface (**Figure 11.15**) to view and add new clips to a videotape. When you are editing to tape, the Viewer window still acts as your source monitor, but the Edit to Tape window replaces the Canvas. That's why the Edit to Tape window has many of the same controls as the Canvas window. You'll find the same transport controls and timecode fields. The editing control buttons and edit overlay operate just as they do in the Canvas, but because you are editing to tape, the edit types available to you in the Edit to Tape window are Insert, Assemble, and Preview—which are the basic edit types in tape-to-tape video editing systems.

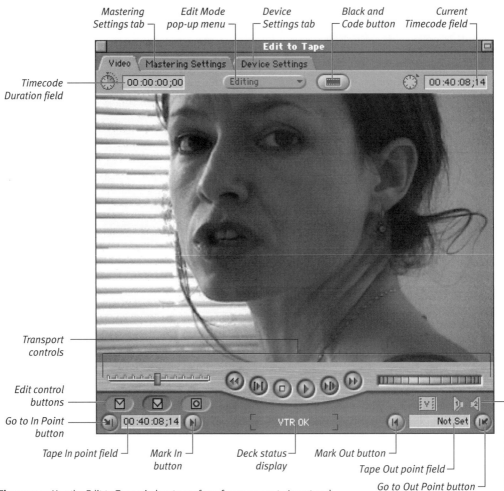

Mastering Settings tab · Edit Mode pop-up menu · Device Settings tab · Black and Code button · Current Timecode field

Timecode Duration field

Transport controls

Edit control buttons

Go to In Point button

Tape In point field · Mark In button · Deck status display · Mark Out button · Tape Out point field · Go to Out Point button · Target track controls

Figure 11.15 Use the Edit to Tape window to perform frame accurate Insert and Assemble edits to videotape, using Final Cut Pro's output as source material.

Onscreen controls and displays

◆ **Mastering Settings tab:** Select this tab to specify pre- and post-program elements to be added to the beginning or end of the sequence. The Mastering Settings tab contains pre-program element options identical to those available in Print to Video. For details on how to configure your settings, see "Print to Video settings checklist" earlier in this chapter.

◆ **Device Settings tab:** Select this tab to switch to a different Device Control or Capture preset, if necessary. The Device Settings tab contains pop-up menus that provide shortcut access to your Device Control and Capture presets. For more information on specifying presets, see Chapter 2, "Welcome to Final Cut Pro."

◆ **Timecode Duration field:** This field displays the duration of the In and Out points you set for the record tape. Enter a timecode duration in this field to set a new Out point.

◆ **Edit Mode pop-up menu:** Select Mastering to include pre-program elements as you output the finished sequence. Select Editing to assemble segments into a longer program, replace a section, or correct part of a sequence.

◆ **Black and Code button:** Use black and code to erase a tape and then record a clean black signal and control and timecode track. See "To prepare a tape with black and code" later in this chapter.

◆ **Current Timecode field:** This field displays the current timecode location of the videotape to which you are recording.

◆ **Edit control buttons:** Perform an Insert, Assemble, or Preview edit by clicking the appropriate button.

◆ **Transport controls:** Use these buttons to control your deck or camcorder transport if you have device control enabled. Transport control operation is described in Chapter 5, "Introducing the Viewer."

◆ **Go to In Point button:** Click this button to shuttle to the recording tape's In point.

◆ **Tape In Point field:** This field displays the timecode location of the recording tape's current In point.

◆ **Mark In button:** Click this button to set an In point for your recording tape.

◆ **Deck status display:** This display shows the status of communication between your deck or camcorder and Final Cut Pro and informs you of any deck or tape malfunction or failure during the editing process.

◆ **Mark Out button:** Click this button to mark an Out point for your recording tape.

◆ **Tape Out Point field:** This field displays the timecode location of the currently marked recording tape's Out point.

◆ **Go to Out Point button:** Click this button to shuttle to the recording tape's current Out point.

◆ **Target track controls:** Click to specify which tracks from your Final Cut Pro sequence are to be recorded on tape. Note that target track specification is not available for DV decks. The default DV target assignment is Video, Audio 1, and Audio 2.

ANATOMY OF THE EDIT TO TAPE WINDOW

Editing controls

Three edit options are available in FCP's Edit to Tape window. Use the Insert, Assemble, or Preview button in the lower-left corner of the window (**Figure 11.16**) to perform drag-and-drop edits from the Viewer or the Browser. You can also click the appropriate editing control button to add a clip or sequence displayed in the Viewer to your tape.

The three edit types that are available as editing control buttons are also available in the edit overlay (**Figure 11.17**). Edit to Tape editing controls operate in the same way as the Canvas editing controls. For operation information, see Chapter 6, "Editing in Final Cut Pro."

Figure 11.16 You'll find the Insert, Assemble, and Preview edit control buttons in the lower-left corner of the Edit to Tape window.

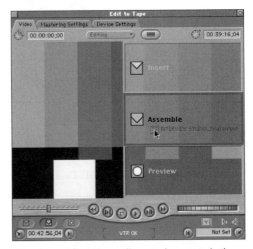

Figure 11.17 Edit to Tape edit controls operate in the same way as the Canvas edit controls. Drag a clip or sequence to the Edit to Tape window and then drop it on the edit overlay to perform Insert, Assemble, and Preview edits to tape.

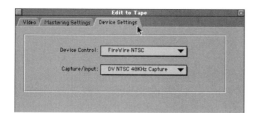

Figure 11.18 The Device Settings tab in the Edit to Tape window offers shortcut access to device control and capture preference settings.

Setting Up for Edit to Tape

The setup procedures for editing a Final Cut Pro sequence to tape include all the steps described in "Setting up for recording to tape," found earlier in this chapter, plus a few additional steps. Here's a checklist:

♦ Calibrate your timecode signal input. If there's any discrepancy between a time-code location on your videotape and that timecode location as it appears in FCP's Edit to Tape window, your edits won't be frame accurate. To learn how to calibrate your timecode, see "Calibrating the time-code signal input" in Chapter 3.

♦ Perform the setup procedures listed in "Setting up for recording to tape," found earlier in this chapter.

♦ Check that your deck or camcorder is responding to Final Cut Pro's device control. Edit to Tape requires device control over your video deck to cue the tape and perform precise edits. If you find that your deck is not responding to the Edit to Tape window's transport controls, check your current device control settings on the Device Settings tab of the Edit to Tape window (**Figure 11.18**). For more information on specifying device control presets, see Chapter 2, "Welcome to Final Cut Pro."

♦ On the Device Settings tab of the Edit to Tape window, check the Capture/Input pop-up menu to make sure the tape deck to which you want to record is selected as the input source.

♦ If your videotape doesn't already have timecode recorded on it, you'll need to prepare the tape by recording continuous clean black signal and control and time-code tracks. See "Using the Black and Code feature," in the following section.

✔ Tip

■ Why are you matching your input set-tings to the output destination for your Final Cut Pro sequence? When you edit to tape, you need to be able to view the material that's already on the tape to select your record In and Out points. The only way FCP can preview your edits to tape is to "capture" the material that's on your tape. You're not actually capturing the tape material and digitizing it to your computer; FCP's just using the capture settings to display the tape material in the Edit to Tape window.

Using the Black and Code feature

You must have timecode already recorded on a tape before you can perform an Insert or Assemble edit.

If you are performing Insert edits on to a previously unrecorded tape, you'll need to record a continuous clean black signal and control and timecode track for more than the entire length of the program you're editing.

If you are performing Assemble edits on a previously unrecorded tape, you'll need to black and code at least 30 seconds at the head of the new tape. Even though Assemble edits record new timecode as part of the operation, you need to start with enough black and coded tape to start the first edit.

Depending on the capabilities of the deck you are using, you may be able to specify a starting timecode. Otherwise, your tape will automatically rewind, and Final Cut Pro will start laying down black and code from the beginning of your tape, erasing anything that you have previously recorded.

✔ Tip

- One question before you kick off a black and code operation: Do you have the correct tape loaded in your video deck?

Figure 11.19 Click the Black and Code button In the Edit to Tape window.

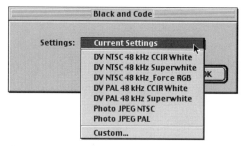

Figure 11.20 In the Black and Code Settings window, confirm that the output settings are compatible with your video card and then click OK.

Figure 11.21 To rewind your tape and overwrite it with timecode and black, click OK.

To prepare a tape with black and code:

1. In the Edit to Tape window, click the Black and Code button (**Figure 11.19**).

2. If your deck supports a remote timecode setting, you'll see a dialog box. Enter a starting timecode for your videotape and click OK.

3. The Black and Code settings window appears. A list of settings based on the sequence presets appear in the Settings pop-up menu. The Current Settings option is based on the sequence preset in your current Easy Setup. Choose a preset that matches the sequence settings of your FCP sequence and then click OK (**Figure 11.20**).

4. If your deck does not support any options, you'll see a dialog box telling you that your tape is about to be rewound to the beginning and overwritten with time-code and black. Click OK (**Figure 11.21**).

   The tape rewinds to the beginning and then records black and timecode, starting from the timecode specified.

✔ Tip

■ To cancel a black and code operation in progress, press the Esc key.

Preparing your sequence for editing to tape

The same rendering protocols that apply to Print to Video apply also to the Edit to Tape window. The Edit to Tape function also prints source material to tape at the currently selected render quality. It will also automatically render any material that is required before performing an edit to tape. Review "Print to Video: Rendering Tips" earlier in this chapter for protocol information and tips.

Performing an Edit to Tape

Before you perform an edit to tape, be sure you have checked and enabled your device controls, black and coded your recording tape (if necessary), and checked to see that your external video device is receiving Final Cut Pro's video output properly.

To simplify the task description, the tasks presented here describe editing to tape using sequences, but you can use clips as well as sequences for your source media.

✔ Tips

- Check out the rendering tips in "Setting up for recording to tape" before you start laying down edits.

- Clips or sequences can be dragged to the Edit to Tape window from the Browser as well as from the Viewer.

To perform an Assemble edit to tape:

1. Follow the setup guidelines in the section "Setting Up for Edit to Tape" earlier in this chapter.

2. Choose Tools > Edit to Tape (**Figure 11.22**).
   The Edit to Tape window appears.

3. *Do one of the following:*

   ▲ If you want your edit to include mastering options, such as pre- or post-program elements, select Mastering from the Edit Mode pop-up menu. Then configure your mastering settings on the Mastering Settings tab (**Figure 11.23**). Your mastering options are detailed in "Print to Video settings checklist" earlier in this chapter.

   ▲ If you do not want to include mastering options, select Editing from the Edit Mode pop-up menu (**Figure 11.24**).

Figure 11.22 Choose Tools > Edit to Tape.

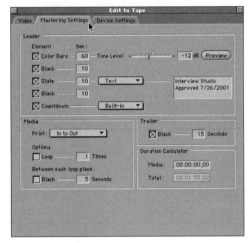

Figure 11.23 The Mastering Settings tab of the Edit to Tape window offers mastering options identical to those available in Print to Video.

Figure 11.24 Select Editing from the Edit Mode pop-up menu to edit to tape only the material you select and exclude any mastering elements.

Figure 11.25 Use the transport controls to cue the tape to the point where you want your first edit to start; then click the Mark In button.

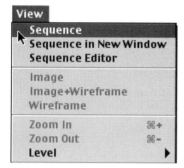

Figure 11.26 Select the sequence in the Browser and then choose View > Sequence.

Figure 11.27 Drop the clip on the Assemble edit area of the edit overlay.

Figure 11.28 Click OK to perform the edit. The tape will shuttle to the pre-roll point and record the Final Cut Pro sequence to tape, starting at the Tape In point.

4. In the Edit to Tape window, use the transport controls to cue the tape to the point where you want your first edit to start and then click the Mark In button or press I to set an In point (**Figure 11.25**).

5. In the Browser, select the sequence you want to edit to videotape and then choose View > Sequence (**Figure 11.26**). If the sequence is open in the Timeline or Canvas, it will close automatically when you load it into the Viewer.

Your edited sequence opens in the Viewer window, ready to be used as source media.

6. Select the portion of the sequence you want to edit to tape by setting In and Out points for the sequence. If you want to use the whole sequence, you don't need to set In and Out points. (See Chapter 5, "Introducing the Viewer.")

Final Cut Pro calculates the edit using three-point editing rules. For more information, see "FCP Protocol: Three-Point Editing" in Chapter 6.

7. Click and drag the sequence from the image area of the Viewer to the Edit to Tape window.

The edit overlay menu appears.

8. Drop the sequence on the Assemble edit area (**Figure 11.27**).

Final Cut Pro automatically renders any unrendered sequence material, plus any additional program elements you've specified.

When the rendering is complete, a dialog box appears.

9. To perform the edit, click OK (**Figure 11.28**).

The tape shuttles to the pre-roll point, and then the edit is performed.

✔ Tip

■ To interrupt an edit in progress, press Esc.

To perform an Insert or Preview edit to tape:

1. Follow steps 1 through 3 in "To perform an Assemble edit to tape" in the preceding section.

2. In the Edit to Tape window, use the transport controls to cue the tape to the point where you want your first edit to start and then click the Mark In button or press I to set an In point.

3. Cue your tape to the end point of your edit and then click the Mark Out button or press O to set an Out point (**Figure 11.29**).

4. Click the target track controls to specify which tracks from your Final Cut Pro sequence are to be recorded on tape. You can specify any combination of Video, Audio 1, and Audio 2 (**Figure 11.30**).

   After you make your track selection, you'll still hear and see all three tracks, but only the tracks you select will be recorded on the tape when you perform the edit.

5. In the Browser, select the sequence you want to edit to videotape and then choose View > Sequence. If the sequence is open in the Timeline, you must close it first, or you won't be able to load it into the Viewer.

   Your edited sequence opens in the Viewer window, ready to be used as source media.

6. Select the portion of the sequence you want to edit to tape by setting In and Out points for the sequence (**Figure 11.31**).

   If you want to use the whole sequence, you don't need to set In and Out points. (See Chapter 5, "Introducing the Viewer.") Final Cut Pro calculates the edit using three-point editing rules.

Figure 11.29 Cue your tape to the end point of your edit and then click the Mark Out button to set an Out point for your Insert edit.

Figure 11.30 Click the target track controls to specify which tracks from your Final Cut Pro sequence are to be recorded on tape. Target track selection is disabled when FCP detects DV decks or camcorders.

Figure 11.31 In the Viewer window, select the portion of the sequence you want to edit to tape by setting In and Out points for the sequence.

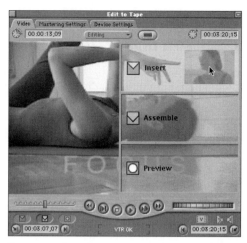

Figure 11.32 Drop the sequence on the Insert edit area to perform an Insert edit to tape.

Click OK to start recording media onto deck.

Cancel   OK

Figure 11.33 Click OK to perform the edit. The tape will shuttle to the pre-roll point and record the Final Cut Pro sequence to tape, starting at the tape In point.

7. Click and drag the clip from the image area of the Viewer to the Edit to Tape window.

The edit overlay menu appears.

8. *Do one of the following:*

▲ Drop the clip on the Preview edit area if you want to see a simulation of your edit without actually recording it.

▲ Drop the sequence on the Insert edit area to perform an Insert edit to tape (**Figure 11.32**).

Final Cut Pro automatically renders any unrendered sequence material, plus any additional program elements you've specified.

When the rendering is complete, a dialog box appears.

9. To perform the edit, click OK (**Figure 11.33**).

The tape shuttles to the pre-roll point, and then the edit or preview is performed.

✔ Tips

■ To interrupt an edit in progress, press Esc.

■ If you are having trouble controlling your deck or camcorder, consult the troubleshooting tips in Chapter 3, "Input: Getting Digital with Your Video."

■ If your external video monitoring is not functioning properly, consult "Troubleshooting" in Chapter 1.

PERFORMING AN EDIT TO TAPE

Data Export Modes

You can export just the editing and clip information from a Final Cut Pro sequence as a formatted text file. Both types of exported text files, batch lists and EDLs, can be used to re-create your edit on another editing system. EDLs can be used for linear and nonlinear editing systems, while batch lists, (lists of clips exported from the Browser), can be used to recapture media in Final Cut Pro or another nonlinear editing system, such as an Avid system.

Exporting an Edit Decision List (EDL)

An Edit Decision List (EDL) is a sequential list of all the edits and all individual clips used in a sequence or project. EDLs are used by video post-production facilities to perform online edits on linear (tape-based) editing systems. If you are editing your program in Final Cut Pro, but you are planning to re-create your edits on another editing system, you'll need to produce an EDL.

An EDL is a text file. In a perfect world, you would be able to take that text file to any editing system in the world—linear or nonlinear—and re-create your sequence. In this world, there are many different systems, and each has its own requirements for the formatting of that text file: the way the edit and source media data are arranged.

If you're planning to finish your program at a post-production facility, you should check with the facility's technical personnel at your earliest opportunity to get a complete description of the capabilities of the editing system and its technical requirements. You should also request complete specifications for the EDL you are providing. EDL format specifications can extend to the type of disk that the EDL is stored on and the software used to format that disk, so be sure to ask.

In Final Cut Pro, you create an EDL by exporting a sequence. A single EDL can have up to two video tracks and four audio tracks. You can use standard dissolves and up to 20 wipe patterns in transitions. Some of the more complicated elements in a sequence can't be represented in an EDL.

For information on importing an EDL, see Chapter 3, "Input: Getting Digital with Your Video."

You EDL What You Edit: Hints for Better EDLs

If you know your FCP project is destined to be exported as an EDL, you should start strategizing right from the beginning stages of your edit. If you can, get detailed EDL specifications from the facility where you plan on doing your online edit.

◆ Before you log your first clip, you should be sure you have calibrated timecode between your deck and your FCP system, because your edits will be based on the your source media's timecode numbers *as captured to disk*. See "Calibrating the timecode signal input" in Chapter 3.

◆ Use short, unique reel names and clip names. Each EDL format has different naming requirements, so err on the side of caution when naming.

◆ If you have DV source tapes with timecode breaks in them, assign a unique reel name to each section.

◆ When you're ready to start editing, consider using FCP's Cutting Station mode. This simplified editing mode disables many of FCP's editing features that don't translate to EDLs.

◆ Don't use transitions on video tracks other than V1—EDLs ignore them.

◆ The audio level and video opacity level information exported to your EDL can be interpreted accurately only by selected online systems. Check with your online facility.

◆ Your chances of successfully exporting a useful and accurate EDL increase significantly if you simplify your sequence before you try to export it. Clips with speed changes, nested sub-sequences, multilayered effects, titles, and stills are also risky elements to leave in.

◆ Use the EDL's audio mapping features to sort out large numbers of audio tracks. Make a test version of your simplified sequence and try it out before your online editing session, if you can.

◆ After you've exported your EDL, open it and examine the contents; do you have the information you need to re-create your sequence in the online session?

◆ If you've had to simplify your sequence quite a bit to successfully export an EDL, you should make a tape copy of your original sequence, as well as the simplified version, and take it with you to the online session. Your online editor might find it useful to refer to the FCP version when she's trying to re-create that Martian dream sequence you concocted.

To export a sequence as an EDL:

1. Select a sequence in the Browser or Timeline.

2. Choose File > Export > EDL (**Figure 11.34**).

3. In the EDL Export Options window, specify options (detailed in "EDL export options checklist" in the next section) and then click OK (**Figure 11.35**).

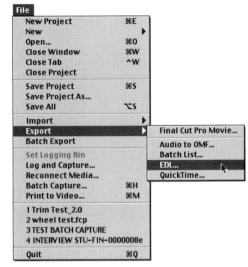

Figure 11.34 Choose File > Export > EDL.

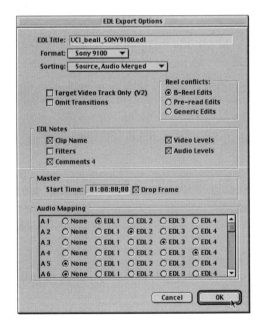

Figure 11.35 In the EDL Export Options window, specify format options for your EDL and click OK.

Figure 11.36 Type a name for your EDL in the Export As field and then select a destination folder from the pull-down menu at the top of the Export dialog box.

Figure 11.37 A second Save dialog box appears if you specified a separate EDL for B-reel edits, or if your EDL exceeds the maximum number of edits allowed.

4. Back in the Export dialog box, type a name for your EDL in the Save As field and then select a destination folder from the pull-down menu at the top of the dialog box (**Figure 11.36**).

5. Click Save.

6. If you specified a separate EDL for B-reel edits, or if your EDL exceeds the maximum number of edits allowed in your selected EDL format, a second Save dialog box appears. Click Save (**Figure 11.37**).

✔ Tips

■ If your sequence will not export in the EDL format you have specified, you'll get a General Error message when you try to save it.

■ If your sequence exceeds the maximum number of events for a specified EDL format, Final Cut Pro will create additional files.

EXPORTING AN EDIT DECISION LIST (EDL)

EDL export options checklist

EDL export options should be specified in strict accordance with the EDL format specifications you receive from your post-production facility.

Figure 11.38 Choose an EDL format that corresponds to the format required by the linear editing system that will use the EDL.

- ◆ **EDL Title:** This field displays the title of the EDL, which appears at the top of the EDL text file and may be different from the file's name on the disk.

- ◆ **Format:** Choose an EDL format (**Figure 11.38**). It should correspond to the format required by the linear system that will use the EDL.

Figure 11.39 Select a sorting format to determine how video and audio edits are sorted in the EDL.

- ◆ **Sorting:** Choose an option to determine how video and audio edits are sorted in the EDL (**Figure 11.39**). The following options are available:

  - ▲ **Master, Audio Merged:** This option sorts the sequence edits chronologically. Linked video and audio appear on the same line, even if the audio ends before the video.

  - ▲ **Source, Audio Merged:** This option sorts edits first by source reel number and then by sequence chronology. Linked video and audio appear on the same line, even if the audio ends before the video.

- ◆ **Target Video Track Only:** Check this box to export edits from only your sequence's current target video track, plus all audio edits.

- ◆ **Omit Transitions:** Check this box to exclude transitions from the EDL.

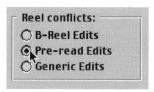

Figure 11.40 Check the Pre-read Edits box to allow the EDL to place transitions between two clips on the same reel.

Figure 11.41 Check boxes next to the data that you want to include in your exported EDL.

◆ **Reel Conflicts:** Check the Pre-read Edits box to allow transitions between two clips on the same reel (**Figure 11.40**). Only certain digital video decks support this feature. Check with your post-production facility to see if the facility's equipment can pre-read edits. If this option is not selected, Final Cut Pro creates a B-reel EDL, if necessary.

◆ **EDL Notes:** Select information to include in your exported EDL (**Figure 11.41**). The following types of notes can be exported:

▲ **Clip Name:** Check this box to include the name of the source media file on disk for the clips used in the sequence. This name appears in the EDL each time the clip is used.

▲ **Filters:** Check this box to include the name of filters that are applied to a clip or a range in the sequence.

▲ **Comments 4:** Check this box to include the contents of the Browser's Comments 4 column in the exported EDL.

▲ **Video Levels:** Check this box to export opacity levels including the timecode location of level changes (based on the master tape's timecode).

▲ **Audio Levels:** Check this box to export audio levels, including the timecode location of level changes (based on the master tape's timecode).

◆ **Master:** Specify the following export mastering options:

▲ **Start Time:** Specify a starting time-code for the master reel in the EDL. By default, the starting timecode of the sequence is used.

▲ **Drop Frame:** Check the box to specify drop-frame timecode as the master tape's timecode format. Uncheck the box to specify nondrop-frame format.

continues on next page

EXPORTING AN EDIT DECISION LIST (EDL)

◆ **Audio Mapping:** These settings determine how audio is mapped to EDL channels. Each sequence audio track can be mapped to one of a maximum of four EDL channels, or it can be turned off.

You can map multiple sequence tracks to a single EDL channel (**Figure 11.42**). (Note that some formats, such as Sony 5000 and CMX 340, do not support more than two channels.)

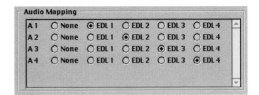

Figure 11.42 Click the radio buttons to configure your audio track mapping.

✔ Tip

■ If the name of a clip as you use it in your sequence is different from the name of its source media file on disk, you still can include the clip's name in your EDL. Control-click the clip in the Timeline and open its Item Properties window. Enter the clip's name in the Comment 4 field on the Logging Information tab. The Comment 4 field also appears as a Browser column, so you could also enter the clip name there. You can include Comment 4 fields when you export your sequence as an EDL (**Figure 11.43**).

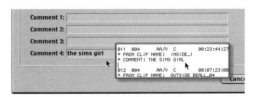

Figure 11.43 If you enter a clip's name in Comment Column 4, it will appear in your EDL.

To open an EDL text file:

1. Choose File > Open; or press Command-O.

2. Navigate to the folder where you saved your EDL and then select it and click Open (**Figure 11.44**).

   Your EDL opens in a text window (**Figure 11.45**), and you can review its formatting. Be extremely cautious about making any changes to your EDL. The EDL's formatting has been set up in accordance with the requirements of the EDL format type.

Figure 11.44 Select your EDL and then click Open.

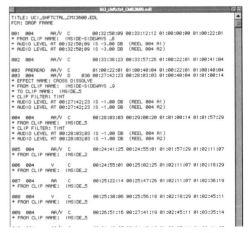

Figure 11.45 Your EDL opens in a text window. You can use Final Cut Pro's text editor to make modifications, but remember that EDLs are finicky about formatting.

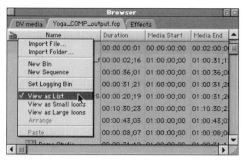

Figure 11.46 Control-click in the Browser's Name column and then select View as List from the shortcut menu.

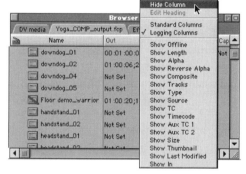

Figure 11.47 Control-click in the header of any column you want to exclude from the batch list and choose Hide Column from the shortcut menu.

Exporting a Batch List

A batch list is a tab-delimited text file containing the clip data listed in the Browser window. This makes batch lists a good choice for exporting clip data that can be used to re-capture media on another nonlinear editing system, such as an Avid system.

While a batch list can include many more types of information about a clip than an EDL, you cannot export a batch list of a sequence.

✔ Tip

- FCP can only export the entire contents of a Browser bin; you cannot select items within a bin for inclusion in a batch list. If you want to export a batch list of selected clips only, you must place the selected clips in their own bin first.

To export a sequence as a batch list:

1. Set your Browser display to View as List (**Figure 11.46**) and then select a project tab.

2. Place all the clips you want to include in your batch list in their own Browser bin, and then open it, making that bin the front tab of the Browser.

3. All columns that are visible at the time of export will be included in the batch list, in the order they appear in the Browser display. To prepare your Browser column display for export, do any of the following:

   ▲ Arrange the Browser columns in the order you want them to appear in your list.

   ▲ Control-click column headers and select any currently hidden columns you want to include.

   ▲ Control-click the header of any column you want to exclude from the batch list and choose Hide Column from the shortcut menu (**Figure 11.47**).

continues on next page

4. Choose File > Export > Batch List (**Figure 11.48**).

All columns that are visible at the time of export are included in the batch list.

5. In the Export dialog box, type a name for your batch list in the Export As field and then select a destination folder from the pull-down menu at the top of the dialog box.

6. Click Save (**Figure 11.49**).

✔ Tip

■ If you are moving your Final Cut Pro project to another nonlinear editing system, a properly formatted batch list will maximize the amount of clip information that transfers to the new system. Try a little reverse engineering. Start by exporting a batch list from the system you are moving to and then opening it in the text editor and/or spreadsheet program to get a look at the format. You might try importing it into FCP to see how it translates into Browser columns. You'll get a better idea of how to format your FCP batch list.

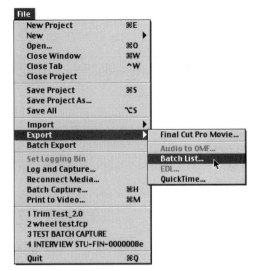

Figure 11.48 Choose File > Export > Batch List.

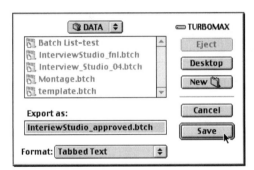

Figure 11.49 Type a name for your batch list in the Export As field and then select a destination folder from the pull-down menu at the top of the dialog box and click Save.

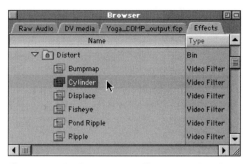

Figure 11.50 On the Browser's Effects tab, select the effect you want to export.

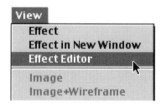

Figure 11.51 Choose View > Effect Editor.

Figure 11.52 Choose FXBuilder > Export Text.

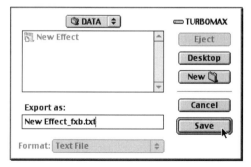

Figure 11.53 Type a name for your FX Builder script in the Export As field; then select a destination folder from the pull-down menu at the top of the dialog box and click Save.

Exporting FXBuilder scripts as text

You can save FXBuilder scripts—the scripts that build Final Cut Pro filters and transitions—as text files. Saving an FXBuilder script as a text file makes it portable: You can take custom effects you've created along with you when you move to another Final Cut Pro system.

For more information about editing FXBuilder scripts, see Chapter 13, "Compositing and Special Effects."

To export an effect as text:

1. On the Browser's Effects tab, select the effect you want to export (**Figure 11.50**).

2. Choose View > Effect Editor (**Figure 11.51**).

   The text version of the effect is loaded into FXBuilder, and the FXBuilder Menu appears in the menu bar.

3. Choose FXBuilder > Export Text (**Figure 11.52**).

4. In the Export dialog box, type a name for your effect script in the Export As field and then select a destination folder from the pull-down menu at the top of the dialog box.

5. Click Save (**Figure 11.53**).

Exporting Sequences and Clips

If you want to convert your Final Cut Pro sequence to another digital format for use in computer-based media, exporting is the right choice for you. You can also export sound files, snippets of clips, or single-frame images. Final Cut Pro offers a variety of format options.

When you export, Final Cut Pro uses Quick-Time's compression codec and file format conversion features to generate a media file on your hard drive in the format you choose.

Here's how FCP's export options are organized:

When you choose File > Export, along with the two data export options you'll see three media export options: Final Cut Pro Movie, Audio to OMF, and QuickTime (**Figure 11.54**).

◆ The Export > Final Cut Pro Movie command is designed to streamline your export configuration chores by offering you limited settings options (**Figure 11.55**). Use Export > Final Cut Pro Movie to export your sequence as a single movie using the same settings as your sequence preset or using another size and codec that you use often.

The Final Cut Pro Movie format is the only export format that allows you to export your sequence as a reference movie. (See "What's a Reference Movie?" in the following section).

Figure 11.54 When you choose File > Export, you'll see FCP's three media export options.

Figure 11.55 Use Export > Final Cut Pro Movie to your export your sequence as a single movie using one of your sequence presets or to export a reference movie for use with a third-party compression program. The Export dialog box displays settings options based on your FCP sequence presets.

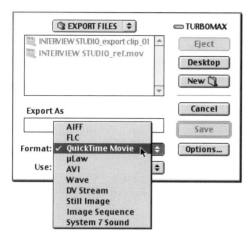

Figure 11.56 One your QuickTime export format options, the QuickTime Movie format, is a good choice for producing highly compressed QuickTime movies for multimedia or web.

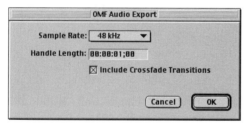

Figure 11.57 Use the Export > Audio to OMF command to export the audio tracks from your sequence as OMF-format files.

◆ The Export > QuickTime command gives you access to the full range of QuickTime-supported file formats. Export > QuickTime is your starting point when you want to export anything, from still images to compressed audio files.

One of the QuickTime format options, the QuickTime Movie format (**Figure 11.56**), is a good choice for producing highly compressed QuickTime movies or media files in full-resolution, uncompressed formats. The QuickTime Movie format option also offers video filters that you can apply as you export a sequence.

◆ The Export > Audio to OMF command can export the audio tracks from your sequence as OMF-format files (**Figure 11.57**). The exported Open Media Framework (OMF) file contains the audio files, plus the audio edit information from your project file. That means you can export your audio tracks with the original track separations, edit points, cross-fades, and video sync intact and then import them into an OMF-compatible digital audio workstation (DAWs), the kind used at most professional audio post-production facilities.

EXPORTING SEQUENCES AND CLIPS

✔ Tips

■ When you're facing a big exporting job involving many clips, you can call on FCP's Batch Export feature. You can queue up multitudes of files, even if they require different export settings, and batch process them while you're busy elsewhere. See "Batch Exporting" later in this chapter.

■ Apple's *Final Cut Pro 2 User's Manual* has an entire 45-page chapter devoted to exporting the various QuickTime file formats—recommended reading for FCP users faced with an export format decision.

■ The two tables that follow provide a sketch of the codecs and file formats you are most likely to use with Final Cut Pro and the way they're most commonly used. Note that these tables do not contain a complete list of QuickTime formats and codecs, and the summary of uses and characteristics is not comprehensive. **Table 11.1** lists the codecs most commonly used with Final Cut Pro. **Table 11.2** lists the most commonly used file formats.

■ Need more information on file formats to decide which output format is best for your needs? Current information on today's array of file formats and compression codecs is available on the Web at the superb Codec Central site, at http://www.codeccentral.com.

■ When you export a clip or sequence, Final Cut Pro includes only the material between the In and Out points in the exported file. You can set In and Out points to select a portion of your clip or sequence, but be sure to clear In and Out points before you export if you want to export the entire clip.

What's a Reference Movie?

The Export > Final Cut Pro Movie feature offers the option of exporting your FCP clip or sequence as a reference movie. A reference movie is a bit of QuickTime media-handling wizardry. A small file that contains no media (except for a render file of your mixed sequence audio, plus video render files for parts of your exported sequence that haven't been rendered yet), a reference movie simply points to the original media files used in the exported sequence. Third-party media compression programs, such as Cleaner, can use the reference movie pointer information from that small file to process the compressed version of your sequence using the larger original media files.

Reference movies will work with any QuickTime-compatible compression application that's installed on the same computer as your Final Cut Pro system. The compression program must have access to the original QuickTime source media files for your reference movie to work.

You won't see a "Make Reference Movie" option in the Export Final Cut Pro Movie dialog box. The only way to export your Final Cut Pro clip or sequence as a reference movie is to leave Make Movie Self-Contained unchecked. Pretty esoteric, huh?

Table 11.1

Some Useful QuickTime Codecs

FILE FORMATS	TYPE	USED FOR	ALPHA CHANNEL?
Sorenson	A/V	CD-ROM	No
Cinepak	A/V	Older CD-ROM	No
QuickTime Fast Start	A/V	Web movies	No
QuickTime Streaming	A/V	Web movies	No
Animation	V	High-res digital export	Yes
Uncompressed	V	Uncompressed digital export	Yes
M-JPEG A/M-JPEG B.	V	Compressed files for editing	No
DV-NTSC/DV-PAL	A/V	Importing DV into FCP	No
MPEG-2*	V	DVD video	No

*DVD Studio Pro required for MPEG-2 processing from FCP 2.

Table 11.2

Some Useful QuickTime File Formats

FILE FORMATS	TYPE	USED FOR	ALPHA CHANNEL?	COMPRESSION?
QuickTime Movie	A/V/Graphic/+	Cross-platform multimedia	Yes	Available
DV stream	A/V	iMovie DV media files	No	Yes
JPEG	Graphic	Graphics, video still frames	No	Available
Photoshop	Graphic	Multilayered graphics	Yes	No
PICT	Graphic	Mac format	Yes	Available
PNG	Graphic	Graphics	Yes	No
TIFF	Graphic	Graphics	Yes	Available
AIFF	A	Common audio format	N/A	Available
WAVE	A	Windows audio format	N/A	No

Codec versus File Format

A codec is an algorithm, or mathematical formula, for compressing and decompressing digital media. The word "codec" is techie shorthand for COmpression/DEcompression. Whenever you see "compression" options in the QuickTime interface, you're looking at a list of codecs.

A file format is one standardized way of organizing data so it can be recognized and used by an application or operating system. You could use the same compression codec in a variety of file formats, and vice versa. QuickTime Movie is an example of a file format that supports many, many codecs.

Exporting a Final Cut Pro Movie

The Export > Final Cut Pro Movie command is the right choice when you want to export a rendered sequence using the same sequence settings or the settings from another sequence preset.

The Export Final Cut Pro Movie dialog box opens with your current sequence preset settings already loaded, but you can select any other sequence preset as an export format. Choose a render quality and specify whether to include audio or video, or both, and you're done.

You can create sequence presets for export formats that you use regularly and then select one of those when you are ready to export. (It's okay to select a different sequence preset when exporting—the preset is just a quick way to specify the format of your exported file without having to manually configure all your QuickTime settings.)

Final Cut Pro Movie is the only export format that offers the option of exporting your sequence as a QuickTime reference movie.

To export a clip or sequence as a Final Cut Pro movie:

1. *Do one of the following:*

   ▲ Select a clip or sequence in the Browser.

   ▲ In the Timeline, open the sequence you want to export.

2. Set In and Out points in your clip or sequence to mark the section you want to include in the exported file (**Figure 11.58**). If you want to export the entire item, clear any In and Out points from the item before export.

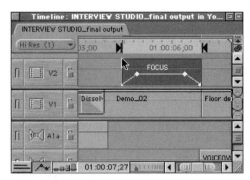

Figure 11.58 Set In and Out points in your sequence to mark the section you want to include in the exported file.

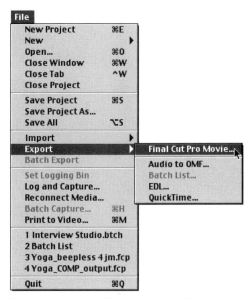

Figure 11.59 Choose > File > Export > Final Cut Pro Movie.

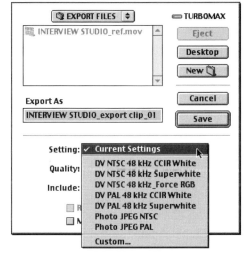

Figure 11.60 Choose Current Settings to use the current QuickTime sequence settings, as defined in the sequence preset in which your sequence was created.

3. Choose File > Export > Final Cut Pro Movie (**Figure 11.59**).

The Export dialog box appears. This is your opportunity to review and confirm the export format settings.

4. From the Setting pop-up menu, choose Current Settings to use the current sequence preset settings (**Figure 11.60**), or choose another sequence preset to recompress your clip or sequence in a different format.

5. From the Quality pop-up menu, choose a render quality for the item you are exporting.

6. From the Include pop-up menu, choose Video and Audio, Audio Only, or Video Only.

7. *Do one of the following:*

▲ Check Recompress All Frames to re-render all frames as you export. Note that Recompress All Frames is available only if you've checked Make Movie Self-Contained.

▲ Leave Recompress All Frames unchecked (**Figure 11.61**) to export a copy of your clip or sequence's existing render files. Copying is much faster than re-rendering.

continues on next page

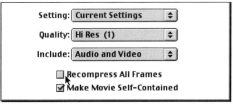

Figure 11.61 Uncheck the Recompress All Frames box to export a copy of the sequence at the render quality you select, using the existing rendered files. Material that does not require rendering will be copied from its source media file.

EXPORTING SEQUENCES AND CLIPS

8. *Do one of the following:*

▲ Check Make Movie Self-Contained to export a QuickTime movie that duplicates all audio, video, and render files in one self-contained media file.

▲ Leave Make Movie Self-Contained unchecked to export a reference movie—a small movie file that contains only pointers to the original audio, video, and render files.

9. In the Export dialog box, type a name for your file in the Export As field and then select a destination folder from the pull-down menu at the top of the dialog box and then click Save.

✔ Tips

■ If you want to export a disk file copy of a rendered sequence you are working on, you should choose Current Settings, select the same render quality that you have already rendered the sequence in, and uncheck Recompress All Frames. Final Cut Pro will copy the rendered files, and you'll have a "hard copy" (an actual media file on disk) of your edited rendered sequence. Exporting a hard copy of a rendered file is a good way to make a backup of long or complex rendered sequences.

■ If your clip or sequence doesn't have an audio track, select Video Only from the Include pop-up menu. Even empty audio tracks will increase the file size of your exported clip.

Figure 11.62 Select the sequence in the Browser.

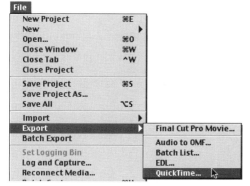

Figure 11.63 Choose File > Export and then choose an export file format from the submenu. Choosing QuickTime gives you access to the full range of QuickTime's output formats.

Exporting Other QuickTime Formats

The Export > QuickTime option gives you access to the full range of QuickTime-supported file formats. Use this option to convert your FCP media into any of the following:

◆ Compressed QuickTime movies (use the QuickTime Movie format)

◆ Uncompressed, full-resolution file formats that include an alpha channel

◆ Still images in a variety of graphics file formats

◆ Audio tracks in a variety of compressed and uncompressed formats

To export a clip or sequence in another QuickTime format:

1. *Do one of the following:*

▲ Select a clip or sequence in the Browser (**Figure 11.62**).

▲ In the Timeline, open the sequence you want to export.

2. Set In and Out points in your clip or sequence to mark the section you want to include in the exported file. If you want to export the entire item, clear any In and Out points from the item before export.

3. Choose File > Export > QuickTime (**Figure 11.63**).

The Export dialog box opens.

continues on next page

4. In the Export dialog box, choose an export file format from the Format pop-up menu (**Figure 11.64**); *then do one of the following:*

▲ Choose one of the export settings presets from the Use pop-up menu (**Figure 11.65**).

▲ Click the Options button to access the full QuickTime settings for the format you have selected. In the settings window, confirm or modify the export format settings and then click OK. Export options will vary according to the format you have selected (**Figure 11.66**).

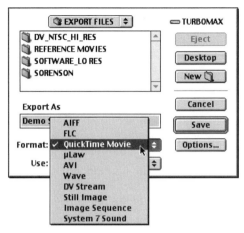

Figure 11.64 Choose an export file format from the Format pop-up menu.

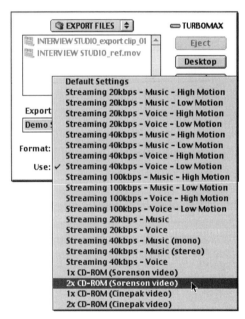

Figure 11.65 Choose one of the export settings presets from the Use pop-up menu. These are the export presets available for the QuickTime Movie export format.

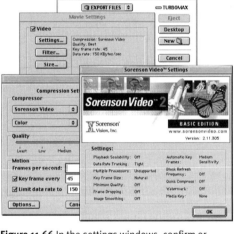

Figure 11.66 In the settings windows, confirm or modify the export format settings and then click OK. Export options will vary according the format you have selected. These are the settings windows for the Sorenson video codec.

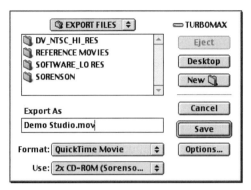

Figure 11.67 Type a name for your file in the Export dialog box's Export As field.

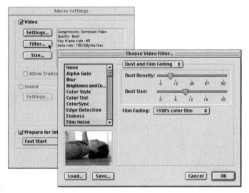

Figure 11.68 Click the Filters button in the Movie settings window to access a palette of QuickTime filters you can apply as part of your export operation. QuickTime filters are available only in the QuickTime Movie format.

5. In the Export dialog box, type a name for your file in the Export As field (**Figure 11.67**) and then select a destination folder from the pull-down menu at the top of the dialog box.

6. Click Save.

✔ Tip

- The QuickTime Movie format option gives you the option of applying QuickTime's suite of video filters. There's a range of effects and image control filters to choose from. (Check out the Film Noise filter!) Select the filters as you are configuring your export options, and they will be processed as part of the export operation. You can access the filters by clicking the Filter button in the Movie Settings window (**Figure 11.68**).

FCP Alert: Web Video Uses the Whole Video Frame

If you are converting your FCP sequence to a compressed format for Web or CD-ROM distribution, be aware that your exported file will show the entire video frame when viewed on a computer screen.

External video monitors typically don't display the edges of the video frame; that's why you're advised to keep your titles inside the "title safe area." If you have unwanted elements, such as microphones, hovering about the edges of your video frame, you may never have seen them if you've been monitoring your framing only on an external video monitor.

So check your whole video frame by viewing it on your computer monitor. If you do find that your frame has unsightly edges, you can always crop your frame before you export.

To export a still image
from a Canvas or Viewer frame:

1. In the Canvas or Viewer, position the playhead on the frame you want to export (**Figure 11.69**).

2. Choose File > Export > QuickTime.

3. In the Export dialog box, choose Still Image from the Format pop-up menu (**Figure 11.70**) and then *do one of the following:*

   ▲ Choose one of the Still Image settings presets from the Use pop-up menu.

   ▲ Click the Options button to access a complete list of QuickTime still image formats and their settings. In the Export Image Sequence Settings dialog box, select an export format from the pull-down menu at the top of the dialog box (**Figure 11.71**) and then click OK.

4. In the Export dialog box, type a name for your still frame in the Export As field and then select a destination folder from the pull-down menu at the top of the dialog box.

5. Click Save (**Figure 11.72**).

   Final Cut Pro automatically adds the correct image file extension to the name you typed.

✔ Tips

■ If you want to export multiple still frames in a batch process rather than exporting them directly (as outlined in this task), you'll first need to use the Modify > Make Freeze Frame command to create FCP still clips. When you're done selecting your freeze frames, you can use the batch-export feature to convert them all to graphic files in one operation.

■ Whenever you're exporting a still frame, you can ignore the frames-per-second settings—they don't apply to still-frame export.

Figure 11.69 Position the Canvas or Viewer playhead on the frame you want to export as a still frame.

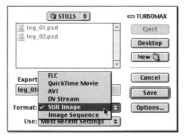

Figure 11.70 Select an Export format from the Format pull-down menu.

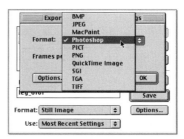

Figure 11.71 Selecting Photoshop as the export format from the pull-down menu in the Export Image Sequence Settings dialog box.

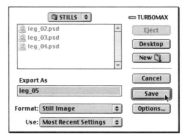

Figure 11.72 In the Export dialog box, type a name for your still frame in the Export As field; then select a destination folder from the pull-down menu at the top of the dialog box and click Save.

Figure 11.73 Set In and Out points in your clip or sequence to mark the section you want to include in the exported image sequence file.

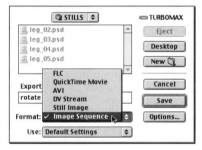

Figure 11.74 Select Image Sequence from the Format pop-up menu.

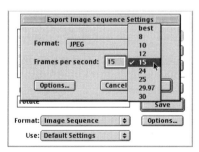

Figure 11.75 Select an export format from the pull-down menu at the top of the dialog box, select a frame rate for your image sequence, and then click OK.

To export an image sequence:

1. *Do one of the following:*

   ▲ Select a clip or sequence in the Browser.

   ▲ In the Timeline, open the sequence you want to export.

2. Set In and Out points in your clip or sequence to mark the section you want to export as a numbered image sequence (**Figure 11.73**). If you want to export the entire item, clear any In and Out points from the item before export.

3. Choose File > Export > QuickTime.

4. In the Export dialog box, choose Image Sequence from the Format pop-up menu (**Figure 11.74**); then *do one of the following:*

   ▲ Choose one of the Image Sequence settings presets from the Use pop-up menu.

   ▲ Click the Options button to access a complete list of QuickTime still image formats and their settings. In the Export Image Sequence Settings dialog box, select an export format from the Format pull-down menu at the top of the dialog box, select a frame rate for your image sequence, (**Figure 11.75**), and then click OK.

5. In the Export dialog box, type a name for your still frame in the Export As field and then select a destination folder from the pull-down menu at the top of the dialog box.

6. Click Save.

   Your image sequence is saved as a series of still graphics in the file format you selected.

To export audio only from a clip or sequence:

1. Select a clip or sequence in the Browser, or open the sequence in the Timeline.

2. Set In and Out points in your clip or sequence to mark the section you want to export as an audio file.

3. Choose File > Export > QuickTime.

4. In the Export dialog box, choose an audio export file format from the Format pop-up menu (**Figure 11.76**); *then do one of the following:*

   ▲ Choose one of the audio export settings presets from the Use pop-up menu.

   ▲ Click the Options button to access the full QuickTime settings for the format you have selected. In the Sound Settings window, select sample rate (**Figure 11.77**) and compression settings and then click OK.

5. In the Export dialog box, type a name for your audio file in the Export As field; then select a destination folder from the pull-down menu at the top of the dialog box.

6. Click Save.

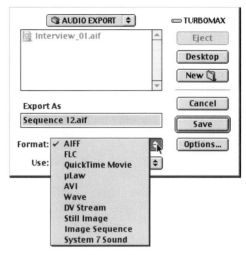

Figure 11.76 Choose File > Export QuickTime and then select an audio format from the Format pop-up menu. AIFF, WAVE, _Law, and System 7 are all audio formats.

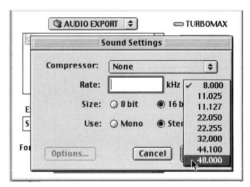

Figure 11.77 Select sample rate and compression settings from the Sound Settings window and then click OK.

✔ Tips

■ You can use the export method just described to convert the 44.1 KHz sample rate of a CD audio track. In the Sound Settings window (see step 4 in the preceding procedure), choose 48 (or 32) kHz—the sample rate that matches your sequence audio's rate. Once you have completed the export/sample rate conversion, import the exported copy back into your project.

■ Final Cut Pro allows you to mix audio tracks with different sample rates in the same sequence. The program can convert the sample rate of nonconforming audio on the fly as you play back a sequence. Real-time sample rate conversion does take processor power, however, and can occasionally produce nasty audible artifacts. So for best results, you should convert the sample rates of all your audio tracks to match the sequence settings.

Figure 11.78 Choose QuickTime Movie from the Format pop-up menu; then click the Options button.

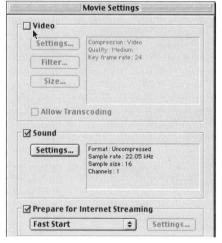

Figure 11.79 In the QuickTime Settings window, deselect the box next to Video and then click the Sound Settings button.

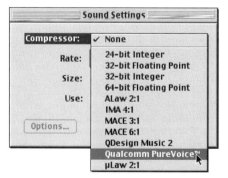

Figure 11.80 Choose a compression codec from the Compressor pop-up menu in the Sound Settings window and then configure codec settings.

To export audio from a clip or sequence in a compressed QuickTime movie format:

1. Select a clip or sequence in the Browser, or open the sequence in the Timeline.

2. Choose File > Export > QuickTime.

3. In the Export dialog box, choose QuickTime Movie from the Format pop-up menu.

4. Click the Options button (**Figure 11.78**).

5. In the Movie Settings window, deselect the box next to Video (**Figure 11.79**) and then click the Sound Settings button.

6. In the Sound Settings window, choose a compression codec from the Compressor pop-up menu; then click OK (**Figure 11.80**). Export settings options will vary according the format you have selected (**Figure 11.81**).

7. Click OK in the Movie Settings window.

8. In the Export dialog box, type a name for your audio file in the Export As field; then select a destination folder from the pull-down menu at the top of the dialog box.

9. Click Save.

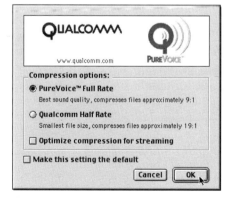

Figure 11.81 Codec settings options will vary depending on the codec you select.

EXPORTING OTHER QUICKTIME FORMATS

429

Batch Exporting

You can use the Batch Export feature to assemble groups of clips and sequences and then export them as QuickTime files in a single operation. You organize and specify export settings for your items in the Export Queue, which appears as a tab in the Batch Export window. Each top-level bin in the Batch Export window can contain multiple clips and sequences, individually or arranged in separate folders. All items and folders of items contained in a top-level bin in the Batch Export window will be exported with the same export settings, so you need a separate top-level export bin for each settings configuration you use. You don't need to export all the items in the export queue at once; you can select items and process only items you select. The Status column in the Export Queue window tracks which items have been exported.

The batch export process exports only QuickTime files.

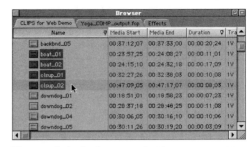

Figure 11.82 In the Browser, select items you want to include in a batch export. You can include items from more than one project in the same batch.

Figure 11.83 Add items to the export queue by selecting clips, sequences, or folders in the Browser and dragging them directly to a folder in the Export Queue window. You can add items to existing export bins or create new ones.

✔ Tip

■ Be sure to complete your batch export operations before you quit Final Cut Pro. All items will be deleted from the Export Queue when you quit the application.

To prepare items for batch export:

1. In the Browser, select the items you want to export (**Figure 11.82**).

2. Choose File > Batch Export.

   The Export Queue window opens, displaying the export queue with your selected items contained in a new top-level export bin.

3. You can add items to the export queue by selecting clips, sequences, or folders in the Browser and dragging them directly to a folder in the Export Queue window (**Figure 11.83**). Items from different projects can be placed in the same export bin.

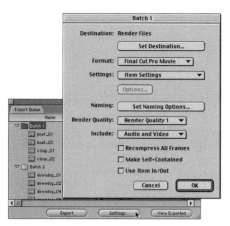

Figure 11.84 Use the Export Settings window to specify export settings for each top-level export bin in the export queue.

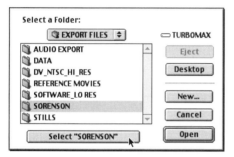

Figure 11.85 Navigate to the folder location where you want the exported files to be saved and then click the Select button.

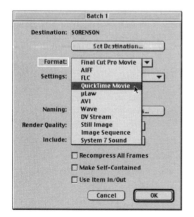

Figure 11.86 Back in the Export Settings window, choose an export file format for this batch from the Format pop-up menu.

4. To configure export settings for the items in an export bin, select the bin and then click the Settings button at the bottom of the window.

The Export Settings window appears with the name of the currently selected batch in the window's title bar (**Figure 11.84**). The current folder destination is displayed at the top of the window.

5. In the Export Settings window, click the Set Destination button; then navigate to the folder location where you want the exported files to be saved and click the Select button (**Figure 11.85**).

6. Back in the Export Settings window, Choose an export file format for this batch from the Format pop-up menu (**Figure 11.86**).

The export settings options displayed in this window will vary, depending on the export format you select. Each export format offers the same settings options as in the Export menu.

continues on next page

7. To specify the export compression settings and other movie options, select a preset from the Settings pull-down menu (**Figure 11.87**).

8. Click the Set Naming Options button and then specify a file extension for your exported items in the Set Naming Options dialog box and click OK. These are your options:

▲ Strip Existing Extension: This option excludes any existing file name extensions from the base file name when the export file name is created.

▲ Add Custom Extension: This option appends a custom extension to the file names of all of the exported items in this bin. Enter the extension in the field.

▲ Add File Type Extension: This option appends the default file name extension for the specified export output type (**Figure 11.88**).

9. If you have selected Final Cut Pro Movie as your export format, you can specify any of the following settings:

▲ Select Item Settings to use each item's original sequence settings as the export settings.

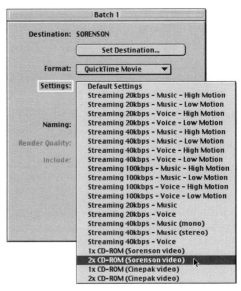

Figure 11.87 Selecting the Sorenson CD-ROM 2X preset from the Settings pull-down menu.

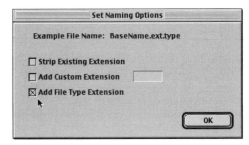

Figure 11.88 Choose Add File Type Extension to append the default file name extension for the specified export output type.

BATCH EXPORTING

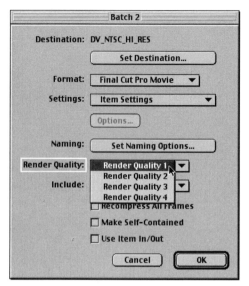

Figure 11.89 Selecting a render quality from the Render Quality pull-down menu will specify the export render quality for all items exported in Final Cut Pro Movie format.

▲ Select a render quality from the Render Quality pull-down menu (**Figure 11.89**). Your selection will specify the export render quality for all items in the selected export bin. You can have items from more than one project in an export bin.

Note that because clips may be exported from several projects with different customized render-quality names, Final Cut Pro assigns generic render-quality names to the four render-quality levels: Render Quality 1 through Render Quality 4. The export operation will observe the individual render-quality settings associated with that render-quality level for each item included in the batch.

▲ From the Include pull-down menu, select Audio and Video, Audio Only, or Video Only to specify which elements will be included in the exported file.

▲ Check Recompress All Frames if you want Final Cut Pro to re-render files that are being exported in the same codec as their source media. Uncheck this option if you want Final Cut Pro to simply copy directly from the source file to the destination file. Files that are being exported in a different codec from their source media will be recompressed in all cases.

▲ Check Make Movie Self-Contained to export a QuickTime movie that duplicates all audio, video, and render files in one self-contained media file. Leave Make Movie Self-Contained unchecked to export a reference movie—a small movie file that contains only pointers to the original audio, video and render files. For more information, see "What's a Reference Movie?" earlier in this chapter.

continues on next page

10. Check Use Item In/Out if you want to export only the portion of the clip or sequence between marked In and Out points.

11. When you have finished configuring your export settings for this export bin, click OK.

12. Repeat steps 4 though 11 for each top-level export bin that requires export settings for a different format.

To export multiple items in a batch process:

1. Follow the item selection and configuration procedures described in the previous section, "To prepare items for batch export."

2. *Do one of the following:*

▲ Select items or folders you want to export now.

▲ Select nothing if you want to process the entire contents of the Export Queue.

3. Click Export (**Figure 11.90**).

The export bins or individual items you selected are processed in their respective formats.

A dialog box appears, with a progress bar indicating the status of export processing. After your batch-export operation is completed, the processed bins' Status column displays Done (**Figure 11.91**).

4. To cancel a batch export, click Cancel.

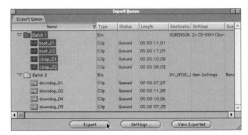

Figure 11.90 Click Export to perform a batch export operation on all items selected in the export queue. You can select individual items from multiple bins, entire bins, or the entire contents of the export queue.

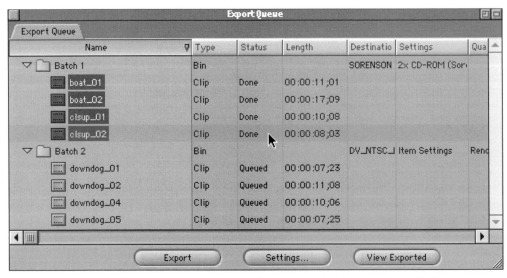

Figure 11.91 After your batch export operation is completed, the processed bin's Status column displays Done.

To open an exported file in the Viewer:

◆ In the Export Queue window, select any item marked Done and click the View Exported button at the bottom of the window.

The exported file opens in a new Viewer window.

Using the Export Queue window display

The columns in the Export Queue window display all of the details about the batch export items and operate in the same way as the Browser columns. Some columns display the settings you have specified in the Export Settings dialog box. You can modify some settings batch exportby Control-clicking a column entry (**Figure 11.92**). Some entries can't be modified.

◆ **Name:** This column displays the item name.

◆ **Type:** This column displays the item type.

◆ **Status:** This column displays the current export status for the item:

 ▲ **Queued:** The item has been added to the batch queue.

 ▲ **Done:** The item has been successfully exported. Items marked Done won't be reprocessed if you perform another batch export process.

 ▲ **Canceled:** The item's export process has been canceled.

 ▲ **Error:** The item's export process encountered an error.

◆ **Base Output Filename:** Enter a different file name to be used for this item's export file, or enter nothing and FCP will use the item's current name. File name extension options specified in the Export Settings dialog box will be applied to the file name specified here.

continues on next page

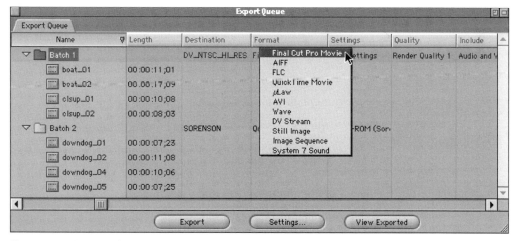

Figure 11.92 Columns in the Batch Export window display details about the batch export items and operate in the same way as Browser columns. Some export settings can be modified directly by Control-clicking in the data column.

BATCH EXPORTING

- **Length:** This column displays the total duration of the clip or sequence.

- **Destination:** This column indicates the destination folder for saving the exported files generated by items in this top-level export bin. The last specified batch export folder is used by default. Double-click the column entry to modify it.

  (If no location was specified, the export files will be saved in the first render scratch location.)

- **Format:** This column displays the current export type. You can access export formats by Control-clicking the column and then selecting an export type from the shortcut menu to apply to individual or multiple bins.

- **Settings:** This column displays the export settings selection you made in the Export Settings window. You can also access existing presets by Control-clicking this column.

- **Quality:** This column specifies the render quality level to be used for the items in this bin. This level applies only to sequences that are using the current settings. Note that because clips may be exported from several projects with customized render quality names, Final Cut Pro assigns generic render quality names to the four render quality levels: Render Quality 1 through Render Quality 4. Render Quality 1, which corresponds to Hi-Res quality, is used by default. Render quality settings apply only to the Final Cut Pro Movie export format.

- **Include:** Specify whether to include Audio and Video, Audio Only, or Video Only. You can access these options through the column's shortcut menu.

- **Recompress All Frames:** Check Recompress All Frames if you want Final Cut Pro to re-render all the frames in files that are being exported in the same codec as their source media. Uncheck this option if you want Final Cut Pro to simply copy directly from the source file to the destination file. If you are not switching codecs, copying the files without recompressing is faster and will give you better quality. Files that are being exported in a different codec from their source media will be recompressed in all cases.

- **Make Movie Self-Contained:** Check Make Movie Self-Contained to export a QuickTime movie that duplicates all audio, video, and render files in one self-contained media file. Leave Make Movie Self-Contained unchecked to export a reference movie—a small movie file that contains only pointers to the original audio, video, and render files. For more information, see "What's a Reference Movie?" earlier in this chapter.

- **Use Item In/Out:** This column indicates that only the portion of the item between its marked In and Out points will be included in the exported file.

- **Naming Options:**
  - ▲ Strip .ext corresponds to the Strip Existing Extension option.
  - ▲ Custom .ext corresponds to the Add Custom Extension option.
  - ▲ Type .ext corresponds to the Add File Type Extension option.

Figure 11.93 Use Audio to OMF export to generate a file containing your audio tracks and edit information. You can then convert that file to a Pro Tools session file.

Exporting Audio in OMF Format

Final Cut Pro 2 adds a powerful new format conversion tool: the option to export the audio tracks from a FCP sequence in Open Media Framework (OMF) format. An OMF file exported from your FCP sequence contains the audio files, plus the audio edit information from your project file. That means you can export your audio tracks with the original track separations, edit points, cross-fades, and video sync intact.

Once your audio tracks are in an OMF-formatted file, you can then import them into any OMF-compatible digital audio workstation (DAW) (**Figure 11.93**). OMF export builds a much-needed bridge between FCP and professional audio post-production tools (and the audio professionals who use them).

FCP Protocol: OMF Audio Export

Here's a list of FCP's protocols governing export of sequence audio to OMF format:

◆ Disabled sequence audio tracks (tracks with Track Visibility toggled off) are not included in the export.

◆ Any disabled individual audio clips are also excluded from export. To learn how to disable audio clips and tracks, see "Making a Timeline track invisible" in Chapter 7.

◆ All cross-fades are exported as linear cross-fades. Some OMF import utilities can't handle cross-fade data at all, so do a test conversion of your OMF file. If you can't test, configure your export OMF options to exclude cross-fade data.

◆ Speed and Reverse effects that you have applied to your sequence audio clips will also be applied to the exported sound media.

◆ All the audio tracks contained within a nested sequence will be exported as a single, mixed audio item.

◆ Audio level, pan, and audio filter settings from your sequence audio tracks are not included in the OMF export.

To export audio from a clip or sequence in OMF format:

1. Select a clip or sequence in the Browser (**Figure 11.94**), or open the sequence in the Timeline.

2. In the Timeline, turn on track visibility for each audio track you want to export by clicking the Track Visibility button. Turn off visibility on any audio tracks you want to exclude (**Figure 11.95**).

3. Choose File > Export > Audio to OMF.

4. In the OMF Audio Export dialog box, specify the following options; then click OK (**Figure 11.96**).

   ▲ **Sample Rate:** Choose a sample rate that matches your sequence audio sample rate. If your destination audio program can't work with files at that sample rate, choose the highest compatible rate. All sequence audio tracks will export at the sample rate you select. Sequence audio with different sample rates will be sample rate converted. The bit depth is always 16-bit.

   ▲ **Handle Length:** Specify a duration for handles added to the audio clips. Clips used in their entirety will be exported without handles.

   ▲ **Include Crossfade Transitions:** Check this box to include cross-fade transition data in your export file. Because cross-fade transition data is incompatible with some OMF importing tools, you should test before you include transition data in your OMF export. When this option is disabled, extra source media is substituted for the duration of the cross-fade. The source media added to cover the area of the cross-fade will be in addition to extra source media added by the Handle Length option.

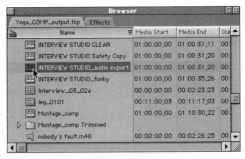

Figure 11.94 Select a clip or sequence in the Browser.

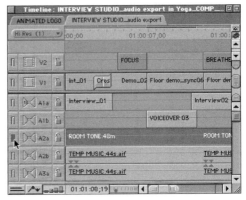

Figure 11.95 Click the Track Visibility button to turn off visibility on audio tracks you want to exclude from OMF export.

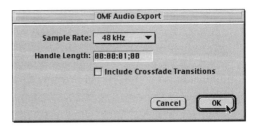

Figure 11.96 In the OMF Audio Export dialog box, specify sample rate, handle duration, and cross-fade options; then click OK

Figure 11.97 Select a destination folder from the pull-down menu at the top of the dialog box, type a name for your OMF file, and then click Save.

5. In the Export dialog box, type a name for your OMF audio file in the Export To field and then select a destination folder from the pull-down menu at the top of the dialog box. Remember that the exported file contains the audio media as well as edit information, so it may be quite large.

6. Click Save (**Figure 11.97**).

Destination: Pro Tools?

There's a good chance that your audio post-production facility will be using Digidesign's Pro Tools—the most widely used DAW program—to edit, sweeten, and mix your audio tracks.

The Export > Audio to OMF procedure itself is simple, but there are many versions of Pro Tools, each with different capabilities.

To make the OMF-to-Pro Tools conversion, you'll need one of the two helper applications available from Digidesign: OMF Tool or DigiTranslator.

All the many specifics, and "gotchas" are detailed in Apple TIL article 25294, "Final Cut Pro 2.0: Exporting Audio in OMF Format for Use with Pro Tools," available online at http://til.info.apple.com/techinfo.nsf/artnum/n25294.

Big Picture: Managing Complex Projects

Media management in a complex project requires creative solutions. Final Cut Pro has a few tools to help you keep your wig on straight as your current project snowballs toward the finish line, even as you're gearing up for the next one.

This chapter covers techniques for working with multiple sequences, including the Nest Items command, which you use to convert a selection of clips in an existing sequence into a self-contained sub-sequence (known as a nested sequence) that's already placed in the existing sequence.

You'll be introduced to Final Cut Pro's media management tools: the Media Manager, and the Reconnect Media and Make File Offline features. You'll also find tips on how to delete files—and how to save them.

Final Cut Pro is a nondestructive, nonlinear editing system, and that design has an impact on the way it handles file management. You'll be much more effective as a media manager if you understand how Final Cut Pro tracks media files and project data before you use the media management tools described in this chapter.

Two sidebars in the book explain Final Cut Pro's file management protocols and how they affect the way the program operates. This information is key to understanding how Final Cut Pro works. If you haven't read them, see "What Is Nondestructive Editing?" in Chapter 2, and "FCP Protocol: Clips and Sequences" in Chapter 4.

Working with Multiple Sequences

There are two approaches to placing one sequence inside another.

One approach is to edit a sequence into another sequence in the same way you would a clip: Drag the entire sequence from the Browser to another open sequence in the Timeline or Canvas. Alternatively, you can drag the sequence from the Browser and drop it on the Viewer's image area and then edit it into your open sequence as you would a clip.

The other approach is to create a sub-sequence: Select a group of clips within a sequence that's already open in the Timeline and then use the Nest Items command to create a new *nested* sequence—containing just the clips you selected—at the selected clips' former location in the Timeline. Any sequence that has been placed inside another sequence is called a nested sequence (or a sub-sequence).

Unlike clips, nested sequences are actually pointers or references to the original sequence, not copies. You can nest a sequence into multiple projects; then if you change the original sequence, all the projects in which that sequence is nested will be updated.

Assembling multiple sequences into a master sequence is useful for a number of purposes, from reusing a previously edited and rendered segment such as a logo or a credit sequence to assembling a final master sequence from shorter segments produced by multiple editors.

Nesting and Sequences: A Glossary

What's the difference between a nested sequence and a sub-sequence? Here's a short glossary of terms related to nesting sequences as used in this book.

Main sequence: A sequence containing one or more nested sequences. Sometimes referred to as a *parent sequence*.

Nested sequence: Any sequence that has been nested within another sequence. Sometimes referred to as a *child sequence*. A nested sequence can range from a clip on a single track to an entire sequence. What designates a sequence as nested is its placement in a parent sequence. The word *nest* can also be used as a verb, as in "nest a sequence," which refers to selecting all or a portion of an existing sequence and invoking the Nest Items command from the Sequence menu.

Sub-sequence: Can be used interchangeably with the term *nested sequence*. Nested sequences function as sub-sequences in their parent sequences.

Creating nested sequences

You can select a group of sequence clips or a portion of a Final Cut Pro sequence and, by using the Nest Items command, convert that selection to a self-contained sub-sequence. Converting a group of clips to a nested sequence has several advantages:

◆ Nesting a group of clips can simplify the process of moving them around within a sequence or placing them in another sequence.

◆ Using Nest Items to convert a series of edited clips into a single nested sequence allows you to create a single motion path for the nested sequence rather than having to create separate motion paths for each clip.

◆ Nesting a group of clips allows you to apply and adjust a single copy of a filter to a series of clips, rather than having to apply and adjust filters for each individual clip.

◆ You can nest clips that are stacked on multiple tracks (such as layered title elements) and animate them as a single sub-sequence.

◆ Nesting a single clip allows you to apply the attributes of that clip to an entire sequence.

◆ You can nest a clip containing an element you want to blur. By increasing the frame size when you nest, you can create a roomier bounding box that will accommodate the larger size of your blurred element.

◆ Nested sequences can help preserve your render files—most render files associated with the nested sequence are preserved within the nested sequence, even if you move it around or change its duration. This feature is particularly useful in dealing with audio files, which lose their render files when they are moved unless they are contained in a nested sequence. For more information on nested sequences and rendering protocol, see "Using nested sequences to preserve render files" in Chapter 10, "Rendering."

◆ In a sequence with multiple effects applied, nesting a clip can force a change in the rendering order.

WORKING WITH MULTIPLE SEQUENCES

FCP Protocol: Selecting Items for Nesting

◆ FCP includes any video and audio sequence material that you select in the nested sequence; you can include as many multiple tracks as you wish.

◆ Any linked audio and video will be included in the nested sequence unless you turn off linked selection.

◆ Only whole clips can be selected.

◆ All nested audio will appear as a stereo pair on two tracks, even if the sub-sequence contains only a single channel of audio.

To nest items in a sequence:

1. In the Timeline, select the items to be nested (**Figure 12.1**).

2. Choose Sequence > Nest Item(s) (**Figure 12.2**).

   The Nest Items dialog box appears.

3. In the Nest Items dialog box (**Figure 12.3**), *do any of the following*:

   ▲ Enter a name for the new nested sequence.

   ▲ Specify another frame size, but only if you want the nested sequence to have a frame size different from that of the main sequence. (This is specifically useful for increasing the frame size of a sequence to accommodate a blur that exceeds the size of the current item.) All other sequence properties are copied from the parent sequence.

   ▲ If you've selected only one clip, leave Keep Effects, Markers, and Audio Levels with Clip deselected if you want the clip's current effects to be applied to the entire nested sequence.

   ▲ Check Mixdown Audio if you want to create a render file of any audio tracks included in the nested sequence.

4. Click OK.

   A new, nested sequence appears as a subsequence at the selected clips' former location in the Timeline (**Figure 12.4**). The new sequence also appears in the same Browser bin as the main sequence.

✔ Tip

■ Nesting audio tracks has its own set of advantages and its own protocols. For details on strategic use of nested audio tracks, see "Using nested sequences to preserve audio render files" in Chapter 10, "Rendering."

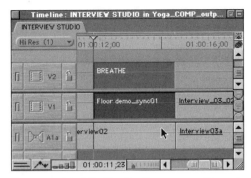

Figure 12.1 Select the Timeline items you want to nest.

Figure 12.2 Choose Sequence > Nest Item(s).

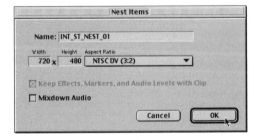

Figure 12.3 Specify settings for your nested sequence in the Nest Items dialog box.

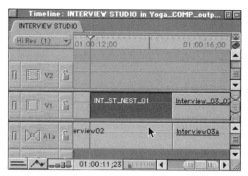

Figure 12.4 A new, nested sequence appears as a sub-sequence at the selected clips' former location in the Timeline.

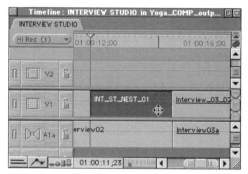

Figure 12.5 Double-click the nested sequence in the Timeline.

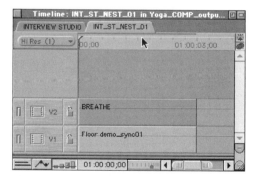

Figure 12.6 The nested sequence opens as the front tab of the Timeline.

To make changes to a nested sequence:

Do one of the following:

◆ In the main sequence in the Timeline, double-click the nested sequence (**Figure 12.5**).

◆ In the Browser, double-click the icon for the nested sequence.

The nested sequence opens as the front tab of the Timeline (**Figure 12.6**). If you opened the nested sequence from inside the main sequence, the main sequence is still open on the rear tab (**Figure 12.7**).

✔ Tip

■ There's no "Un-nest" command in Final Cut Pro. If you want to replace a nested sequence that you have placed in your main sequence with the clips contained in that nest, you should first open the nest in the Timeline as just described and then copy the clips from the open nest and paste them back over the nested sequence's original location in the main sequence. For more information, see "Copying and pasting from sequence to sequence" later in this chapter.

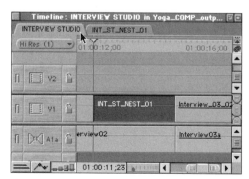

Figure 12.7 The main sequence is still open on the rear tab of the Timeline.

FCP Protocol: Updating Nested Sequences

When you insert a clip from the Browser into a sequence, the clip is copied into the sequence. The copy of the clip you placed in the sequence refers directly to the actual media file on the disk and is not a reference to the clip in the project file. Changes you make to the sequence version of the clip will not be reflected in the Browser version.

Nested sequences update globally

The protocol governing sequence versions is different, and it is also central to understanding the program. Unlike clips, sequences nested inside another sequence are actually pointers, or references, to the original sequence, not copies. *If you make changes to a sequence after you've edited it into a number of other master sequences, any changes you make to the original* **will be reflected** *every place you have used it. You'll need to make a duplicate of the sequence and make changes to the copy if you want to avoid a global update.*

For example, you could create a standard credit sequence and edit that sequence into every program in your series. If your credits require any last-minute changes, you can make the changes in the original sequence, and all the projects in which that sequence is nested will be updated.

But duplicate sequences are independent copies

Keep a close watch on nested sequences that you're using in multiple locations.

Multiple nested copies of the same sequence will point to the original sequence IF (that's a big *if*) you always use the original Browser version of your sequence as your source when you nest the sequence into multiple locations.

If you duplicate the original sequence in the Browser, the duplicate sequence you create is an independent copy of the original sequence that **will not reflect** *changes you make to the original.* Duping a sequence is good way to preserve render files, but bad news if you want to nest an identical sequence in multiple locations and take advantage of the global updating feature.

Copying and pasting a nested sequence to multiple locations within the master sequence in the Timeline produces the same result: independent duplicates of the original that don't update.

If you need to place multiples of a nested sequence you created in the Timeline, always use the Browser version of your nested sequence (it appeared when you performed the Nest Items command) to place the sequence in multiple locations.

Other limitations

There are two important limitations to automatic updating of sequences:

- If you change the overall duration of a sequence that you have already nested, the change in duration won't be updated in the main sequence. You have to update the nested sequence's length manually in the main sequence.

- You cannot extend the total duration of a nested sequence beyond its duration at the time it was first nested. To extend would require additional clip media— media that may exist in your source media file but that is not available to the sequence once you nest. If you know you'll need some flexibility later, add extra media handles at the start and end of sequences before you nest them.

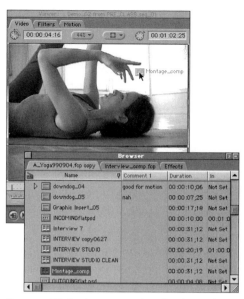

Figure 12.8 To load a sequence into the Viewer, drag the sequence's icon from the Browser and drop it on the image area in the Viewer window.

Figure 12.9 Your edited sequence opens in the Viewer window. You can edit the sequence into an open sequence in the Timeline, just as you would a clip.

Editing a sequence into another sequence

You can use sequences as source clips and edit them into another sequence. Your source clip sequence could be a preexisting sequence you drag into the Viewer or Timeline from the Browser, or it could be a nested sequence located inside a parent sequence in the Timeline. Opening a sequence in the Viewer is not quite as easy as opening a clip. Once you've loaded a sequence into the Viewer, however, you can edit it into a sequence just as you would a clip.

If you need more information on how to perform edits in Final Cut Pro, see Chapter 6, "Editing in Final Cut Pro."

To load a sequence into the Viewer:

◆   In the Browser, select the sequence you want to edit into your main sequence; then *do one of the following:*

  ▲   Choose View > Sequence.

  ▲   Drag the sequence's icon from the Browser and drop it on the image area in the Viewer window (**Figure 12.8**).

Your edited sequence opens in the Viewer window, ready to be used as source media (**Figure 12.9**). If the sequence you select is open in the Timeline and the Canvas, it will close automatically when you load it into the Viewer.

To load a nested sub-sequence into the Viewer:

◆ In the Timeline, *do one of the following:*

▲ Control-click the nested sequence and then choose Open Viewer from the shortcut menu (**Figure 12.10**).

▲ Double-click the nested sequence while holding down the Option key.

Your nested sequence opens in the Viewer window, ready to be used as a source clip.

✔ Tip

■ When you load a nested sequence from the Timeline and edit it back into your main sequence, you are creating a duplicate of the nested sequence—an independent copy of that original sequence that will not reflect changes you make to the original. If you want all copies of your nested sequence to update when you make changes, use the Browser version of your nested sequence as your source clip instead.

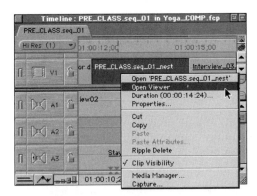

Figure 12.10 Control-click the nested sequence in the Timeline and then choose Open Viewer from the shortcut menu.

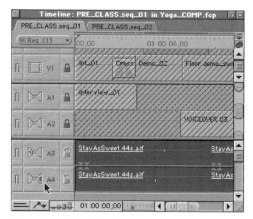

Figure 12.11 In the Timeline, set the target track controls to the track or tracks you are copying from.

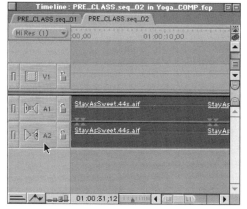

Figure 12.12 Press Command-V to paste the sequence tracks into your destination sequence.

Copying and pasting from sequence to sequence

If you don't want to use the Nest Items feature to help you move material between sequences, you can simply copy material from one sequence and paste it into another sequence. You can copy and paste the entire contents of a sequence, or you can select a single clip. Final Cut Pro has a tricky protocol that governs copying between sequences: When you paste, the clips will paste themselves into the new sequence in the same relationship to the target track that they held when they were copied. So you need to be aware of which track is targeted when you copy and also when you paste.

To copy and paste clips between sequences:

1. In the Timeline, set the target track controls to the track or tracks you are copying from (**Figure 12.11**).

2. Select the clips you want to copy into the destination sequence and then press Command-C.

3. In the destination sequence, set the target track control to the track or tracks you are pasting into; then press Command-V (**Figure 12.12**).

✔ Tips

- You can also select and then Option-drag items from one sequence to another.

- Edit decision lists (EDLs) can't handle nested sequences. Opening a nested sequence and then copying and pasting the nested clips into your main sequence is the way to "un-nest" nested material when you are preparing a sequence for EDL output.

Assembling Nested Sequences with Transitions

Building your program as a series of separate sequences and then assembling your sequence "scenes" into a final master sequence is a common FCP post-production strategy. If you want to use transitions to join your scenes together, you'll need to allow extra media handles at the start and end of your nested sequences. When you're ready to assemble your master sequence, load each sub-sequence into the Viewer. Mark the frames you want to appear as the center point of your scene-to-scene transition as the sub-sequence's In and Out points before you edit them into the final master sequence, (**Figure 12.13**).

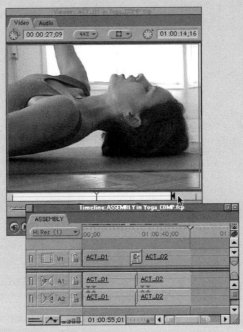

Figure 12.13 If you want to use a transition to join two sub-sequences, Mark In and Out points that allow handles on your sub-sequences to establish the extra frames your transition will require.

Figure 12.14 Choose Tools > DV Start/Stop Detection.

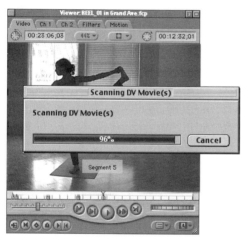

Figure 12.15 Final Cut Pro places a marker at every point where it detects a Stop/Start signal in your clip's media file.

Using DV Start/ Stop Detection

The DV Start/Stop Detection feature automatically sets markers in a previously captured DV clip each time it detects a Start/Stop (Record/Pause) signal in that clip. Because FCP can use markers to break a clip into individual subclips, you can use the technique outlined here to capture long sections of DV tape and break it into usable subclip chunks. After you've "subclipped" your long captured clip, you can use the Media Manager to delete the unused master clip footage from your subclips.

As you might guess from its name, DV Start/Stop Detection works on DV format source media only.

For more information, see "About Subclips" in Chapter 5.

To divide a captured DV clip into subclips based on starts and stops:

1. Open your previously captured DV clip in the Viewer.

2. With the Viewer active, choose Tools > DV Start/Stop Detection (**Figure 12.14**). Final Cut Pro places a marker at every point where it detects a Stop/Start signal in your clip's media file (**Figure 12.15**).

3. If you want, you can add more markers at any point in the clip where you'd like to create a subclip.

continues on next page

4. Locate your clip's icon in the Browser; then click its twirldown triangle to view the markers you just added to the clip (**Figure 12.16**).

5. If you want, you can rename markers with the name you'd like your subclip to have.

6. Select all the markers; then choose Modify > Make Subclip.

New subclips, derived from your marked clip, appear in the Browser (**Figure 12.17**). If you renamed your markers, your new subclips will use those names.

7. Review your new subclips and delete any with material you don't need.

✔ Tip

■ This DV Start/Stop technique is handy for converting a long clip into a group of smaller subclips, but when you're done, you still have a batch of subclips on your hands, and all of those subclips are still referencing the full length of your original media file. You can use the Media Manager to convert your subclips into full-fledged clips that reference discrete media files and then delete your unwanted extra footage. See "Trimming unused media from subclips" later in this chapter.

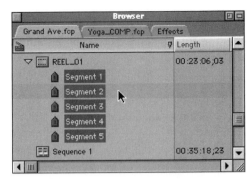

Figure 12.16 Click the twirldown triangle next to the clip to view the new markers.

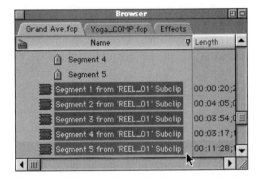

Figure 12.17 New subclips, derived from the markers in your marked clip, appear in the Browser.

USING DV START/STOP DETECTION

Using Media Management Tools

The amount of media you must handle seems to expand with your capacity to handle it. Digital video files are huge—you need over 1 gigabyte of disk space to store 5 minutes of full-resolution DV. Even a large disk array can be overwhelmed by the storage demands of a single digital video project.

Even if you have more than enough storage space to handle your project, you can reach a point where the number and complexity of sequence versions, clips, and render files in an open project can start to slow Final Cut Pro's performance. That's the time to think about shedding some excess baggage.

Final Cut Pro has powerful tools to help you manage your projects' media files: the Media Manager, the Render Manager, and the Reconnect Media and Make File Offline features.

Like a Swiss Army knife, the Media Manager is a powerful, flexible tool for copying, moving, and trimming unused footage from your projects and their associated media files. Invest some time exploring the Media Manager's capabilities early in your project—before you need it.

Use the Render Manager to delete render files for obsolete projects or to remove obsolete render files from your current projects. The Render Manager finds and lists files from unopened projects as well as open projects. For more information, see "Using the Render Manager to manage rendered files" in Chapter 10, "Rendering."

You can use the Reconnect Media feature to reestablish the links between the clips and sequences in your FCP project and their source media. If you accidentally break the link between a project, sequence, or clip and its underlying media files, you can use the Reconnect Media command to reestablish the connection. You can also use Reconnect Media to redirect online clips to use different source media.

Make File Offline offers options for deleting media files, or just breaking the links between clips and sequences and their media files while leaving the media files on disk.

Using the Media Manager

The Media Manager is a multifunction tool for copying, moving, trimming, and deleting unused media from your Final Cut Pro projects, sequences, and clips. The flexibility of the Media Manager options allows you to customize media management operations for a wide variety of needs.

This section includes:

◆ An overview of Media Manager procedure

◆ A list of your options in the Media Manager window

◆ A description of the Media Manager operation processing order

◆ Information on the Additional Items Found dialog box

◆ Step-by-step instructions for performing four common media management operations:

▲ Copying or moving an entire project and its media

▲ Deleting media from a project

▲ Trimming unused media from subclips

▲ Creating an offline trimmed sequence

New in 2: Media Management

Media management has undergone a major overhaul. The way that Final Cut Pro 2 tracks your actual source media files on disk and the virtual clips and sequences you edit inside FCP have received a lot of attention. The result is that much more Finder information and functionality has made its way inside the program.

◆ Final Cut Pro 1 offered a pair of media management tools with discrete functions: the Sequence Trimmer for trimming sequences for batch recapture, and the Media Mover for copying a sequence and its associated media and render files to a different disk location.

◆ The new Media Manager replaces the Sequence Trimmer and Media Mover and offers other powerful new features as well. You can still trim sequences for batch recapture, and copy or move sequences and clips, along with their source media files. New in FCP 2 is the power to delete all or part of a media file from inside the program. You can trim off the unused portions of the clips you're using in your sequence and actually delete the media from your drive.

◆ Reconnect Media replaces FCP 1's Relink Media command (please update your glossaries). Reconnect Media is smarter—you don't have to lead FCP to the correct location of your source media files any more. FCP 2 searches out your source media files automatically when you reconnect. If FCP 2 detects that a project has lost links to its render files, you'll be offered an opportunity to reconnect those render files.

◆ FCP 2 offers new options for deleting media files. Control-click a clip (or multiple clips) and choose the new Make Offline command. You'll have three options: you can break that clip's link to its source media file but leave the source file on disk; you can move the source file to the Trash; or you can delete the source file from the disk.

◆ Find Unused Media, a new feature in the Find window, allows you select a sequence or multiple sequences and then search the project for clips you haven't used yet.

Overview of Media Manager Procedure

A media management operation involves your precious files, so you should plan your procedure before you proceed. Here's an overview of the process and recommended objectives; you'll find a few step-by-step examples of specific types of media management processes later in this chapter.

Setting up for a Media Manager procedure

Media management is a lot like house painting—you get the best results by investing most of your time in careful preparation. Here are some recommended prep steps:

◆ Figure out what you want to accomplish. Do you need a trimmed offline version of your sequence because you want to batch recapture your footage? Do you need to delete unused media from your project because you're running short of disk space? Develop a clear, detailed idea of the project and media that's going to best serve you as you move on to the next stage of your post-production work; then design a media management process that produces that project.

◆ Clean up before you operate. If you're processing all the elements in your project, follow the procedures recommended in "To streamline a project in progress" later in this chapter. If you are managing multiple projects that all reference the same media files, remember to include all relevant projects in your clean-up and inspection.

continues on next page

- Give unique names to clips with duplicate names. If you've used a lot of subclips and razorbladed (divided) clips in your sequences, consider renaming subclips with a system of names that are brief, consistent, and easy to identify (**Figure 12.18**).

- Final Cut will look in all projects open at the time you run your Media Manager operation. If you want Final Cut Pro to track items from other projects that might be affected by media files you're moving or deleting, open those projects before you proceed (**Figure 12.19**). You should also close any projects you want to exclude from item tracking.

✔ Tip

- One final important step: before you proceed with your Media Manager operation, make a safety copy of your cleaned-up project files. If FCP should crash during Media Manager processing, your project files and/or media files could become damaged.

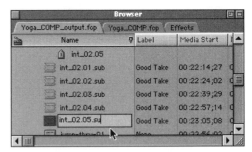

Figure 12.18 Give unique names to clips with duplicate names. Use names that are brief, consistent, and easy to identify.

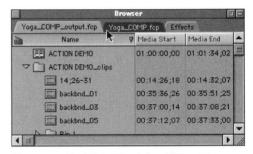

Figure 12.19 Final Cut will look for additional items that reference your media files in all projects open at the time you run your Media Manager operation. Open all projects you want FCP to include in its scan.

Figure 12.20 Select the clips and sequences you want to operate on; then Control-click a selected item and choose Media Manager from the shortcut menu. You can select items from the Browser or from the Timeline, as pictured here.

Performing a Media Manager operation

1. Select the clips and sequences you want to operate on. You can even select a clip you've used in a sequence.

2. Choose Sequence > Media Manager; or Control-click the item and choose Media Manager from the shortcut menu (**Figure 12.20**).

3. Configure your options in the Media Manager window and keep checking the Results feedback at the bottom to see that you've designed your media management operation correctly, that you're getting the results you want, and that you have enough disk space to accommodate any new files you're creating (**Figure 12.21**).

continues on next page

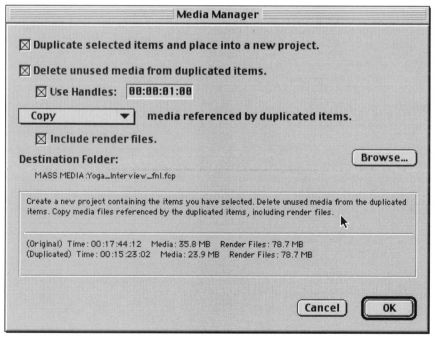

Figure 12.21 While you're setting options in the Media Manager window, keep checking the results feedback at the bottom to see that you've designed your media management operation correctly.

OVERVIEW OF MEDIA MANAGER PROCEDURE

4. When you click OK to start the process, Final Cut Pro examines the clips and sequences you've selected. Any requests for additional information or warnings will appear now.

5. After you've responded to any warnings or prompts, processing begins. A status window displays the progress of each stage in the operation (**Figure 12.22**). If the operation encounters an error, processing stops, and Final Cut Pro displays an error message.

6. When the Media Manager operation is complete, go to the processed files' location on disk and check out the results (**Figure 12.23**). If the product of your media management procedure is a new project and trimmed sequence, you should open the sequence, play it, and check your media thoroughly before you throw away your old files. Is it in sync? Are the handles you specified present? Are all your graphics and digital audio files present and intact?

Figure 12.22 During Media Manager processing, a status window displays the progress of each stage in the operation.

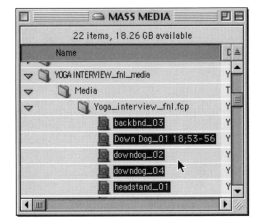

Figure 12.23 When your Media Manager process is complete, open the folder containing the processed media files and spot-check your new files.

Media Manager window options

After you've selected the items in your project that you want to process, you open the Media Manager window to configure the media management procedure you want to perform. The Media Manager window offers a lot of options, but the dialog box is well designed, with a feedback section at the bottom that summarizes the results of your choices.

The top section of the Media Manager window lists your file management options. Your choice of individual options determines how FCP will process the items you've selected. Media Manager options are context sensitive; options that aren't compatible with your currently selected settings are dimmed.

As you move down the options list, keep your eye on the status area—the feedback section at the bottom of the window. The upper feedback section displays a descriptive sentence for each process option you've

specified. The lower feedback section displays the total time and file size of the media you've selected—before and after processing.

You can fine-tune your media management process specifications by selecting and deselecting various combinations of options and then checking the feedback section to see whether you're getting the results you need.

Figure 12.24 shows an overview of the Media Manager window.

✔ Tip

- The first option in the Media Manager window, Duplicate Selected Items and Place into a New Project, lets you specify how you want to process the selected items (the virtual clips and sequences) in your project file. In the Process Mode drop-down option, you specify how you want to process the actual media files attached to the virtual clips and sequences in your project.

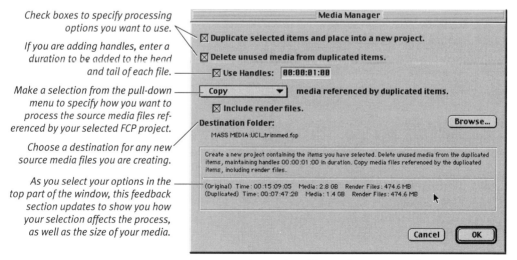

Check boxes to specify processing options you want to use.

If you are adding handles, enter a duration to be added to the head and tail of each file.

Make a selection from the pull-down menu to specify how you want to process the source media files referenced by your selected FCP project.

Choose a destination for any new source media files you are creating.

As you select your options in the top part of the window, this feedback section updates to show you how your selection affects the process, as well as the size of your media.

Figure 12.24 An overview of the Media Manager window.

- **Duplicate Selected Items and Place into a New Project:** Check the box to create a new project file that contains duplicates of the sequences and clips you've selected. The duplicate items in the new project will reflect any trimming you've specified. Any new media files you create will be linked to this new project.

  Creating a duplicate project that reflects your changes is generally a good idea. Because the duplicate you're creating is a project file containing edit information only, it's not very big. When your process is complete, you can compare the new project to the original to see that your Media Manager process produced the results you wanted.

- **Delete Unused Media from Duplicated Items:** Check the box to analyze any media files attached to the items you've selected for processing and remove any media outside the In and Out points. If you're copying or moving your files, checking this option means that the unused media won't be included in the new copies. If you're trimming existing files, the unused media will be deleted from your hard disk.

- **Use Handles:** Check the box to add handles (extra frames beyond the In and Out points) to files that will have unused media removed. Use Handles is available only if you've checked the Delete Unused Media option. To set the handles' duration, enter a value in the field. The default duration is one second. If your files have insufficient media to accommodate the handles, Final Cut Pro will make the handles as long as the existing media allows.

  If you have enough footage, and if your disk space will allow it, it's a good idea to include handles when you trim your media files. You'll be glad to have the flexibility later.

- **Process Mode:** Choose a process mode from this pop-up menu. This option specifies how you want to process the source media files on disk that are linked to your selected clips and sequences. *Select one of the following* four process modes:

  - ▲ **Copy:** Copies the source media files attached to the clips in your sequence. The original source media files are not touched. Make sure you have enough disk space available to use the Copy option.

  - ▲ **Move:** Moves the source media files to the new location you specify and removes them from their current locations on disk. All projects that reference these media files must be open at the time you move the media, or they will lose their links to these media files.

  - ▲ **Use Existing:** The program creates a trimmed version of each clip by copying just the portion you've marked from the original file, and then it deletes the full-length original. When you select a batch of clips or a sequence to trim, the Media Manager performs trim operations one clip at a time.

    Even though you are deleting unused media from existing clips, you will need enough extra drive space to accommodate the first trimmed media file copy. You can't undo this operation.

  - ▲ **Create Offline:** Performs all project data processing as specified and then produces offline copies of your selected clips and sequences that reflect your changes. The new offline clips and sequences have no links to existing media files and are ready to be used for batch recapturing.

◆ **Include Render Files:** Check the box to include render files in any Copy or Move operation.

◆ **Destination Folder:** Click Browse and then navigate to the drive location where you want to save any new media files created by a Copy or Move operation.

◆ **Status Area:** This area displays a description of the media management process specified by the current options settings. The status area updates every time you change your Media Manager window settings.

FCP Protocol: Media Manager Operation Processing Order

When you're planning (or troubleshooting) a media management operation, it can help to know the specific order of events in a Media Manager operation *after* you've selected your options and clicked OK.

Media Manager events are processed in the following order:

1. If you've chosen Duplicate Selected Items and Place in New Project, you're prompted for a name and location for the new project file containing your processed clip and sequence data.

2. If you've chosen to delete unused media from any existing media files, all items outside your current selection are scanned to see if they use those same media files. FCP will look in all projects open at the time you perform the Media Manager operation, but will not check any closed projects.

3. If FCP detects other clips or sequences that refer to the media files you're about to alter, the Additional Items Found dialog box appears, asking if you want to add these items to the current selection, exclude them from your selection and risk making them offline, or cancel the operation. For more information, see "Additional Items Found'—What Are your Options?" later in this chapter.

4. FCP checks your selected destination disk to see if there is enough available disk space to hold any new media files generated by the media processing options you've selected. If there's not enough available disk space, a dialog box appears, asking you to specify a new destination disk or cancel the operation.

5. If items outside your selection were found and you chose to exclude additional items from your selection in Step 2 (by selecting Continue), those items are taken offline now.

6. FCP copies or moves your specified media files to your selected destination. If you selected Delete Unused Media from Duplicated Items, the unused media is removed.

7. If you included render files, they're copied or moved to the selected destination.

8. If you chose Duplicate Selected Items and Place in New Project, FCP creates a new project and copies all selected sequences and clips.

9. Sequence and clip items in your original or newly created project are relinked with any copied or moved media files.

"Additional Items Found"—What Are Your Options?

Many clips, one source media file: that's a common situation in FCP projects.

Both the Browser version of a clip and the copy you place in a sequence refer to the same source media file. And if you use subclips in your projects, divide clips with the razor blade, or simply use a number of different sections from the same clip, you end up with many, many clips in a project all referring to the same source media file.

If you specify a Media Manager operation that trims or deletes media files that are referenced by additional clips or sequences that weren't included in your selection for the Media Manager procedure in progress, the Additional Items Found dialog box appears before your media file processing operation proceeds (**Figure 12.25**).

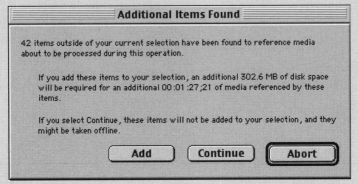

Figure 12.25 If you're about to delete or move files referenced by additional clips and sequences outside your selection, for example, Browser versions of clips in your sequence, FCP displays the Additional Items Found dialog box.

continues on next page

You'll typically encounter this dialog box if you select only your sequence and then set up the Media Manager to trim the parts of your media files unused by your sequence clips. The Additional Items Found dialog box is FCP's means of saying, "Hey! What do you want me to do about the Browser versions of these clips?"

You're also likely to encounter the AIF dialog box when you batch recapture the media for a trimmed sequence, because the trimmed "sequence" versions of the clips reference the same media files as the full-length Browser versions of those clips.

This dialog box is a little vague, and your options are not always obvious. What are your options? Here's a translation:

Click Continue to proceed with your original item selection. Any additional clips that reference media files you're moving or trimming will be made offline (meaning the additional clips' links to these media files will be broken) if the new trimmed media file is written to the same folder location on disk as the original media file.

Click Add to include the additional clips in this Media Manager operation. The Media Manager process will retain any part of your media file that's used—not only by your originally selected clips, but by the additional clips as well—and thus maintain the additional clip's links to the processed media files. If the "additional items found" are the untrimmed Browser versions of your clips, clicking Add will cause the full length of the clip's media files to be copied or moved and then relinked. When you examine the new project produced by your Media Manager operation, you'll find not only the sequence(s) you selected, but the Browser version of the clips you used in those sequences.

Click Abort to abort this Media Manager operation. Your project and media files remain untouched, but the items you selected for processing will be deselected, and you'll need to start your Media Manager operation from scratch.

Copying or moving an entire project and its media

If you have been working on a project with media files scattered across a number of different drives, you might want to copy your entire project and all the media files associated with it to a single drive as part of general project streamlining and maintenance. Or you might copy an entire project onto an external drive to hand off the project to another editor.

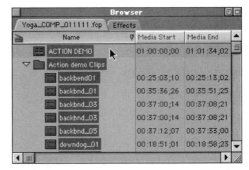

Figure 12.26 Select all the items on the project's tab in the Browser.

✔ Tip

■ Do you really need to preserve every scrap of media and every old duped sequence in your project? Redundant copies of project items may seem valuable now, but will you remember why you saved them when you return to this project in a year? Consider some project streamlining before you pack up and move. Check out the "Deleting media" and "Project Maintenance Tips" sections later in this chapter for ideas.

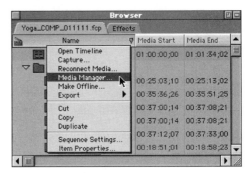

Figure 12.27 Control-click one the selected items in the Browser; then choose Media Manager from the shortcut menu.

To move or copy a project and its media to another location:

1. In the Browser, select all the items on the project's tab (**Figure 12.26**); *then do one of the following:*

   ▲ Choose Sequence > Media Manager.

   ▲ Control-click a selected item in the Browser; then choose Media Manager from the shortcut menu (**Figure 12.27**).

OVERVIEW OF MEDIA MANAGER PROCEDURE

2. In the Media Manager window, configure your options as shown here (**Figure 12.28**). For details on option settings, see "Media Manager window options" earlier in this chapter.

▲ Check Duplicate Selected Items and Place into a New Project to select it.

▲ Uncheck Delete Unused Media from Duplicated Items to deselect it.

▲ The Use Handles option is unavailable, because you are copying the full length of all of your clips.

3. *Do one of the following:*

▲ Choose Copy from the Process Mode pop-up menu if you want the Media Manager to make a copy of your project and files in the new location and leave your original project and files untouched.

▲ Choose Move from the Process Mode pop-up menu if you want the Media Manager to make a copy of your project and files in the new location and then delete your original project and files from their current locations.

continues on next page

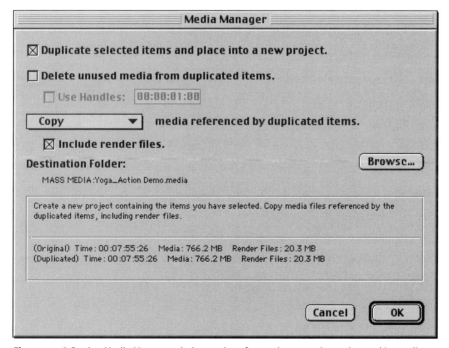

Figure 12.28 Setting Media Manager window options for moving an entire project and its media files to a new location.

4. Check Include Render Files to include any render files associated with your project.

5. Click Browse; then navigate to the disk location where you want to copy or move the project's media files (**Figure 12.29**).

6. Check the status area at the bottom of the window to see that you have configured your settings correctly.

7. Click OK.

8. In the dialog box, enter a name in the Save Project As field, choose a location to save your new project file, and then click Save (**Figure 12.30**).

The Media Manager operation proceeds. A status window displays the progress of each stage in the operation. If the operation encounters an error, processing stops, and Final Cut Pro displays an error message.

When the process is complete, your new project appears on the front tab of the Browser (**Figure 12.31**).

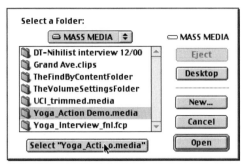

Figure 12.29 Select the disk location where you want to copy or move the project's media files.

Figure 12.30 Enter a name and choose a location to save your new project file; then click Save.

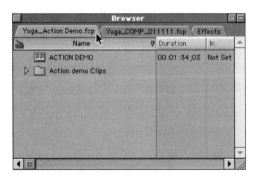

Figure 12.31 When the process is complete, your new project appears on the front tab of the Browser.

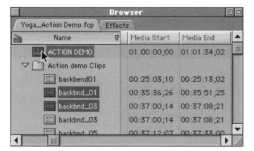

Figure 12.32 Select all sequences and clips from which you want to delete unused media.

Figure 12.33 Media Manager window options configured to delete unused media from an existing project.

Deleting media from a project

You can use the Media Manager to delete just the parts of your media files that you're not using in your project and free up disk space. When you delete unused portions of existing media files, the Media Manager creates the trimmed version of each media file by copying just the used portion from the original file and then deletes the original. Even if you select a batch of clips or a sequence to trim, the Media Manager performs this trim operation one file at a time, so you need only enough drive space to accommodate a copy of your single largest trimmed media file.

To delete unused media from a project:

1. In the Browser, select all sequences and clips from which you want to delete unused media (**Figure 12.32**); *then do one of the following:*

   ▲ Choose Sequence > Media Manager.

   ▲ Control-click a selected item in the Browser; then choose Media Manager from the shortcut menu.

2. In the Media Manager window, configure your options as shown here (**Figure 12.33**). For details on option settings, see "Media Manager window options" earlier in this chapter.

   ▲ Uncheck Duplicate Selected Items and Place into a New Project to deselect it.

   ▲ Check Delete Unused Media from Selected Items to select it.

   ▲ If you want to maintain handles beyond the In and Out points of your media, check the Use Handles option; then enter a timecode duration.

   ▲ Choose Use Existing from the Process Mode pop-up menu.

3. Click OK.

continues on next page

467

4. If the files you've selected for trimming are referenced by additional clips or sequences you didn't select, the Media Manager displays the Additional Items Found dialog box (**Figure 12.34**) and offers you an opportunity to add those items to your selection. See "'Additional Items Found'—What Are Your Options?" earlier in this chapter for more information. Click Add or Continue to complete the operation.

If you choose to continue the process, the Media Manager operation proceeds. A status window (**Figure 12.35**) displays the progress of each stage in the operation. If the operation encounters an error, processing stops, and Final Cut Pro displays an error message.

Your source media files are trimmed to include only the media actually used in your selected sequences and clips (plus handles, if specified) and remain in the same disk location.

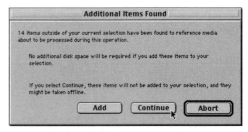

Figure 12.34 If the files you've selected for trimming are referenced by additional clips or sequences you didn't select, the Media Manager displays the Additional Items Found dialog box.

Figure 12.35 While the Media Manager is processing, a status window displays the progress of each stage in the operation.

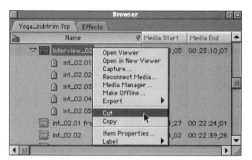

Figure 12.36 When you cut the master clip from the Browser, you're not deleting the master clip's media file, just removing the master clip that references it.

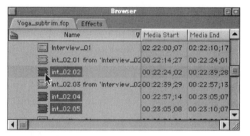

Figure 12.37 Select the subclips you created from your master clip and exclude any subclips containing footage you want to discard.

Trimming unused media from subclips

This Media Manager operation is designed to delete unwanted extra footage from one or more subclips and convert those subclips into full-fledged clips that reference discrete media files. If you like to capture long sections of raw footage and then select the usable bits by creating subclips, this technique can simplify your project management by removing the outtake footage from your drive and producing discrete clips that don't all reference the same source media file. See "Using DV Start/Stop Detection" earlier in this chapter for tips on converting markers to subclips.

To trim unused media from subclips:

1. In the Browser, Control-click the master clip that you derived your subclips from and choose Cut from the shortcut menu to remove the master clip from the Browser (**Figure 12.36**).

   You're not deleting the master clip's media file, just removing the master clip that references it.

2. Select the subclips you created from that master clip, excluding any subclips containing footage you want to discard. (**Figure 12.37**); *then do one of the following:*

   ▲ Choose Sequence > Media Manager.

   ▲ Control-click a selected subclip in the Browser; then choose Media Manager from the shortcut menu.

   continues on next page

3. In the Media Manager window, configure your options as shown here (**Figure 12.38**). For details on option settings, see "Media Manager window options" earlier in this chapter.

- ▲ Uncheck Duplicate Selected Items and Place into a New Project to deselect it.

- ▲ Check Delete Unused Media from Selected Items to select it.

- ▲ Uncheck the Use Handles option to deselect it.

- ▲ Choose Use Existing from the Process Mode pop-up menu.

4. Click OK.

5. If the files you've selected for trimming are referenced by additional clips or sequences you didn't select, the Media Manager displays the Additional Items Found dialog box and offers you an opportunity to add those items to your selection. See "'Additional Items Found'— What Are Your Options?" earlier in this chapter for more information. Click Add or Continue to complete the operation.

If you choose to continue the process, the Media Manager operation proceeds. A status window displays the progress of each stage in the operation. If the operation encounters an error, processing stops, and Final Cut Pro displays an error message.

The unused footage from your master clip's media file is deleted, leaving just the media in your selected clips (**Figure 12.39**).

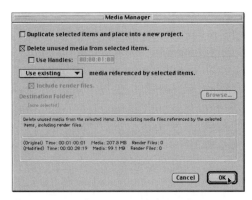

Figure 12.38 Media Manager window options configured to delete unwanted extra footage from one or more subclips and produce clips that reference discrete media files.

Figure 12.39 The unused footage from the master clip's media file is deleted, leaving just the media in your selected clips.

Creating an offline trimmed sequence

You can use the Media Manager to analyze a sequence and then create a new offline version of the sequence that includes only the clips you actually used in the sequence, plus handles (extra frames) of a length you can specify. The new offline sequence also includes all your clip names, filter settings, transitions, keyframes, titles, generators, and so on.

Creating a trimmed offline sequence is the first step in a commonly used media management plan. The second step is to use the new, offline sequence as a batch list to batch recapture your source media from the original tapes. You recapture only the media you need for the trimmed sequence; then your sequence is re-created, and you're ready to perform the third step, which is to re-render and carefully check your re-created sequence. If you're satisfied, and if you are short of drive space, you can then delete the old version of your sequence and the old, untrimmed media files associated with it. (Be careful that you don't toss your graphics and music files, though!)

Creating a trimmed offline sequence is an important part of any media management plan that involves capturing and editing a project with lower-resolution media and then recapturing the media at a higher resolution at the final output stage.

Any source media used in your sequence that doesn't have a timecode reference (such as Adobe Photoshop files or digital audio from a CD) is not trimmed. The sequence clips in the new, trimmed version of the sequence retain their links to those source media files in their present disk location, but the clip icons don't appear on the new project tab in the Browser.

For more information on batch capturing, see "Batch Capturing Clips" in Chapter 3, "Input: Getting Digital with Your Video."

OVERVIEW OF MEDIA MANAGER PROCEDURE

To create a trimmed offline sequence:

1. Select the sequence in the Browser; *then do one of the following:*

   ▲ Choose Sequence > Media Manager.

   ▲ Control-click the selected sequence in the Browser; then choose Media Manager from the shortcut menu (**Figure 12.40**).

2. In the Media Manager window, configure your options as shown here (**Figure 12.41**). For details on option settings, see "Media Manager window options" earlier in this chapter.

   ▲ Check Duplicate Selected Items and Place into a New Project to select it.

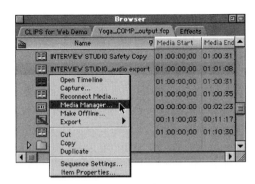

Figure 12.40 Control-click the selected sequence in the Browser; then choose Media Manager from the shortcut menu.

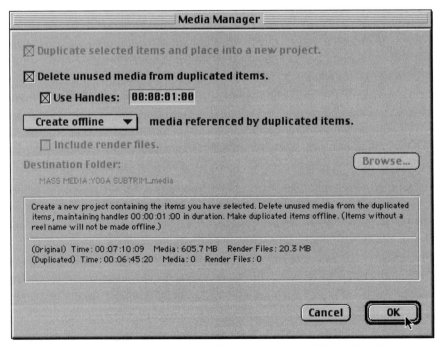

Figure 12.41 Media Manager window options configured to create an offline version of your sequence, ready for batch recapturing.

Figure 12.42 Enter a name for the project containing your new offline sequence, choose a location to save your new project file, and click Save.

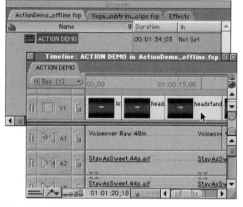

Figure 12.43 When processing is complete, a new project file containing your offline sequence appears on the front tab of the Browser.

▲ Check the Delete Unused Media from Duplicated Items check box to select it.

▲ If you want to maintain handles beyond the In and Out points of your sequence clips, check the Use Handles option; then enter a timecode duration.

▲ Choose Offline from the Process Mode pop-up menu.

3. Click OK.

4. In the dialog box, enter a name for the project containing your new offline sequence, choose a location to save your new project file, and click Save (**Figure 12.42**).

The Media Manager operation proceeds. A status window displays the progress of each stage in the operation. If the operation encounters an error, processing stops, and Final Cut Pro displays an error message.

When processing is complete, a new project file containing your offline sequence appears on the front tab of the Browser. Clips with reel designations appear in the Timeline as offline clips, but items that do not have a reel name, such as graphics and digital audio files, are not taken offline, so your links to those elements remain intact (**Figure 12.43**).

OVERVIEW OF MEDIA MANAGER PROCEDURE

Reconnecting Offline Files

In Final Cut Pro, the links between your clips and sequences in the Browser and the underlying media source files on disk are based on the media file's location. If you rename the source media files used in a project or sequence, the next time you open your project, you'll be greeted with the Offline Files window full of clips marked "missing." Don't panic. You can reconnect clips to media on your disk using the Reconnect Media command.

It's important to understand how Final Cut Pro's protocols governing clip versions affect the reconnection process. Remember that the clips in your sequence are considered separate copies of the clips in the Browser. If a clip is used in a sequence, you must reconnect both the sequence version and the Browser version of the clip. This is a little tricky, because in FCP, the sequence icon in the Browser doesn't display the red diagonal offline indicator to warn you that it contains offline clips. When you are reconnecting offline files, be sure to select the sequence in the Browser as well as the clips. Selecting the sequence when you are reconnecting allows you to locate files for all offline clips in the sequence.

✔ Tip

■ You can use Final Cut Pro's Find function to search for all the offline clips and sequences in a project (search the Offline Yes/No column for Yes) and then select and reconnect the offline clips and sequences right in the Find Results window.

FCP Protocol: Broken Links

How did your clips get thrown offline? Here's a list things you might have done that severed the link between your FCP project and its source media files:

◆ You renamed your source media files.

◆ You renamed the folder containing your source media files

◆ You moved your source media files to another disk.

◆ You deleted your source media on disk.

FCP is actually pretty good at tracking "unofficial" relocation of source media folders (try it some time), but forcing FCP to do so is not recommended procedure.

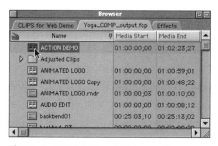

Figure 12.44 Select the clip you want to reconnect to its source media file.

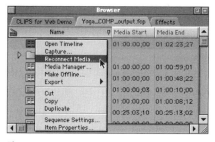

Figure 12.45 Control-click the clip; then choose Reconnect Media from the shortcut menu.

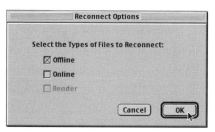

Figure 12.46 In the Reconnect Options dialog box, check the box for each type of file you want to reconnect; then click OK.

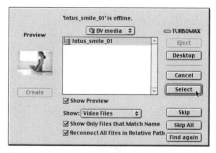

Figure 12.47 Final Cut Pro searches your media drives for the first file in your selection and then opens the Reconnect dialog box with that source file displayed in the file window.

To reconnect offline files:

1. Select the file or files to be reconnected (**Figure 12.44**). You can select a clip or sequence in the Browser or clips in an open sequence in the Timeline.

2. *Do one of the following:*
   - ▲ Choose File > Reconnect Media.
   - ▲ Control-click the clip or sequence; then choose Reconnect Media from the shortcut menu (**Figure 12.45**).

3. In the Reconnect Options dialog box, Offline, Online, or Render file options may be available, depending on your current file selection. Check the box for each type of file you want to reconnect; then click OK (**Figure 12.46**).

   Final Cut Pro searches your media drives for the first file in your selection. If FCP successfully locates the source media file for your first offline clip, the Reconnect dialog box appears with that source file listed in the file window (**Figure 12.47**). If FCP cannot locate the first source media file, a prompt at the top of the window displays the name of the clip and the first file you should locate.

continues on next page

4. *Do any of the following:*

▲ Check Show Preview to view thumb-nails of your files.

▲ Select a file type from the Show pop-up menu to limit the file list display to the selected file type.

▲ Check Show Only Files that Match Name to limit the file list display to an exactly matching name. Disable this feature to see a complete list of the folder's contents.

▲ Check Reconnect All Files in this Path to automatically reconnect any other clips in the sequence that are associated with files located in the same folder. You must reconnect the first file manually by clicking Select.

▲ Click Select to reconnect the clip and its source media (**Figure 12.48**).

▲ Click Skip to bypass the clip currently displayed in the prompt at the top of the dialog box.

▲ Click Skip All to bypass all remaining clips that can't be located automatically.

▲ Click Find Again to search for the same clip after you've navigated to its folder location.

5. The prompt indicates the next file to locate. Continue until the dialog box closes.

✔ Tip

■ The prompt area at the top of the Reconnect dialog box is too often too small to display the full directory path for the clip you're searching for. When you're searching for many clips with similar names, the partial display is pretty use-less. Where can you see the full directory path name for your stray clip? Your best bet is the Source column in the Browser (**Figure 12.49**).

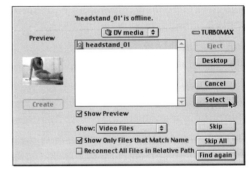

Figure 12.48 Click Select to reconnect the file to the clip.

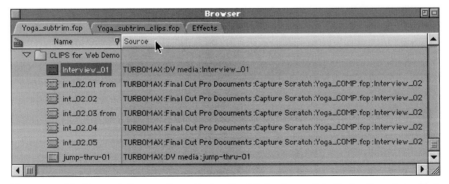

Figure 12.49 The Browser's Source column displays the full directory path to the location of your files.

Reconnecting online files

The Reconnect Media feature offers an option to reconnect online as well as offline files. Reconnecting missing or offline clips is the most common use of the Reconnect Media command, but you could have occasion to reconnect online files, too. Here are a couple of examples:

◆ You've been using low-resolution versions of your source media files to produce an edited version of your program. You could use Reconnect Media to redirect your sequence clips to high-resolution versions of the same media files.

◆ You want to replace the media in a clip you've used in a sequence with a revised version of the same media element or with another element entirely.

Note that if you do want to relink a clip in your sequence with an entirely different source media file, the new source file must be at least long enough to cover the current marked duration of the clip you're relinking it to. If your new source file is too short, you'll see an error message.

Using the Offline Files window to reconnect

Final Cut Pro displays the Offline Files window to alert you that media files have gone missing since the last time you saved a project. Any time you open a project or switch back to FCP from the Finder, Final Cut Pro rechecks the status of your media files. If FCP detects missing files, the Offline Files window appears automatically to alert you and offer you options for restoring order to your FCP project.

To reconnect using the Offline Files window:

1. Final Cut Pro displays the Offline Files window (**Figure 12.50**), which contains a list of all media files missing from the current project and their most recent hard disk location. This listing could include:

   ▲ Missing source media files

   ▲ Render files lost because they reference a missing media file

   ▲ QuickTime Reference movies made invalid by a missing media file.

   ▲ A segment of a spanned media file.

2. Do any of the following:

   ▲ Use the Forget Files buttons (**Figure 12.51**) to change the status of the files listed in the window from "missing" to "offline" and remove them from this list of missing files. Final Cut Pro will continue to post alerts about missing media each time you launch the project, until you reconnect the media and clips or make the clips offline.

   ▲ Click the Movie button to change the status of all the source media files in the list from "missing" to "offline." All clips referencing these files will be marked as offline clips in your project, but you can still relink the files later.

   ▲ Click the Render button to remove all of the render files from this list. If you choose to forget render files, you won't have the opportunity to reconnect them later.

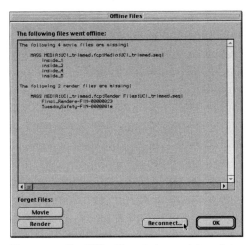

Figure 12.50 The Offline Files window contains a list of all media files missing from the current project and their most recent hard disk location.

Figure 12.51 Use the Forget Files buttons to change the status of the files listed in the window from "missing" to "offline" and remove them from this list of missing files.

RECONNECTING OFFLINE FILES

Figure 12.52 Click the Reconnect button to access the Reconnect Media feature and try to locate and reconnect the missing files.

3. To finish the process, choose one of the following options:

▲ Click the Reconnect button (**Figure 12.52**) to access the Reconnect Media feature and then try to locate and reconnect the missing files. The Reconnect Media operation is described earlier in this chapter.

▲ Click OK to exit the Offline Files window leaving all the files remaining in the list classified as missing or invalid. The next time you launch this project, FCP will display the Offline Files window again, and you can choose to reconnect or to take files offline at that time.

FCP Protocol: Offline versus Missing Clips

Missing clips and offline clips look the same in the Browser, Viewer, Timeline, and Canvas.

What's the difference?

Offline clips are listed as offline in your project's item tracking data, so Final Cut Pro doesn't look for them the next time you open that project.

Missing clips are listed as online in your project's item tracking data, but FCP can't find the clip's underlying media file. FCP will search for missing files each time you open a project until you reconnect them or make them official offline files by clicking Forget in the Offline Files window.

Deleting Media

The Make Files Offline command is the right tool to use when you want to remove clips and their associated source media from your project. It's acceptable to delete media files outside Final Cut Pro by dragging them directly from your media drives to the Trash, but using the Make Files Offline feature accomplishes the same thing and keeps the file tracking in your FCP project up-to-date.

Make Files Offline offers three options. All the options start by making your selected clip or sequence offline. Making a clip offline breaks the link between that clip and its media file.

Once the clip has been decoupled from its media file, you can choose to move the media file to the Trash or delete it from your disk.

FCP Protocol: Deleting Media

How do you delete media files from Final Cut Pro the right way?

Before you toss that folder full of source media files in the Trash, take a moment to review the way Final Cut Pro tracks files. Remember that the Browser clips you use to construct sequences in your project are not actually media files; they are pointers to the actual media files on disk, and Final Cut Pro's links to those underlying source media files are location dependent. If you open the Item Properties window for any clip in Final Cut Pro, you'll see the directory path to the underlying source media (the clip's directory path also appears in the Browser's Source column). If you have created subclips, repeated the same clip in a sequence, divided a clip with the razor tool, or created multiple versions of your sequence, you can have quite a few different clips all pointing to the same media file on disk.

If you delete a clip from the Browser bin or a Timeline sequence, you haven't thrown out the underlying media source file on disk. You can re-import the file to reconnect it to your project, or if you've already used that clip in a sequence, you can drag a copy of the sequence version of the clip back into the Browser. Dragging a clip from an open sequence in the Timeline back into the Browser places a copy of the sequence version of the clip in your project.

Your source media files stay on disk until you use the Make Files Offline feature to move them to the Trash or delete them from your hard drive.

Using Make Files Offline is the recommended way to delete files from inside FCP. Should you need to delete source media files outside FCP, by dragging them to the Trash in the Finder, it's best not to delete media files linked to an open project while Final Cut Pro is running. You should save and close the project before you delete media files in the Finder. Determine your own comfort level here, but quitting Final Cut Pro before you trash any media files would be the safest course.

Once you've deleted a source media file, all clips referring to that file will be marked as offline. Final Cut Pro will warn you that the clips are offline each time you open the project until you delete the clip references, including any versions of the clips that appear in sequences, or tell FCP to "forget" the offline clips. See "Using the Offline Files window to reconnect" earlier in this chapter.

Use the Render Manager to delete render files. For more information, see Chapter 10, "Rendering."

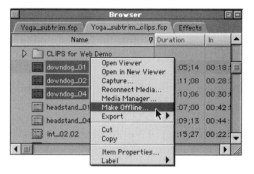

Figure 12.53 Control-click a selected item; then choose Make Offline from the shortcut menu.

Figure 12.54 Click Move Them to the Trash to make the file offline and move the source media files to the Trash.

Figure 12.55 If you choose to move or delete the files, a warning message tells you this action cannot be undone. To continue, click OK.

To make files offline:

1. In the Browser or Timeline, select the clips or sequences you want to make offline.

2. *Do one of the following:*

   ▲ Choose Modify > Make Offline.

   ▲ Control-click a selected item; then choose Make Offline from the shortcut menu (**Figure 12.53**).

3. In the Make Offline dialog box, choose one of the following three options; then click OK.

   ▲ Click Leave Them on the Disk to make the files offline and leave the original media files on your disk.

   ▲ Click Move Them to the Trash to make the files offline and move the source media files to the Trash (**Figure 12.54**). To finally delete the files, you'll need to empty the Trash manually. If you change your mind later, before you empty the Trash, and want to retrieve the files, drag them out of the Trash and reconnect them to your project by using the Reconnect Media command. If you empty the Trash, your files are finally deleted.

   ▲ Click Delete Them from the Disk to make the files offline and then immediately delete the media files from your disk. This action cannot be undone. You'll have to recapture the media to restore to your project.

4. If you choose to move or delete the files, a warning message tells you this action cannot be undone. To continue, click OK (**Figure 12.55**).

DELETING MEDIA

Project Maintenance Tips

Even if you are not forced to reorganize your project's media elements because you have run out of disk space, it's a good idea to streamline a project as you go, especially if you're working on a long, complex project. As your project accumulates clips, sequences, edits, render files, multiple tracks of audio, and effects, more and more of your available RAM is needed just to open the project. At some point, you could experience a drop in Final Cut Pro's speed or video playback performance.

To streamline a project in progress:

1. With the project open in the Browser, choose File > Save All (**Figure 12.56**).
   The current version of the project is saved.

2. Choose File > Save Project As.
   The File dialog box appears.

3. Use the pull-down menu at the top of the dialog box to navigate to the folder where you want to store your project file, enter a name for the new project version in the Save Project As field, and then click Save (**Figure 12.57**).
   The new version of your project replaces the older one on the front tab of the Browser window (**Figure 12.58**).

Figure 12.56 Choose File > Save All to save the current version of the project.

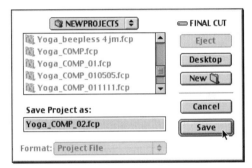

Figure 12.57 Enter a name for the new project version in the Save Project As field; then click Save.

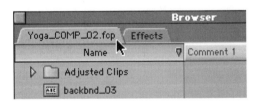

Figure 12.58 The new version of your project replaces the old one on the front tab of the Browser window.

PROJECT MAINTENANCE TIPS

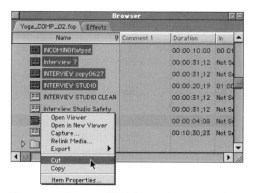

Figure 12.59 Remove all but the most current versions of your sequences and delete any excess clips. If you need the old versions later, you still have them in the project version you saved in step 1.

4. Remove all but the most current versions of your sequences and delete any excess clips (**Figure 12.59**). If you are short of disk space, you could choose to delete the clips' source media files as well, but you don't need to delete the source media files to get the benefits of a streamlined project.

5. Choose Tools > Render Manager and delete any obsolete render files. Remember that the Render Manager gives you access to render files for all of your projects (**Figure 12.60**), so be careful as you select the files you want to delete.

6. With the new streamlined project open in the Browser, choose File > Save.

7. If you streamlined your project to improve Final Cut Pro's performance, you'll need to close and then reopen the project to recapture the available RAM and start enjoying improved performance.

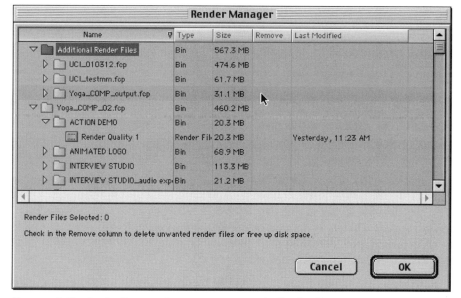

Figure 12.60 The Render Manager gives you access to render files for all your projects, so be careful which files you delete.

PROJECT MAINTENANCE TIPS

Editing in stages

If you are trying to assemble a long project in Final Cut Pro on a modest system, you may find that you have much more media than hard drive space to store it on. Here are some project management strategies for editing a project in stages.

The simplest approach to a staged editing process is to edit one sequence at a time, print it to video, clear off the media, and then edit the next sequence.

Here's a checklist for taking a completed sequence offline and preparing your drives for the next sequence:

- After you have completed a sequence and printed it to tape, make sure you save the project file that contains the final version of your sequence.

- You should also save a backup copy of the project file on a Zip disk, CD, or some other form of removable media.

- Back up any media elements in your sequence, such as graphics files or digital audio from CD, that won't be restored in a batch recapturing process.

- In the Browser, select all the clips and sequences that reference media files you no longer need. Use the make Offline command, described earlier in this chapter, to delete all of the media source files you no longer need.

- The clips and sequences referring to the deleted media files will be marked offline, but the clip data will remain in your completed project file. This clip and sequence data takes up very little room, so you don't need to delete it; you can store it in a single Browser bin.

- Capture the next batch of media files and start work on your next sequence.

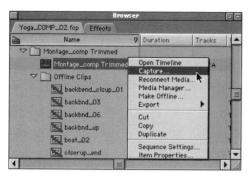

Figure 12.61 In the Browser, select the sequence, plus any clips that you want to restore.

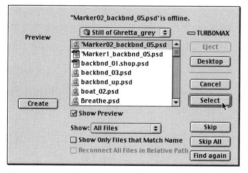

Figure 12.62 Follow the steps for reconnecting offline files.

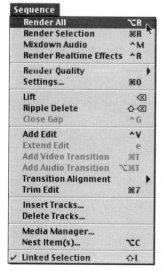

Figure 12.63
To restore the render files, you must re-render any sequence material requiring rendering.

Restoring a sequence

If you find you need to go back and modify a sequence after you have deleted its underlying media files, you can use the sequence data you saved in the project file to batch recapture your footage and re-create the sequence.

All filters, motion paths, keyframes, transitions, nested items, and audio mixing are reconstituted when you batch recapture the media files for a sequence. Your render files will be gone, however, and you'll need to re-render any sequence material requiring it.

To restore a sequence:

1. Select the sequence in the Browser and choose File > Batch Capture. If you want to recapture any Browser clips, select those as well (**Figure 12.61**).

2. Follow the steps in "To batch capture clips" in Chapter 3," and batch recapture your footage from tape.

3. Restore to your hard disk any media elements in your sequence, such as graphics files or digital audio from CD, that won't be restored in the batch recapturing process.

4. Select the sequence in the Browser and choose File > Reconnect Media.

5. Follow the steps described in "To reconnect offline files" (**Figure 12.62**) earlier in this chapter and reconnect the media elements you restored.

6. To restore the render files, re-render any sequence material requiring rendering (**Figure 12.63**).

Modifying an offline clip before recapture

Here's a technique that can streamline your project and save you some drive space. Let's say you have refined your edited sequence and discover that you are using just the audio track (or just the video) from a large number of audio+video clips. You can recapture your audio+video clips as audio only or video only without relogging by adjusting the clips' formatting in the Tracks column of the Browser. You need to take the clips offline first.

To learn how to modify the audio/video format (or other types of settings) for logged offline clips, see "Modifying logged clip data" in Chapter 3.

Tracking used and unused clips

If you just want to do a little housecleaning in your project's media file folder, it's handy to have an inventory of every clip that's currently being used in a sequence in your project and another list of every element in your project that remains unused. How can you create complete lists of used and unused elements in your project? It's simple. You can use the Find feature to assemble these lists—you can even inventory multiple projects in a single Find operation. Powerful stuff.

Removing a project from your drives

Final Cut Pro doesn't generate separate preview or temporary files when you use the Print to Video or Edit to Tape function. The only files you need to clean up after a project are the project file, media files, render files, and thumbnail and waveform cache files (**Figure 12.64**).

Figure 12.64 Looking for the Thumbnail and Waveform Cache folders? You'll find the directory path to their disk location listed on the Scratch Disk Preferences tab of the Preferences window.

The Last Mile: Tips for Final Assembly of BIG Projects

You can tell when the size of your project is taxing the limits of FCP's performance. Everything takes longer—opening and saving the project, screen refresh, even moving around the Timeline. If you have no choice but to press FCP's capacity to handle large amounts of media and multiple long sequences, try this:

◆ Split your show into a series of separate sequences and complete all rendering inside the individual sequences.

◆ Create a new project and drag just the finished individual sequences from your old projects into the new project; then close the old projects.

◆ Create the master sequence assembly of all your finished segment sequences in the brand-new project containing just the master sequence and keep all other projects closed as much as possible.

◆ Back up your project file frequently.

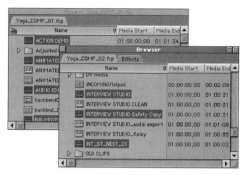

Figure 12.65 On each project's tab in the Browser, Command-click to select the sequences you want to include in your search.

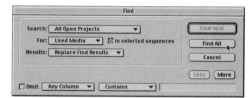

Figure 12.66 The Find window, configured to find unused clips in selected sequences. Click Find All to perform the search.

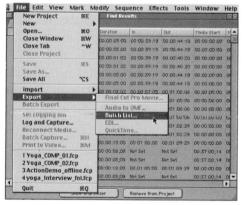

Figure 12.67 Export a text file of your used clip list directly from the Find Results window.

To get a complete list of elements used in a group of sequences:

1. Open all the projects you want to search.

2. On each project's tab in the Browser, Command-click to select the sequences you want to include in your search (**Figure 12.65**).

3. Choose Edit > Find; or press Command-F.

4. In the Find window, configure the options as follows:

   ▲ Choose All Open Projects from the Search pull-down menu.

   ▲ Choose Used Media from the For pull-down menu and check the box next to In Selected Sequences.

   ▲ Choose Replace Find Results from the Results pull-down menu.

5. Click Find All (**Figure 12.66**).

   A list of all the clips used in the sequences you selected is displayed in the Find Results window.

✔ Tips

■ You can export your used clip list directly from the Find Results window and convert it to a text file. With the Find Results window active, choose File > Export > Batch list (**Figure 12.67**).

■ If your clip's name is different from the name of the underlying media file, you can find the underlying media file (and its location) for any clip in the clip's Item Properties window or the Browser's Source column.

PROJECT MAINTENANCE TIPS

487

Setting Up for Multiple Projects and Multiple Users

Here are a couple of procedures for setting up a Final Cut Pro system shared by multiple users working on different projects.

A single Final Cut Pro system can track multiple project files, but each individual user will need to set the Scratch Disk preferences to refer to his or her own media files at the start of a session. (You might want to post a day-glow reminder on the monitor!)

To set yourself up as a new user, create your personal project folder in the Finder before your first Final Cut Pro session; then set the Scratch Disk preferences to refer to your personal project folder. Reset the Scratch Disk preferences to point to your personal project folder at the start of each subsequent session. Your captured media will be easier to manage when it's easier to locate.

To create a personal or project folder:

1. In the Finder, navigate to the correct scratch disk location.

2. Choose File > New Folder.

3. Enter a name for your personal project folder (**Figure 12.68**).

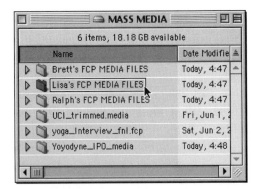

Figure 12.68 Enter a name for your personal project folder.

Figure 12.69 To access Scratch Disk preferences, choose Edit > Preferences and then click the Scratch Disks tab.

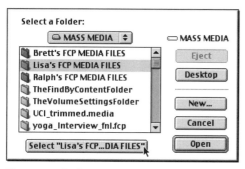

Figure 12.70 Navigate to your personal folder and set it as the default Capture Scratch folder before you start your editing session.

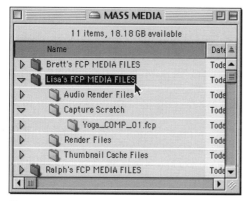

Figure 12.71 Your captured media will be gathered in one folder location inside your personal project folder.

To select a personal folder as a storage directory for captured media files:

1. Launch Final Cut Pro.

2. Choose Edit > Preferences and then select the Scratch Disks tab(**Figure 12.69**).

3. Follow the instructions in "To specify scratch disk preferences" in Chapter 2, "Welcome to Final Cut Pro."

4. Navigate to your personal folder and set it as the Capture Scratch folder (**Figure 12.70**).

Even if you're working on multiple projects, your captured media will be gathered in one folder location (**Figure 12.71**).

COMPOSITING AND SPECIAL EFFECTS | 13

Final Cut Pro's effects tools are like a whole program within a program. This chapter provides basic information and a few step-by-step procedures to give you a feel for how techniques are combined to create simple effects. It also includes some single-purpose tasks that show how the interface and tools operate. However, this chapter is not a comprehensive survey of Final Cut Pro's effects capabilities. There are many more options, adjustments, keyboard commands, and possibilities than are described in this chapter, but you will be in a better position to explore them yourself after going through the basic procedures described here.

You won't find lists of the available filters or composite modes in this chapter. You should refer to the Final Cut Pro manual or Web site for comprehensive lists.

As you start to apply effects to your clips and sequences, it's important to keep this in mind: Adding a clip from the Browser window to a sequence in the Timeline places a copy of the clip in the sequence. By placing a clip in a sequence, you create a new instance of the clip. Before you modify a clip with effects, be sure you have selected the correct copy of the clip you want to change. This rule is central to understanding editing in Final Cut Pro. For more information, see "FCP Protocol: Clips and Sequences" in Chapter 4.

Basic Building Blocks of Effects Creation

The basic building blocks you use to create video effects are fairly simple. You can generate complex video effects by combining and then animating images using the basic processes described in here.

Layering is an arrangement of multiple clips at one point in time, each in its own track. Superimposing a title over a video clip is a simple example of layering, with the video clip forming the background layer and the title forming the foreground layer. Other layering arrangements require making the upper layers semitransparent, so you can see the image in the background layer.

Compositing can be any process that combines two or more image layers to create an effect. Compositing techniques can include adjusting the transparency of one or more of the image layers and the selection of a Composite mode, which is the algorithm that controls the way the image layers are combined.

Motion properties are a collection of image modification tools that include tools that control a clip's size and shape, its position in the frame, and its designated center point. The tools that are grouped together on the Motion tab don't always have an obvious connection to moving images; for example, the Opacity controls are located on the Motion tab. However, making incremental adjustments to a clip's size, position, and angle of rotation are basic steps in animating a static element—that's when things start to move.

Filters are image modifiers that process the image data in a clip. Over time, filters have developed into a diverse effect category that includes everything from basic tools, such as brightness, contrast, and color controls, to complex 3D simulators.

Opacity refers to a clip's level of transparency. A clip with an opacity level of 100 percent is completely opaque; one with an opacity level of 0 percent is completely transparent. Adjusting opacity is a basic procedure in compositing layers of images. Alpha channels and mattes are a means of adjusting opacity in selected portions of an image. You can adjust a clip's opacity on the Viewer's Motion tab or by using the opacity clip overlay in the Timeline.

Generators are a class of effects that create (or generate) new video information, rather than modify existing video. Generators are useful for producing utility items such as black frames (known as slug), a plain-colored background, or text titles.

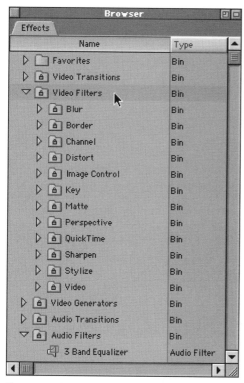

Figure 13.1 The Browser's Effects tab organizes available effects in bins.

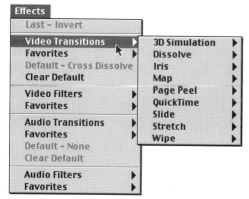

Figure 13.2 The same library of effects is available from the Effects menu.

Locating and Applying Effects

You can access Final Cut Pro's effects features in a variety of places:

- The Browser's Effects tab (**Figure 13.1**) displays bins containing all the types of effects available in Final Cut Pro except motion properties.

- The same effects found on the Browser's Effects tab are also available from the Effects menu (**Figure 13.2**).

- Motion properties are automatically applied to every clip. Open a clip in the Viewer and click the Motion tab to access a clip's motion controls.

You can apply effects to clips and sequences in the following ways:

- Select a clip in the Timeline and then choose an effect from the Effects menu.

- Select an effect from a bin on the Effects tab of the Browser and drag it onto the clip.

- Select a customized effect or motion from the Favorites bin on the Effects tab of the Browser and drag it to the clip to apply it.

- Choose a generator from the Generator pop-up menu in the lower-right corner of the Viewer.

- Open a Timeline or Browser clip in the Viewer; then use the controls on the clip's Motion tab to apply motion effects.

Onscreen effects controls

You can make adjustments to effects you've already applied in the following ways:

◆ Double-click the clip in the Timeline; then select the Audio, Filters, Motion, or Controls tab in the Viewer window and use the controls to make your adjustments. **Figures 13.3 and 13.4** illustrate the operation of the controls found on the Filters, Motion, and Control tabs.

◆ In the Timeline, adjust keyframe locations in the clip's Filters and Motion bar. **Figure 13.5** shows an overview of the effects tools and procedures available in the Timeline window.

◆ In the Canvas, turn on Wireframe mode and make adjustments to a clip's motion properties.

Effects Production Shortcuts

Creating effects can be time consuming and repetitive. Here are a few production shortcuts.

Copying and pasting clip attributes: Clip attributes are settings applied to a particular media file in Final Cut Pro. You can copy and paste selected settings from one clip to another clip in the Timeline or in the Canvas. For more information, see Chapter 7, "Using the Timeline and the Canvas."

Nesting sequences: When you place, or create, a Final Cut Pro sequence within another sequence, it's called *nesting* a sequence. Nested sequences can streamline and enhance your effects work in a variety of ways. You can use nested sequences to protect render files, to force effects to render in a different order, or to group clips so you can apply a single filter or motion path to all of them in one operation. Nested sequences are discussed in Chapter 12, "Big Picture: Managing Complex Projects."

"Effecting" multiple clips: FCP allows you to adjust opacity levels for a group of clips. You can also adjust audio levels for multiple clips in a single operation. See "Setting a clip's opacity in the Timeline" later in this chapter.

Favorites: Favorites are customized effects presets. For example, if you need to apply the same color correction to a large group of clips, you can tweak the settings once and then save that filter configuration as a Favorite and apply it to the whole group without having to make individual adjustments. Favorites are discussed later in this chapter.

Effects tabs:
Click to access a tab containing effects controls and keyframe graphs.

Triangle:
Click to show or hide controls.

Toggle switch:
Check box to turn effect on or off.

Filter In point:
Drag to adjust filter duration.

Sequence marker:
Sequence markers placed in the Timeline also appear here; used to align keyframes over multiple tracks.

Filter Out point:
Drag to adjust filter duration.

Clip control:
Drop other clips here to affect the filtering of this clip.

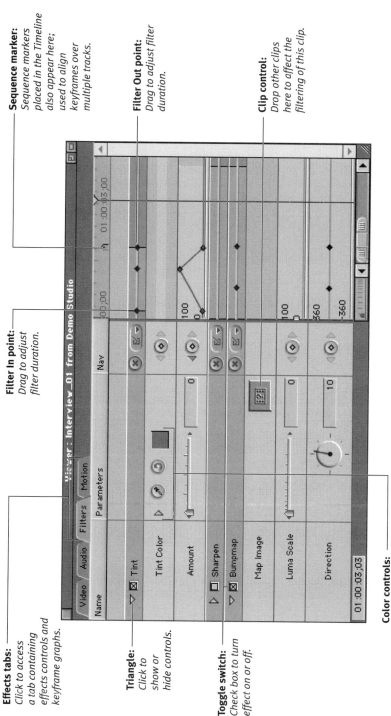

Color controls:
- *Click the triangle to oper. HSB controls.*
- *Use the eyedropper to pick colors from Video windows.*
- *Click the arrow to perform color cycling for sweep direction.*
- *Click the square to bring up the Apple Color Picker.*

Figure 13.3 Overview of the effects controls found on the Filters, Motion, and Controls tabs in the Viewer window.

LOCATING AND APPLYING EFFECTS

495

LOCATING AND APPLYING EFFECTS

Adjustable column width:
Drag separator lines.

Reset button:
Click to reset all controls
to default values.

Playhead:
Shows current frame location;
linked to Timeline playhead.

Keyframe ruler:
Displays the timecode for
the current sequence.

**Incremental
controls:**
Click tiny arrows to
change value by one.

Slider controls:
Drag slider to
set value.

Dial controls:
Drag the needle
to set value.

Text field:
Enter exact
parameter values.

**Current
Timecode field:**
Shows playhead's
timecode location;
enter time to move
playhead.

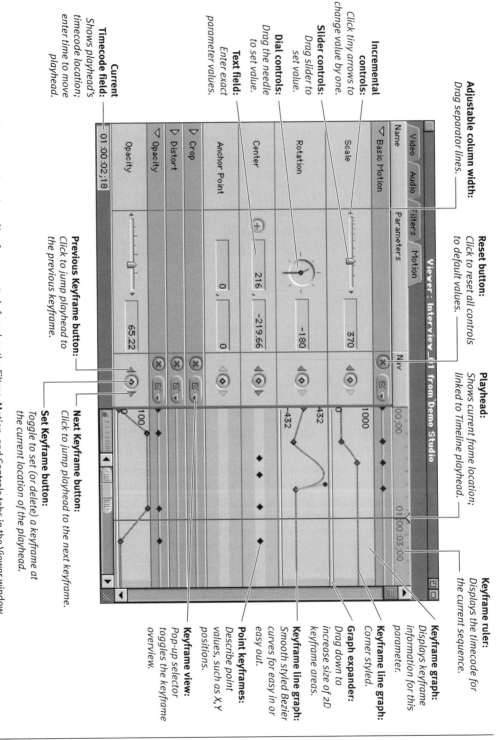

Previous Keyframe button:
Click to jump playhead to
the previous keyframe.

Next Keyframe button:
Click to jump playhead to the next keyframe.

Set Keyframe button:
Toggle to set (or delete) a keyframe at
the current location of the playhead.

Keyframe graph:
Displays keyframe
information for this
parameter.

Keyframe line graph:
Corner styled.

Graph expander:
Drag down to
increase size of 2D
keyframe areas.

Keyframe line graph:
Smooth styled Bezier
curves for easy in or
easy out.

Point keyframes:
Describe point
values, such as X,Y
positions.

Keyframe view:
Pop-up selector
toggles the keyframe
overview.

Figure 13.4 Overview of keyframe controls found on the Filters, Motion, and Controls tabs in the Viewer window.

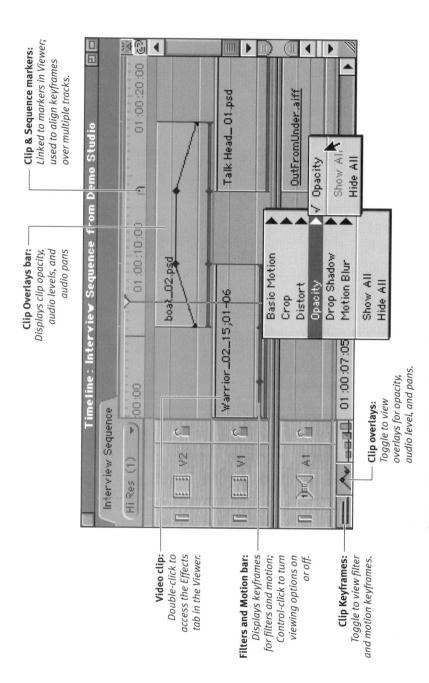

Clip & Sequence markers:
Linked to markers in Viewer; used to align keyframes over multiple tracks.

Clip Overlays bar:
Displays clip opacity, audio levels, and audio pans

Video clip:
Double-click to access the Effects tab in the Viewer.

Filters and Motion bar:
Displays keyframes for filters and motion; Control-click to turn viewing options on or off.

Clip overlays:
Toggle to view overlays for opacity, audio level, and pans.

Clip Keyframes:
Toggle to view filter and motion keyframes.

Figure 13-5 Overview of effects tools in the Timeline.

Saving effects settings as Favorites

You can designate an effect, transition, or motion as a Favorite. Favorite effects are placed in the Favorites bin on the Browser's Effects tab and are also available from the Effects menu. Favorites provide an easy way to save an effect that you want to reproduce later. Favorite motions are particularly useful for streamlining animation. For more information on creating and using favorites, see "Working with Default and Favorite Transitions" in Chapter 9.

To create a Favorite effect by saving its settings:

1. In the Timeline, double-click the clip with the effect you want to make a Favorite. The clip opens in the Viewer.

2. Select the Filters, Motion, or Controls tab to access the selected effect's controls;

3. Select the effect in the Name column (**Figure 13.6**); then *do one of the following*:

   ▲ Choose Modify > Make Favorite Effect.

   ▲ Choose Modify > Make Favorite Motion to save motion properties settings.

   ▲ Click and drag the effect's name from its control bar to the Favorites bin on the Browser's Effects tab.

✔ Tip

■ If you've created a set of Favorite effects for use in a particular project, you can archive those effects by dragging the Favorites folder (or selected Favorite effects) from the Browser's Effects tab onto your project tab. Your project's Favorite effects will be saved with the project file.

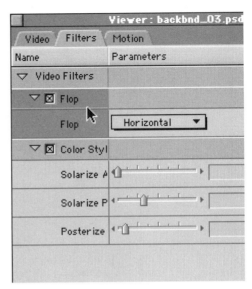

Figure 13.6 Save customized effects settings by selecting an effect in the Name column and choosing Modify > Make Favorite Effect.

Tuning in Effects: Using Dial, Slider, and Point Controls

Here are some keyboard/mouse combos you can use to enhance your control over any effect parameter with a dial interface:

◆ You can hold down the Shift key to constrain the dial to 45-degree increments.

◆ Hold down the Command key to "gear-down" the dial's movement and make precise adjustments.

◆ Drag way, way out of the dial to reset the effect to the previous value.

Here are a few tips for effect parameters with slider interfaces:

◆ You can expand the horizontal throw of any slider by widening the Parameters column in the Nav bar. A longer slider makes it easier to adjust values.

◆ Hold the Command key to "gear-down" the slider's movement and make precise adjustments.

◆ Hold down the Shift key to add two decimal places of accuracy to a slider's value. This command could be more useful if it incorporated "gear-down" as well. You need to expand the horizontal throw of the slider by widening the Parameters column in the Nav bar before the "double-digit accuracy" becomes useful. Maybe they'll fix this one in FCP 3....

◆ The Point control is that little crosshairs button you use to select location coordinates for a clip's Center point. You can select the Point control and then click in the Canvas to specify a center point. Very handy. Here's a way to use the point control that's even better. Once you've clicked, keep the mouse button pressed, and you can drag your center point location around the canvas until you get a positioning you like. The Canvas will update even while you still have the mouse button down.

To create a Favorite effect before changing its settings:

1. On the Effects tab in the Browser, select an effect and drag it to the Favorites bin (**Figure 13.7**).

2. Open the Favorites bin; then double-click the effect.

   The effect opens in the Viewer.

3. Adjust the effect's settings (**Figure 13.8**); then close the Viewer.

4. In the Favorites bin, rename the new effect (**Figure 13.9**).

✔ Tip

■ You can also select an effect in the Browser and then choose Edit > Duplicate. A copy of the effect appears in the Favorites submenu of the Effects menu.

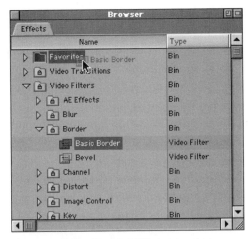

Figure 13.7 On the Browser's Effects tab, select an effect and drag it to the Favorites bin.

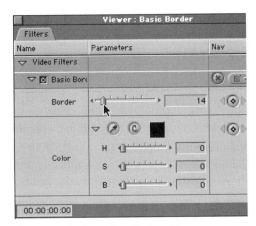

Figure 13.8 Configure the effect's settings.

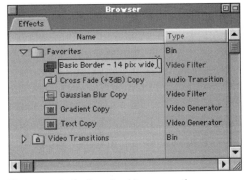

Figure 13.9 In the Favorites bin, rename the customized effect.

Using Wireframes

The wireframe shows the outline of the clip that is currently selected in the Timeline, which comes in handy when you are trying to sort and identify several layers of clips. When you adjust motion properties in the Viewer or Canvas, you must be in one of the two available Wireframe modes.

Wireframe mode represents the selected clip as a simple rectangle on a black background. Wireframe mode always plays back in real time and is very useful for sculpting motion paths efficiently, but you can't see the clip's image.

Image+Wireframe mode combines the Wireframe mode with your clip image. This mode takes longer to update previews, but sometimes you need to see how your clips' images are interacting.

The elements of the wireframe aren't just indicators; they're also on-screen controls you can use to manipulate your clip's motion properties. Select the appropriate tool from the Tool palette; then click and drag a handle on the clip's wireframe in the Canvas or Viewer. **Figure 13.10** offers a key to wireframe handles and tools.

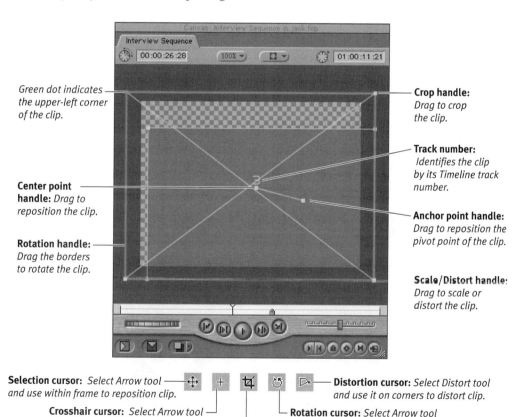

Green dot indicates the upper-left corner of the clip.

Crop handle: Drag to crop the clip.

Track number: Identifies the clip by its Timeline track number.

Center point handle: Drag to reposition the clip.

Anchor point handle: Drag to reposition the pivot point of the clip.

Rotation handle: Drag the borders to rotate the clip.

Scale/Distort handle: Drag to scale or distort the clip.

Selection cursor: *Select Arrow tool and use within frame to reposition clip.*

Distortion cursor: *Select Distort tool and use it on corners to distort clip.*

Crosshair cursor: *Select Arrow tool and use on corner points to resize clip.*

Rotation cursor: *Select Arrow tool and use it on borders to rotate clip.*

Crop cursor: *Select Crop tool and use it on borders or corners to crop clip.*

Figure 13.10 To manipulate motion properties in Wireframe mode, select a tool; then click and drag the appropriate handle on the clip's wireframe.

Wireframe keyframe indicators

Wireframe mode uses green highlighting to indicate whether a keyframe is present on a frame and what type of keyframe it is (**Figure 13.11**).

To enable Wireframe mode:

Do one of the following:

◆ Choose View > Wireframe.

◆ Choose Wireframe (or Image+Wireframe) from the View pop-up menu at the top of the Viewer or Canvas (**Figure 13.12**).

◆ Press W once to place the Viewer or Canvas in Image+Wireframe mode.

◆ Press W again to turn on Wireframe mode.

◆ Press W again to return to Image mode.

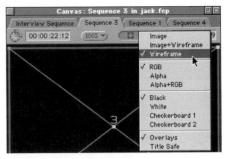

Figure 13.12 Choose Wireframe from the View pop-up menu at the top of the Viewer or Canvas.

✔ Tip

■ While you are working in Wireframe mode, note that the selected track's number appears just above the clip's center point. The track number helps you keep track of which layer you have selected. If you're working on an effects sequence with many layered elements, that's a big help.

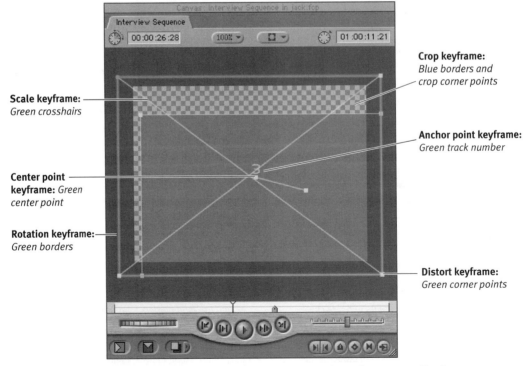

Crop keyframe:
Blue borders and crop corner points

Scale keyframe:
Green crosshairs

Anchor point keyframe:
Green track number

Center point keyframe: *Green center point*

Rotation keyframe: *Green borders*

Distort keyframe:
Green corner points

Figure 13.11 Wireframe mode uses highlighting to indicate the presence of keyframes.

USING WIREFRAMES

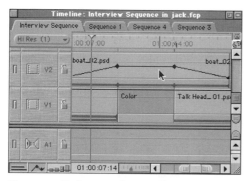

Figure 13.13 Keyframe overlays are displayed as line graphs right on top of the track display in the Timeline. The overlay in this figure controls opacity.

Using Keyframes

Whenever you create motion paths, change filters over time, sculpt audio levels, or just fade to black, you need to use keyframes. Think of a keyframe as a kind of edit point: You set a keyframe at the point at which you want to change the value of an effect's parameter. Keyframes work the same way wherever they are applied.

When you use a keyframe to change a parameter, you have the option of making that keyframe a "curve-type." Curve-type keyframes have two added controls: *Bézier handles*, which you can use to fine-tune the shape of the motion path's curve, and *ease handles*, which you can use to fine-tune a clip's speed immediately before and after the keyframe location. You can also use curve-type keyframes to fine-tune the rate of change in an effect parameter's level. Converting a keyframe from a "corner type" to a "curve-type" is sometimes called "smoothing" a keyframe. For more information on keyframe types, see "Adjusting motion path curves and corners," later in this chapter.

Final Cut Pro has two types of keyframe graphs: keyframe overlays and keyframes:

Keyframe overlays are a special subset of keyframe graphs that are displayed as line graphs right on top of the track display in the Timeline (**Figure 13.13**) and over the waveform display on the Viewer's Audio tab. You set and adjust them in those two locations as well. Keyframe overlays indicate clip opacity (for video clips) and volume level and stereo pan position (for audio clips).

Keyframes also appear in the keyframe graphs located on the various eeffects tab in the Viewer, on motion paths in the Canvas (or in the Viewer), and on the Filters and Motion bars in the Timeline.

This section describes how to set and adjust keyframes in the keyframe graphs on the Viewer's Filters, Motion, and Controls tabs.

The Viewer's effects tabs display the keyframes on a keyframe graph (**Figure 13.14**), which extends to the right of each effect parameter control. Each effect parameter has its own separate set of keyframes, so you have individual control of every parameter and the way that parameter changes over time. The flexibility offered is limited only by your imagination.

After you have added the first keyframe to a clip, Final Cut Pro adds a new keyframe automatically whenever you change an effect setting for that clip at a different point in time.

The Nav column on the Viewer's Filters and Motion tabs lets you navigate through, add, or delete keyframes.

All of the tasks described here take place on the Viewer's Filters, Motion, or Controls tab.

For information about working with keyframes in the Timeline, see Chapter 7, "Using the Timeline and the Canvas."

For information about working with motion paths, see "Creating Motion Paths" later in this chapter.

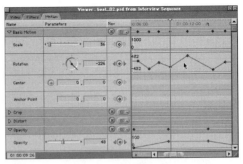

Figure 13.14 Keyframes appear on the keyframe graphs located on the various Effects tabs in the Viewer, on motion paths on the Canvas (or Viewer), and on the Filter and Motion bars in the Timeline.

Table 13.1

Keyboard Shortcuts for Keyframes	
Go to Next Keyframe	Shift-K
Go to Previous Keyframe	Option-K
Add Motion Keyframe	Control-K
Add Audio Level Keyframe	Command-Option-K

Keyframing Cheatsheet

Here's a quick summary of the basic keyframing steps in order:

1. Open the selected clip or sequence in the Viewer.

2. On the clip's Motion, Filters, or Controls tab, move the playhead to location A.

3. Enter value A for the parameter.

4. Click the Add Keyframe button.

5. Move the playhead to location B.

6. Enter value B.

The second keyframe is added automatically.

Figure 13.15 The Opacity bar is located on the Motion tab of the Viewer.

Figure 13.16 Click the Add Keyframe button in the Nav column to the left of the keyframe graph.

Using keyframes to set a single parameter

This task explains how to set keyframes for a single parameter on the Motion tab. As an example, we'll control the opacity of a clip to create a fade-in, fade-out effect.

To use keyframes to set a single parameter:

1. In the Timeline, double-click the clip that you want to fade in and out.

   The clip opens in the Viewer window.

2. In the Viewer, click the Motion tab; then locate the Opacity bar. The Opacity bar is the fourth main Motion control (**Figure 13.15**).

3. Click the triangle next to the Opacity bar. The Opacity Options settings open.

4. In the keyframe ruler, drag the playhead to the point where you want to set the clip to 100 percent opacity.

5. Click the Add Keyframe button in the Nav column to the left of the keyframe graph (**Figure 13.16**).

6. To set the Opacity level to 100 percent, *do one of the following:*

   ▲ On the keyframe ruler, click in the keyframe graph and drag up to set the keyframe value to 100 percent.

   ▲ In the Opacity Options settings, drag the slider to the right to set the keyframe value to 100 percent

   ▲ Enter 100 in the Opacity text field.

   continues on next page

USING KEYFRAMES

7. Drag the playhead to the point in the clip where you want to start the fade out. Click the Add Keyframe button. Again, enter 100% as the keyframe value.

    The second keyframe is set with a value of 100 percent (**Figure 13.17**).

Figure 13.17 Set the second keyframe to a value of 100 percent.

8. Press Home to go to the beginning of your clip.

9. Click the Add Keyframe button.

10. Enter 0% as the keyframe value.

    You can see a graphic representation of your fade-in as a diagonal line in the keyframe graph (**Figure 13.18**).

Figure 13.18 Your fade-in is represented by a diagonal line in the keyframe graph.

11. Press End to go to the end of your clip.

12. Add another keyframe and then enter 0% as the keyframe value (**Figure 13.19**).

Figure 13.19 At the end of your clip, add another keyframe and then set it to 0 percent.

13. You must render your clip before you can play it back. Select the clip; then choose Sequence > Render Selection.

14. Play back your fade-in and fade-out effect.

✔ Tip

■ For a wider view of your effects controls tab, try dragging the tab out of the Viewer and then stretching the display. When you're done, drag it back to the Viewer.

Setting keyframes with timecode entry

Even spacing of keyframes is essential to achieve smooth, even changes in your effects or precision synchronization to music or other effects. This is especially true for motion effects. When you are animating a program element, using timecode ensures that your keyframes will be set at precise intervals. This task shows you how to rotate a clip using timecode entry to set keyframes.

Figure 13.20 Click the Add Keyframe button, located to the right of the Rotation parameter control.

Figure 13.21 Click the Current Timecode field at the bottom left of the Motion tab; then type +30 to add 30 frames to the playhead location.

Figure 13.22 You have set three keyframes, exactly 30 frames apart, that cause your clip to complete two full 360-degree rotations in 2 seconds.

To set keyframes using timecode entry:

1. In the Timeline, double-click the clip you want to rotate to open it in the Viewer.

2. In the Viewer, click the Motion tab; then press Home to set the playhead in the key-frame graph to the first frame of your clip.

3. Click the Add Keyframe button that is located to the right of the Rotation control (**Figure 13.20**).

   The clip's first Rotation keyframe is set on the first frame.

4. Check to see that the Rotation control is set to zero.

   This establishes the clip's orientation at the beginning of the rotation.

5. Click the Current Timecode field at the bottom left of the Motion tab; then type +30 to move the playhead 30 frames forward (**Figure 13.21**).

   The playhead advances 30 frames in the keyframe graph.

6. Click the Add Keyframe button again; then *do one of the following:*

   ▲ On the keyframe ruler, click in the keyframe graph and drag up to set the keyframe's value to 360.

   ▲ In the Rotation parameter control, drag the dial needle to the right to set the keyframe value to 360.

   ▲ Enter 360 in the Rotation text field.

7. Repeat Steps 5 and 6, increasing the keyframe value to 720.

   You have set three keyframes, exactly 30 frames apart, which cause your clip to complete two full 360-degree rotations in 2 seconds (**Figure 13.22**).

8. You must render your rotating clip before you can play it back. Select the clip; then choose Sequence > Render Selection.

9. Play back your rotation effect.

USING KEYFRAMES

507

Working with keyframes on the Viewer's effects tabs

The Nav bar and keyframe graphs (to the right of the effects controls on the Viewer's Filters, Motion, and Control tabs) offer the most detailed control over individual keyframes. Here's a rundown of basic keyframe commands.

To set a keyframe:

1. On the Motion tab of the Viewer, position the playhead at the point in the keyframe graph where you want to set the keyframe.

2. Click the Set Keyframe button.

3. To set additional keyframes, move the playhead to the next location where you want to set a keyframe; then *do one of the following:*

   ▲ Click the Set Keyframe button.

   ▲ Click the Add Keyframe button in the Canvas or in the Viewer (**Figure 13.23**).

   ▲ Click the keyframe graph with the Arrow or Pen tool.

   ▲ Make an adjustment to an effects tab parameter control.

   Final Cut Pro adjusts the values and then automatically adds the keyframe.

✔ Tip

■ Click the Add Keyframe button in the Canvas or in the Viewer window to set a motion keyframe across all motion parameters for the current frame.

Figure 13.23 Move the playhead to the next location; then click the Add Keyframe button on the Canvas or in the Viewer.

Figure 13.24 To move the playhead to the next keyframe in either direction, click the Previous or Next Keyframe button.

Figure 13.25 To smooth a corner-type keyframe to a Bézier curve type, Control-click the keyframe and choose Smooth from the shortcut menu.

Figure 13.26 Drag the small blue circle at the end of the Bézier handle to adjust the motion path leading away from the keyframe.

To move a keyframe:

1. Click the keyframe graph with the Arrow or Pen tool.

2. *Do one of the following:*

    ▲ Drag the keyframe up or down to adjust the value.

    ▲ Drag the keyframe left or right to adjust the timing.

To navigate between keyframes:

◆ Click the Previous or Next Keyframe button (**Figure 13.24**).

    The playhead will move to the next keyframe in either direction. The arrows are dimmed if no other keyframes are in the clip.

To delete a keyframe:

Do one of the following:

◆ In the keyframe graph, position the playhead on the keyframe you want to remove; then click the Set Keyframe button (the button is green when it's on a keyframe).

◆ In the keyframe graph, Option-click the keyframe with the Arrow or Pen tool.

To refine a keyframe:

1. Control-click the keyframe and choose Smooth from the shortcut menu (**Figure 13.25**).

    The keyframe will change into a curve type, and Bézier handles appear.

2. Drag the small blue circle at the end of the Bézier handle to adjust the motion path leading up to (or away from) the keyframe (**Figure 13.26**).

✔ Tip

■ Double-click a Filters bar or a Motion bar in the Timeline with the Arrow tool to open the effect in the Viewer, with the correct tab already displayed.

USING KEYFRAMES

Precision control of a keyframe's positioning

Even in a compact screen layout, FCP offers a variety of techniques to help you get a grip on your keyframe's positioning:

◆ You can expand the vertical scale of most keyframe line graph displays on the Viewer's Effects tabs. Drag the separator bar at the bottom of a keyframe line graph to make a roomier keyframe graph (**Figure 13.27**).

◆ Here's another keyframe graph trick: You can adjust a keyframe while the playhead is located at a particular target frame, and the effect's parameter readout will show the value *at the playhead position*, so you can set a keyframe that results in a position or size at that target frame (**Figure 13.28**).

◆ Use the incremental controls (the tiny arrows at either end of effect parameter control sliders) to nudge values by + or –1, or enter an exact numeric value in the parameter's text field.

◆ In the Timeline or Viewer, hold down the Command key while you drag a keyframe. This enables "gear-down" dragging, which allows you to move the keyframe in precise increments.

◆ Shift-drag to change both the value and the keyframe's point in time simultaneously (**Figure 13.29**).

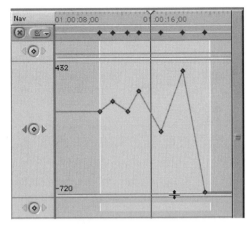

Figure 13.27 Drag the separator bar at the bottom of a keyframe line graph to expand the vertical scale.

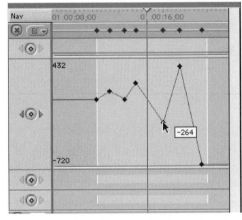

Figure 13.28 Adjust a keyframe while the playhead is located on a different frame, and the effect's parameter readout will show the value at the playhead position.

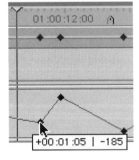

Figure 13.29 Shift-drag the keyframe to change both the value and the keyframe's point in time simultaneously.

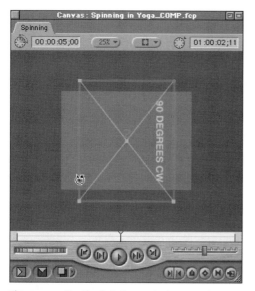

Figure 13.30 Use the Rotation control as a static composition tool to set a title clip at a 90-degree angle.

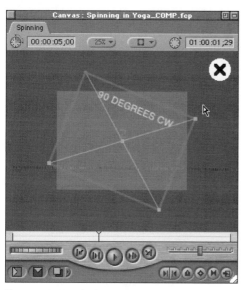

Figure 13.31 Use the Rotation control to animate the title clip's rotation by setting incrementally increasing values over time.

Using Motion

Unlike filters or generators, motion properties are already present on every clip. You can access them by loading a clip or sequence into the Viewer and then selecting the Motion tab.

A few of the controls you find on the Motion tab of the Viewer don't have any obvious connection to movement: The Opacity control is located on the Motion tab, as well as Crop, Distort, and Drop Shadow.

Some of the tools perform basic image modifications when used as static composition tools, but they also create motion effects when you adjust their values over time. For example, you might use the Rotation control as a static composition tool to display a title at a 90-degree angle (**Figure 13.30**) or animate rotation by setting incrementally increasing values over time (**Figure 13.31**).

This section introduces the image modification tools, which can be used in static or animated compositions, and then discusses motion paths: the time-based uses of motion properties.

Setting motion properties

Motion properties are present automatically on every clip, and their controls can be adjusted on the clip's Motion tab (**Figure 13.32**) in the Viewer, or on the clip's Wireframe mode overlay in the Canvas (**Figure 13.33**) or in the Viewer. The Motion properties are listed here.

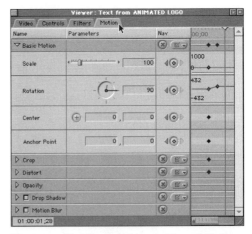

Figure 13.32 Use the controls on the Viewer's Motion tab to adjust motion properties.

◆ **Scale:** Adjusts the size of the clip to make it smaller or larger than the sequence frame size.

◆ **Rotation:** Rotates the clip around its anchor point without changing its shape. Clips can be rotated up to plus or minus 24 complete rotations.

◆ **Center:** X,Y coordinates specify the center point of the clip.

◆ **Anchor Point:** X,Y coordinates specify another point relative to the clip's center point to use as a pivot point for rotating, scaling, or animating the motion path of the clip.

◆ **Crop:** Crops (removes) a portion of the clip from the side you specify. Use the Edge Feather option to create a soft border at the crop line.

◆ **Distort:** Changes the shape of the clip by adjusting its corners. The Aspect Ratio parameter sets the clip's Height:Width proportions.

◆ **Opacity:** Makes a clip opaque or translucent; 100 percent is completely opaque, and 0 percent is completely transparent.

◆ **Drop Shadow:** Places a drop shadow behind the selected clip of a color, softness, and opacity you specify. You also specify the drop shadow's offset.

◆ **Motion Blur:** Blurs moving images by a specified percentage, by combining the images of adjacent frames to create the effect.

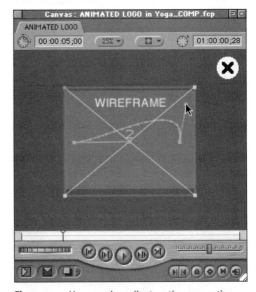

Figure 13.33 You can also adjust motion properties graphically, using the Canvas wireframe overlay.

Locating X,Y coordinates

Final Cut Pro uses X,Y coordinates to specify a clip's position in the frame. For example, in the DV-NTSC (720 by 480 pixel) frame size, you can specify locations outside the visible frame by using coordinate values greater than plus or minus 360 on the X axis, or plus or minus 240 on the Y axis. You'll often see X,Y coordinates specified like this (50,25). The first number (50) is the X coordinate, and the second number (25) is the Y coordinate.

Figure 3.34 is a diagram of X,Y coordinate locations in a DV-NTSC (720 by 480 pixel) frame.

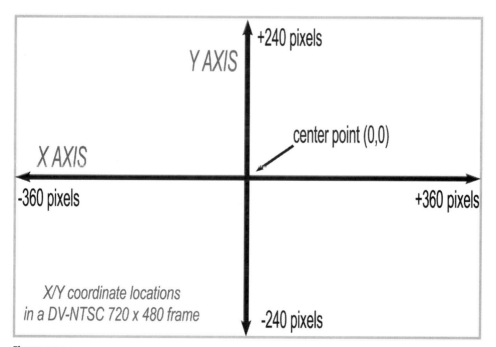

Figure 13.34

Scaling and Positioning Clips

In Final Cut Pro, clips start out positioned at the center of the Canvas or Viewer. You can reposition a clip's center point by dragging it to a new position in the Canvas or in the Viewer (**Figure 13.35**), or you can specify new center point coordinates on the clip's Motion tab (**Figure 13.36**). You can position a clip partially or completely outside the sequence frame.

Most of the tasks described in this section can be performed in two different places: on the clip's wireframe in the Canvas or Viewer window, or on the clip's Motion tab in the Viewer. Start each task by following the general setup procedure for each respective mode; the setup tasks are described in the following sections.

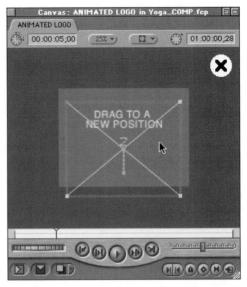

Figure 13.35 You can reposition a clip's center point by dragging it to a new position on the Canvas or in the Viewer.

Figure 13.36 Specify new center point coordinates on the clip's Motion tab.

Pressin', Clickin', and Draggin': Using Keyboard Shortcuts with Wireframes

Many of the scaling and positioning tools have keyboard modifiers—keys you press as you drag the tool on the wireframe handles in the Canvas or in the Viewer—that you can use to create complex alterations to a clip.

Option key: Use this modifier to force automatic rendering while you drag the clip.

Shift key: Use this modifier to enable nonproportional scaling (modification of a clip's aspect ratio while scaling). You can use the Shift and Option modifiers together.

Command key: Use this modifier to rotate and scale the clip simultaneously. You can use the Command and Option modifiers together.

SCALING AND POSITIONING CLIPS

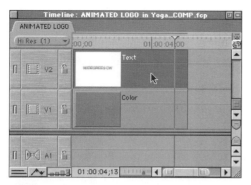

Figure 13.37 Select the clip you want to reposition in the Timeline.

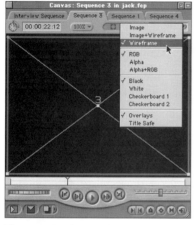

Figure 13.38 Select Wireframe mode from the View pop-up menu on the Canvas.

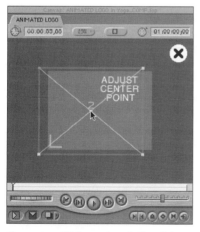

Figure 13.39 Click anywhere in the clip's wireframe and drag it to a new position.

To set up for motion properties adjustment in Wireframe mode:

1. In the Timeline, select the clip you want to reposition (**Figure 13.37**). If you are working with a layered composition, be sure to choose the layer you want to affect.

2. From the Tool palette, choose the Arrow tool.

3. In the View pop-up menu of the Viewer or Canvas, select Wireframe or Image+ Wireframe to turn on Wireframe mode (**Figure 13.38**).

   The outline of the selected clip appears in Wireframe mode.

To set up for motion properties adjustment on the Viewer's Motion tab:

1. Double-click the clip in the Timeline or Browser to open it in the Viewer.

2. In the Viewer, click the Motion tab.

To adjust a clip's center point using Wireframe mode:

◆ Follow the setup steps for Wireframe mode presented earlier; then click anywhere inside the clip's wireframe and drag it to a new position (**Figure 13.39**).

To adjust a clip's center point on the Viewer's Motion tab:

Follow the setup steps for the Motion tab mode described earlier; then *do one of the following:*

Figure 13.40 Click the Point Select button located to the left of the Center value field.

◆ Enter new X,Y coordinates for the clip's center location. Enter the X coordinate in the left value field and the Y coordinate in the right value field.

◆ Click the Point Select (+) button (**Figure 13.40**) (located to the left of the Center value field) and then specify new center coordinates by clicking the new center location in the Canvas (**Figure 13.41**) or on the Video tab of the Viewer.

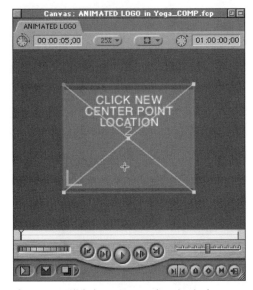

Figure 13.41 Click the new center location in the Canvas to specify new center coordinates.

FCP Protocol: Center Point vs. Anchor Point vs. Origin Point

All three of these points—the center point, anchor point, and origin point—are used to define position, but each serves a different purpose:

Center Point: Establishes the clip's position inside the Canvas area. The center point's default position (0,0) is the same as the Anchor point.

Anchor Point: Establishes the pivot point for a clip's movement inside the Canvas area. Rotation and Scale properties and motion paths are all based on the anchor point. The anchor point's default position (0,0) is the same as the Center point.

Origin Point: Origin appears on the Controls tab for text generators and establishes the positioning of the text elements placed inside the clip.

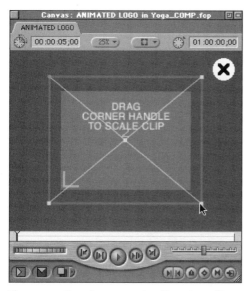

Figure 13.42 Dragging a corner handle scales a clip while maintaining its proportions.

Scaling clips

A clip placed in a Final Cut Pro sequence plays at the same frame size at which it was captured, regardless of the sequence frame size. Clips whose native size is smaller than the sequence frame size appear in the center of the sequence frame, and clips whose native size is larger than the sequence frame size will show only the portion of the clip that is within the sequence frame dimensions.

You can adjust the scale of a clip to change its frame size (for the current sequence only). If you want to create a media file of your clip at a different size that does not need to be rendered before it can be played back, you should export a copy of the clip at the frame size you need.

To scale a clip in Wireframe mode:

1. Follow the setup steps for Wireframe mode presented earlier.

2. Drag a corner handle to scale a clip while maintaining its proportions (**Figure 13.42**).

✔ **Tips**

■ Smooth your keyframes with Bézier curves when you animate scale. Curve-type keyframes produce a change in the rate of scale at the beginning and end of the scaling animation, making the movement less mechanical. To learn how to convert a keyframe to a Bézier curve type, see "To refine a keyframe" earlier in this chapter.

■ When you're scaling a clip, it's easy to drift away from the clip's original aspect ratio, but not easy to find the control that resets your clip to its native proportions. Go to the clip's Motion tab and scroll down to the Distort controls. That's where you'll find the Aspect Ratio parameter. Reset the value to 0, and you'll restore height/width sanity to your scaled clip.

SCALING AND POSITIONING CLIPS

517

To scale a clip on the Viewer's Motion tab:

Follow the setup steps for the Motion tab mode presented earlier; then *do one of the following:*

◆ Adjust the Scale slider (**Figure 13.43**).

◆ Enter a percentage in the text field located to the right of the slider; 100 percent is equal to the clip's native size.

To scale a clip to conform to the sequence frame size:

◆ Select the clip in the Timeline or Browser; then choose Modify > Scale to Sequence (**Figure 13.44**).

Rotating clips

Rotation is an important part of modern video effects (as you know if you've watched a TV commercial break recently).

A clip rotates around its anchor point. The default anchor point location matches the clip's center point, but you can rotate a clip around a different pivot point by changing the location of the anchor point. You can position a clip at the edge of your sequence frame and rotate your clip partially or completely outside the Canvas, so it appears on the screen for only a portion of its rotation. You can also rotate a clip up to 24 revolutions in either direction or use the Rotation control to angle a clip as part of a static composition.

To rotate a clip in Wireframe mode:

Follow the setup steps for Wireframe mode presented earlier; then *do one of the following:*

◆ Click an edge of the border and drag in an arc around the clip's center point (**Figure 13.45**).

Figure 13.43 Adjust the Scale slider on the Motion tab to scale the clip.

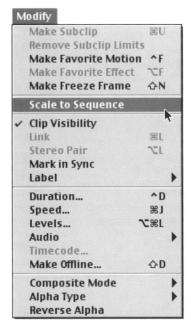

Figure 13.44 Choose Modify > Scale to Sequence to make a clip frame size conform to the sequence frame size.

Figure 13.45 To rotate a clip in Wireframe mode, drag in an arc around the clip's center point.

Figure 13.46 Drag around the rotation control dial needle to set a rotation position. The black hand indicates the current angle of the clip, and the small red hand indicates how many total rotations forward or backward have been specified.

◆ Click and drag further away from the clip's center point to get more precise control over the rotation.

◆ Hold down the Shift key while dragging to constrain the rotation positions to 45-degree increments.

◆ Drag around the clip multiple times without releasing the mouse to specify a number of rotations.

To rotate a clip on the Viewer's Motion tab:

Follow the setup steps for the Motion tab mode described earlier; then *do one of the following:*

◆ Drag around the rotation control dial needle to set a rotation position (**Figure 13.46**).

◆ Enter a new value in the text box.

The clip will realign at the new rotation angle for the selected frame. To create an animated rotation effect on the Motion tab, you must set individual keyframes for each rotation angle value.

Cropping clips

You can crop a clip either by dragging with the Crop tool or by specifying the number of pixels to crop from the borders. You can also feather the edges of the frame to make them blend smoothly with the background.

When you use the Crop tool to remove part of a clip's image, the selected parts are hidden, not deleted. You can restore the cropped sections to view by clicking the Reset button next to the crop controls on the Viewer's Motion tab.

continues on next page

To crop a clip in Wireframe mode:

1. Follow the setup steps for the Wireframe mode presented earlier; then select the Crop tool from the Tool palette.

2. *Do one of the following:*

   ▲ Click and drag from the edges of the clip to hide elements in the image (**Figure 13.47**).

   ▲ Shift-drag to constrain the clip's aspect ratio as you crop.

   ▲ Command-drag to trim both horizontal edges or both vertical edges simultaneously.

   ▲ Use Option in combination with Shift and Command to force rendering while performing a crop operation.

To crop a clip on the Motion tab:

1. Follow the setup steps for the Motion tab mode described earlier; then open the Crop Control bar by clicking the triangle on the left (**Figure 13.48**).

2. To crop the clip from a specific side, *do one of the following:*

   ▲ Drag the slider for that edge to a new value (**Figure 13.49**).

   ▲ Enter a new value in the text field.

3. To soften the cropped edges of the clip, *do one of the following:*

   ▲ Adjust the Edge Feather slider to specify the width of the feathered edge.

   ▲ Specify a value in the Edge Feather text field.

   ▲ Click in the Edge Feather keyframe graph and drag up to set the value.

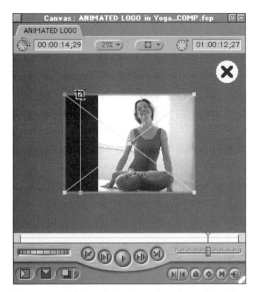

Figure 13.47 Click and drag from the edges of the clip to crop out elements in the image.

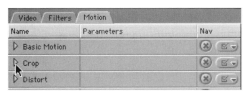

Figure 13.48 Open the Crop Control bar by clicking the triangle on the left.

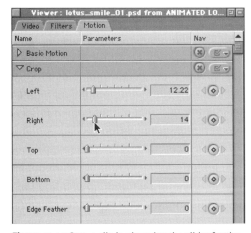

Figure 13.49 Crop a clip by dragging the slider for the side you want to crop and setting it to a new value.

Figure 13.50 Select the Distort tool from the Tool palette.

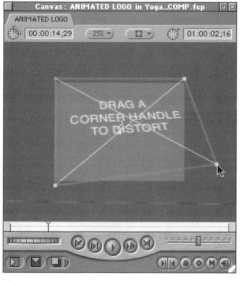

Figure 13.51 Drag a corner handle of the clip's wireframe to distort it.

Distorting a clip's shape

The Distort tool gives you independent control over each corner point of the clip's wireframe, or you can specify X,Y coordinates for the location of each of the four corner points numerically on the Viewer's Motion tab.

To distort the shape of a clip in Wireframe mode:

1. Follow the setup steps for the Wireframe mode presented earlier; then select the Distort tool from the Tool palette (**Figure 13.50**).

2. To distort the clip's image, *do one of the following:*

   ▲ Drag a corner handle of the clip's wireframe (**Figure 13.51**).

   ▲ Shift-drag to change the perspective of the image.

To distort a clip on the Viewer's Motion tab:

1. Follow the setup steps for the Motion tab mode presented earlier; then open the Distort Control bar by clicking the triangle on the left.

2. To specify new locations for the corner points, *do one of the following:*

   ▲ Enter new values for the corner points you want to move.

   ▲ Adjust the Aspect Ratio parameter to change the clip's height:width ratio, relocating all four corner points. A clip's original aspect ratio has a value of zero.

Adjusting Opacity

Final Cut Pro clips start out 100 percent opaque (**Figure 13.52**). If you superimpose a clip over another clip in the base track of your sequence, the background image will be completely hidden until you adjust the opacity of the superimposed clip to less than 100 percent, making it semitransparent (**Figure 13.53**).

Layering multiple, semitransparent images is a basic compositing technique, and one you may be familiar with if you have ever worked with Adobe Photoshop.

You can adjust a clip's opacity on the Viewer's Motion tab or with the opacity clip overlay in the Timeline.

Figure 13.52 The title is 100 percent opaque and completely obscures the background.

Figure 13.53 The superimposed title with opacity set to less than 100 percent appears semitransparent.

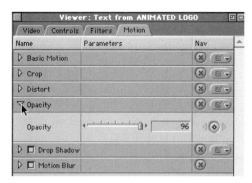

Figure 13.54 Click the triangle to open the opacity controls.

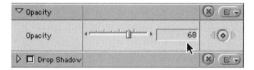

Figure 13.55 Enter a value between 0 and 100 in the Opacity text field.

To set a clip's opacity on the Viewer's Motion tab:

1. In the Timeline, double-click the sequence clip to open it in the Viewer window.

2. In the Viewer, click the Motion tab; then locate the Opacity bar. The Opacity bar is the fourth main motion control.

3. Click the triangle next to the Opacity bar. The Opacity Options settings open (**Figure 13.54**).

4. To set the opacity level, *do one of the following:*

   ▲ In the Opacity Options settings, drag the slider to the right to set the keyframe value.

   ▲ Enter a value between 0 and 100 in the Opacity text field (**Figure 13.55**).

   ▲ To use keyframes to set opacity levels, see "Using keyframes to set a single parameter" earlier in this chapter.

Setting a clip's opacity in the Timeline

A clip's opacity can be adjusted directly in the Timeline using the clip overlay for opacity, a level line graph that appears over the clip icon in the Timeline. To display clip overlays, click the Clip Overlays button in the lower-left corner of the Timeline.

For information on adjusting clip overlays in the Timeline, see "Working with Keyframes in the Timeline" in Chapter 7.

Use the Modify > Levels command to adjust opacity levels for a group of Timeline clips in a single operation.

To adjust opacity levels on a group of clips:

1. In the Timeline, select a group of clips whose levels you want to adjust (**Figure 13.56**).

2. Choose Modify > Levels.

3. In the Opacity Adjust dialog box, *do one of the following:*

   ▲ Choose Relative from the pop-up menu. Adjust each clip's opacity relative to its current level by specifying the percentage value (**Figure 13.57**).

   ▲ Choose Absolute from the pop-up menu; then set an absolute value for all clips' opacity by specifying a percentage value.

4. Click OK.

Adding a drop shadow to a clip

Drop shadows add the illusion of dimensional depth to the 2D television screen (**Figure 13.58**). Titles pop out from the backgrounds, or clips softly float over other clips; complex silhouettes can add a special depth to your sequences. You can add a drop shadow to any clip whose display size is smaller than the sequence frame size.

You can apply drop shadows to clips that were captured at a smaller frame size and to clips that have been scaled, cropped, moved, or distorted. You can also display a drop shadow on a full-size clip with an alpha channel.

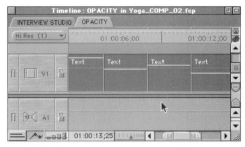

Figure 13.56 Select the clips to be adjusted in the Timeline.

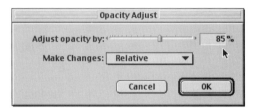

Figure 13.57 Choose Relative in the Opacity Adjust dialog box to adjust the opacity of all the selected clips by the percentage you specify.

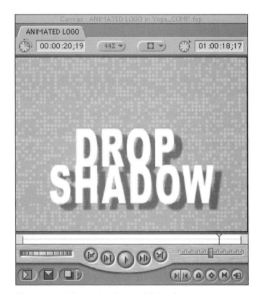

Figure 13.58 Drop shadows add depth to a superimposed title.

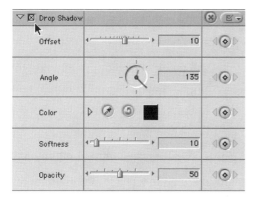

Figure 13.59 Check the box to enable the Drop Shadow option.

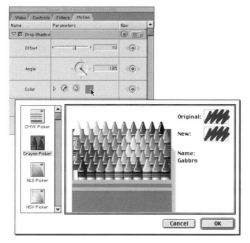

Figure 13.60 Click the color swatch; then choose a color from one of the color pickers.

To add a drop shadow to a clip:

1. Double-click the clip in the Timeline or Browser to open it in the Viewer.

2. In the Viewer, click the Motion tab; then check the box next to the Drop Shadow option to enable this option (**Figure 13.59**).

3. To adjust the settings that control the appearance of the drop shadow, *do any of the following:*

   ▲ Enter Offset settings to specify the shadow's distance from the clip.

   ▲ Enter Angle settings to specify the position of the shadow relative to the clip edge.

   ▲ Enter Softness settings to specify the degree of blending in the shadow's edge.

   ▲ Enter Opacity settings to specify the shadow's degree of transparency.

4. On the Color control, click the triangle to the left to reveal the full set of color controls; then *do one of the following:*

   ▲ Drag the hue, saturation, and brightness sliders to new values.

   ▲ Enter color values numerically in the text fields.

   ▲ Click the eyedropper and click in the Canvas to sample a color.

   ▲ Click the color swatch and use one of the color pickers to choose the desired color (**Figure 13.60**).

Adding a motion blur effect

The motion blur effect enhances the illusion of movement by compositing the images of adjacent frames (**Figure 13.61**). This is definitely one control to experiment with, particularly for creating interesting animated soft-focus background textures. If you're using graphics or stills, you'll need to combine motion blur with other motion effects— scaling, rotation, or motion paths, for example—to see the motion blur effect, but you can use it to create a lot of action in your composition, even with static elements (**Figure 13.62**).

✔ Tip

■ Nest a clip containing an element you want to blur. By increasing the frame size when you nest, you can create a roomier bounding box that will accommodate the larger size of your blurred element.

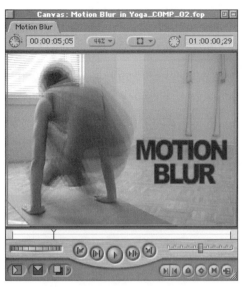

Figure 13.61 Motion blur produces soft focus effects based on movement within your video image.

Figure 13.62 You can apply motion blur to a static graphic as well, but you need to animate the graphic with a motion path first.

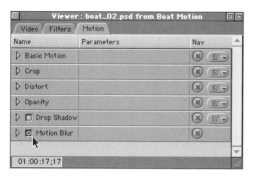

Figure 13.63 Check the box next to the Motion Blur option to enable this option.

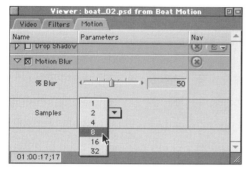

Figure 13.64 Specify a number of samples by selecting a value from the pop-up menu. The sample rate changes the quality of the motion blur.

To add motion blur to a clip:

1. Double-click the clip in the Timeline or Browser to open it in the Viewer.

2. In the Viewer, click the Motion tab; then check the box next to Motion Blur (at the bottom of the tab) to enable this option (**Figure 13.63**).

3. Open the Motion Blur control bar by clicking the triangle on the left.

4. Use the % Blur slider or enter a value in the text field. Values range from 1000%, which blurs a frame's image across 10 frames, to 100%, which blurs the image on a single frame.

5. To change the quality of the motion blur, adjust the sample rate. Specify a number of samples by selecting a value from the pop-up menu (**Figure 13.64**).

   The sample rate is the number of in-between images FCP calculates when it compares two adjacent frames to calculate motion blur. A low sample rate produces more visible intermediate steps; a high sample rate produces a smoother look, but takes longer to render.

✔ Tip

■ Using curve type keyframes to animate motion properties gives the timing of motion blur effects a more organic feel. To learn how to convert a keyframe to a Bézier curve type, see "To refine a keyframe" earlier in this chapter.

Creating Motion Paths

If you are new to motion paths, try one—working in Wireframe mode first. You can play wireframes back in real time without rendering, and it will help you get a feel for how the Canvas function changes when you are working in Wireframe mode. You can work in Wireframe mode in the Viewer as well.

When you animate the center point, you move the whole clip. The basic steps for animating a simple motion path are explained in the following section.

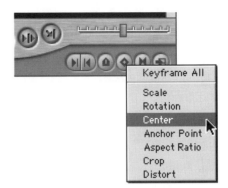

Figure 13.65 Control-click the Add Keyframe button on the Canvas; then select Center from the shortcut menu.

✔ Tip

- Motion paths are limited to single sequence clips; you must nest sequence clips if you want to create a motion path that includes two or more clips that have been edited together. For more information on nesting items, see Chapter 12.

To create a motion path in the Canvas:

1. In the Timeline, select a sequence clip; then position the playhead on the first frame in your clip.

2. Make the Canvas active; then choose View > Level > 25%.

3. Choose View > Image+Wireframe.

4. To add the first keyframe, Control-click the Add Keyframe button in the Canvas; then select Center from the shortcut menu (**Figure 13.65**) to specify which parameter you are animating.
   Final Cut Pro sets the first keyframe on the Center motion parameter for that sequence frame.

5. In the Canvas, click and drag the wireframe's center handle to the left until the right side of the wireframe is aligned with the left edge of the black background. Hold down the Shift key while you drag to

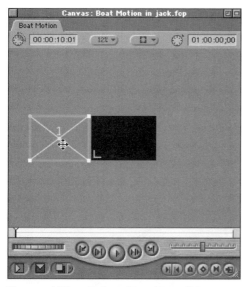

Figure 13.66 Your clip is positioned just off the screen, at the left.

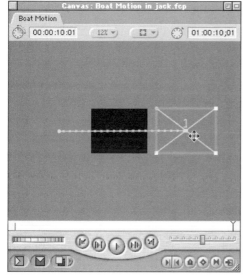

Figure 13.67 The white line indicates the motion path of your clip's center point.

constrain the motion path. This makes it easier to drag in a straight line.

Your clip is now positioned just off the screen, at the left (**Figure 13.66**).

6. In the Timeline, position the playhead on the last frame in your sequence clip.

7. In the Canvas, click inside the wireframe and Shift-drag it to the right. Drag the wireframe across the black background until its left side is aligned with the right edge of the black background.

   As you drag, the motion path appears across the center of the screen. The white line indicates the motion path of your clip's center point (**Figure 13.67**).

8. To preview your motion path, hold down the Option key while you scrub the Canvas Scrubber bar from side to side. You'll see your finished product play back at a reduced frame rate.

9. You must render your moving clip before you can play it back at its actual frame rate. Select the clip; then choose Sequence > Render Selection.

✔ Tips

- You can use the Add Keyframe button in the Canvas to delete keyframes. Locate your Canvas playhead at the timecode location of the keyframe you want to delete. Control-click the Add Keyframe button to bring up the shortcut menu and deselect the checked motion parameter.

- When your clips and motion paths are so spread out that you need to make the Canvas or Viewer view smaller than the smallest level listed on the Zoom control (12 %), choose Fit All, which will zoom out as far as necessary to fit all elements of your multilayered composited sequence within the window.

To add curves to a motion path:

1. If you don't already have a sequence clip with a motion path applied, follow steps 1 through 8 in the previous task, "To create a motion path in the Canvas."

2. To create a curve in your straight motion path, click the motion path and drag in the direction you want the path to curve.

   As you drag the motion path into a curve, additional keyframes automatically appear on the motion path; the keyframes have little handles, called Bézier handles, that you use to sculpt the motion path's curves (**Figure 13.68**).

3. Click the Canvas Play button to play back the first draft of your edited motion path. Watching real-time playback in Wireframe mode is the best way to evaluate your clip's speed and movement.

4. To adjust the curve, click a keyframe's Bézier handle; then *do any of the following:*

   ▲ Drag the handle away from the keyframe to deepen the curve.

   ▲ Drag the handle toward the keyframe to reduce the curve.

   ▲ Rotate the handle to change the direction of the curve relative to that keyframe (**Figure 13.69**).

   ▲ Command-drag to restrict rotation to one side of the curve (**Figure 13.70**). Release the Command key to set the new relationship between the two curves.

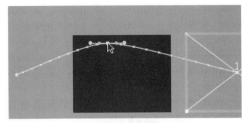

Figure 13.68 As you drag the motion path into a curve, the additional keyframes appear with little handles, called Bézier handles, that you click and drag to sculpt the motion path's curves.

Figure 13.69 Rotate the handle to change the direction of the curve relative to that keyframe.

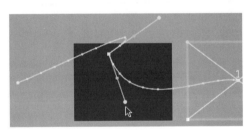

Figure 13.70 Command-drag to restrict rotation to one side of the curve.

Editing a Motion Path

Once you have created it, you can make adjustments to a motion path directly in the Canvas (or Viewer) by moving or deleting motion path keyframes. When you're working with a motion path in the Canvas, the playhead doesn't need to be over a keyframe for you to move or delete it, nor does the playhead location prohibit you from adding a motion path keyframe.

Remember that a keyframe is like an edit point: It signals a change in an effect. In a motion path, keyframes are placed automatically only when a motion path changes direction. A straight motion path requires only two keyframes: a start keyframe and an end keyframe.

The two motion path variables you are adjusting are your clip's speed of travel (determined by the ratio of duration to distance between keyframes) and the path's route (indicated by the shape of the white line that connects the start and end keyframes). The little round dots that appear in between the keyframes indicate the duration between path points.

Adjusting motion path curves and corners

Final Cut Pro has two types of motion path keyframes: corners and curves. The default motion path keyframe is a corner, which creates an instant change in direction. If you want a smoother motion effect, the curve keyframes have Bézier handles, which you can use to fine-tune the shape of the motion path's curve, and ease handles, which you can use to fine-tune your clip's speed immediately before and after the keyframe location.

You switch a corner-type motion path keyframe to a curve type as the first step in smoothing your motion path and finessing its timing.

✔ Tips

■ You can use the Shift and Command keys while dragging a Bézier or ease handle to influence the connections between the angles of the curve.

■ When you're adjusting curves in the Viewer's keyframe graph, try expanding the keyframe area. The larger size makes fine adjustments much easier.

To toggle a keyframe between corner and curve types:

Do one of the following:

◆ In the keyframe graph of the Viewer's Motion tab, Control-click a keyframe and then choose a keyframe type from the shortcut menu.

◆ Choose Smooth to toggle to a curve keyframe (**Figure 13.71**).

◆ Choose Corner to toggle to a corner keyframe (**Figure 13.72**).

◆ Choose Clear to delete the keyframe.

To toggle a keyframe between corner and curve types in Wireframe mode:

With your clip displayed in Wireframe mode in the Canvas, Control-click a keyframe and *choose one of the following options:*

◆ Make Corner Point, which toggles the keyframe from a curve type to a corner type (**Figure 13.73**).

◆ Ease In/Ease Out to access the ease handles, which are discussed later in this section.

◆ Linear, which applies a constant rate of speed to the path immediately before and after the keyframe location.

◆ Delete Point, which deletes the keyframe.

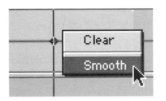

Figure 13.71 Control-click a corner keyframe and then choose Smooth to toggle to a curve keyframe.

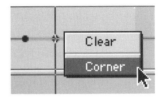

Figure 13.72 Control-click a curve keyframe in the keyframe graph; then choose Corner to toggle to a corner keyframe.

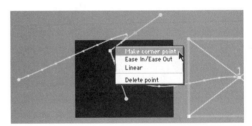

Figure 13.73 Control-click a keyframe on the Canvas; then choose Make Corner Point, which toggles the keyframe from a curve type to a corner type.

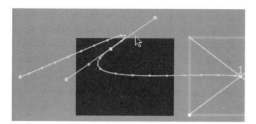

Figure 13.74 Ease handles are located about midway between the Bézier handles and the keyframe's position point.

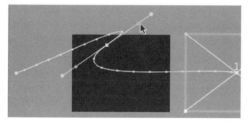

Figure 13.75 Drag the ease handle away from the keyframe to increase a clip's speed as it passes through the keyframe's location on the motion path.

Adjusting speed along a motion path

You can increase the speed of a clip between two keyframes by shortening the timecode duration between two keyframes without changing their spatial coordinates. The clip's speed will increase, as it takes less time to travel between the two locations on your motion path. Or keep the time interval the same and move the keyframes farther apart on the motion path, so the clip travels farther in the same amount of time. Other timing factors in your sequence composition will dictate your choice.

Ease handles, located in the Canvas between the Bézier handles and the keyframe's position point (**Figure 13.74**), fine-tune the rate of speed at which a clip approaches and leaves a curve keyframe. The default Ease In and Out setting slows the speed on the motion path by 33 percent before and after the keyframe, but you can customize your Ease In or Out setting. Drag both handles to set the clip's ease in and ease out to the same rate, or drag the handles separately to set different ease-in and ease-out rates.

To make a clip ease in and out of a keyframe:

1. With the Canvas in Wireframe mode, start with a curve motion path keyframe.

2. Select the Arrow tool.

3. Click the curve keyframe; then *do one of the following:*

   ▲ Drag the ease handle away from the keyframe to increase the clip's speed as it passes through the keyframe's location on the motion path (**Figure 13.75**).

   ▲ Drag the handle toward the keyframe to slow the clip's speed as it passes through the keyframe's location on the motion path.

continues on next page

▲ Drag either ease handle to adjust the path's timing on both sides of the keyframe equally (**Figure 13.76**).

▲ Shift-drag one ease handle to adjust the path's timing only on the selected side.

4. Play back in Wireframe mode to see your results.

✔ Tip

■ You can copy and paste Motion Paths between clips or sequences by using Paste Attributes. Check the Scale Attributes box when you go to paste attributes onto your destination clip, and you can reuse a motion path on a different clip that's shorter or longer than the original.

Setting motion paths for multiple clips

How can you easily apply a single motion path to multiple clips? There are a couple of different techniques available; your choice depends on whether you are dealing with a series of clips on a single track or multiple clips stacked in layers on Timeline tracks.

The Nest Items command allows you to select a series of clips in an edited sequence and apply a single motion path to the entire series.

If you want to apply the same motion path to multiple layers, such as a layered Photoshop file containing title elements, you can select all the tracks you want to include and apply the Nest Items command. You also have the option of copying a clip and pasting its motion path alone using the Paste Attributes function.

For more information on the Nest Items feature, see Chapter 12, "Big Picture: Managing Complex Projects."

For more information on the Paste Attributes feature, see Chapter 7, "Using the Timeline and the Canvas."

Figure 13.76 Drag the ease handle toward the keyframe to decrease a clip's speed as it passes through the keyframe's location on the motion path.

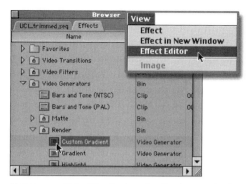

Figure 13.77 Select the Custom Gradient generator in the Browser's Effects tab; then choose View > Effect Editor to open the generator in FXBuilder.

```
                    FXBuilder
  FXBuilder Text Entry    FXBuilder Input Controls
generator "Custom Gradient", 120;
group "Render";
AlphaType(kAlpha);

input SHAPERAMP, "Shape", popup, 1, "Linear", "Radial";
input STARTRAMP, "Start", point, -0.5, 0;
input RAMPDIRECTION, "Gradient Direction", angle, 90, -360, 360 de
input RAMPWIDTH, "Gradient Width", slider, 100, 0, 100 detent 100;
input STARTCOLOR, "Start", color, 255, 255, 255, 255;
input ENDCOLOR, "End", color, 255, 0, 0, 0;
input DITHRAMP, "Dither", checkbox, 0;
input GAUSRAMP, "Gaussian", checkbox, 0;

code
    on fabs (value _n)
        return (_n<0 ? -_n : _n);
    end;
```

Figure 13.78 This is the FXBuilder script for the Custom Gradient generator. Replace the highlighted values with the custom values highlighted values in Figure 13.79.

About FXBuilder

You can use Final Cut Pro's FXBuilder effects scripting utility to create, test, and modify custom video filters, generators, or transitions. You can build effects, modify existing Final Cut Pro effects, or combine several effects into one FXBuilder script. FXBuilder scripts can be saved in a copy-protected format that allows them to be run but prevents anyone from viewing their code. For more information about FXBuilder, see Chapter 31 in Apple's *Final Cut Pro 2 User's Manual.*

Editing FXBuilder scripts

Many of FCP's working filters can be viewed and modified within FXBuilder. Even if you're not yet ready to write your own effects, editing existing FXBuilder effects can be a snap. Modifying existing FXBuilder scripts is a good way to get started with FXBuilder.

Here's an example. Making simple changes to an existing generator script creates a custom Gradient generator that looks like the twilight sky.

To edit an existing FXBuilder script:

1. On the Browser's Effects tab, select the Custom Gradient Generator (**Figure 13.77**), and then choose View >Effect Editor to open the generator's script in FXBuilder.

2. On the FXBuilder Text Entry tab, change the default settings of the Custom Gradient generator (**Figure 13.78**) by editing the Custom Gradient FX Builder script as follows:

   ▲ Change the name of the new generator from Custom Gradient to Twilight Sky by replacing the word *Custom Gradient* with the words *Twilight Sky*.

   ▲ Change the default "Gradient Direction" setting by replacing the 90 with a 0 (zero).

continues on next page

▲ Change the default "Start" point setting by replacing the -0.5, 0 settings with 0, 0.5.

▲ Change the default Start color of the new gradient to sky blue by changing the R,G, and B values from - 255, 255, 255, 255 (RGB settings for pure white) to the RGB values for sky blue: 255, 100, 100, 255 (**Figure 13.79**). (The first of the four values in the string, 255, is the generator's default alpha value.)

▲ Change the default End color of the new gradient to midnight blue by changing the R,G, and B values from 255, 0, 0, 0 (RGB settings for pure black) to the RGB values for midnight blue: 255, 0, 0, 105.

3. Choose FXBuilder > Export Text and save this new file as Twilight Sky inside your Plugins > FXScripts > Generators > Render folder.

4. Quit Final Cut Pro and relaunch the application. After relaunch, your new custom color matte, Twilight Sky, joins the list of generators appearing in the Generator > Matte pop-up menu in the Viewer (**Figure 13.80**).

✔ Tips

■ If you use FCP's RGB color picker to select custom colors for an effect, you'll need to multiply those color values by 2.55 to convert the RGB color picker setting, which uses a range of 0 to 100%, to an RGB level that works in FXBuilder, which uses a range of 0 to 255.

■ Want a user's-eye view of FXBuilder scripting? Check out Joe Maller's fine FXBuilder reference site at http://www.joe.maller.com.

Figure 13.79 This is the FXBuilder script for the customized "Twilight Sky" gradient generator. The replacement values are highlighted.

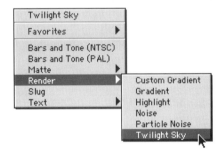

Figure 13.80 Your new custom gradient, Twilight Sky, appears in the list of generators in the Viewer's Generator pop-up menu.

Figure 13.81 Final Cut Pro comes with a library of more than 50 filters.

Applying Filters

Just as the term *motion properties* is used to describe a collection of tools that do a lot more than move things, so the term *filters* applies to a lot more than just tools for tinting or texturing an image. Final Cut Pro comes with more than 50 video filters, with a wide variety of uses (**Figure 13.81**). In addition to a suite of image-control filters for color correction or tinting, Final Cut Pro provides filters you can use to blur, twirl, emboss, ripple, flip, mask, and key. When you're done, you can apply another filter to generate visible timecode over your final results! For a complete list of filters, refer to Chapter 22 in Apple's *Final Cut Pro 2 User's Manual.*

But wait—there's more. Final Cut Pro can also make use of the QuickTime effects that are installed with QuickTime, and the program is compatible with many of After Effects' third-party filters.

For more information about After Effects third-party filters, see "Using Third-Party After Effects Filters" later in this chapter.

You'll find filters on the Browser's Effects tab or in the Effects menu. After installation, QuickTime effects and third-party After Effects filters are stored in separate bins within the main Video Filters bins.

To apply a filter to a clip:

1. *Do one of the following:*

   ▲ Drag the filter from the Browser's Effects tab and drop it on the clip in the Timeline (**Figure 13.82**).

   ▲ Select the clip in the Timeline, choose Effects > Video (or Audio) Filters, and make your filter selection from the submenu.

2. Position the playhead over a frame in the selected clip to see a preview of the effect in the Canvas (**Figure 13.83**).

✔ Tip

■ Many filters' default settings have no visible effect on a clip. You will need to make settings adjustments before you can detect a difference.

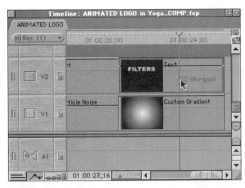

Figure 13.82 Drag the filter from the Effects tab and drop it on the clip in the Timeline.

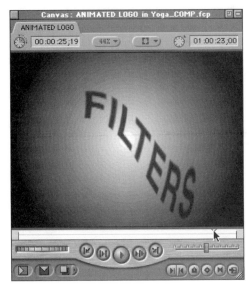

Figure 13.83 Position the playhead over a frame in the filtered clip to see a preview of the effect on the Canvas.

APPLYING FILTERS

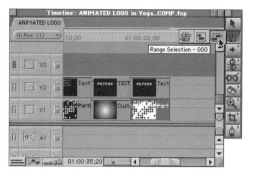

Figure 13.84 Choose the Range Selection tool from the Tool palette.

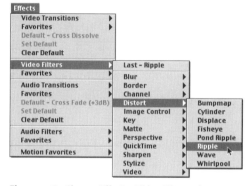

Figure 13.85 Choose Effects > Video Filters; then select a filter from the submenu.

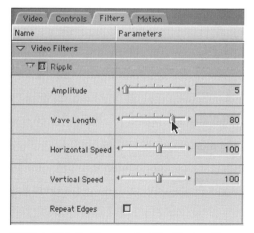

Figure 13.86 In the Viewer, adjust the filter's settings on the clip's Filters tab.

To apply a filter to a range of clips or part of a clip:

1. From the Tool Palette, choose the Range Selection tool (**Figure 13.84**).

2. In the Timeline, drag to select whole or partial clips.

3. Choose Effects > Video (or Audio) Filters and select a filter from the submenu (**Figure 13.85**).

   If you selected multiple clips, Final Cut Pro adds a separate copy of the filter to each clip.

4. Position the playhead over a frame in the selected clip range to see a preview of the effect in the Canvas.

To adjust a filter:

1. In the Timeline, double-click a clip to which you've added a filter to open it in the Viewer.

2. In the Viewer, click the Filters tab to access the filter's controls.

3. Configure the filter's settings (**Figure 13.86**). (The items you can change vary according to the type of filter.)

4. To see the changes you've made, use the arrow keys to move through the clip frame by frame. You must render the clip before you can play it with a video filter applied. You can use keyframes to make additional changes in a filter over time.

continues on next page

APPLYING FILTERS

✔ Tips

■ You can turn off a filter by unchecking the box next to the filter's name on its control bar on the Viewer's Filters tab. The filter is disabled but is still applied to the clip. To toggle it back on, just recheck the box. You can also configure render qualities to exclude filters during rendering. See Chapter 10, "Rendering."

■ Final Cut Pro renders a clip's filters in the order they appear on the Filters tab. You can click and drag the filter names to rearrange the filter order in the list, which specifies the rendering order for multiple filters. Rendering order affects your final results.

■ If you need more space to adjust sliders (or just to read the full name of some of the filter controls), you can expand the width of the columns containing the effect controls on the Filter, Control, and Motion tabs. Drag the column headers to adjust their width (**Figure 13.87**).

To adjust the position or duration of a filter in a clip:

Open the clip in the Viewer and click the Filters tab. Locate the Duration bar for the selected filter; then *do one of the following:*

◆ To set a filter's In and Out points within a clip, use the Arrow tool to drag the ends of the Duration bar (**Figure 13.88**). Default In and Out points are at either end of the Duration bar.

◆ Drag between the In and Out points on the Duration bar to slip the position of the filter's duration within the clip.

Using keyframes to animate filters

You can use keyframes to animate filter settings over time. Learn about keyframes in "Using Keyframes" earlier in this chapter.

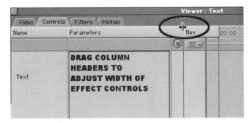

Figure 13.87 Drag the column headers on the Filter, Control, and Motion tabs to adjust the width of the effect controls.

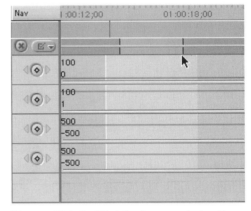

Figure 13.88 In the filter's keyframe graph, drag the ends of the Duration bar to set In and Out points for a filter.

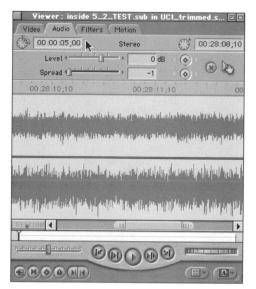

Figure 13.89 Make a short test clip from a representative section of your audio track.

Adjusting audio filters

Final Cut Pro's suite of audio filters are geared toward repairing problems in production audio. That's good, because production audio frequently has problems—problems that don't come to light until you're reviewing your footage in the editing room. FCP's equalization, compression, and noise reduction filters are tools you can use to reduce rumble in an exterior street recording or improve the crispness in a dialogue track (before you ask, there is no filter that will strip background music out of dialogue).

You apply FCP's audio filters in the same way that you apply video filters.

Like video filters, most audio filters in FCP have to be rendered before you can hear the results of your settings adjustment. Unfortunately, the lack of real-time feedback makes adjusting audio filters in FCP more challenging. Try the method described here to reduce the lag time between adjusting an audio filter's setting and hearing the results.

To adjust an audio filter's settings:

1. Make a short test clip from a representative section of your audio track (**Figure 13.89**). If you're trying to fix a problem, pick out a worst-case section and then maybe an average-case section to try your worst-case settings on. Make the section long enough so you can evaluate your work, say 5 to 10 seconds.

2. Open your test clip in the Viewer, apply the filter, and start tweaking the filter settings.

3. You'll hear a series of beeps (FCP's rendering indicator for audio) when your test clip requires rendering. You'll need to render the audio before you can hear the effect of the audio filter you've applied. Your short test clip should render quickly.

continues on next page

4. Enable looped playback and then try to get into a rhythm of adjusting, rendering, and listening. When you think you've zeroed in on your filter settings, copy and paste the filter (and its settings) from the test clip to your full-length audio track in the sequence (**Figure 13.90**). Use the Paste Attributes command to paste just the filters (**Figure 13.91**).

If you need more control over your audio tracks than you can get inside FCP, you can export your sequence audio tracks out of Final Cut Pro in Open Media Framework (OMF) format. The exported OMF file contains the audio files, plus the audio edit information from your project file. That means that you can export your audio tracks with the original track separations, edit points, cross-fades, and video sync intact and then import them into an OMF-compatible digital audio workstation (DAW), the kind used at most professional audio post-production facilities. For more information, see "Exporting Audio in OMF Format" in Chapter 11.

✔ Tips

- Audio filters applied to audio that is formatted as a stereo pair are applied to both channels equally, and only one set of controls appears on the Viewer's Filters tab.

- You can copy an audio filter and all of its current settings and paste it onto other clips or onto an entire nested sequence. If you perfect the EQ setting that cancels out the sound of your camera, you can easily apply the same filter setting wherever it's needed. See "Copying and pasting clip attributes" in Chapter 7.

- Chapter 17 of Apple's *Final Cut Pro 2 User's Manual* contains a complete list of FCP's audio filters and a 145-page chapter on working with audio in FCP.

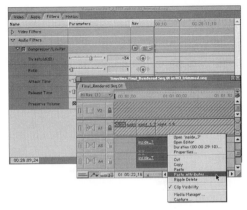

Figure 13.90 When you've tuned in filter settings, copy and then use the Paste Attributes command to paste the filter and its settings from the test clip to your full-length audio track in the sequence.

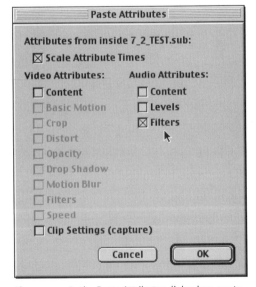

Figure 13.91 In the Paste Attributes dialog box, paste just the filters from your test audio clip onto the longer audio clip you're filtering.

Useful Filters

There's a boatload of filters in Final Cut Pro. Some of them do really useful and cool things that you might not normally associate with the idea of a "filter."

Here's the rundown of a few interesting ones that you might have missed:

Flop: A Perspective filter that flip-flops the image horizontally, vertically, or both directions at the same time. John Huston used this effect in his WWII documentary "The Battle of San Pietro" to keep the Allied Forces heading right-to-left, and the Axis Forces heading left-to-right, regardless of which direction they were actually moving.

De-interlace: A Video filter that can improve the stability of still images by duplicating either of the two fields that make up a video frame. De-interlace is also useful for correcting jittery high-speed movement, if you can accept a slightly softened image quality.

Timecode Print: A Video filter that simplifies making "window burns" (copies of your FCP sequence with visible timecode printed in the frame) for production outside of FCP, or for client review copies. Nest a sequence, apply this effect, and render a quick dub for your music composer. This effect can also be combined with the **View Finder** filter to simulate footage from security cameras, home cameras, or pre-production screen tests. Other filters in the Video group—**Blink, Strobe, and Image Stabilization**—are also interesting and can be applied creatively. Check 'em out.

Sepia: An Image Control filter that tints the clip to an old-time faded film color. Why use this filter when the Tint filter does that as well? Well, with Sepia, you can change the color in the same way as you can using the Tint filter, but you have the advantage of being able to tweak the contrast as well, which you can't do using the Tint filter. If you need to adjust color *and* contrast, why not have just one filter doing the math instead of two?

Echo and Reverb: Two Audio filters that help make that pickup dialogue you recorded in your bedroom sound believable when you cut it into the scene you shot in the gymnasium.

Boris Script LTD: An After Effects third-party filter for creating complex text effects. It's not in the usual place you find text generators. See "Creating titles with Boris Script LTD" later in this chapter.

Film Noise: This QuickTime filter adds hair, scratches, dust, and the look of old film to your video. Lots of people skip the dust and scratches completely and use Film Noise just for a faded-color-film look that renders quickly. This is not, however, a filter that can be found on the Effects tab in the Browser. To use Film Noise, you'll need to export your clip as a QuickTime movie and access the Filters as described in "To export a clip or sequence in another QuickTime format" in Chapter 11. Be sure to set your movie settings to match your audio and video sequence settings. Re-import your processed clip back into your project and enjoy your film noise.

APPLYING FILTERS

Compositing

Compositing can be any process that combines two or more image layers to create an effect. A compositing process can also include filters and motion that have been applied to modify individual layers or the composited image.

When you're compositing multiple layers and working with special effects, the program adjusts window size and position to give you ready access to images and controls in the Viewer, Canvas, and Timeline windows.

To arrange windows for compositing:

◆ Choose Window > Arrange > Compositing.

Setting Composite mode

A Composite mode is an algorithm, a mathematical formula that controls the way the colors in a clip will be combined with the clip colors in underlying video layers.

All compositing happens from the top down; the highest-numbered track's image sits on the front plane and obscures the image on a track beneath it, unless the foreground image is made transparent. Each clip's opacity setting influences the final effect of the Composite mode.

For a complete list of Final Cut Pro's Composite modes, refer to Chapter 20 of Apple's *Final Cut Pro 2 User's Manual.*

To set the Composite mode for a clip:

1. Select the clip in the Timeline.

2. Choose Modify > Composite Mode and then select a Composite mode from the submenu (**Figure 13.92**).

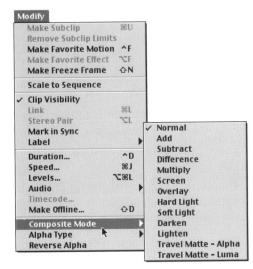

Figure 13.92 Choose Modify > Composite Mode and then select a composite mode from the submenu.

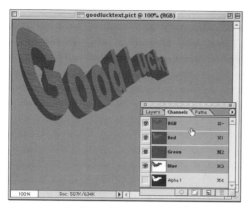

Figure 13.93 A still graphic image.

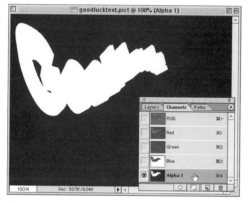

Figure 13.94 The graphic's alpha channel. With the alpha channel set to Straight, the black area will be interpreted as transparent.

Figure 13.95 The graphic frame superimposed over video. With the frame's alpha channel set to Straight, the black areas in the alpha channel shown in Figure 13.94 are made transparent in this figure, allowing the video background to show through.

Using alpha channels

An RGB image is composed of three 8-bit gray-scale images—the red, green, and blue color channels—that express color information as a gray scale: 256 brightness values (ranging from 0 for black to 255 for white), plus an alpha channel. An alpha channel is a fourth 8-bit channel that can be assigned to an RGB image to keep track of which areas of the image are transparent.

Figures 13.93, 13.94, and **13.95** illustrate the ways an alpha channel can be manipulated to mask selected areas in an image.

Alpha channels are useful critters with a variety of applications in digital imaging. Final Cut Pro video clips have alpha channels assigned to them; it's the alpha channel that's being manipulated when you adjust the opacity of a clip or apply a key or matte filter.

◆ When you import an image that has an alpha channel, Final Cut Pro interprets the clip's alpha channel and sets the alpha channel to Straight, Black, or White (corresponding to the background setting for the clip at the time the clip was created).

◆ When you place a clip in a sequence, Final Cut Pro automatically makes the alpha channel area transparent. You can override the automatic setting by modifying the alpha channel type.

◆ You can reverse an alpha channel if you want to invert the transparency of an image, or you can choose to ignore the clip's alpha channel altogether.

To view a clip's alpha channel:

◆ Choose View > Channel > Alpha.

To modify the alpha channel type:

1. Select the clip.

2. Choose Modify > Alpha Type and select a different alpha channel type from the submenu (**Figure 13.96**).

✔ Tip

■ DV clips will not retain their alpha channel information if you export them in a DV format. If you want to save a clip's alpha channel when you export, use the Animation codec, set to Millions Colors+. If you're exporting FCP elements to process in After Effects, this is the way to go. Use the Animation codec again when you export from After Effects.

Working with mattes

Mattes are filters that you shape to define which areas of opaque video clips are to be made transparent during compositing. For example, a circular matte can be used to isolate a clock face from its background, or a matte in the shape of a keyhole can be used to simulate peeking through a door keyhole.

In another example, say you have a video clip that shows a weather forecaster standing against a solid blue wall. A color key filter can matte out the solid color of the wall so that a clip with weather map graphics can be placed behind the forecaster.

There are many different types of matte filters. Some are "garbage mattes," used to quickly rough out large areas of the frame. Some are keys, a type of matte that uses a clip's color or luminance information to determine which opaque areas will be made transparent (bluescreen effects are created with color key mattes set to make blue areas transparent). And others are based on existing alpha channels of clips. You can combine layers of different types of mattes to create very complex composite shapes.

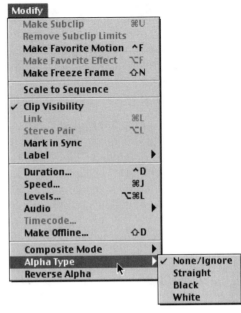

Figure 13.96 Choose Modify > Alpha Type and select a different alpha channel type from the submenu.

COMPOSITING

Figure 13.97 Drag your background clip to track V1.

Figure 13.98 Drag your matte clip to track V2. The white areas in this clip will define the opaque areas of the foreground clip.

To apply a matte:

1. *Do one of the following:*

   ▲ Drag the Key or Matte filter from the Browser's Effects tab and drop it on the clip in the Timeline.

   ▲ Select the clip in the Timeline, choose Effects > Video Filters, and select a filter from the Key or Matte submenu.

2. Position the playhead over a frame in the selected clip to see a preview of the effect in the Canvas.

Travel mattes

A travel matte allows one video clip to play through another. The alpha information in a third clip is used as a matte that defines the transparent and opaque areas of the composited image.

When you create a travel matte effect, there are usually three video tracks involved; this is sometimes called a "matte sandwich." The background clip is placed on V1, or the lowest video track available. The Matte clip, preferably a high-contrast grayscale motion clip or still image, goes on the video track just above the background clip, on V2, and the foreground clip sits on V3, or the video track above the Matte clip. A Composite mode specifically for creating travel mattes, called Luma, is applied to the foreground clip. If the matte clip is placed on video track V1 without a background clip, then the background is automatically black.

To create a travel matte:

1. In the Timeline, drag your background clip (**Figure 13.97**) to V1.

2. Drag the clip selected to be the matte clip (**Figure 13.98**) to V2.

continues on next page

COMPOSITING

3. Drag your foreground clip (**Figure 13.99**) to V34. To establish the travel matte, select the foreground clip on V3 (**Figure 13.100**) and choose Modify > Composite Mode > Travel Matte – Luma.

The completed travel matte effect (**Figure 13.101**) uses the matte clip's luminance (or grayscale) levels as the mask. The matte clip's black area creates the shape of the foreground clip's transparent areas, and the matte clip's white area creates the shape of the foreground clip's opaque areas—that's where you see the foreground clip's video.

✔ Tips

■ After you composite your travel matte, you can refine the effect by adjusting the matte clip's brightness and contrast.

■ You can apply motion filters and effects, as well as any other standard clip motion, to the travel matte in V2 for some very interesting looks.

■ Play with Edge Feather and Edge Thin to soften the halo effect you might find around your matted objects when working with Color Keys.

■ DV video is not the best video format for creating effects that require critical color key mattes, for example, blue or green-screen effects. DV compression throws out too much color information to give you the best control over edges.

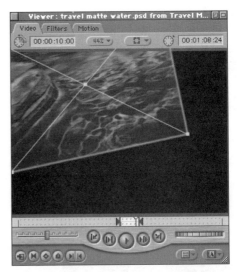

Figure 13.99 Place your foreground clip on track V3.

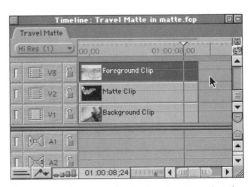

Figure 13.100 To composite the travel matte, select the foreground clip on V3 and choose Modify > Composite Mode > Travel Matte – Luma. The foreground clip on V3 is now composited with the matte clip on V2.

Figure 13.101 The completed travel matte effect.

COMPOSITING

Using Generators

Generators are a class of effects that create (or generate) new video information rather than modify existing video. After you have generated it by rendering, a generated clip can be used just like any other clip. Text is a high-profile member of the generator class of effects; how to use the text generator to produce titles is covered later in this chapter.

Final Cut Pro's generators include the following:

- Bars and Tone, which generates NTSC or PAL color bars and includes a 1-KHz audio tone. (There are no controls for this effect.)

- Matte, which generates solid single-color clips.

- Render, which generates color gradients and different types of "noise."

- Slug, which generates solid black (0 IRE) frames and silent audio. (There are no controls for this effect.)

- Text, which generates simple titles using TrueType fonts you have loaded in your system.

Always Be Title Safe!

Every TV set is different: different colors, different screen geometries, different projection skews—never the same color, never the same combinations. Since even the middle area of the screen is not reliably centered (especially on home sets!), it's important to keep your text and graphics elements within a screen area that television engineers call *title safe*.

With the Title Safe overlay on, you will see two boxes superimposed on your clip—the inside border outlines the Title Safe boundary. Keep your graphic elements inside this box, and you'll know that the edges won't get cropped off, even on consumer TVs. The slightly larger box surrounding the Title Safe boundary is known as the Action Safe boundary. Any visual elements critical to your project should not occur outside the Action Safe region.

For details on turning Title Safe mode on or off, see "Viewing Title and Action Safe boundaries" in Chapter 5.

When creating graphic elements in an external program (such as Photoshop), remember to respect the Title Safe area. Import a quick test screen into Final Cut Pro before you invest too much time on your layout.

One final note: Title Safe and Action Safe areas apply only to program material display on a TV (both NTSC and PAL). If you plan on showing your FCP project on the Web or other computer-based format, remember that Web video will display the entire frame, so check the edges of your frame for unexpected surprises—microphones, shadows, dolly grips, and so on. The same caveats apply if you're compositing a Picture in Picture (PiP) effect: every pixel in your frame will be included. (In fact, a PiP effect is likely to show some of the edges of the technical part of the video stream, so try experimenting with cropping a pixel or two into your clip or adding a border.)

To add a generator to a sequence:

1. In the Viewer, choose an item from the Generator pop-up menu in the lower-right corner (**Figure 13.102**).

   The generator effect is loaded into the Viewer as an unrendered clip.

2. Click the Controls tab to access the generator controls.

3. Adjust the generator's controls (**Figure 13.103**); then click the Video tab to view the generator clip in the Viewer.

4. Edit the generator into your sequence just as you would a clip.

5. Render your generated clip. You must render it before you can play it back. Select the clip; then choose Sequence > Render Selection.

✔ Tip

■ When you are configuring settings for a generator clip, it's much easier to see what you're doing if you drag the generator clip's Controls tab out of the Viewer window first. Now you can view the generator image on the Viewer's Video tab as you configure the settings on the Controls tab.

To edit a generator in a sequence:

1. Double-click the generator clip in the Timeline to open it in the Viewer.

2. Click the Controls tab; then make your adjustments.

Figure 13.102 Choose a generator from the Generator pop-up menu in the lower-right corner of the Viewer window.

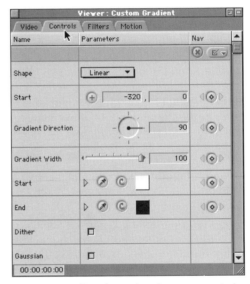

Figure 13.103 Adjust the settings for your generated clip on the clip's Controls tab.

Always Be Color Safe!

It's a fact of life: It's easy to produce video with colors and luminance levels that look great on your Macintosh, but look scary, overblown, and distorted on a home television set. With DV cameras and properly calibrated analog tapes, you shouldn't need to worry about their levels, but images created in the computer need to be created correctly. Many colors, including black, white, and quite a few reds, are considered outside the color-safe guidelines. While this may not matter so much if you are creating content for the Web, it will matter if you are intending your masterpiece to be premiered on broadcast or cable TV.

Use the built-in vectorscope and waveform monitor (on the Clip Settings tab of the Log and Capture window) to check levels on your video output. Although you can't adjust DV video levels as you're capturing, you can at least watch your levels on previously captured video clips.

Marked on the waveform monitor are levels of IRE—a unit of luminance. DV video IRE levels can range from –10 to 110, but the NTSC legal limits (in the United States) are a strict 7.5 to 100 IRE. When you produce external graphics, you will want to keep your IRE and color saturation within the sight of the scopes. It's easy to exceed NTSC broadcast limits; Photoshop and other programs allow you to create images with colors and levels well outside the legal broadcast limits. Make sure to apply the Photoshop NTSC Colors filter before saving your final artwork. See "Recommendations for creating artwork" later in this chapter.

Be sure to check your work on an external TV monitor as you proceed. The best way to get out of trouble is not to get in.

Of course, if your project is really headed for national broadcast, you might want to bring your tapes and EDL to a professional post-production house for a proper online session, where all the technical demands of broadcast TV can be honored in style.

For more information on FCP's role in handling the conversion of digital video lvels to analog video levels, see Apple Tech Info Library article # 60864, "Final Cut Pro: About Luminance", available online at the Apple web site: http://til.info.apple.com/techinfo.nsf/artnum/n60864.

USING GENERATORS

Generating Text

Use text generators to create text elements and title screens in Final Cut Pro. A text generator can create titles using any TrueType font currently loaded in your System Folder. You can specify text size, style, color, tracking, and kerning.

Final Cut Pro offers six text generator options, available from the Viewer's Generator pop-up menu (**Figure 13.104**):

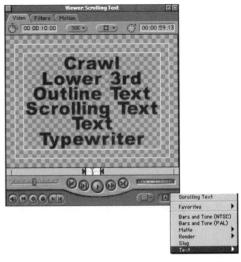

Figure 13.104 Six text generator options are available from the Generator pop-up menu in the Viewer window.

◆ **Text:** Generates static text in a single size and style. This option allows carriage returns.

◆ **Lower 3rd:** Generates two lines of static text. Each line has separate font, style, and size controls. The Lower 3rd generator is designed to create the standard titles used to identify interview subjects in news and documentary programs.

◆ **Crawl:** Generates a single line of animated text that scrolls horizontally across the screen. Crawl speed is determined by the duration of the clip. A longer clip duration results in a slower crawl speed.

◆ **Outline Text:** Generates static text with an adjustable outline stroke and background matte. You can also matte graphics into the text, outline, or background elements.

◆ **Scrolling Text:** Generates animated text that scrolls vertically up or down the screen. A longer clip duration results in a slower scrolling speed. Scrolling text allows carriage returns.

◆ **Typewriter:** Generates animated text that appears on the screen one letter at a time, as if typed.

Assembly-Line Text Generation

If you have a big stack of title or text screens to produce, this assembly-line production technique may help:

1. To produce a title template, create a standard text generator that specifies all basic formatting: font, size, color, position, and so on. Save it as a Favorite Effect.

2. Select all the clips that get titled and apply your template Favorite to all of them in one operation.

3. Choose File > Open and open a text document window that contains all your title copy.

4. Open your text generator clips one at a time; then copy and paste from the title copy in the text window to the Text field in the text generator clip.

These built-in generators are the simplest means of adding text to your sequences, but there are some limitations: Although text generators offer extensive control over the font, size, style, and positioning of text, with the exception of the Lower 3rd generator, you're limited to a single font per text generator.

You can edit a text generator clip into a sequence in the Timeline and apply effects, just as with other clips. You can also animate static text by using keyframes to make dynamic adjustments to your text generator's effects parameters.

Your animation applies to all text in the generator—you cannot individually control each letter, word, or sentence.

✔ Tip

- The simplest way to fade titles in and out is to keyframe opacity at the head and tail of the text generator clip. If you're building a title sequence, you can save your fade in/fade out opacity settings as a Motion Favorite, or copy and paste attributes to ensure a consistent look.

Complex Text: Other Options

If you need to build more complex text elements, your best bet is to use the (free) Boris Script LTD filter that is included on your Final Cut Pro CD. This filter offers a number of additional titling features you can use within FCP. For more information, see "Creating titles with Boris Script LTD" later in this chapter.

Here's another option: Create your text outside of FCP in a professional graphics program, such as Adobe's Photoshop, Illustrator, or After Effects, or Macromedia FreeHand, and then import the text elements as motion clips.

Advanced third-party plug-ins, such as Boris Script, Red, or Graffiti, are all-in-one solutions that allow you to create complex elements while remaining within FCP.

GENERATING TEXT

Text generator options checklist

On the Controls tab, you can specify the following text control settings (**Figure 13.105**):

◆ **Text:** Enter your text in this field or cut and paste from a word processing program.

◆ **Font:** Choose a font from this pop-up menu.

◆ **Size:** Use the slider or enter a point size for your type; values are expressed in pixels.

◆ **Style:** Choose a font style (Plain, Bold, Italic, and so on) from this pop-up menu.

◆ **Alignment:** Choose Center, Left, or Right alignment from this pop-up menu.

◆ **Font color:** Click the triangle at the left to reveal the full set of color controls; then *do one of the following:*

  ▲ Drag the hue, saturation, and brightness sliders to new values.

  ▲ Enter color values numerically in the text fields.

  ▲ Click the eyedropper and click in the Canvas to sample a color.

  ▲ Click the color swatch and use one of the color pickers to select a color.

◆ **Origin:** Click the Point Select (+) button (located to the left of the Origin value field) and then specify new coordinates for your text's origin point relative to the frame by clicking the new Origin location in the Canvas or on the Video tab of the Viewer. Animating the Origin point (rather than the Center point) of your text allows you to position your text at a starting point outside your frame.

◆ **Tracking:** Use the slider or enter a value to specify the space between letters.

◆ **Leading:** Use the slider or enter a value to specify the space between lines of text.

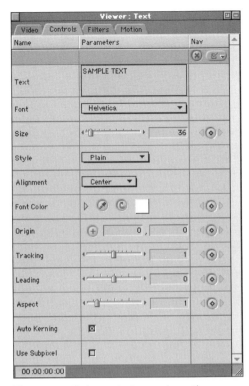

Figure 13.105 Style your text generator on the Viewer's Controls tab.

GENERATING TEXT

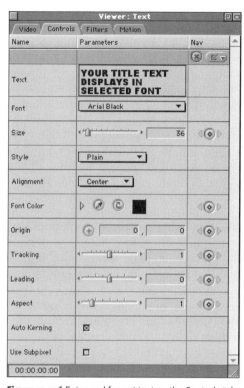

Figure 13.106 Enter and format text on the Controls tab.

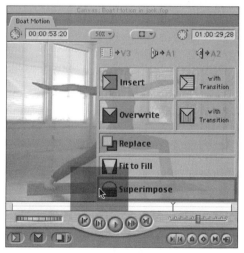

Figure 13.107 Drop the text clip on the Superimpose area of the edit overlay. A Superimpose edit automatically places your text clip on a new Timeline track above the target track, starting at the sequence In point.

◆ **Aspect:** Use the slider or enter a value to specify the height-to-width proportion of your selected font.

◆ **Auto Kerning:** Check the box to enable automatic adjustment of the spacing between individual letters.

◆ **Use Subpixel:** Check the box to enable subpixel accuracy in your rendered text generator. Subpixel rendering takes longer.

To generate a basic title screen:

1. To generate a title screen, *do one of the following:*

   ▲ From the Generator pop-up menu in the lower right of the Viewer window, choose Text.

   ▲ On the Browser's Effects tab, choose Text from the Video Generator bin.

   The text generator appears in the Viewer.

2. In the Viewer, click the Controls tab to access the generator's controls; then specify your text control settings as outlined in the previous section, "Text generator options checklist" (**Figure 13.106**).

   Although you can use keyframes to animate parameters such as size, origin point, colors, and tracking, you can specify only one font per text generator.

3. Click back to the Viewer's Video tab and edit the text clip into your sequence in the Timeline. If you want to superimpose your text over video, choose the Superimpose edit type when you perform your edit (**Figure 13.107**).

   You can edit, filter, and animate text clips as you would any other video element.

   continues on next page

GENERATING TEXT

✔ Tips

■ Text size should be larger than 24 points if you want your text to be legible. Always check your type on an actual television monitor (if you are outputting for home viewing on videotape, preferably test it on the absolute worst-case television set and VCR you can find in the nearest back alley junkyard.)

■ Don't forget the simple drop-shadow effect found on the Motion tab of any clip. Try animating it over time. With some tweaks, you can create a professional-quality drop shadow that will really pop your title out from any background.

The wonders of outline text

The Outline Text generator offers three customizable elements in one text generator: text, an outline stroke, and a rectangular background matte (**Figure 13.108**)—perfect for punching titles over hard-to-read backgrounds or creating subtitles that maintain their legibility. You can insert clips into any of the three elements by dropping the clip on the element's clip well on the Controls tab; the clip's image will be matted into the outline text element you specify (**Figure 13.109**).

Figure 13.108 The Outline Text generator is composed of three customizable elements: text, an outline stroke, and a rectangular background matte.

Figure 13.109 You can matte graphics into any of the generator's three elements. This composition has a clip matted into the text element.

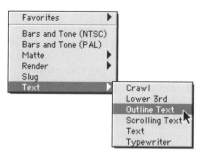

Figure 13.110 Choose Outline Text from the Viewer's Generator pop-up menu.

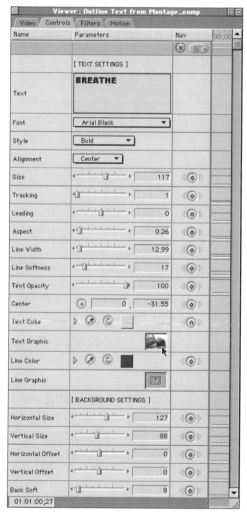

Figure 13.111 Specify your text control settings as outlined in the "Text generator options checklist."

To create outline text:

1. To generate an outline text title, *do one of the following:*

   ▲ From the Generator pop-up menu in the lower right of the Viewer window, choose Outline Text (**Figure 13.110**).

   ▲ On the Browser's Effects tab, choose Outline Text from the Video Generator bin.

   The new Outline Text generator appears in the Viewer.

2. In the Viewer, click the Controls tab to access the generator's controls; then specify your text control settings as outlined earlier in the section "Text generator options checklist" (**Figure 13.111**).

3. You can also specify any of the following outline text parameters:

   ▲ **Line Width:** Specify the width of the text's outline.

   ▲ **Line Softness:** Specify the amount of edge feathering applied to the text's outline.

   ▲ **Text Opacity:** Specify the text's transparency level.

   ▲ **Center:** Specify (X,Y) coordinates for the text's center point.

   ▲ **Text Color:** Select a color for the text.

   ▲ **Text Graphic:** Drag and drop a graphic clip to be matted into the text element.

   ▲ **Line Color:** Select a color for the text's outline.

   ▲ **Line Graphic:** Drag and drop a graphic clip to be matted into the outline element.

continues on next page

GENERATING TEXT

4. Use the sliders in the Background settings section to specify size, edge feathering, opacity, color, and graphic for an optional rectangular matte that sits behind the text and outline. The default Size values are set to zero, so you must increase the Size settings to see the background matte.

5. Click back to the Viewer's Video tab and edit the text clip into your sequence in the Timeline. If you want to superimpose your text over video, choose the Superimpose edit type when you perform your edit.

✔ Tip

■ You can drop a motion clip into the clip well, and moving video will appear inside the element you've specified. But the circumstances under which you can use motion clips in the Outline Text generator are quite limited. The outline text clip will need to be put on the V2 track in the Timeline, with a motion clip under it on the V1 track, and you can't specify the In and Out points of the motion clip. Bug or feature?

Using Animated Text Generators

Final Cut Pro offers three animated text generators: Scrolling Text, Crawl, and Typewriter. These generators offer the font styling and positioning controls of the static text generators, plus simple animation routines built into the generator. You set up the animation on the text generator's Control tab.

Like the other parameters on the generator's Control tab, the animation controls can be keyframed to change over time, but you don't need to use keyframes at all to throw together a simple scroll, crawl, or typewriter title effect.

Because these animated titles typically start offscreen, you will not see any text onscreen if your playhead is parked at the beginning or end of the clip. You will need to scrub the playhead through the clip to see how your animated title is shaping up.

Creating scrolls

Scrolls are most often found as credit sequences at the end of a show (or at the beginning of *Star Wars* parodies). Scrolling text displays a lot of information in a little time, but take care not to roll your text too quickly. If you set your scroll speed too high, the titles will stutter (won't appear to scroll smoothly), and no one will be able to read them.

There are several ways to create the scrolling graphic elements. The easiest is to use the Scrolling Text generator found in the Video Generator list, but if you plan to use multiple fonts or specialized tracking, sizing, and kerning, then your best bet is to use the free Boris Script LTD filter found on your Final Cut Pro CD. See "Creating titles with Boris Script LTD" later in this section.

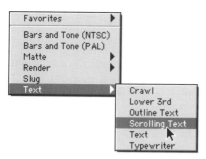

Figure 13.112 Choose Scrolling Text from the Viewer's Generator pop-up menu.

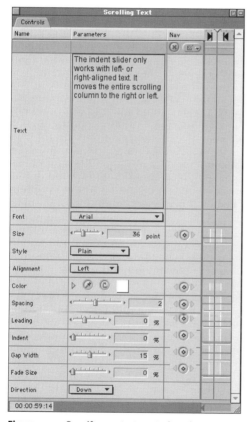

Figure 13.113 Specify your text control settings as outlined in the "Text generator options checklist."

To generate a scrolling text title:

1. *Do one of the following:*

   ▲ From the Generator Pop-up menu in the lower right of the Viewer window, choose Scrolling Text (**Figure 13.112**).

   ▲ On the Browser's Effects tab, choose Scrolling Text from the Video Generator bin.

   The Scrolling Text generator appears in the Viewer.

2. In the Viewer, click the Controls tab to access the generator's controls; then specify your text control settings as outlined earlier in the section "Text generator options checklist" (**Figure 13.113**).

3. You can also specify any of the following scrolling text parameters:

   ▲ **Spacing:** Use the slider or enter a value to specify the space between letters (as with Tracking).

   ▲ **Leading:** Use the slider or enter a value to specify the space between lines of text.

   ▲ **Indent:** Use the slider or enter a value to set the X axis (left-right) positioning of the scroll's aligned edge, expressed as a percentage of the screen. Indent is enabled only for left or right-aligned scrolls. The title-safe area begins inside 10% of the screen.

   ▲ **Gap Width:** Use the slider or enter a value to specify the width of the gap between any two text entries separated by an asterisk (*) symbol.

   ▲ **Fade Size:** Use the slider or enter a value to set the vertical display area of your scrolling text, expressed as a percentage of the screen. The scrolling

continues on next page

USING ANIMATED TEXT GENERATORS

text will fade in as it enters (and fade out as it exits) the vertical display area you specify.

▲ **Direction:** Choose Up or Down from this pop-up menu to specify the direction in which the generated text will scroll.

4. Click back to the Viewer's Video tab and edit the text clip into your sequence in the Timeline. If you want to superimpose your text over video, choose the Superimpose edit type when you perform your edit.

✔ Tip

■ Use the Gap Width setting to create a double-column credit scroll with a center gutter. Here's how: Set the Gap width parameter to specify the width of the gap between any two text entries separated by an asterisk (*) symbol. When you assemble the text for your credit scroll, type *Production Credit*Name*, for example `Visual Effects*Xochi Studios`, and the gutter in your credit scroll will be set to the Gap Width value.
How*about*that?

Creating crawl titles

Like the stock market tickertape creeping along at the bottom of your TV screen, a text crawl is an animated title that scrolls horizontally. Text crawls can be useful for displaying short phrases—but keep them short, unless you are trying to annoy your audience.

Stuttering is more pronounced during a text crawl than during any other type of text effect. Take care to test your crawl on an NTSC monitor and watch for optical jumpiness. Possible remedies include using a wider-stroked font, a larger font size, a slower crawl speed, or motion blur.

USING ANIMATED TEXT GENERATORS

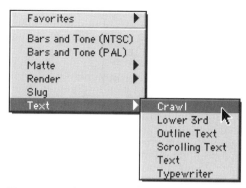

Figure 13.114 Choose Crawl from the Viewer's Generator pop-up menu.

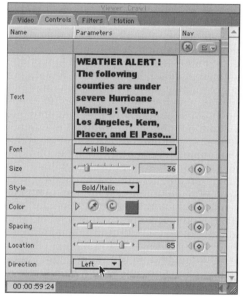

Figure 13.115 On the generator's Controls tab, specify your text control settings as outlined in the "Text generator options checklist."

To generate a crawl text title:

1. *Do one of the following:*

   ▲ From the Generator Pop-up menu in the lower right of the Viewer window, choose Crawl (**Figure 13.114**).

   ▲ On the Browser's Effects tab, choose Crawl from the Video Generator bin.

   The Crawl Text generator appears in the Viewer.

2. In the Viewer, click the Controls tab to access the generator's controls; then specify your text control settings as outlined earlier in the section "Text generator options checklist" (**Figure 13.115**).

3. You can also specify any of the following crawl text parameters:

   ▲ **Spacing:** Use the slider or enter a value to specify the space between letters (as with Tracking).

   ▲ **Location:** Use the slider or enter a value to specify the Y axis (top-bottom) positioning of your crawl.

   ▲ **Direction:** Choose Left or Right from this pop-up menu to specify the direction in which the generated text will scroll.

4. Click back to the Viewer's Video tab and edit the text clip into your sequence in the Timeline. If you want to superimpose your text over video, choose the Superimpose edit type when you perform your edit.

Creating animated typewriter text

The cute little Typewriter Text generator automates the animation of single letters popping onto the screen; that's why it's called Typewriter. It's a real timesaver, as anybody who has manually animated simulated typing will tell you.

To generate a typewriter text title:

1. *Do one of the following:*
   - ▲ From the Generator Pop-up menu in the lower right of the Viewer window, choose Typewriter (**Figure 13.116**).
   - ▲ On the Browser's Effects tab, choose Typewriter from the Video Generator bin.

   The Typewriter Text generator appears in the Viewer.

2. In the Viewer, click the Controls tab to access the generator's controls; then specify your text control settings as outlined earlier in the section "Text generator options checklist" (**Figure 13.117**).

3. You can also specify any of the following typewriter text parameters:
   - ▲ **Spacing:** Use the slider or enter a value to specify the space between letters (as with Tracking).
   - ▲ **Location:** Use the slider or enter a value to specify the Y axis (top-bottom) positioning of your text element.
   - ▲ **Indent:** Use the slider or enter a value to specify the X axis (left-right) positioning of your text element, expressed as a percentage of the screen.

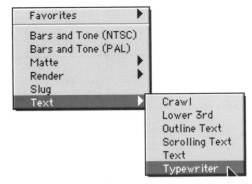

Figure 13.116 Choose Typewriter from the Viewer's Generator pop-up menu.

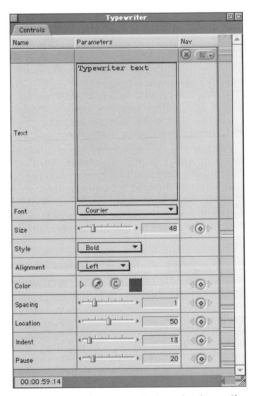

Figure 13.117 On the generator's Controls tab, specify your text control settings as outlined in the "Text generator options checklist."

▲ **Pause:** Use the slider or enter a value to specify the timing of your type-writer animation. A larger Pause value results in a longer hold at the end of the clip. The speed of the type-on effect is calculated based on the over-all duration of the generator clip minus the pause value you set here.

4. Click back to the Viewer's Video tab and edit the text clip into your sequence in the Timeline. If you want to superimpose your text over video, choose the Superimpose edit type when you perform your edit.

✔ Tips

■ If you're looking for an old-fashioned typewriter font, try Courier.

■ Use a techno-style font like Andale Mono or VT 100 for simulating computer input (and don't forget the Blink filter!).

■ Keyframing the Pause value of your Typewriter Text generator will vary the rate that the letters appear on the screen and give your typing a nice human touch.

Creating titles with Boris Script LTD

Boris Script LTD, a limited-feature version of Boris Script, is a third-party filter plug-in available for installation from your Final Cut Pro CD. You'll find Boris in the Third Party Demo Software folder.

Unlike the FCP text generators, which you select from the Generator pop-up menu, Boris Script is a filter. You must apply the Boris Script filter to the clip. (You can gener-ate a slug or matte clip if you want your title to have a plain background). You access the Boris Script controls in the same way you access any filter you apply to a clip.

Boris Script may appear on the Filter tab, but it offers the capabilities of a specialized titling application.

Here's a rundown of features. You can:

◆ Enter text in a larger text-entry field.

◆ Create static titles.

◆ Set font, size, style, and color properties for individual characters.

◆ Apply drop shadows and borders.

◆ Create auto-animated rolls and crawls.

◆ Choose from other 2D title animation options.

◆ Copy and paste text from a word proces-sor program.

Note that you can set individual parameters such as font, size, colors, and tracking for every character, but you can cannot animate individual character properties over time. You can, however, keyframe changes in motion properties, roll, crawl, rotation, scale, and opacity for the entire text block.

For more information about Boris Script LTD, see the "Script LTD User Manual," an Acrobat PDF file, on the Final Cut Pro CD.

USING ANIMATED TEXT GENERATORS

To create a title using the Boris Script LTD filter:

1. Follow the instructions for installing Boris Script LTD from your Final Cut Pro CD.

2. In the Timeline, select the clip you want to superimpose text on. If you want your title to appear over a plain background, generate a slug or color matte clip and edit it into the sequence.

3. Choose Effects > Video Filters > AE Effects > Boris > Boris Script LTD.

4. Double-click the clip to open it in the Viewer; then click the Filters tab.

   The Boris Script FX filter appears on the Filters tab of the Viewer.

5. On the Filters tab, click the Text Entry & Text Style logo to open the filter's Text window; then specify your text settings (**Figure 13.118**). Click the tabs on the left side of the Text window to access more settings options.

6. When you are finished entering and styling your text, click Apply in the bottom-right corner of the Text window to apply your changes and close the window. Your title appears in the Canvas.

7. Back on the Filter tab, you can specify more Boris Script filter settings, including keyframes for animation.

✔ Tip

■ The simplest way to use Boris Script LTD to create titles on a blank transparent clip is to apply it to a standard text generator clip and then delete the "Sample Text" text from the text entry field on the text generator's Controls tab. Your Boris clip will be labeled "Text" when it's in the Timeline, and by placing the text clip with the Boris filter on a higher track, you can superimpose a single Boris Script title across a series of clips in your sequence.

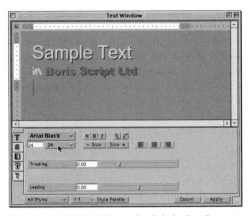

Figure 13.118 On the Filters tab, click the Text Entry & Text Style logo to open the Boris Script LTD filter's Text window; then specify your text settings.

Creating Artwork in Adobe Photoshop

Adobe Photoshop is a highly recommended tool for creating graphic elements for use in Final Cut Pro. Its file format compatibility with Final Cut Pro makes importing your artwork's layers and alpha channels easy.

Recommendations for creating artwork

Images that look beautiful in print or on a computer screen may not display well on a television monitor. The NTSC broadcast video standard cannot tolerate extreme contrast shifts on many of the colors that you can create and display in Photoshop. However, Photoshop comes with a filter that you can apply to your artwork to make it color safe for TV sets.

For more information, see "Always be Color-Safe!" earlier in this chapter.

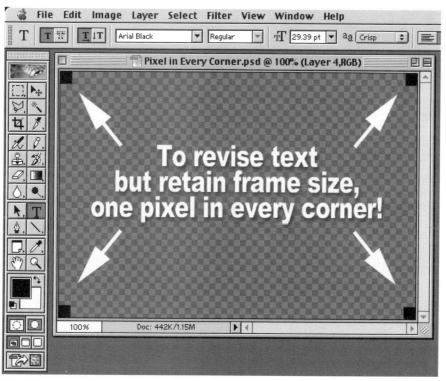

Figure 13.119 Place a single nontransparent pixel in each corner of each layer of your Photoshop composition. If you need to revise your Photoshop text later, those corner pixels will maintain a constant frame size, and when you re-import or reconnect your revised Photoshop file, FCP will recalculate your previously applied effects with the correct frame size. Hey—it's a workaround.

FCP Protocol: Updating Photoshop Files in FCP

It's easy to import Adobe Photoshop files into FCP, but if you need to make a change to a Photoshop file you've already used in a sequence, there are some hoops to jump through. Get ready to jump....

When you import a multilayer PS file into your FCP project for the first time, Final Cut Pro constructs a description of this file that includes the number of layers and the frame size of each layer.

First hoop: It's not easy to get Final Cut to update its description data of your Photoshop file. If you revise your existing PS file in Photoshop and save changes in the original file, you may not see the changes reflected when you return to Final Cut Pro. FCP protocol dictates that the original proxy description of your PS file is used.

How do you get FCP to refresh its memory and update your PS file's description? Suggested workarounds include:

◆ After you've revised your Photoshop file, rename the file when you save your changes and then re-import it into FCP. Because you're re-importing the file with a new name, FCP will create a new description of your PS file. The good news? Your Photoshop file revisions are showing up in FCP. The bad news? Now you have to manually replace the PS file with the revised file everywhere you've used it.

◆ If your PS file has the same number of layers, and those layers have the same frame size, you should be able to select the PS clip wherever you've used it in your sequence and then use the Reconnect Media command to manually reintroduce the clip and the PS source media file.

Second hoop: FCP uses the frame size data it recorded when you first imported your PS file in all effect calculations that use X,Y coordinates—motion paths, scaling, warp filters, and so on. However (get ready to jump...), FCP does not include transparent pixels when it calculates a PS layer's frame size. Say you have created text on a transparent background in Photoshop, imported your PS file into FCP, and then applied effects. Should you need to revise your text when you return to it, the frame size of your text layer has changed. Even if you successfully reconnect your revised PS file to your FCP sequence, FCP will use the data description from the original import (with the old frame size) to calculate your effects. The result? Your text effects will look distorted, and you'll briefly consider quitting the business.

There's a workaround for this dilemma. It's not pretty, but you can save yourself some headaches down the road by anticipating changes to your text. Get ready to jump....

◆ When you build your original Photoshop file, place a single nontransparent pixel in each corner of the frame (**Figure 13.119**). You'll need to do this for each and every layer. FCP will use the rectangle created by those four placeholder pixels to calculate the frame size. You can change text to your heart's content inside the bounding box created by the four corner pixels, and your FCP frame size will not change. So if you can reconnect your PS file, your effects will be calculated with the correct frame size data.

◆ The best workaround? Once you've imported your PS graphics, don't change your mind. Or get ready to jump....

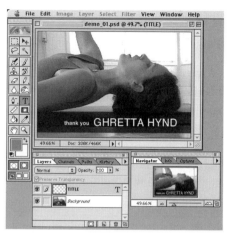

Figure 13.120 Open your file in Adobe Photoshop.

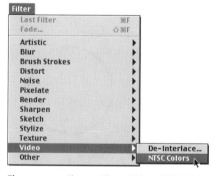

Figure 13.121 Choose Filter > Video > NTSC Colors.

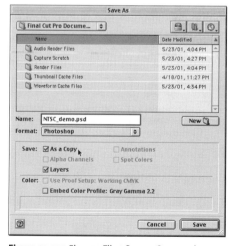

Figure 13.122 Choose File > Save a Copy and name your NTSC-ready Photoshop file; then click Save.

To make artwork NTSC color safe in Photoshop:

1. Open the file in Adobe Photoshop (**Figure 13.120**).

2. Select a layer that you will be using in your Final Cut Pro sequence.

3. Choose Filter > Video > NTSC Colors (**Figure 13.121**).

4. Repeat steps 2 and 3 for each layer you will be using in Final Cut Pro. The NTSC filter must be applied individually to each layer.

5. Save your Photoshop file as a copy, name your NTSC-ready Photoshop file, and click Save (**Figure 13.122**).

✔ Tip

■ Applying the NTSC Colors filter to your Photoshop file should be the very last step in your process. If you modify colors, contrast, or brightness after you've applied the NTSC Colors filter and then use the filter a second time, you duplicate the effects of the filter on your original graphic elements. Save a version of your Photoshop file before you apply the NTSC filter. If you need to modify the file later, make your adjustments to the prefiltered version (and don't forget to save a copy of your new version before you apply the NTSC filter!).

Setting the target resolution

Target resolution refers to the actual pixel count of an image's frame size in its final delivery (or target) format. The best way to preserve image quality in digital image formats is to maintain the same frame size and resolution from beginning to end. You will get best results by creating your art with the required pixel dimensions in mind, but if you

continues on next page

create artwork on a computer for display on broadcast television, you'll find that you must jump through a few hoops.

The native frame size of DV is 720 by 480 pixels. However, if you create your artwork in Photoshop at that size, your image looks squeezed when it's displayed on a TV monitor after printing to video. This is because of a difference in the pixel aspect ratio between the computer world and the broadcast television world.

Computer monitors use square pixels, where the height is perfectly proportional to the width. NTSC television monitors use a system that has a nonsquare pixel aspect ratio of 1.33:1, where the height is just a little bit greater than the width.

To accommodate the difference between these two frame sizes, you must create your full-frame graphic elements at a slightly larger size than your target resolution and then size them down to the target resolution in Photoshop before you import your image into Final Cut Pro.

To create a Photoshop file at DV NTSC target resolution:

1. In Photoshop, choose File > New; or press Command-N.

2. Enter a width of 720 pixels, a height of 534 pixels, and a resolution of 72 pixels per inch (**Figure 13.123**).

   This ratio of 720:534, or 1.33, is the proper proportion for creating text and graphics that will look the same on your NTSC monitor as on your computer monitor.

3. Create your image file (**Figure 13.124**).

4. Save the file as your original image file.

   Use this original graphic file to make any subsequent changes to the artwork.

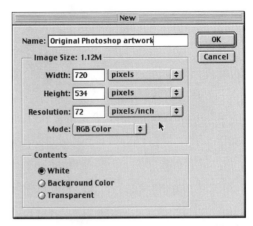

Figure 13.123 In the New dialog box, enter a width of 720 pixels, a height of 534 pixels, and a resolution of 72 pixels per inch.

Figure 13.124 The original Photoshop image at 720 by 534 pixels, before resizing.

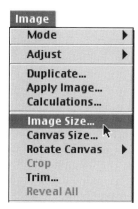

Figure 13.125 Choose Image > Image Size.

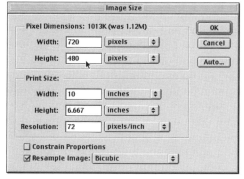

Figure 13.126 In the Image Size dialog box, specify a width of 720 pixels and a height of 480 pixels.

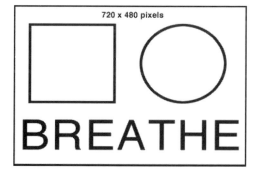

Figure 13.127 The "squashed" Photoshop image at 720 by 480 pixels, after resizing.

5. Choose Image > Image Size (**Figure 13.125**).

6. In the Image Size dialog box, uncheck Constrain Proportions to turn off this option.

7. In the Pixel Dimensions section, enter a width of 720 pixels and a height of 480 pixels (**Figure 13.126**).

8. Click OK.

   The vertical aspect of the image shrinks, which makes it look squashed (**Figure 13.127**).

9. Save the file as your production graphic file. Use this production graphic file in your project.

10. If you make need to make changes to the artwork, use the original graphic file, which has the unaltered aspect ratio; then when you're ready to save, repeat steps 4 through 9.

✔ Tips

- You don't have to import an entire full-screen image if your image uses only a small portion of the frame. Arrange your elements in position in full-screen format, resize for the pixel aspect ratio difference, and then crop down the artwork.

- You can import a variety of file formats, but the most common are the native Photoshop format (for images with multiple layers) and the standard PICT format (for single-layer images with alpha channels).

- You can also resize imported graphics clips and sequences in Final Cut Pro, but you'll get better results using Photoshop's bicubic scaling for resizing because it uses a better resampling algorithm.

Importing a Photoshop file into Final Cut Pro

Adobe Photoshop files are imported into Final Cut Pro with their original layer, Opacity mode, and Composite mode settings preserved. Layer effects and masks are not imported.

When you import a layered Photoshop file into Final Cut Pro, it appears in the Browser as a new sequence. You can double-click to see it in the Timeline, where you can choose individual layers to manipulate. Each layer is found on its own video track. If you want to treat an individual Photoshop layer as a clip, you can drag individual layers out of the Photoshop sequence, and drop them into a bin or into another sequence. They will appear as clips.

For more information, see "Importing layered Photoshop files" in Chapter 3.

Because layered Photoshop files are treated as sequences in Final Cut Pro, you should review a few protocol tips before you start editing. For more information, see "Working with Multiple Sequences" in Chapter 12.

To import a Photoshop file:

1. Choose File > Import > File; or press Command-I.

2. Navigate to the folder where you saved your Photoshop file, select it, and click Open.
   The Photoshop file appears in the Browser.

✔ Tip

■ If you're unsure about whether your image is going to be displayed in its proper proportions on an NTSC monitor, import an early test into Final Cut Pro and display it on your monitor to check your work.

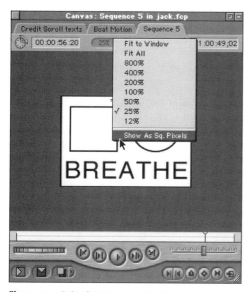

Figure 13.128 On the Canvas, select Show as Square Pixels from the View selector pop-up menu.

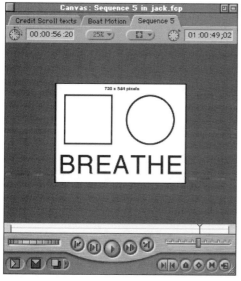

Figure 13.129 With Show as Square Pixels checked, the Canvas image simulates the way the Photoshop image will look when displayed on an NTSC monitor.

To simulate the display of a Photoshop file on an NTSC monitor:

1. Drag the Photoshop clip from the Browser and drop it into an open sequence in the Timeline; then position the playhead somewhere on the clip.

   The Photoshop image is displayed in the Canvas.

2. In the Canvas, select Show as Square Pixels from the View selector pop-up menu (**Figure 13.128**).

3. When Show as Square Pixels is checked, the Canvas image will simulate the way your Photoshop image will look displayed on an NTSC monitor (**Figure 13.129**).

Setting the default duration for stills

Photoshop files are still images, and like all stills, they must be rendered before you can play them back in Final Cut Pro. Even though you have to render them first, still images and generators are assigned a duration at the time they're imported into Final Cut Pro. You specify the default duration for still images on the General tab of the Preferences window.

No matter what duration you set, your Final Cut Pro clip is referencing a single still image, so you won't create large, full-length video files until you render or export your stills at their edited lengths.

The default still duration is applied at the time you import the still into Final Cut Pro. If you have imported a still image and want the duration to be longer, you must modify the preference setting and then re-import the still.

To change the default still duration:

1. Choose Edit > Preferences; or press Option-Q.

2. On the General tab of the Preferences window, enter a new default duration in the Still/Freeze Duration field (**Figure 13.130**).

3. Click OK.

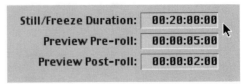

Figure 13.130 On the General tab of the Preferences window, type a new default duration in the Still/Freeze Duration field.

CREATING ARTWORK IN ADOBE PHOTOSHOP

Figure 13.131 The Commotion DV compositing program is included on your Final Cut Pro 2 CD.

Using Commotion DV

Commotion DV 1.0 is a free application that's included on your Final Cut Pro CD (**Figure 13.131**). It's an excellent compositing program with some advanced features that remove some of the drudgery from making movie magic.

DV clips can be imported directly into Commotion after being captured in FCP. All manipulations and settings can be saved for all the multiple revisions, retractions, and client re-dos that usually occur on a special effects project.

Commotion DV features include:

◆ **AutoPaint**: You can record and play back a series of paint strokes and create a hand-animated look without the hours of tedious frame-by-frame hand painting. You can make animated strokes smooth or wiggly.

◆ **Rotoscoping**: Rotoscoping is a process of hand tracing an area for manipulation. Rotoscoped areas can be composited with motion clips, effects, and/or filters. Commotion allows easy animation of the vector paths that mark the rotoscoped areas.

◆ **Super-cloning**: Like a rubber stamp tool that can be applied across successive frames in a clip or between multiple clips, Super-cloning offers an efficient way to replace parts of your image. Common uses of Super-cloning include removal of wires and boom operators from special-effects shots.

For details on using Commotion DV, see the PDF manual in the application folder.

✔ Tips

■ Commotion DV is a RAM-hungry program. The amount of RAM you can make available to Commotion determines the maximum number of frames loaded into RAM at any one time. One option is to close any other programs and provide more RAM for Commotion; however, it is possible to work on small pieces at a time without having to load the entire clip into memory.

■ Commotion DV can save alpha channels for easy use in FCP, but the DV video codec does not support alpha channel information. To best save your clips (and your alpha channel as well), use the Animation codec, set at Millions of Colors+.

Using Third-Party After Effects Filters

Final Cut Pro is compatible with many of Adobe After Effects' third-party image filter plug-ins. Standard plug-ins that come with After Effects, however, are not compatible with Final Cut Pro. Once you've installed them, After Effects-compatible plug-ins will appear in the Video Filters section of the Effects menu and can be used just like any other Final Cut Pro filter (**Figure 13.132**).

There may be some trial and error involved in determining which third-party filters will work and weeding out the ones that don't. Make sure you have the latest versions of the filters installed—check the Final Cut Pro Web site for a current list of compatible filters.

To install third-party video filters:

1. In the Finder, locate and open the AfterEffects Plug-ins folder; then *do one of the following:*

   ▲ Duplicate the third-party After Effects filters and then drag the copies to the Final Cut Pro Plugins folder.

   ▲ Create aliases of your third-party filters' folders and then move the aliases to the Final Cut Pro Plugins folder (**Figure 13.133**).

   ▲ Create aliases of individual third-party filters and move them to the Final Cut Pro Plugins folder.

2. If any of your third-party filters requires a hardware key or dongle, refer to the filter's installation instructions.

3. Launch Final Cut Pro.

4. Choose Effects > Video Filters (**Figure 13.134**) and then locate and test your third-party filters.

Figure 13.132 Even custom interfaces used by third-party After Effects image filter plug-ins can be used on the Filters tab of the Viewer.

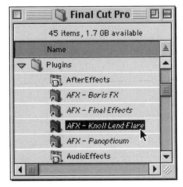

Figure 13.133 Create aliases for individual third-party filters and move them to the Final Cut Pro Plugins folder.

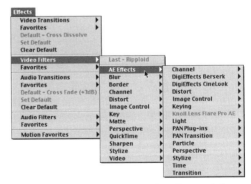

Figure 13.134 Choose Effects > Video Filters and then locate and test your third-party filters.

If you cannot load particular third-party filters, remove those individual files or aliases from your Plugins folder and contact the manufacturer for details about compatibility with Final Cut Pro.

✔ Tips

■ Save your work before using a third-party filter for the first time. Some filters may surprise you with a system crash that will require you to restart Final Cut Pro. These filters involve some pretty complicated math, so it's always better to play with new filters after you save.

■ Not all third-party plug-ins work successfully, and the dialog boxes that come up every time you start (until you remove the incompatible filters from the Final Cut Pro Plugins folder) don't explain much.

To apply third-party After Effects filters:

Do one of the following:

◆ In the Browser, click the Effects tab; then drag a third-party filter from the Video Filters folder to a clip in the Timeline.

◆ In the Timeline, choose the clip; then choose Effects > Video Filters > AE Effects to locate the third-party filters.

FCP Protocol: Third-Party After Effects Filters

Your third-party After Effects filters may not operate in Final Cut Pro and After Effects in exactly the same way. It's important to note differences in how the two programs use the same filter plug-in.

◆ Final Cut Pro assigns the (X,Y) origin point of a filter to the center of a clip, whereas After Effects assigns the origin point to the upper-left corner.

◆ Custom interfaces for third-party filters are supported on the Filters tab of the Viewer.

◆ Final Cut Pro's Clip control, similar in function to After Effects' Track Matte, allows you to use the image information in another clip to affect the filtering of the selected clip. Drag the first clip to the clip control icon of the selected clip. Not all filters, however, use this control.

ONLINE RESOURCES

Apple Computer Links

http://www.apple.com/finalcutpro/

Apple's Official Final Cut Pro Home Page is the place to go for program updates; the latest FCP news; updates on Final Cut Pro and QuickTime; and the list of Apple approved video hardware and software. Check in at the FCP home page on a regular basis.

http://til.info.apple.com/

Apple's Tech Info Library (TIL) is Apple's knowledge base with product information, technical specifications, and troubleshooting information. Search the TIL with keywords "Final Cut Pro" for a complete list of Apple technical documents relating to FCP.

✔ Tip

■ Check the Tech Info Library regularly. Apple posts updates on "known issues" (a.k.a. bugs) affecting Final Cut Pro in the TIL—and nowhere else.

http://www.apple.com/finalcutpro/directory.html

The **Final Cut Pro Directory page** contains links to discussion groups, general DV reference resources, and developers of software and plugins you can use in conjunction with Final Cut Pro.

http://www.apple.com/finalcutpro/specs.html

The **Technical Specifications page** contains—well, FCP 2 technical specifications of course—but you'll also find links to the developers of FCP-compatible capture cards and real time systems.

http://www.apple.com/quicktime/
Apple's QuickTime Home Page

http://www.apple.com/firewire/
Apple's FireWire Home Page

Online Users Forums

http://www.2-pop.com/

When Final Cut Pro was released in April 1999, the **2-pop.com site** quickly became the central exchange forum for Final Cut Pro users to share information. This is the place to go for answers, FCP News, new ideas, and product critique. A gold mine.

http://www.2-pop.com/boards/index.html

This is a direct link to a complete listing of **2-pop's discussion forums**.

Be sure to take advantage of the Search feature located at the top of most discussion boards; you'll find a wealth of detailed information by **searching the archives** of the 2-pop message boards.

http://discuss.info.apple.com/boards/finalcut.nsf/by+Topic

This is **Apple's Final Cut Pro Discussion Forum**, Apple's official online support forum for Final Cut Pro.

Hardware

http://www.matrox.com/

Matrox manufactures the RTMac, the first real-time system certified for use with Final Cut Pro.

http://www.pinnaclesys.com

Pinnacle Systems manufactures the Targa Cinewave capture/playback board, an analog video capture system Apple-certified for use with Final Cut Pro.

http://www.digitalvoodoo.net/

Digital Voodoo manufactures FCP-compatible analog capture/playback boards.

http://www.auroravideosys.com/

Aurora Video Systems manufactures FCP-compatible analog capture/playback boards.

Reference

http://www.dv.com/site.shtml

DV Live Magazine would be my first stop if I were looking for product reviews, industry analysis, and "long view" technical evaluations of the current state of the digital video world. This URL takes you directly to the DV site directory; it's not always easy to find what you want from DV's home page.

http://www.codeccentral.com/

Codec Central is Terran Interactive's reference database of information on multimedia codecs and technologies.

http://www.adobe.com/

In addition to product specific information on Photoshop and After Effects, **Adobe's Web site** is a great source of general information on digital imaging.

http://www.techweb.com/encyclopedia/

Simple to use, the **TechEncyclopedia** offers more than 20,000 definitions of computer terms and concepts.

Mavens

If you are seeking alternatives to marketing department hype, these sites offer a bracing dose of opinionated candor and experienced insight, along with valuable reference material and more great links.

http://desktopvideo.about.com/ compute/desktopvideo/

David Simpson's DV Home Page has links to most of the sites listed on this page, along with fresh news from the DV world. A great resource. David hosts Ross Jones' fab "Golden List of Macintosh DV and FireWire Nonlinear Editing Solutions." You'll also find links to other FCP discussion groups.

http://www.adamwilt.com/DV.html

Adam Wilt's Amazing DV FAQ. I'm an Adam Wilt fan. See for yourself.

http://www.nonlinear4.com/

Michael Rubin (and co-editor Ron Diamond) are keepers of the **nonlinear4.com**, a great reference and resource site for all things digital and video. You should also visit this site to purchase *Nonlinear4* (the fourth edition of Michael Rubin's really good "field guide to digital video and film editing").

http://www.joemaller.com/

Joe Maller's FXScript Reference is a great resource for anyone interested in using FXBuilder to create filters and transitions for Final Cut Pro. The site started from notes he made while building Joe's Filters, his set of shareware utility filters. Joe also offers a free set of Debugging and Exploration scripts to help understand how FXScript works.

http://www.dvcentral.org/

Get subscription information at **DV & FireWire Central** for the excellent DV_L mailing list.

FCP User Groups

http://www.2-pop.com/boards/ board.html?groups.cgi

2-pop's User Groups Announcement Forum is the best place to check for user group action in your town. If you don't see any users posting from your area, this is a good place to try and round up your neighborhood FCP users and start a user group of your own.

http://www.lafcpug.org

The **Los Angeles Final Cut Pro User Group** is a triumph of ad-hocracy (and a tribute to the energy of its prime mover, Michael Horton). Founded in June 2000, LAFCPUG now has over 800 members on its mailing list. LAFCPUG holds well-attended monthly meetings. The LAFCPUG web site is updated regularly, and is worth a visit for the archive of fine "how-to" articles contributed by community-minded FCP mavens.

http://www.sfcutters.org/

The **San Francisco Final Cut Pro User Group Web site**. These guys started the first FCP user group, and gleefully nagged Southern California FCP users until they started the LAFCPUG. The rest is history.

KEYBOARD SHORTCUTS

Keyboard Shortcuts

General controls

FUNCTION	KEY COMMAND
Open file	Cmd O
Open selected item	Return
Open in separate window	Shift Return
Open item editor	Option Return
Close window	Cmd W
Help	Cmd ?
Quit	Cmd Q
Save	Cmd S

General controls *(continued)*

FUNCTION	KEY COMMAND
Save all	Option S
Undo	Cmd Z
Redo	Cmd Y
Audio scrub on or off	Shift S
Edit render quality	Shift Y
Snapping on or off	N
Looping on or off	Ctrl L
Close Tab	Ctrl W
Open text generator	Ctrl X

To open application windows

FUNCTION	KEY COMMAND
Viewer	Cmd 1
Canvas	Cmd 2
Timeline	Cmd 3
Browser	Cmd 4
Audio Meters	Option 4
Effects	Cmd 5
Favorites bin	Cmd 6
Trim Edit	Cmd 7
Log and Capture	Cmd 8
Item Properties	Cmd 9
Sequence Settings	Cmd 0 (zero)
Preferences	Option Q

Select, cut, copy, and paste

FUNCTION	KEY COMMAND
Copy	[Cmd] C
Cut	[Cmd] X
Duplicate	[Option] D
Make In/Out a selection	[Option] A
Paste	[Cmd] V
Paste attributes	[Option] V
Paste Insert	[Shift] V
Select all	[Cmd] A
Deselect all	[Cmd] D

Navigation

FUNCTION	KEY COMMAND
Forward one frame	[→]
Back one frame	[←]
Forward one second	[Shift] [→]
Back one second	[Shift] [←]
Match frame	F
Next edit	[Shift] E
Previous edit	[Option] E
Next gap	[Shift] G
Previous gap	[Option] G
To beginning of media	HOME
To end of media	END *or* [Shift] HOME
To next edit or In/Out	[↓]

Navigation *(continued)*

FUNCTION	KEY COMMAND
To previous edit or In/Out	⬆
To next marker	Shift ⬇
To previous marker	Shift ⬆
To master clip	Shift F
Shuttle backward fast	J (tap repeatedly to increase speed)
Shuttle backward slow	J + K
Pause	K
Shuttle forward fast	L (tap repeatedly to increase speed)
Shuttle forward slow	L + K
Next edit	' (single quote)
Previous edit	; (semicolon)

Finding items

FUNCTION	KEY COMMAND
Find	Cmd F
Find Next (in Find results)	Cmd G *or* F3
Find previous (in Find results)	Shift F3

Scrolling

FUNCTION	KEY COMMAND
Horizontal scroll left	Shift Page Up
Horizontal scroll right	Shift Page Down
Vertical scroll up	Page Up
Vertical scroll down	Page Down

Screen layout and display

FUNCTION	KEY COMMAND
Custom layout 1	[Shift] U
Custom layout 2	[Option] U
Standard Layout	[Ctrl] U

Projects and sequences

FUNCTION	KEY COMMAND
New project	[Cmd] E
New sequence	[Cmd] N
New Sequence with Presets prompt	[Cmd] [Option] N
Import file	[Cmd] I

Browser

FUNCTION	KEY COMMAND
Insert bin	[Cmd] B
Open bins (list view)	[→]
Close bins (list view)	[←]
Make Favorite	[Option] F
Show logging columns	[Option] B
Show standard columns	[Shift] B
Toggle list/icon view	[Shift] H
Make Favorite motion	[Ctrl] F

Timeline

FUNCTION	KEY COMMAND
Create or break link	Cmd L
Create or break stereo pair	Option L
Toggle track sizes	Shift T
Clip Keyframes on or off	Option T
Clip overlays on or off	Option W
Delete and leave gap	Delete
Ripple delete (no gap)	Shift Delete
Ripple Cut to Keyboard	Shift X
Fit sequence in window	Shift Z
Lock video track + track number	F4 + track number
Lock all video tracks	Shift F4
Lock audio track + track number	F5 + track number
Lock all audio tracks	Shift F5
Turn on Audio Waveforms	Cmd Option W
Linked selection on or off	Shift L
Modify Duration	Ctrl D
Zoom Timeline In	Option - (minus sign)
Zoom Timeline Out	Option + (plus sign)

Logging and capturing

FUNCTION	KEY COMMAND
Log clip	F2
Batch capture	Cmd H
Capture Now	Shift C

Playing video

FUNCTION	KEY COMMAND
Play	L *or* Spacebar
Pause/Stop	K *or* Spacebar
Play around current	\ (backslash)
Play every frame	Option P
Play here to Out	Shift P
Play in reverse	Shift Spacebar *or* J
Play In to Out	Shift \ (backslash)

In and Out points

FUNCTION	KEY COMMAND
Set In point	I *or* / (slash) on keypad
Set Out point	O *or* * (asterisk) on keypad
Clear In	Option I
Clear Out	Option O
Clear In and Out	Option X
Make selection an In or Out	Shift A
Mark clip	X
Go to In point	Shift I
Go to Out point	Shift O
Set video In only	Ctrl I
Set video Out only	Ctrl O
Set audio In only	Cmd Option I
Set audio Out only	Cmd Option O

Tool selection

FUNCTION	KEY COMMAND
Tool Selection	A
Tool Edit Select	G
Tool Group Select	G+G
Tool Range Select	G+G+G
Tool Track Forward Select	T
Tool Track Backward Select	T+T
Tool Track Select	T+T+T
Tool All Tracks Forward Select	T+T+T+T
Tool All Tracks Backward Select	T+T+T+T+T
Tool Roll Edit	R
Tool Ripple Edit	R+R
Tool Slip	S
Tool Slide	S+S
Tool Razor Blade	B
Tool Razor Blade All	B+B
Tool Hand	H
Tool Zoom In	Z
Tool Zoom Out	Z+Z
Tool Crop	C
Tool Distort	D
Tool Pen	P
Tool Pen Delete	P+P
Tool Pen Smooth	P+P+P

Markers

FUNCTION	KEY COMMAND
Add marker	M
Add and name marker	M + M
Delete marker	[Cmd] ` (accent grave)
Extend marker	[Option] ~ (tilde)
Reposition marker	[Shift] ` (accent grave)
Next marker	[Shift] M
Previous marker	[Option] M
Clear All Markers	[Ctrl] ` (accent grave)

Editing

FUNCTION	KEY COMMAND
Select Closest Edit	V
Add Edit	[Ctrl] V
Toggle Ripple / Roll Tool Type	U *or* [Shift] R
Apply Default Video Transition	[Ctrl] T
Apply Default Audio Transition	[Cmd] [Option] T
Extend edit	E
Insert edit	[F9]
Insert with transition	[Shift] [F9]
Overwrite	[F10]
Overwrite with transition	[Shift] [F10]
Replace	[F11]
Fit to fill	[Shift] [F11]

Editing *(continued)*

FUNCTION	KEY COMMAND
Superimpose	[F12]
Make subclip	[Cmd] U
Slip edit	[Shift] Click In *or* Out point
Split edit	[Option] Click In *or* Out point
Set target video + track number	[F6] + track number
Set target video to None	[Shift] [F6]
Set target Audio 1 + track number	[F7] + track number
Set target Audio 1 to None	[Shift] [F7]
Set target Audio 2 + track number	[F8] + track number
Set target Audio 2 to None	[Shift] [F8]
Trim backward one frame	[(left bracket) *or* , (comma)
Trim backward x frames	[Shift] [(left bracket) *or* [Shift] , (comma)
Trim forward one frame	] (right bracket) *or* . (period)
Trim forward x frames	[Shift]] (right bracket) *or* [Shift] . (period)

Output

FUNCTION	KEY COMMAND
Toggle render quality	Y
Display frame	[F15] *or* [Shift] [F12]
Print to video	[Cmd] M

Compositing and special effects

FUNCTION	KEY COMMAND
Nest Items	[Option] C
Add Motion Keyframe	[Ctrl] K
Next Keyframe	[Shift] K
Previous Keyframe	[Option] K
Make still frame	[Shift] N
Render effect (FXBuilder)	[Cmd] K
Render selection	[Cmd] R
Render sequence	[Option] R
Render single frame on or off	[Caps Lock]
Speed	[Cmd] J
Toggle Image/Wireframe view	W
Toggle RGB/RGB+A/Alpha	[Shift] W
Fit in window	[Shift] Z
Nudge position down	[Option] [↓]
Nudge position left	[Option] [←]
Nudge position right	[Option] [→]
Nudge position up	[Option] [↑]
Sub pixel down	[Cmd] [Shift] [↓]
Sub pixel left	[Cmd] [Shift] [←]
Sub pixel right	[Cmd] [Shift] [→]
Sub pixel up	[Cmd] [Shift] [↑]
Zoom in	[Cmd] = (equal sign)
Zoom out	[Cmd] - (minus sign)

Compositing and special effects *(continued)*

FUNCTION	KEY COMMAND
Add Motion Keyframe	Ctrl K
Add Audio Level Keyframe	Cmd Option K
Mixdown Audio	Ctrl M

Quick Navigation Keys and Modifiers

This group of Keyboard shortcuts for marking and navigation are arranged in what is known as a "Set-Clear-Go" scheme.

- ◆ The simple key command sets the edit, marker, or point.
- ◆ Shift plus the key command advances to the next edit, marker, or point.
- ◆ Option plus the key command advances to the previous edit, marker, or point.
- ◆ Ctrl Shift plus the key command also advances to the previous edit, marker, or point.

KEY	NO MODIFIER	Shift + KEY	Option + KEY OR Ctrl Shift + KEY
I	Set In	Go To In	Clear In
O	Set Out	Go To Out	Clear Out
M	Set Marker	Next Marker	Previous Marker
E	Extend Edit	Next Edit	Previous Edit
G		Next Gap	Previous Gap
K		Next Keyframe	Previous Keyframe
Ctrl K	Add Motion Keyframe		

INDEX

E

INDEX

INDEX

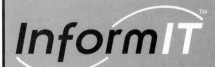